INAUSPICIOUS BEGINNINGS

FOREIGN POLICY, SECURITY, AND STRATEGIC STUDIES

Editors: Alex Macleod and Charles-Philippe David

The Foreign Policy, Security, and Strategic Studies Series seeks to promote analysis of the transformation and adaptation of foreign and security policies in the post–Cold War era. The series welcomes manuscripts offering innovative interpretations or new theoretical approaches to these questions, whether dealing with specific strategic or policy issues or with the evolving concept of security itself.

Canada, Latin America, and the New Internationalism
A Foreign Policy Analysis, 1968–1990
Brian J.R. Stevenson

Power vs. Prudence
Why Nations Forgo Nuclear Weapons
T.V. Paul

From Peacekeeping to Peacemaking
Canada's Response to the Yugoslav Crisis
Nicholas Gammer

Canadian Policy toward Krushchev's Soviet Union
Jamie Glazov

The Revolution in Military Affairs
Implications for Canada and NATO
Elinor Sloan

Inauspicious Beginnings
Principal Powers and International Security Institutions after the Cold War, 1989–1999
Edited by Onnig Beylerian and Jacques Lévesque

PROCEEDINGS

The Future of NATO
Enlargement, Russia, and European Security
Edited by Charles-Philippe David and Jacques Lévesque

Inauspicious Beginnings

Principal Powers and International Security Institutions after the Cold War, 1989–1999

Edited by

ONNIG BEYLERIAN and
JACQUES LÉVESQUE

The Centre for Security and Foreign Policy Studies
and
The Raoul-Dandurand Chair of Strategic and Diplomatic Studies

McGill-Queen's University Press
Montreal & Kingston · London · Ithaca

© McGill-Queen's University Press 2004
ISBN 0-7735-2625-0 (cloth)
ISBN 0-7735-2626-9 (paper)

Legal deposit second quarter 2004
Bibliothèque nationale du Québec

Printed in Canada on acid-free paper that is 100% ancient forest free
(100% post-consumer recycled), processed chlorine free.

This book has been published with the help of a grant from the
Centre for Security and Foreign Policy Studies.

McGill-Queen's University Press acknowledges the support of the
Canada Council for the Arts for our publishing program. We also
acknowledge the financial support of the Government of Canada
through the Book Publishing Industry Development Program (BPIDP)
for our publishing activities.

National Library of Canada Cataloguing in Publication

Inauspicious beginnings : principal powers and international security
institutions after the Cold War, 1989–1999 / edited by Onnig Beylerian
and Jacques Lévesque.

(Foreign policy, security, and strategic studies 7)
Co-published by the Centre for Security and Foreign Policy Studies
and the Raoul-Dandurand Chair of Strategic and Diplomatic Studies.
Includes bibliographical references.
ISBN 0-7735-2625-0 (bnd)
ISBN 0-7735-2626-9 (pbk)

1. Security, international.   2. Balance of power   3. World politics –
1989–   . I. Beylerian, Onnig, 1947–   . II. Lévesque, Jacques,
1940–   . III. Université du Québec à Montréal. Centre d'études des
politiques étrangères et de sécurité.   IV. Raoul-Dandurand Chair of
Strategic and Diplomatic Studies.   V. Series.

JZ5588.I53 2004   327′.09′049   C2003–905081–5

Typeset in 10/12 Sabon by True to Type

Contents

Preface

With *Inauspicious Beginnings*, the Centre d'études des politiques étrangères et de sécurité (CEPES) of the Université du Québec à Montréal (UQAM) publishes its third collective work with McGill-Queen's University Press and the second in its series of team projects on the major powers and changes in international relations since the end of the Cold War. The first of these projects, published as *Role Quests in the Post–Cold War Era*, was led by Philippe Le Prestre and dealt with how the collapse of the Soviet Union affected the major powers' own conceptions of the roles they played in the international system. In the present volume, the contributors have continued these reflections by examining how these states have acted through international security organizations since the early 1990s. A third project that is now well under way is looking at the extent to which the principal states within the transatlantic area (including Russia, of course) have reshaped their national identities in response to transformations in the international system that have taken place since the symbolic fall of the Berlin Wall.

Inauspicious Beginnings is also the seventh publication in the Foreign Policy and Strategic Studies Series, which were created by CEPES and the Raoul-Dandurand Chair of Strategic and Diplomatic Studies (also of UQAM) at McGill-Queen's in 1998. This series was established with the aim of publishing works dealing with changes in the foreign and security policies of the major states since the end of the Cold War. It was, of course, subjected to the same rigorous and anonymous evaluation process as all other books published by McGill-Queen's.

All the CEPES team research projects fall within the Centre's general mission. CEPES was created in 1991 with the help of a subsidy from the then Military and Strategic Studies Program of the Canadian Department of National Defence – now known as the Security and Defence Forum – which has concentrated on the foreign and security policies of the major powers, including Canada, since the end of the Cold War. It began as a research group of five members, four from UQAM's Political Science Department and one from the now defunct Royal Military College in Saint-Jean-sur-le-Richelieu, Quebec, and it has since blossomed into a group of some ten active members, which includes three from the Political Science Department of Concordia University. It fosters research into foreign and security policy on the part of their members, and strongly encourages the participation of graduate students, especially as research assistants. CEPES is also generally involved in organizing activities aimed at increasing public awareness of the issues of the day through its two publications, *Points de mire* (Focus Points) and the *Bulletin du maintien de la paix* (Peacekeeping Bulletin,) which appear throughout the academic year, and its annual conferences, several of which have already led to publications.

However, its long-term research projects, financed by the Quebec government research grant program Fonds pour la formation de chercheurs et l'aide à la recherche (FCAR), now called the Fonds québécois pour la recherche sur la culture et la société (FQRCS), constitute the Centre's main research activity. Around the same nucleus of three members of CEPES, teams of some six researchers have been formed for each project. Every one of them has been included because of their particular regional expertise or knowledge of the foreign and security policies of a chosen country. They have, in turn, appointed their own research assistants to work with them over a period of three to four years and to produce the individual chapters of a planned book, as well as articles and conference papers based on their research. The key to the success of any such exercise is undoubtedly the leadership provided by the colleague or colleagues who agree to direct the process.

In the case of *Inauspicious Beginnings* it was Onnig Beylerian, a research fellow at CEPES and in the Political Science Department of UQAM, who, in collaboration with Jacques Lévesque, a long-time director of CEPES, undertook the daunting task of bringing together a team of specialists from three different universities who had very different theoretical outlooks to produce the present book and to give it the necessary coherence, without sacrificing the diversity of views and theoretical approaches one is bound to find in such a group. Onnig Beylerian's role was particularly important because he prepared the general framework and research design of the project and was in charge of day-to-day administration, including regular meetings with the research assistants and providing them with advice on questions of international relations theory.

Finally, as someone who has been connected closely with the production of this book at all its stages, I would like to extend my thanks and the thanks of the editors to FCAR/FQRCS for having provided us with the financial backing to carry out this project and to the Security and Defence Forum for allowing us to put in place and maintain the physical and administrative infrastructure without which no team project of this dimension could have been undertaken. Our thanks also to Aurèle Parisien and Joanne Pisano of McGill-Queen's, who guided our original manuscript through all the stages from submission to publication. We would also like to acknowledge the contribution of our anonymous evaluators, whose judicious suggestions helped us to present a much-improved final version. Last, but by no means least, a special thanks to Louis Bouchard, a graduate student in political science at UQAM, who painstakingly went through each chapter to make sure that they all followed the same format, checked every reference, and generally made sure the book was ready for the final editing process.

Needless to say, *Inauspicious Beginnings* is very much a team effort, and consequently, all contributors share the responsibility for both its strengths and its weaknesses.

Alex Macleod
Director, Centre d'études des politiques étrangères et de sécurité
Université du Québec à Montréal

Abbreviations

APEC	Asia Pacific Economic Conference
ARF	ASEAN Regional Forum
ASEAN	Association of Southeast Asian Nations
ASEM	Asia-Europe Meeting
AWACS	Airborne Warning and Control System
CCP	Chinese Communist Party
CCW	Convention on Conventional Weapons
CDU	Christliche Demokratische Union (Christian Democratic Union
CFE	Conventional Armed Forces in Europe
CIS	Commonwealth of Independent States
CSCE	Conference on Security and Cooperation in Europe
CTBT	Comprehensive Test Ban Treaty
EAPC	Euro-Atlantic Partnership Council
ECOSOC	Economic and Social Council
EEZ	Exclusive Economic Zone
FDP	Freie Demokratische Partei (Free Democratic Party)
FRG	Federal Republic of Germany
G7/G8	Group of Seven/Group of Eight (most important industrialized countries)
GDR	German Democratic Republic
GIA	Group Islamique Armé (Armed Islamic Group)
IAEA	International Atomic Energy Agency
ICBC	International Campaign to Ban Landmines
IFOR	Implementation Force (in Bosnia)

IMF	International Monetary Fund
IO	International Organisation
ISAF	International Security Assistance Force
ISI	international security institution
JDA	Japanese Defence Agency
KEDO	Korean Peninsula Energy Development Organisation
KFOR	Kosovo Force
LDP	Liberal Democratic Party
LWR	Light-Water Nuclear Reactor
METI	Ministry of Economy, Trade, and Industry
MIPONU	United Nations Civilian Police Mission in Haiti
NACC	North Atlantic Cooperation Council
NATO	North Atlantic Treaty Organisation
NDPO	National Defence Program Outline
NGO	nongovernment organisation
NORAD	North American Air Defence Command
NPT	Non-Proliferation Treaty
NTBT	Nuclear Test Ban Treaty
OAS	Organisation of American States
ODA	official development assistance
OEWG	Open-ended Working Group
OSCE	Organisation for Security and Cooperation in Europe
P5	The five permanent members of the United Nations Security Council
PfP	Partnership for Peace
PKO	peacekeeping operations
SACEUR	Supreme Allied Commander in Europe
SCAP	Supreme Commander for the Allied Powers (in Japan)
SDF	Self-Defence Forces
SFOR	Stabilization Force (in Bosnia)
SLOC	Sea Lines of Communication
TMD	Theater Missile Defense
UNITAF	United Task Force (in Somalia)
UNMIH	United Nations Mission in Haiti
UNOSOM	United Nations Mission in Somalia
UNPROFOR	United Nations Protection Force (in Bosnia)
UNSC	United Nations Security Council
UNSCPM	United Nations Security Council Permanent Member
UNSMIH	United Nations Support Mission in Haiti
UNTAC	United Nations Transitional Authority in Cambodia
UNTMIH	United Nations Transition Mission in Haiti
WEU	West European Union
WTO	World Trade Organisation

INAUSPICIOUS BEGINNINGS

Security Institutions after the Cold War

ONNIG BEYLERIAN

Although the Soviet Union had clearly been disintegrating for some time, no one had anticipated the final collapse on Christmas of 1991. So, too, no one had suspected that on a sunny September morning in 2001 a clandestine Islamist terrorist group would plunge two passenger jets into the twin towers of the World Trade Center in New York and another one into the Pentagon in Washington and thus abruptly change the course of history. Along with the entire world, the United States was shocked to witness the loss of over three thousand of its citizens and to see its overwhelming power contested in such a fundamental way in its own homeland.

The reaction to this tragic event was swift. All the principal powers expressed support for the United States, Russia among the first. Even China, whose relations with the United States had recently been strained, did not hesitate to lend assistance. Enjoying the support of all the principal powers and of others as well, the United States resolved to undertake major military operations in Afghanistan to root out members of the Islamist organization al-Qaeda, which was believed to be responsible for the tragedies of September 11 and other acts of global terrorism. As all the major international security networks, including the United Nations Security Council, joined in a coalition to fight global terrorism, any doubts about the existence of a unipolar system of international relations was dissipated for the moment by this unusually widespread backing of the world's only superpower.

But this almost universal approval of u.s. counterterrorist actions and policies soon ran into trouble because of Washington's intention to extend its campaign against what President George Bush called the "axis of evil," consisting of Iraq, Iran, and North Korea. Nearly all members of the coalition opposed converting the struggle against global terrorism into an all-out assault against these countries. Several members began to suspect that the United States was simply seeking to use its formidable military capabilities to subdue recalcitrant powers that would not comply with its wishes and, in the process, to increase its own power.

Indeed, after September 11 the world community was dealing with a different United States. During much of the 1990s, as we shall see in this volume, the United States was a minimalist superpower. It reaped the fruits of its victory over the Soviet Union, sought to build a zone of peace and democracy, minimized as much as possible the impact of the sudden rise of its relative power and maintained a low profile. But after September 11 the United States shed this minimalist role and demonstrated the full range of its global power. With the tragic events engraved in the American psyche and with the concomitant rebirth of American patriotism, the Bush administration undertook wide-ranging initiatives to protect the security of the United States, both at home and around the world. Faced with a unilateralist United States, the principal powers were now searching for ways to restrain the United States and prevent it from embarking on a path that could generate unmanageable international instability, especially in the greater Middle East.

Influential commentators for several of the principal powers suggested that one solution would be to build on the work done during the 1990s to develop multilateral networks of international security institutions, networks in which the United States was still active and playing a leading role. At first glance this might appear to be an inappropriate solution, given the sheer superiority of the power of the United States in almost every respect. But a close examination of the behaviour of principal powers during much of the 1990s may help to explain why they thought that security institutions could redirect the United States to act multilaterally.

THE EBB AND FLOW OF SECURITY INSTITUTIONS IN THE 1990S

Well before the collapse of the Soviet Union international security mechanisms and procedures were receiving new life and energy, as is exemplified by the Nobel Peace Prize awarded to UN peacekeepers in 1988. The unprecedented level of cooperation between the principal powers provided a major impetus for the creation and development of security institutions. In 1990–91 the United States and the Soviet Union cooperated within the framework of the United Nations Security Council as they responded to Iraqi aggression in Kuwait. With Germany unified in October 1990, security institutions in Europe changed significantly. At Maastricht in 1991 the European Community could now proceed with its plan for a European Union, and it looked forward to defining a distinct European defence and security identity. Long considered no more than a debating forum, in November 1990 the Conference on Security and Co-operation in Europe (CSCE) was set to become a full-fledged organization complete with a permanent structure and headquarters in Prague. Still stunned by the speed of the end of the Cold War, NATO could now seek to expand its mandate, if not its membership.

The end of bipolarity was to amplify even more the willingness of major powers to extend and deepen the mandate of security institutions. They now thought it was possible to create a new generation of security institutions, while also reforming existing ones, such as the United Nations Security Council. Indeed, the success of the coalition against the president of Iraq, Saddam Hussein, in March 1991 allowed them to foresee a world where the basic security of states could be achieved at a reasonable cost. This new-found enthusiasm for world order and organization prompted the United States and other leading powers to send an expeditionary force to Somalia in December 1992 to assist the relief work of humanitarian NGOs. But the euphoria soon waned when UNOSOM (United Nations Operations in Somalia) proved unable to act consistently, with clear and realistic objectives. UNPROFOR (the United Nations Protection Force) proved to be similarly inept in Bosnia-Herzegovina in 1992–95 when frequent disagreements arose among the Allies over how to deal with ethnic cleansing and Russia joined the fray not knowing exactly what interest to defend. Perhaps it was in Rwanda in the spring of 1994 that the Security Council's dysfunction became most apparent. In just ten weeks more than eight hundred thousand Tutsis and moderate Hutus met violent deaths in what was to be the last case of genocide of the twentieth century.

These security breakdowns and massive humanitarian disasters not only demonstrated the weaknesses of security institutions but also revealed disagreements between the major powers, the main providers of international security and the initiators of previous major wars. Each major power defended its peculiar perspectives on how to meet the growing needs of international security, and there were extensive debates about institutional preferences and the appropriate roles of international security organizations. Despite their institutionalist rhetoric, the principal Western powers gave priority first and foremost to their alliance system by increasing the membership in NATO, reshaping its doctrine, and defining missions outside its traditional geographic areas. As expected, Russia opposed NATO expansion, since it would reduce its traditional influence in European security affairs and jeopardize the institutional development of the Commonwealth of Independent States (CIS), which was considered by Moscow to be the only security institution of the former Soviet republics. The Western powers were less concerned with Moscow's displeasure than with reducing the probability of instability in Eastern Europe, right next to a recently unified Germany. Although Western capitals understood that Russia was in serious trouble and although they agreed that the expansion of NATO might threaten Russia's security, they expected it to be self-disciplined enough to act responsibly. In the end, Russia had to be content with a seat at the G7/G8 summit roundtable. It agreed, in a founding act signed with NATO in April 1997, to participate with NATO countries in a permanent council to discuss issues related to European security.

This new venue, however, proved to be less than useful in the spring of 1999 when the major Western powers decided on a military campaign by NATO to drive Serbian military and police forces from Kosovo. Russia and China were opposed: they would have preferred to see the problem handled peacefully in the UN Security Council. Moscow and Beijing had previously found themselves defending similar positions in the Security Council when they favoured lifting sanctions against Iraq, opposed a U.S.-British bombing campaign against Iraq's radar installations, and urged a final settlement for the disarmament of Iraq. With the massive bombing campaign in Kosovo, which destroyed China's embassy in Belgrade, Moscow and Beijing saw clear confirmation of their fears that Western powers wished to expand their influence well beyond their national territories.

In the Asia Pacific region, security institutions made little headway. China was still smarting from Western condemnations of its suppression of the prodemocracy and student movements in Tiananmen Square in 1989, and in an attempt to regain its lost position it pursued a policy of engagement towards its neighbours, and other states as well. But this strategy did not include an institutional dimension. Opportunity would knock in 1994 when the Southeast Asian states, having recently formed their multilateral Regional Security Forum within the framework of ASEAN, invited Beijing to participate. Although suspicious at first, Beijing was eventually satisfied with the informal nature of the gathering, which, among other advantages, did not require a major commitment on its part. Several issues were earnestly broached, most importantly the status of the Spratlys Islands (on this issue, see chapter 7), but also other confidence-building measures. In the main, ASEAN countries succeeded in engaging China in multilateral activities until the Asian financial crisis struck in the autumn of 1997. Since then – and despite reduced ASEAN institutional activities – China's interest in multilateralism has increased, and it has taken on some institutional security responsibilities.[1] But East Asia remains without a significant system of security institutions because Japan and China seem reluctant to take the irrevocable step of founding such a system on a lasting and historic reconciliation. To Japan, a renewed and close alliance with the United States has seemed a cheaper way to provide for its national security than playing a leading role in institution-building in East Asia. To China, even though the presence of the United States in East Asia has had unsettling implications for Chinese national security, it has nevertheless prevented the rise of a Japan that might seriously threaten China's security. The continued division of Korea would be yet another obstacle to, and indeed unforeseeable factor in, any institutionalization of security in the Asia Pacific region.

Major institutional innovations and developments did not emerge from relations between principal powers and other states in the United Nations. Most of the energy that was devoted to building security institutions came from Western powers who were attempting to update their security arrangements, and little was done to reform the security functions and structures of the UN. In 1995, at the fiftieth anniversary of the founding of the United Nations, member states were told that the Security Council was not about to be reformed, as had been hoped during the previous two years. In 1993 the General Assembly had decided to explore structural and functional reform of the Security Council, but after extensive consultation between member states over the need to expand the Council and improve its working methods, little progress had been achieved by September 2000,[2] some seven years later.[3] Even without reform, however, the Security Council was able to make modest advances in arms control, nuclear non-proliferation and disarmament, and conflict resolution. With the UN mission in East Timor, for example, the Security Council produced tangible, albeit mixed, results.[4] It also worked to achieve a convention to ban antipersonnel landmines, even though the agreement was concluded outside the chambers of the world organization.[5] Another important milestone was the indefinite extension of the Non-Proliferation Treaty (NPT) in 1995. But the advent of two new nuclear powers, India and Pakistan, in May 1998 worked against the non-proliferation cause. Nor did the continued and unfettered possession of nuclear weapons by the five nuclear powers, notwithstanding their willingness, stated in May 2000 at the end of the Sixth NPT Review Conference, to eventually destroy their nuclear arsenals.[6] North Korea's agreement to suspend its nuclear weapons program may have seemed to be an encouraging sign, but Pyongyang asked for a high price in return. Iraq's failure to comply with the terms of its disarmament agreement, as well as Israel's undeclared possession of nuclear weapons, continued to plague the prospect for a lasting security regime in the Middle East.

In sum, the majority of the principal powers were willing to create new international security institutions and reinforce existing ones. But their commitment and investment did not come close to satisfying the continually increasing demands for security in critical geopolitical areas. Moreover, principal powers had different views of and interests in security institutions. At times they considered them to be unimportant, to the point of neglecting and even avoiding them. At other times, when it suited their interests, they decided to work through them and considered them more valuable. Understanding what drives their differing interest in security institutions is the main goal of this book. It seeks to describe why and under what circumstances principal powers turn to international security institutions to achieve their ends. Although principal powers are the main providers of security goods in most international security institutions, they do not always use them to settle disputes, regulate security relations, or avert security crashes: they do not invest the same resources in security institutions whenever they are needed. Furthermore, they entertain different preferences for one institution over another. Thus their interest in international security institutions in general tends to vary over time, as does their interest in particular security institutions.

THEORETICAL PERSPECTIVES

In this section, we describe briefly how the three main theoretical perspectives in international relations – the institutionalist theory, the constructivist theory, and the realist theory – explain why the major powers would act through security institutions. We argue that each perspective provides a partial, but complementary, explanation of institutional security behaviour.[7] The real difference between them lies in the scale and the angle from which they observe this behaviour: no perspective provides a more complete picture of the complex problem at hand.

Institutionalist Theory

The institutionalist theory considers that the principal powers use security institutions to gain tangible advantages, even though they do not need them, as small states do, to amplify their power or to achieve security at a much lower price. The theory assumes that these powers can achieve their ends without turning to security institutions. A cursory examination of defence planning, for instance, would show that security institutions are of secondary importance to principal powers when they determine the force structure they need to ensure national security.

However, security institutions are useful to principal powers because they substantially reduce the transaction costs of reaching and maintaining agreements. Principal powers want to make sure that agreements are enforced and cheating is deterred through verification mechanisms. In many instances the burden-sharing designs of such mechanisms are crucial, especially when the immediate interests of the powers are not at stake and they are dealing with other international security issues, such as virulent ethnic conflicts.[8]

The principal powers would also turn to security institutions in order to exchange information with their peers and with secondary powers and other states and to find out what other states want and how much they are willing to sacrifice to get what they desire. In other words, institutionalist theory sees security institutions as information clearinghouses. Two main types of information are exchanged. The first is information about defence matters ranging from the structure of armed forces and military exchanges to intelligence-sharing programs. The purpose is to reduce as much as possible the level of uncertainty between nonallied major powers and other states or to ensure normal operation of an alliance infrastructure. The second is information about what constitutes a threat and a security risk and how to respond to it, as well as information about principles of acceptable security behaviour and how to reach a consensus about their legitimacy. The purpose is to discover the optimal level of security for each state, in order to fend off claims to absolute security and settle instead for a window of vulnerability that will assure the others of one's own benign intentions.

According to institutionalist logic, the principal powers would use security institutions to solve problems of collaboration, coordination, assurance, and suasion.[9] In the first two types of problems there is a symmetry of interests; in the latter two, the players' interests are distinctly asymmetrical. The actual function of a security institution is to resolve some or all of these problems, and the function or functions of a security institution determines the form it must take in order to perform its tasks. Three games would be played out by the principal powers in the global security system. First, if a principal power takes the interests of its peers into consideration, we would see collaboration and coordination, depending on where the players find themselves placed in relation to others and the nature and complexity of the security issues at hand. Second, in interactions between major powers and lesser powers and small states, we would probably see assurance and suasion, since there would be an asymmetry of interests between the players most of the time. A third game reflects the exceptional position of u.s. power within the group of principal powers. In this game, there is a mix of interactions, because at times there is an asymmetry of interests between the United States and the rest of the group. We would therefore see some major powers vying for proximity and convergence with the superpower and others trying to constrain the excesses of American power. If the latter phenomenon depicts Russian and Chinese multipolar efforts since 1996, the former represents the behaviour of the major Western European powers before September 11, but with some variations. France is closer to Russia and China insofar as it has also vowed to build a multipolar world as a means to balance the formidable, if not completely overwhelming, influence of the United States on the global equilibrium.[10]

Security institutions also offer a convenient venue for bargaining on issues that have no chance of being resolved elsewhere. They may satisfy the need for transparency and provide civil society with the opportunity to participate in policy-making. The principal powers would find it more appealing to offer concessions in an institutional setting, since the concessions could be accompanied with a host of side payments. Furthermore, they could offer a number of face-saving devices and other types of facilitative procedures that would make the acceptance of agreements more palatable to domestic stakeholders.[11]

But would principal powers willingly accept institutional constraints on their freedom of action in security affairs? Institutionalist theory holds that they would be likely to do so because security institutions provide them with increasing returns on their investment. For example, the defence capabilities of the United States, the strongest of the principal powers, nominally guarantee its own security, and it therefore has the greatest incentive to bypass security institutions. Nevertheless, institutionalist theory sees the United States as engaged in self-imposed "strategic restraint": it enjoys the support of the majority of the other principal powers and of states that receive benefits from the American liberal world order, which rests on limits imposed on u.s. power.[12] The United States achieves this feat principally through international institutions that can lock states into continuous and predictable courses of action. Neither the United States nor the other states can easily disentangle themselves from this process. On the other hand, principal powers, such as China and Russia, that see little immediate benefits from this order will be less likely to accept institutional constraints unless there is tangible evidence that they can obtain major benefits sustainable over time.

Constructivist Theory

Constructivists would see two major reasons for major powers to be interested in solving problems through international security institutions. First, as a major locus of the international social structure, security institutions may well determine the norms that enable states to regulate their security behaviour. By participating in security institutions, principal powers could attempt to ensure that emerging international norms do not put their national values in question. They would also realize that security institutions can provide norms that tell states how they should act, in accordance with their identity. Thus, international security institutions become a place where states seek to influence the process of creating those norms which will eventually affect state identities.[13]

The constructivist approach considers that the international social structure is dominated by Western norms of security behaviour.[14] After the Cold War, the major Western powers set out to reinforce this structure in an effort to better circumscribe emerging threats, especially from "rogue states" that were reputed to have replaced the Soviet threat.[15] Having resolutely shed its Soviet mantle, Russia sought to anchor its security interests to those of the West precisely when Western powers were themselves seeking to redefine their security identity. But to its dismay Russia soon discovered that the Western powers wished to do so without Russian participation. Similarly, before 1989 China enjoyed the trust that the major Western powers had placed in China in their security considerations. Since China was almost considered as a friendly state by the Western powers during the last decade of the Cold War, the Chinese leaders thought they could rely on Western understanding of their country's security requirements and domestic political imperatives. However, after Tiananmen Square, Beijing discovered that Western normative preferences had changed. They now wanted China to behave according to norms from which Beijing thought it was exempted.

In summary, ambitious principal powers will attempt to develop new norms because they know that pleading for such change can eventually bring about a modification in the security behaviour of their peers. The construction of new norms becomes a process of argumentation and deliberation. Institutions are not so much venues for bargaining, as the institutionalist theory would suggest, as they are forums where various sides are able to communicate as freely as possible and forge intersubjective understandings that are then internalized within the domestic system of norms. The reverse process would also take place: a principal power would attempt to influence the international social structure with its home-grown norms and values.[16]

Second, security institutions would help principal powers to define their security interests with like-minded and friendly states or potential and actual adversaries. The major Western powers reinforce their democratic identity by negating illiberal norms of other major powers and states. For example, the Western powers redefined NATO to enlarge the community of democratic states, a step that Russia and China regarded as primarily aimed at states that did not have a democratic lineage or credentials. However, not all identification processes consist of devaluing or rejecting the norms upheld by outside groups. In the case of the European Union's security concerns, the identification process is done largely within NATO's security framework, even though some of the concerns may not coincide with the security identity of NATO's non-European members.

For principal powers that are not part of the Western group, the process of security identification is similar. Thus, we see Russia and China trying to introduce a new counterhegemonic language, as a step in creating a multipolar world. Constructivists would argue that they might just succeed reaching that goal if they can only convince other states that a multipolar world is feasible since it is desirable. Constructivist theory considers that politics is not just an arena in which actors play power games but that it is mainly a construction site where identities are destroyed and new ones created. The theory places emphasis not on material capabilities but on the possibility that once an idea is thought out and launched, the challenge will be to find actors who will embrace it. They would do so if the idea was based on a real human need, not on fictions. Thus, when Russia and China talk about creating a multipolar world, they are not dreaming but are trying to mold the identity of an unsatisfied group of Asian states (India and Iran) that reject the way Western powers identify themselves as a select group of countries with a special mission to accomplish. Whether Moscow and Beijing will succeed in their endeavour is beside the point. What is important is that these two principal powers feel the need to invent a counteridentity that can attract political allegiances in Asia and elsewhere (and perhaps in Japan itself), even though their in material capabilities are inferior to those of the United States and its allies.

Finally, there are similarities between institutionalist and constructivist approaches, insofar as both emphasize that states use institutions for communications. Institutionalists see them as venues for building transparency through information exchange and shaping mutual expectations. They would not foresee a change in the strategy or preferences of principal powers at the end of an institutional process, but they would foresee a reduction of uncertainty in the expectations of the players. They would not be engaged in forging a security identity or even an understanding of what constitutes a threat, although they might exchange information about the nature of a threat and how it affected the national security of various states. In institutionalist theory, security identity does not change as a result of relations established with the interlocutor, because this identity has to do with preferences that are considered as given, whereas on constructivist theory, preferences may change as a result of communication undertaken by both sides.[17]

Realist Theory

For realist theory the key variable is the number of great powers in the international system, along with the distribution of power across the system (polarity). Periodic imbalances in the distribution of power are corrected through the balance of power. But "balance of power" appears to have several meanings, depending on the specific strand of realist theory. With structural realists, balance of power is an objective phenomenon: it takes place automatically, as it were. For Kenneth Waltz, balance is achieved through alliances, through increasing one's own internal capabilities, and, ultimately, through war or various forms of compromise arrangements. In the more traditional strain of realist theory, a balance of power takes place when principal powers agree to settle their differences by balancing their political interests and build the international order on that settlement. The leaders of the principal powers try to find a compromise between the power that is attained and the correlation of interests, against the backdrop of power relations. In the classical version of realist theory, a balance of power should give way to a balance of interests.[18] Security institutions help to define security roles and responsibilities based on the agreed balance of interests. They can also help to alleviate the apprehensions of major powers concerning future imbalances and the uncertainty of outcomes. In sum, for this strain of realist theory security institutions are the principal locus and mechanism of the balance of power.

Three types of structure can emerge in the international system: unipolarity, bipolarity, and multipolarity. In a unipolar world, balance of power is absent and bandwagoning prevalent, given the over-whelming power wielded by the dominant state. The structural-realist assumption is that eventually the dominant power will be opposed by a coalition of principal powers because of the power imbalance across the system.[19] More traditionalist realists would argue that the durability of unipolarity would depend not only on how power is concentrated in the international system but also on how the dominant actor manages this system.[20] The current American unipolarity is quite unique, in that it depends upon regional multipolarities in which states must balance their powers with or without the leadership of American power. The American governance of unipolarity looks like a decentralized, federal form of international power structure, very much like the domestic federal system of the United States itself.[21] But just as the constituent parts can oppose the central power in any federal system, principal powers can also band together to restrain occasional autocratic propensities of the global power. The form of governance of a unipolar system can therefore determine its durability. Consequently, a system of security institutions is required to ensure a predictable and manageable world order, provided that the global power remains always at its core.

In a bipolar structure of world power, security institutions are organized in two distinct sets of security blocs made up of alliances, bilateral security arrangements, and universal security arrangements (e.g., the United Nations). The two power blocs cannot manage world order, because competition drains most of their energies and attention, and a stalemate arises most of the time. Security blocs operate according to a tight schedule and well-defined objectives, while universal security arrangements are in limbo. There is limited room here for manoeuvre for states in the international community. To be sure, two blocs might at times agree to establish principles of behaviour that can regulate their competition in arms production and regional influence. But these episodes will be short-lived, since both sides will revert to their original reflexes. In bipolar systems, security institutions operate in two separate systems, and relations between both systems depend on whether power relations are managed offensively or defensively, in a friendly or confrontational manner.[22]

Finally, in a multipolar structure, security institutions are far less subject to major powers' control and more active and autonomous, depending on the path taken by the search for the elusive balance of power. Principal powers are generally expected to rely more frequently and more intensively on security institutions. Major powers would therefore invest significantly more in security institutions to achieve balance of power and hence avert confrontation and, ultimately, conflict. This cooperation might take the form of "concerts," in which the major powers agree together to maintain international order and stability or other types of security-management systems. But the players may not use security institutions: they may rely instead on other non-institutional methods to either restore the balance of power or achieve hegemony. They might do so if one or more major powers is driven by aggressive ambitions, thus throwing the self-regulating balance-of-power mechanism into complete disarray. This scenario will be more likely when major powers resort to security institutions, not to solve security problems, but to gain or safeguard status and prestige. Not all principal powers are security seekers; more often than not, they may be status-oriented and actively pursue the enhancement of their international reputation.[23]

Unlike institutionalists and constructivists, realists do not think that institutions can change major powers' security preferences, except in an unanticipated way. Generally, realists see institutions most of the time as promoting well-entrenched interests; principal powers would be unlikely to accept any changes arrived at by institutions that run against their established goals. When principal powers cooperate to manage emerging security threats, they are not really changing any of their preferences, although the process may lead them to develop their preferences in directions that may or may not be congruent with institutional preferences. As long as the process of preference formation is under their own control, principal powers are free to select any new institutional suggestions. Only when they face highly complex and unpredictable situations may they find themselves forced to participate in a process of preference formation and to live with the consequences of the outcome.

Security institutions can function as an insurance policy, however, and protect against unanticipated consequences. This function would depend entirely on the political and strategic acumen of the decision makers, as classical and neoclassical realists never tire of repeating.[24] If the leaders are enterprising enough, they will certainly use security institutions to their advantage or skilfully oppose decisions reached within them. If they do not, then security institutions in which major powers are active will likely shape their preferences in an irreversible way. For realists, security institutions are established to reflect major power interests. Whether they can be more or less useful depends on the degree to which leaders appreciate what they can do and devise innovative methods to ensure the security of communities and states.

RESEARCH DESIGN

As we have indicated, the three theories just discussed are in many respects complementary. The most important difference between them resides in their core assumptions and logical inferences. Each approach focuses on different dimensions of international political phenomena, dimensions that the other two approaches may find much less fundamental. Or they may find that the analytical sequence is wrong. Although the three theories depart from different premises, they pursue parallel lines of reasoning. Sometimes their arguments overlap: they may be saying the same thing but in a different form and style. They may use the same labels for their concepts, but the content may be different. Even if the content is the same, its status in the overall analytical framework may be different. The result of this frequent overlapping and parallelism is duplication, redundancy, and noise, especially when defenders of one approach reconstruct a highly simplistic picture of the others' core assumptions in order to dismiss it in a few, fast strokes.

Furthermore, the three theories are also congruent in their choice of analytical methods. For instance, both realists and institutionalists use rationalist arguments and almost invariably resort to interest-based analysis. Institutionalists even use realist power assumptions in their analysis, whereas constructivists may sometimes sound like traditional realists when they depict the extent to which international order is based on principles of legitimacy. Moreover, when constructivists emphasize the international social structure as the starting point for understanding an agent's conduct, their mutual disagreement with the structural realists produces only a marginal difference in understanding. Thus, when structural realists describe the structure of power distribution in material terms, constructivists would describe the same structure in ideational or normative terms. There might seem to be a vast difference between the two, but both are trying to paint the same picture.[25]

Because they are complementary, taken together the three approaches can provide a far more complete picture of the complexity of institutional security phenomena than each does separately. The main question that arises, then, is not so much whether using them simultaneously is methodologically legitimate but how to configure an analytical framework that combines the most robust insights of each approach.[26] We believe it to be possible to combine various analytical models deriving from each approach, provided that we also respect the axioms and the mode of inference of each approach.[27] For instance, if we need to explain the operation of an institutional mechanism and to focus on power relations in order to complete the explanation, it is useful to begin by using institutionalist arguments and then to complement them with realist arguments. Depending on the scale and angle from which the phenomenon is observed, one could begin with a conventional constructivist framework of analysis and then complement it with structural realist arguments. The actual combination of analytical groups, or modules, of arguments will depend on the scale of the phenomenon to be explained – or, to use a geometrical metaphor, on the plane at which the phenomenon reveals itself best – and on what narrative is the most appropriate to explain its occurrence. It does not of course make any sense to combine elements of the three approaches just for the sake of proving they can be combined, for indeed some assumptions of these approaches are incompatible. They should not be combined haphazardly; the combination should, in our judgment, follow an explanatory purpose.

One can use two methods to combine the analytical elements of the three approaches. In the "nesting" method, the objective is to select analytical elements of each of the approaches and arrange them in a suitable configuration to observe the phenomena we seek to elucidate. For instance, if we want to explain American institutional-security conduct, we could use, as Jean-Philippe Racicot and Charles-Philippe David do (chapter 1), arguments from the defensive realist approach and complete them with structural-liberal arguments. In this case, we would seek to complement a defensive realist narrative with structural-liberal arguments or vice versa. Reversing one for the other would not affect the explanation, since both sets of arguments are symmetrical and complementary.

But in some cases this interchangeability is more problematic, if not impossible, because the analyst has no choice but to start with a set of arguments from one specific approach and then continue with arguments from another approach. In this sequencing method, the order in which sets of arguments appear is important, for one approach provides the necessary concepts for the following set of arguments.[28] As Jean-Pierre Lavoie and Jacques Lévesque show in the case of Russian institutional security strategy (chapter 2), even though Russia's first maneuvers were all intended to establish extensive reciprocal relations with Western security institutions, it would be inappropriate to begin an explanation with institutionalist arguments, because Russian leaders soon found out that this objective was out of their reach. Thus, Russian conduct can largely be plotted with realist and then constructivist arguments, with occasional institutional arguments being included along the way. Similarly, if we wish to explain the operation of an institutional mechanism, it makes less sense to begin with realist or constructivist arguments; institutionalist arguments should provide our starting point. Does this mean that institutionalist theory subsumes subsequent arguments? Obviously not, since the sequencing logic is established not by the superiority of institutionalist axiomatic and inferential logic but by the scale at which the phenomenon is examined. This is why constructing and selecting cases becomes all the more important.

Case Selection

There are three classes of cases to consider. In the first class, principal powers must respond to conflicts in a way that circumscribes their effects and provides solutions to them. In some instances major powers may plan to use force to resolve the conflict, or in other instances they may be involved in peacekeeping and peace-enforcement operations, which presuppose a prior agreement by all parties to end hostilities. They may also be involved in relief and reconstruction, which may include returning failed states to political and economic normalcy or averting the imminent collapse of a fragile state. Finally, in their search for solutions to conflicts principal powers may combine the use of force with diplomatic efforts, until a settlement is reached.

In the second class of cases, major powers "regulate" security relations with their peers and other states. In this regulatory class of cases, principal powers interrelate their national security with that of their allies and other states. Examples are the détente agreements reached between the United States and the Soviet Union in 1972–73 and the German-Soviet negotiations that sealed Germany's unification in 1990. This class includes geopolitical and security dialogues between allies and adversaries on emerging threats and the means to deal with them and confidence-building measures that can encourage transparency and mutual trust. Moreover, it includes military exchanges and intelligence-sharing programs and arms-control and disarmament agreements, including agreements about verification and follow-up procedures. Most of these regulatory cases may result either in new security institutions or in new mandates for existing security institutions.

The result just described brings us to the third, institution-building class of cases, in which principal powers invest resources to create or develop international security institutions. This class is different from the previous one in that the decision to reform existing security institutions does not result from a new security arrangement. This class also includes situations in which principal powers undertake reform of norms, rules, operational procedures, and other institutional mechanisms, so as to adapt institutions to new security conditions. Institution-building also includes situations where major powers terminate or phase out security institutions or their own participation in a security institution.

As with many classification schemes, the conceptual tools provided by these three classes of cases should allow us to capture almost all instances where principal powers are involved in security institutions. Reality is of course more complex and much less amenable to neat divisions like the ones proposed here. The cases should therefore be interpreted as ideal types. Furthermore, a particular event may actually involve all three types: the conflict in Bosnia and Herzegovina is one example. In this book we have built our cases with the objective of considering only those elements that fit into our classification scheme, bearing in mind that they are connected with other types of institutional security phenomena that do not follow the same pattern of behaviour.

TYPES OF SECURITY INSTITUTIONS

Classifying security arrangements according to threats and risks or according to inclusivity and exclusivity, is useful, but it tells only part of the story.[29] The difference between a threat and a risk is not sufficient enough to allow us to capture the types of security arrangements that have emerged so far. To begin with, it is of course true that states have an interest in consulting their peers about emerging threats and risks. They also have an interest in establishing strategies for dealing with them, since some states have more resources than others to do so effectively. The strategies may include force planning in collective defence arrangements such as alliances and coalitions. But ultimately states are more interested in knowing whether their national security can be assured by other states or international arrangements should their own defence apparatus fail. States also want to know the costs of access to security arrangements that other states or international entities can provide. Obviously, a state expects to receive security assurance when it is genuinely threatened, not when it is seeking to maximize power.

Therefore, a classification of security arrangements should begin with two fundamental considerations. First, it should consider the type of security goods they can provide and whether they can be delivered on time. By "security goods" we mean, basically, "security guarantees," that is, protection and defence in response to an encroachment on a state's security. Second, a classification should consider that security goods also involve a system of norms, rules, and procedures that states must respect if they wish to have access to them. The rules, norms, and procedures are benchmarks against which a state's security behaviour can be evaluated. If a state violates them, not only should it expect to see its security assurance severely curtailed, but it should also expect sanctions and ostracism on the part of its allies or even the international community itself.

There are six types of security arrangements. The least binding are strategic partnerships; they represent one of the favourite forms of principal powers.[30] In such arrangements, both sides are willing to set aside differences they may have on several issues. They also strive to find a convergence in their perceptions of security threats. Normally, these partnerships are not institutions, since they do not contain implicit or explicit rules and norms, nor do they include security guarantees. But both sides adopt activities and practices that can lead to the establishment of security mechanisms, as well as norms governing their security relationship.

In alignments, the second type of security arrangement, there is more than just a convergence of geopolitical interests; the participants co-ordinate their security policies in the light of definite threats and risks. They undertake joint international security activities and missions, very often according to a joint program. No formal security guarantees are granted to anyone. Implicit rules and norms govern security relations among the aligned states, and the possibility of defecting from alignments is real. Nevertheless, the alignments are more binding than strategic partnerships, in that the states must honour their security commitments if they wish to avoid incurring the costs of defection.

In alliances or collective defence arrangements, the third type, we find security guarantees. To this end, alliances are equipped with a security and defence infrastructure, along with appropriate military doctrines and force-employment procedures that are supposed to provide the security assurance. Furthermore, alliances include explicit security rules and norms that member states must abide by. Coalitions, which belong to this type, are alliances that have been set up to prosecute a specific mission; they are not supposed to last beyond the period required for dealing with the security contingency at hand.[31]

Unlike the previous types of security arrangements, which occur between friendly allied and nonallied states, a fourth type involves adversaries who still maintain substantial hostility towards one another. They may establish security cooperation institutions to reduce dangerous tensions that may lead to confrontations and war. Although there are no security guarantees at all, because of substantial continuing hostility, the two sides nevertheless create security goods to the extent that they reassure each other in a limited way and are prepared to manage their differences and security rivalry through rules and norms that govern their interactions. The best example can be found in the numerous agreements reached between the Soviet Union and the United States in the 1970s and in late 1980s. The arms-control agreements reached during the détente of the 1970s were monitored by bilateral security institutions.[32] The first intrusive verification procedures for the limitation, reduction, and elimination of nuclear weapons were worked out within the framework of these security interactions.

The fifth type of arrangement, the international security treaty, is intended to establish norms, rules, and standards of security behaviour that are specific to particular issues. Classic examples are the Non-Proliferation Treaty (NPT), the Comprehensive Test Ban Treaty (CTBT),and the chemical and biological weapons-control conventions. There are no security guarantees in these institutions, but states are expected to abide by these international agreements. Nominally, all states, regardless of whether they maintain friendly or nonfriendly security relations with other states, are called upon to devise ways to manage important security risks that concern all of them. These institutions are therefore quintessential security-management institutions, since their main purpose is to manage security risks.

As in the previous types, in a sixth type all states coalesce in a collective security arrangement in order to provide for the security of another state. But unlike alliances, collective security arrangements are not binding and do not have at their disposal security and defence infrastructures, along with force-employment doctrines. Furthermore, since this is a universal type of security institution, the actual implementation of the security assurance for a specific state remains problematic, since not all states will agree that one of their peers is threatened or that it needs to be rescued. However problematic the enforcement of collective security can be, it is nevertheless a universal principle that all states highly value, since it represents a right to basic security.[33]

In the chapters that follow, the contributors to this volume assess the explanatory power of individual theoretical approaches or of a combination of approaches organized into distinct models. In the chapters on France and Japan (3 and 5), the authors consider to what extent the constructivist approach captures the security behaviour of these powers. In the case of the United States and Russia (chapters 1 and 2), the authors evaluate models that combine analytical elements from all three theoretical approaches to international relations. Again, in the case of Germany (chapter 4), the authors explore all three approaches to present a more complete picture of Germany's interest in security institutions. In the case of China and Canada (chapters 6 and 7), the authors test explanatory arguments derived from the structural-realist approach.

The overall purpose of this collective study of security institutions is to elaborate elements of a typological theory that explains the principal powers' institutional security strategy. In the concluding chapter, we therefore compare the findings of each chapter and build a typology of institutional security behaviour that is a step towards broader generalizations about why and under what conditions principal powers act through international security institutions.

Contradictory or Complementary? Defensive Realism, Structural Liberalism, and American Policy towards International Security Institutions

JEAN-PHILIPPE RACICOT
AND CHARLES-PHILIPPE DAVID

More than half a century after the creation of what might be called modern international security institutions, nation-states are more willing than ever to join institutions such as NATO, the United Nations Security Council, the Organisation for Security and Cooperation in Europe (OSCE), and many others. This state of affairs gives rise to many questions. For example, why do nation-states want to join these institutions? What is to be gained? Can they change state behaviour? Are multilateral solutions better suited to solve problems in the current international order? Among all these questions, one strikes us as perhaps the most compelling: Why does a powerful state choose one international security institution (ISI) over another?[1] This question becomes even more intriguing when asked with regard to the (currently) most powerful state of all, the United States.

The United States can arguably be credited with the creation of modern international security institutions. Following the costly Second World War, it used its considerable weight to instigate a new world order in which international institutions would be more effective than they had been in the past. Not wanting to repeat the fiasco of the League of Nations of the previous two decades and hoping, as well, to regulate and foster a new international economic system, the United States actively pursued the formation of the United Nations and the

Bretton Woods Accords. In addition, with the creation of the North Atlantic alliance (NATO), the United States supported Western Europe's attempt to create a security system that would not only stabilize European countries' relations with one another but also present a strong front to a significant Red Army presence in the rest of Europe. In those decisive times, the United States did not hesitate to limit its own power in order to participate in security institutions. Why does it still choose to do so? More importantly, why does it prefer some institutions to others? We will attempt to address this question here by proposing a synthesis of defensive realism and liberal institutionalism.

To examine how the United States interacts with international security institutions, we need to elaborate a theoretical model that would suggest certain outcomes and explain those outcomes or, alternatively, shed some light on the absence of a predicted outcome, as the case may be. We propose an original model that links realism with liberal institutionalism. It is our view that realism can still serve as a useful tool in understanding state behaviour,[2] even though it has been widely criticized for its poor predictive performance and for its failure to anticipate the outcome of the Cold War.[3] The demise of realism has been greatly exaggerated; a survey of recent scientific articles and publications on international relations would surely demonstrate that it is alive and well and that as a theoretical model it is far more intricate and complex than its critics suggest. One aspect of realism that has not been discussed thoroughly (or convincingly, for that matter) is its relationship to international security institutions and to multilateral cooperation in general.

We intend to show that certain variants of realism can be linked with recent liberal institutional theory and to show how this combination can shed new light on the relationship between great powers and international institutions. This synthesis combines the best of both theories and elucidates the often unilateral actions of the American superpower, while also offering a working model of how the United States interacts with international security institutions. As mentioned, to accomplish this synthesis, we will employ the variant of realism called defensive realism and a variant of liberal theory known as liberal institutionalism. Both theories will be tested in studies of three situations that arose during the Clinton administration: the UN reform of the Security Council, U.S. behaviour in Bosnia after the implementation of the Dayton Accords, and NATO enlargement.

The idea of a hybrid between realist and liberal theories may at first seem untenable, but the two theories share various essential premises. Realism identifies the state as the main player in international relations today, as does liberalism. Both liberalism and realism acknowledge that anarchy – the absence of a supreme international authority – characterizes international relations today. As well, defensive realism and liberal institutionalism are not extreme versions of their respective paradigms. The former is a softer version of realism, while the latter depends on the existence of a dominant world player and can be considered a hard variant of liberal theory. Thus, the two theories meet halfway. Finally, from a methodological point of view, both are explanatory, foundational, positivist, and rationalist.[4] They basically see the world through the same lenses, although they do not always agree in their identification of the causal relations in contemporary international relations.

In this study we will address two distinct challenges. First, we will try to demonstrate that realism and neoliberalism can simultaneously provide explanations of cooperation through international institutions.[5] We will refute John Mearsheimer's allegations that international institutions "do not matter" in changing a state's behaviour[6] and we will take up Schweller and Priess's challenge to create "a system theory that can incorporate the characteristics of states, their interactions, and a more comprehensive view of system structure than is captured by the concept of polarity."[7] Our theoretical model is not merely a new version of structural realism or a revamped neorealism but rather a new model based on the merits of these two different but compatible theories. Buzan, Jones, and Little proposed a similar type of project with the creation of structural realism in an attempt to "fuse Neorealism and Liberalism into a full system theory that incorporates process as well as structure."[8] Second, and less ambitiously, our project is designed simply to provide a broad explanation of u.s. foreign policy with regard to international security institutions; it is not intended to create an entirely new international relations theory.

In our view, realist thought has always regarded international institutions as essential tools of foreign policy. To deny this would be to deny the importance to the great powers of constructs such as the Concert of Europe in the nineteenth century. Thus our answer to the neoliberal-neorealist debate would be that neorealism is not in tune with the actual look and feel of international politics.[9] If it was, the logic of neorealism would apply and states would act according to a distinctive pattern. In particular, they would tend to maintain a balance of power or restore it if it should be upset. For example, Kenneth Waltz anticipated the creation of a counterweight against a greater power, but we do not currently see a counterweight developing against the world's superpower, the United States.[10] However, international institutions are still vulnerable to the whims of a powerful state and therefore cannot be considered fully autonomous or strong enough to completely impose a course of action on a reluctant state. The solution to this dilemma is the presence of a benign liberal hegemonic power, such as the United States. Surrounding this power is a cobweb-like structure that directs the ebb and flow of international relations. This structure is made up of various international institutions that depend on, but also limit, the actions of the hegemonic power. We employ a complementary fusion of defensive realism and liberal institutionalism to describe this situation.

The next section of this chapter looks at the theoretical model we have chosen to explain U.S. involvement with international security institutions (ISIS). We briefly describe the roots of defensive realism and structural realism, highlighting the theoretical assumptions that, when combined, can explain U.S. institutional security conduct since the end of the Cold War. In the subsequent section we then proceed to analyze the three cases and assess how they fare in the light of our explanatory model.

COMBINING THEORIES:
DEFENSIVE REALISM AND LIBERAL INSTITUTIONALISM

Various Forms of Realism:
A Brief Survey of a Broad Paradigm

Realism is not monolithic. Regardless of how the critics of realism would like to see it, realism is in fact a varied and multidimensional research program. In this sense, realism is also not a unified theory but a general paradigm consisting of several subtheories. Thus realism is not a single theory that can be tested, confirmed, or refuted as such. However, some unifying premises do link all the various categories of realism. We can identify four of these assumptions.[11] First, the nation-state is not the only player on the current world scene, but it is the only one that can give us proper insight into world politics through its inter-action with other nation-states. Second, nation-states are rational players and their behaviour can be understood as the consequence of strategic and instrumental reflection. Third, realists emphasize state power and national interests. The state seeks power (either to gain rel-ative material capabilities or influence over outcomes) in order to achieve its goals. Fourth, nation-states are inherently competitive as a consequence of anarchy, which forces them to rely on themselves for survival and autonomy.

All realist theories share these assumptions, but they differ in their interpretations of how certain elements of the international system (such as anarchy or the position of one state relative to others) affect state behaviour, as well as in their interpretation of how a state will behave (that is, whether or not state power will be maximized). Broadly, we can identify three realist theories: classical realism, neorealism, and neoclassical realism.

Classical Realism. No other international relations theory has quite the pedigree of classical realism, but what is of interest here is the modern version of classical realism. Reacting to the idealism between and following the two world wars of the twentieth century, writers such as E.H. Carr and Hans Morgenthau brought back concepts like the inherent evil in human nature, the inevitability of war between competing states, the lust for power, and the primacy of the national interest. For classical realists, power is what drives key events in international politics, not justice or lofty moral ideals. The national interest of a state, which is basically determined by its material capabilities and its geography, is best served when it attempts to maximize power. Balance of power is an essential concept for classical realists since weak states will tend to band together to protect themselves from more powerful ones.

Neorealism. Neorealism, or structural realism, arose in the late seventies, after traditional realism had been seriously challenged by two other theoretical approaches. On the one hand, the ideas of interdependence and transnationalism put forward notably by Joseph Nye and Robert Keohane in the seventies (in *Power and Interdependence: World Politics in Transition*), questioned the role of the state as the sole actor in the international system. On the other hand, the behaviourist projects that were very popular in the sixties and seventies in the United States criticised realism's lack of scientific rigour. However, with the end of détente in the late 1970s, realism came back with a vengeance, taking a more parsimonious, systematic, and specific form than ever with Kenneth Waltz's groundbreaking *Theory of International Politics*. Grounded in microeconomics, neorealism presupposes that security, not power, is the highest end of states in the international system. Anarchy and the distribution of capabilities are the basic causal variables to be considered. The biggest difference between neorealism and classical realism is that neorealism is a theory of international politics, not a theory of foreign policy. Waltz and other authors, such as Christopher Layne and John Mearsheimer, focus on the system-wide distribution of capabilities and on the polarity of the system, rather than on the relative inequalities of power between states. In their view, self-help always applies to states under anarchy, and weak states will tend to seek a counterbalance against stronger ones. Finally, neorealism does not place much weight on domestic politics or ideologies.

Neoclassical Realism. Neoclassical realism takes off where neorealism ends. This recent form of realism builds on the weakness of neorealism (i.e., its inability or unwillingness to open the "black box" of domestic politics) and returns to the teachings of classical realism (hence its name). Gideon Rose, who is closely associated with neoclassical realism, in fact coined the term.[12] Neoclassical realism attempts to consider both internal and external variables simultaneously. It attempts to create a new theory of international politics, as well as a new theory of foreign policy. A state's foreign policy is determined by its place in the international system and its relative power capabilities. However, the impact of these characteristics is indirect and complex, because systemic pressures must be translated through intervening variables at the unit (state) level. This implies that similar gross power capabilities in different kinds of states lead to different state actions. By considering the context in which foreign policies are formulated as essential, neoclassical realism tries to fill the gap between neorealism (where there is a clear link between systemic configuration and unit behaviour) and constructivism[13] (on this theory, reality is socially constructed).[14]

Offensive and Defensive Realism. Offensive and defensive realism can be identified, essentially, as interpretations of how the international system fosters or refrains from encouraging aggression.[15] Commentators who view the international system as an arena where conflict and violence rule can be considered offensive realists. According to their view, security is precarious, and wars between states are very likely to occur. Offensive strategies are therefore better suited to this world, because they ultimately offer greater security. Defensive realists, on the other hand, think that cooperation between states is possible and that insecurity is not the only result generated in the international environment. According to defensive realists security is generally plentiful and a defensive strategy can have more productive results than an offensive one. According to Sean Lynn-Jones, defensive realism is essentially a neorealist theory in which the state is the main player in an international system that shapes the pattern of relationships between states. But it lacks classical realism's pessimistic outlook.[16]

The concepts of offensive and defensive realism first appeared in the writings of Jack Snyder.[17] However, Snyder admits that he was inspired by the then unpublished work of Steven Van Evera, who may be considered the father of offensive/defensive realist theory.[18] Another theorist, Fareed Zakaria, disagrees with Snyder and explains that states expand when they are threatened (expansion is broadly defined as having an aggressive international policy and not strictly as territorial expansion).[19] When decision makers perceive an increase in threats, they act aggressively to feel more secure.[20] According to Zakaria, "For the Classical realist, states expand because they can, for the defensive realist, states expand because they must."[21] Sean Lynn-Jones disagrees with Zakaria's interpretation, however, and argues that he fails to refute defensive realism.[22] According to Lynn-Jones, defensive realism contends that a state will attempt to expand only when expansion increases its security and when three conditions are met: 1 a threat exists; 2 expansion will reduce this threat; and 3 the state has the means to pursue its expansionist policy.[23] We agree with this interpretation of defensive realism.

It is also our view that the present international system does not necessarily generate conflict and war. As mentioned, contrary to what Waltzian neorealism predicts, we have not yet witnessed the emergence of a balance of power against the system's superpower, the United States. We can therefore assume that although there are multiple risks in the current international system, none is so significant that it threatens the very existence of that country. If security is generally plentiful and available to the superpower, it will tend to seek it in a cooperative manner, since – as defensive realism claims – defensive strategies are likely to lead to even greater stability and security. If we consider Snyder's arguments that domestic structure and politics are important factors in its response to the international environment, we can assume that the United States did act according to the tenets of defensive realism. Van Evera also offers ten explanations for war that do not represent the present state of affairs and clearly indicate that the actual international system is more "defensive" than "offensive."[24]

So how does cooperation take place in the offensive/defensive realism paradigm? Aggressive, offensive behaviour (or expansionist behaviour) is characterized by constant unilateralism, secret diplomacy, a series of faits accomplis, and a sharp decrease in international agreements. It would be safe to assume that defensive behaviour is exactly the opposite: it is characterized by frequent multilateralism, respect for international law and treaties, and open diplomacy and negotiation. Thus defensive alliance formation, bargaining, and even bandwagoning are considered evidence for defensive realism.[25]

Where do ISIS fit into the defensive realist model? Why should a superpower decide to engage in multilateral security arrangements? The literature on this subject is not very specific, but we can deduce a few possible interpretations. Maintaining ISIS makes conquest and offensive strategies that much harder to accomplish and thus creates a more peaceful international environment. ISIS create a "defense dominant" environment, since they help to control "offense dominant" state reactions.[26] Also, if ISIS encourage stability, maintain international order, and increase and widen communication channels between states, they will be supported by the United States. Benign hegemony theory supports this idea.[27] American behaviour, regardless of the superpower's relative strength, favours regional integration, ISIS, and even stable multipolarity.[28] American efforts to preserve U.S. predominance in the international system include "engaging status quo-oriented states, confronting revisionist states, and [using] multilateral institutions to reinforce the perception that America's power is not being exercised arbitrarily or in a threatening manner."[29] Thus, participating in and fostering the development of ISIS that are beneficial in maintaining the status quo and U.S. predominance are both supported by defensive realism. Defensive realism thus leads us to the following hypotheses concerning American behaviour towards ISIS. First, the hegemonic power will seek security through partnership, not competition. Second, the hegemonic power will mostly support ISIS that maintain world order and the status quo (i.e., the central position of the United States in the international system).

Structural Liberalism

Structural Liberalism is part of the greater liberal tradition. Liberalism, like classical realism, has its roots in classical political philosophy. Strongly influenced by the Enlightenment, liberalism views human nature from a perspective that is very different from the negative and pessimistic outlook of realism. Centred around individual liberty, the state, according to liberals, must exist to protect individuals from themselves and from others, but it must always act as the servant of collective will (and not as its master, as in the case of realism). Like realism, liberalism has evolved over the years in several different theoretical directions.[30] In the interest of brevity, we will not discuss all the different theories. However, we can safely say that all liberal theories, while they do not disregard the power relationship between states, stress that prosperity and security are better attained through cooperation. Stability is provided by cooperative security, democratic peace, and economic interdependence.

In his thought-provoking article "The False Promise of International Institutions," Mearsheimer rekindled a debate that still rages today.[31] Do international institutions really affect and alter a state's behaviour? Do they have an individual impact on the world scene or are they ultimately subservient to a state's desires, tools to be used in time of need but otherwise ignored? Mearsheimer, deliberately (mis)representing realism, claims that institutions are indeed present on the international scene but that they do not have sufficient clout to impose their will on individual states and that it would be foolish to think otherwise. Classical realists and more recent realist studies clearly indicate that Mearsheimer's position is not representative of theoretical realism in general. Liberalism responded forcefully and the debate continues.[32] We will use a recent contribution by Daniel Deudney and John Ikenberry that incorporates the characteristics of a unipolar international system with liberal and institutional structures.[33] The absence of major conflict between Western states is the result of what the authors identify as structural liberalism, or the institutionalization of a system of consensual and reciprocal relations among participating states. American hegemony is essential to the maintenance of structural liberalism.

According to Deudney and Ikenberry, realist and liberal theories both fall short of explaining the contemporary world and the lasting power of international institutions. Structural liberalism seeks to capture the major components of the Western political order and explain their interrelationships. Although major conflict is avoided, conflict between great powers does exist, but it is channelled through international institutions and falls short of violence. Structural liberalism is characterized by five elements that, taken together, describe the Western order.[34] The first element is "security co-binding": through ISIS (NATO, the EU), the great Western power and the world superpower exercise mutual constraint. The second element is the "penetrated" form of American hegemony. It is reciprocal, legitimate, and transparent, and it provides easy access to policy-making. Two factors make this possible: the political structure of the United States and the prevalence of transnational politics.

"Semi-sovereignty" and partial great powers make up the third element of the Western order. Japan and Germany are excellent examples of great powers that limit their sovereignty through peace constitutions, self-constraint, and a wide variety of multilateral arrangements. The fourth element is structural economic openness. Co-binding institutions and practices makes it possible to moderate anarchy without producing hierarchy. Political structures emerge from the contemporary form of capitalism and favour institutions that mitigate anarchy. The final element is civic identity, or the common components of Western identity. The Western powers share the fundamental values of liberalism, democracy, and capitalism. Circulating elites, educational exchanges, and a "business civilisation" foster a cohesive political order. With state interactions, civic and capitalistic identities are created as national and ethnic identities slowly settle into the background. Thus, identities are created rather than assumed. This hint of constructivism makes structural liberalism even more interesting.

We have chosen structural liberalism because it seems to offer a more accurate description of the current international political order and of the position of the United States within this order than the descriptions of either realism or liberalism. Since structural liberalism is already a hybrid of realist and liberal theories, it remains methodologically coherent.

While structural liberalism seems to properly identify the main components of the Western order, one question remains: why would the United States agree to limit its power? Ikenberry again provides a useful answer for our project. He refers to "strategic restraint,"[35] which was originally designed "to convey to America's potential partners credible assurances of its commitments to restrain its power and operate within the agreed-upon rules and principles of the postwar order."[36] This approach facilitated consensus-building among the Allies and achieved the participation of other states. The same system is used today. Three conditions are needed to make strategic restraint possible: bonding between states, binding through institutions, and creating opportunities for other states to have a voice and make their grievances known. Post–Cold War American hegemony can therefore be described as reluctant, open, and self-binding. The United States remains fully at the centre of this structure, but other states are highly integrated into it. Because the structure is legitimate, the United States does not need to exercise coercive power, and other states do not feel the need to seek a counterbalance against the hegemonic power. Some states, such as China, Russia, or France, might disagree and argue that "strategic restraint" is not a good descriptor of u.s. policy, but their general policies and actions do not indicate a strong inclination to challenge u.s. power or to disturb the present status quo.

Structural liberalism suggests that relations between the United States and other participating states will outlast any change in external threats and that the overall cohesion and strength of Western international institutions will grow. According to structural liberalism, isis will flourish and prosper because of the overall structure of the

Western political order. The United States should consequently help to bring about and sustain ISIS that foster a continuing relationship between it and other nations.

Structural liberalism therefore leads us to three additional hypotheses that complete our working model. First, the United States has continued to use strategic restraint in the post–Cold War era. Second, ISIS allow for the co-binding effect to continue and provide opportunities for other countries to have a voice: they are encouraged to do so by the United States. Third, American hegemony is best described as benign, since it is reluctant, open, and self-binding. These hypotheses, in conjunction with the two initial hypotheses from defensive realism discussed above, allow us to construct the basic hypothesis that underlines our explanatory model:

To maintain the status quo and international stability, the United States adopts a defensive strategy that is characterized by a benign form of hegemony, strategic restraint, and the creation and support of ISIS that allow for cooperation, co-binding, and the creation of voice-opportunities.

ISIS are thus both part of the current international order that the United States wishes to maintain and a means of sustaining this order. On the other hand, when an ISI does not serve vital U.S. interests, we believe that domestic politics and domestic political structures interfere with the course of action that our explanatory model would suggest. We would then face a situation best described by neoclassical realism, in which the structure and characteristics of a unit (in this case, U.S. domestic politics), distort systemic influences through its "filtering" capabilities and have a profound impact on the unit's foreign policy and interaction with ISIS.

With this model, we should be able to predict the outcome of our three case studies. UN Security Council reform and UN reform in general should be helped along by U.S. support. With its goal of curbing international violence and increasing interstate communication and cooperation, the United Nations still provides excellent opportunities as an ISI, and it generally benefits U.S. interests. However, we will see that this is not always the case and that our contrary hypothesis is supported in this case study. Second, the maintenance and enlargement of NATO to include all compatible members should also be supported by the United States. NATO is more than just a defensive military alliance; it is also a co-binding institution that needs to be protected at all costs. (The NATO case will also demonstrate the impact of domestic structure on a state's interaction with ISIS.) Finally, American involvement in Bosnia after the Dayton Accords will continue, for the sake of contributing to NATO stability and maintaining an American presence in Europe. American leadership is essential to securing peace in Europe and to creating new opportunities for political ties between past adversaries. The next section of this chapter will test these predictions against each case study.

TESTING THE MODEL: POST-DAYTON BOSNIA, NATO ENLARGEMENT, AND UN SECURITY COUNCIL REFORM

American Involvement in Post-Dayton Bosnia

Signed on 21 November 1995, the Dayton Accords implemented a cease-fire and the beginnings of territorial, legal, and constitutional arrangements in Bosnia. Armed forces from allied NATO nations, as well as member states of Partnership for Peace (PfP) were sent into Bosnia on 14 December of the same year. With the Dayton Accords, the international community hoped it had finally achieved a peaceful and lasting solution to an ethnopolitical conflict that had only worsened since the early 1990s.

Following the Dayton Accords the American military participated in a multilateral force in Bosnia to implement and monitor what was agreed upon in Dayton. This engagement was both multilateral and institutional: multilateral because more than thirty nations participated in the Implementation Force, or IFOR, and institutional because NATO was the ISI chosen to supervise and lead IFOR. American conduct in this operation can be divided into two distinct phases.

Phase one ran from 14 December 1995 to 20 December 1996, when American participation in the NATO Joint Endeavour was limited to military operations: Serb, Croatian, and Bosnian troops were pulled out of indicated areas, the withdrawal of UNPROFOR, the United Nations Protection Force, was implemented, and secure conditions for reconstruction and reconciliation were created. This phase of American institutional behaviour was characterized by four steps. First, it was necessary to establish a precise timetable for American deployment and especially for withdrawal from the Bosnian theatre, because doing so allowed for a national consensus and, at the same time, helped the Clinton administration to fend off congressional attacks. It thus declared that 20 December 1996 would be the deadline for all American forces to leave the area. The objectives of the Joint Endeavour operation would thus have to be achieved within this time frame.[37]

In step two of this phase, IFOR success criteria and the original IFOR mandates were modified in a way that would not only change NATO's role in IFOR but forever alter its traditional institutional mission. This exit strategy was basically a military strategy that did not take into account the political aspects of the Bosnian crisis. The Clinton administration soon realized that without true reconciliation between the parties, an early pullout would lead to renewed fighting, and it thus started to shift its objectives from a purely military perspective to a civilian one. Peacekeeping was being transformed into peacebuilding, and IFOR would be maintained until the civilian goals had been reached.[38]

The third step was the holding of free national elections in the fall of 1996. For the Clinton administration they would be a symbol of the success of IFOR in Bosnia. Pressure was applied to the OSCE in June 1996 to speed up the creation of proper conditions for a September vote, notwithstanding serious misgivings of observers who felt that proper conditions could not be created by that time.[39] For Washington, an early election would have a double benefit. It would show that IFOR troops had created a favourable climate and that a withdrawal within the initial parameters was possible. Clinton's credibility would consequently increase and his success on the foreign policy front on the eve of his possible re-election would be highlighted.

In the final step of phase one the Clinton administration acknowledged that IFOR would probably stay active beyond the original deadline of 20 December. Insufficient progress had been made in Bosnia and an early pullout would prove disastrous. The decision to stay longer than initially expected was also the result of allied pressure. Other NATO members would also leave Bosnia if the United States decided to leave IFOR. Thus, NATO planned for a prolonged operation in the fall of 1996. No official declaration was heard before the U.S. presidential elections, but on 15 November President Clinton explained to the American people the new NATO mission and its goals of preventing new hostilities, allowing for political reconciliation, and assisting in economic reconstruction.[40]

The second phase of U.S. involvement in Bosnia after Dayton took place under the banner of the International Stabilizing Force (SFOR). The beginning of this second phase also marked the rekindling of the debate about an exit strategy. After answering to a congressional inquiry at his confirmation hearing, William S. Cohen, the secretary of defense, made it clear on 25 January 1997 that U.S. troops would be in Bosnia for at least another year and a half.[41] The target exit date was now 30 June 1998. On 10 June 1997 President Clinton issued a statement that U.S. troops could not simply abandon Bosnia after so much effort.[42]

A second characteristic of the SFOR phase was the Clinton administration's recourse to international organizations to put additional pressure on the Serb and Croat nations. After reviewing the lack of progress with certain IFOR/SFOR objectives (i.e., the pursuit and incarceration of war criminals), the Clinton administration suspended international loans and isolated both nations from regional organizations for as long as they would not cooperate in a more complete way with SFOR and the International Criminal Tribunal. Despite congressional opposition, the administration did not hesitate to use NATO, the IMF, and the World Bank to put unrelenting pressure on Slobodan Milosevic and Franjo Tudjman to facilitate the rounding up of individuals accused of war crimes. The complexity of such operations made it clear once again that it was totally unrealistic to expect to fulfill SFOR objectives before June 1998.[43]

Meanwhile, Congress was placing increased pressure on the Clinton administration for an early pullout from Bosnia. Both the House and the Senate found that an engagement until 1998 went far beyond U.S. interests in the region.[44] But once again, the administration proceeded against the advice of Congress and indicated that U.S. forces would stay in the Bosnian area for 1998, and maybe even beyond. At the end of December 1997, President Clinton went so far as to suggest that U.S. troops would remain until the end of his mandate in January 2001.[45] For the Clinton administration the course was set: since its initial objectives had not been met, there was now no turning back.

Realizing that additional efforts at political stabilization were needed in Bosnia, the United States decided to support moderate Serb factions led by Biljana Plavsic, president of the Bosnian Serb Republic. By having NATO adopt proactive measures aimed at reenforcing Plavsic's position, the United States was trying to undermine the negative influence of former Bosnian Serb president, Radovan Karadzic and his political allies. Through nonmilitary means (assuming police functions, confiscating weapons caches, preventing hate-filled television transmissions) NATO directly affected the power base of Karadzic, and through similar operations (improving police effectiveness, protecting the free press, and raising the level of economic aid) NATO helped to foster moderate factions. These actions were a far cry from the original, strictly military role of IFOR. The actions of NATO and the United States in Bosnia were now proceeding well beyond what had been envisioned at Dayton. The lack of rapid progress in a number of key SFOR objectives once again reminded NATO that peacebuilding operations did not follow the same time frame that peacekeeping operations followed and did not require the same commitments. Consequently, on 18 February 1998 NATO members decided to prolong the SFOR mandate yet again. This time, however, no exit date was mentioned in the decision, which indicated that the United States, NATO, and other SFOR members were in Bosnia for the long haul, that is, for as long as it would take to achieve peacebuilding objectives.

Interpreting U.S. Behaviour in Post-Dayton Bosnia

Before we proceed to verify our explanatory model, we can draw several conclusions about American institutional behaviour in Bosnia, conclusions that are in accordance with specific aspects of our hypothesis.

Our first conclusion is that American leadership in this case reflects classic hegemonic behaviour. It was crucial to an American military presence in Bosnia, as was made evident by the rejection of the double-key system of NATO/UN command and control that had been so detrimental to Bosnian peacekeeping operations from 1992 to 1995.[46] With NATO solely in control of IFOR and SFOR, it was clear that the United States was asserting its leadership after years of hesitation. With critical NATO superior officer positions being held either by Americans or by close allies, operations in Bosnia would not be hindered by bureaucratic and diplomatic difficulties associated with the UN.[47]

The NATO-U.S. equation was certainly not in question on 27 November 1995 when President Clinton announced that "America alone can and should make the difference for peace ... If we're not there, NATO will not be there; peace will collapse; the war will reignite."[48] For the Clinton administration, vital American values and interests were at stake in Bosnia, and thus powerful motives dictated American leadership. European stability and the survival of an emerging pan-European liberal system were being threatened by unrest in Bosnia. Instability in Bosnia would lead to instability in Europe, a scenario that the Clinton administration could not allow to unfold.[49]

This leadership role was also supported and encouraged by the main U.S. allies in Europe. Germany recognised that it was only through American leadership that the Bosnian stumbling blocks had been overcome, while France acknowledged that an American presence was necessary both logistically and politically. Without it, Western Europe would probably not even be present in Bosnia.[50] So hegemonic leadership was both necessary and welcome in post-Dayton Bosnia.

Our second conclusion concerns the key roles played by international security institutions and other international organizations employed by the Clinton administration to reduce costs and share responsibilities.[51] NATO was the main tool chosen by the administration to construct and implement workable solutions in Bosnia. During the post-Dayton era, NATO consistently stood head and shoulders above the UN and the OSCE. Through the PfP program it did more to bring East and West together than any other multilateral European security organization, mainly because of the strong American presence in NATO and because of the alliance's ability to achieve consensus rapidly with a little horse-trading, despite considerable divergence between the allies.[52] It is also clear that the Clinton administration had many hopes riding on NATO's performance in Bosnia. Failure in Bosnia would have been followed by a failure of the enlargement process and eventually a failure of the alliance itself. This was not an option for the Americans.

U.S. leadership is obviously integrated into NATO, and it filtered through at all levels during the operations of IFOR and SFOR, but a reciprocal relationship was nonetheless established through fifty years of common action. European members wanted a strong American presence in the Balkans, while the Americans wanted to see more European countries do their share in security matters.[53] NATO was also involved in defining objectives, even if ultimately it had little power to make the United States intervene. American command and control, limited engagements, and subordination of the allies and of other PfP members were American preferences, and by and large they were respected. Thus, rules were dictated and strengthened by the United States inside NATO. Support for the proposed liberal model seemed constant on the part of all partners involved, within NATO, the PfP and the Contact Group.

Even if American leadership was deemed necessary, it nevertheless generally corresponded with what we have described as strategic restraint. American behaviour in post-Dayton Bosnia was indeed open, self-restrained, and reluctant. The Clinton administration was under significant pressure from Congress and from public opinion to leave Bosnia as quickly as possible. This pressure certainly entails a form of restraint and reluctance, since the executive branch of government had no free reign in the Bosnian theater and was under constant scrutiny with regard to its policy decisions. The United States also partly gave way to allied pressure, indicating an openness not usually associated with traditional hegemonic power.

We can therefore conclude that post-Dayton Bosnia has enhanced the appeal of the norms and values (such as multilateral cooperation, collective defense, and democracy) promoted not only by the United

States but also by NATO members and many other European states. IFOR and SFOR have been beneficial to the construction of a European security system linked to a worldwide security system in which the United States is at the centre and in command but in which it also supports a security network essential to its interests. This evidence clearly supports our defensive realist/structural liberal model. By using ISIS and international organizations, the Clinton administration demonstrated its willingness to act openly and in conjunction with other nations to support ideals and values that are certainly close the its own interests but that also form the basis for an international liberal system. Unilateralism was expressed in American leadership, but it was always filtered through international organizations.

This conclusion appears to match our explanatory model. We find no major discrepancy between our hypothesis and this first case study. American involvement was clearly designed to maintain a stable Europe, as well as to support ISIS and other international organizations (IOs). The Clinton administration did not oppose the shift from a purely military NATO presence to more complex operations involving peacebuilding and other civilian-oriented activities. Acceptance of this institutional shift is consistent with the tenets of structural liberalism. The United States also used other international institutions to apply pressure on the Serb and Croat nations. The use of these ISIS and IOs to deny a voice to noncollaborating states indicates the importance of these institutions in the current international system. Although this type of political blackmail can be interpreted as an indication that ISIS and IOs are mostly the tools of the great powers, we believe that their value goes much farther. A rogue state can defy the hegemonic power for a certain time and hope to be able to bear the consequences, but it cannot defy the will of the international community, as expressed through international institutions, for very long. Autarky is simply not a valid option for a state that has been admitted into the various international organizations that facilitate commerce, diplomacy, and security.

NATO Enlargement

As in Bosnia, U.S. behaviour with regard to NATO enlargement was spurred by external pressure and events and not by a specific foreign policy or an overall post–Cold War strategy for the Atlantic alliance. In this case, it was the combined demands of Poland, Hungary, and Czechoslovakia for NATO membership that brought NATO enlargement rapidly onto America's foreign policy agenda.[54] Recognizing the void left by the retreat of the Red Army following the end of the Cold War, both the United States and Germany decided to institutionalize relationships between East and West on a more formal basis. The North Atlantic Cooperation Council was thus created in 1991 and Eastern European countries were asked to participate in peacekeeping missions with NATO members in the former Yugoslavia as of 1992.[55]

Under the Clinton administration, however, NATO enlargement went far beyond what had been timidly suggested by the previous administration. Following the tenet of providing unflagging support for newborn democracies, especially in Eastern Europe, Clinton and his National Security Advisor, Anthony Lake – and later the State Department – plotted a course of action that necessarily included NATO enlargement.

Expansion would serve two of the Clinton administration's goals. The first was to export the rule of law, respect for international norms, and the spread of democratic values to Eastern European states. With this goal in mind, the Clinton administration would leave tentative measures behind and fully engage itself in NATO enlargement, especially after 1993–94.

The second goal was to create a new institutional tool for improving relations with Moscow. NATO enlargement, especially in the view of the Defense Department and certain factions of the State Department, would entail a modification of U.S.-Russian relations by adding another forum for discussion between East and West. Since NATO enlargement was essentially perceived in a negative light by Moscow, a parallel objective was to create a new dialogue between NATO and Russia. Reaching this objective would help manage an already fragile Russia by maintaining a special status for the battered giant state.

We identify 1993 as a pivotal year for U.S. interest in NATO enlargement. Closer ties with the new Eastern European democracies were no longer sufficient. It was decided that an official, institutional commitment was now necessary. This decision was mainly directed from the White House. It seems that what jumpstarted President Clinton's involvement in this issue was a trilateral meeting between himself and Lech Walesa and Vaclav Havel in Washington in the spring of 1993. Clinton seems to have been impressed with these two leaders' advocacy for NATO membership for Poland and Czechoslovakia respectively. The political records of these two great reformers must have also struck a chord with the President. With the help of Anthony Lake, an initial bureaucratic nexus was created to pursue this endeavour.[56]

Ironically, despite the White House's initial enthusiasm, the first concrete American proposition that was directed at soothing Eastern European anxieties about being left out of Western institutions came from the Pentagon. In April 1993 the supreme allied commander in Europe (SACEUR), General John Shalikashvili, proposed the creation of what would later be called the Partnership for Peace (PfP).[57] This organization would support military cooperation between Eastern European states, former U.S.S.R. states, and NATO members. The PfP was more than merely a consultative body like the North Atlantic Cooperation Council (NACC); it would put troops in contact with each other in the field through joint exercises, and it would help create common planning.[58] For Defense Department planners, the PfP was a safer option than outright NATO enlargement. It would provide and maintain a stabilizing American presence in Europe and would therefore be an immediate response to Eastern European states, who were growing increasingly impatient about being left in the security void of Soviet withdrawal.[59] What the Defense Department wanted to avoid, above all, was the creation of a new dividing line in Europe between NATO members and nonmembers. Another disadvantage of NATO enlargement was the negative Russian reaction to penetration into what it still considered its sphere of influence. Finally, the integration of several new national armies into the NATO superstructure could very well be disadvantageous.[60]

Although Shalikashvili's proposal was welcome, NATO enlargement nonetheless remained on the Clinton administration's list of top priorities, even though the State Department was divided over the issue. Many observers (such as Strobe Talbott, special ambassador for the CIS) believed that NATO enlargement would create unnecessary tensions between Washington and Moscow, compromise what little reform had been achieved, and give fuel to nationalist or ultranationalist movements within Russia. A more prudent and gradual approach had to be taken with Russia. In spite of these fears, a second faction in the State Department seemed to rally around the president and his national security advisor. For this segment of the Clinton administration, the choice was clear: NATO had to accept the new Eastern European democracies, in order to promote the expansion of democracy throughout Europe and make sure that liberal values, such as political and economic openness, would take root in these countries. To prevent these new democracies from floundering and straying from reform, a strong Western institutional link had to be offered, and NATO enlargement fit the bill exactly.[61]

Secretary of State Warren Christopher decided to opt initially for the middle ground between the Pentagon and the White House and to present the PfP proposal at the next NATO summit in Brussels in January 1994, while still considering enlargement. Clinton went along with this plan and officially stated in Brussels that the American attitude towards NATO enlargement was positive, although he was not very specific at that point as to how it should proceed.[62] Enlargement was still at the working stage. From the summer of 1994 on, the twin objectives of NATO enlargement were set: expand membership to include the new Eastern European democracies and improve relations with Russia.

In spite of his interest in expanding NATO, President Clinton was not insensitive to Russia's plight and its deep concerns about the project. While Russia was not rejecting the PfP, it wanted to negotiate on an equal basis with the alliance. According to Russia, the OSCE was still the institution of choice to help create a new security structure for Europe. Russia nevertheless signed the PfP agreement on 22 June 1994, since it realized that the advantages of the program outweighed the costs. For the Clinton administration, this step was again a sign that efforts to spur democratization and liberalisation in Russia would not be in vain.[63]

While the Clinton administration was still hesitating to designate the new NATO candidates, Congress went ahead with a full-fledged campaign for the inclusion of Poland, Hungary, and the new Czech Republic. With the election of a new Republican majority in Congress in the fall of 1994, Congress had now become a major player in the NATO-enlargement process.[64] In 1994 and 1995 Congress passed several bills that clearly indicated that it wanted as many fledgling democracies to join NATO as soon as possible. It now conceived of a much larger enlargement wherein the Baltic states, Albania, Romania, Bulgaria, Slovenia, and even the Ukraine could join NATO if they so desired and if conditions were right.[65]

During the fall of 1995, after an outburst by the Russian president, Boris Yeltsin, threatening war in Europe over NATO enlargement, NATO decided that there would be no new permanent troops and no nuclear weapons deployed on the territory of Eastern European NATO members.[66] Enlargement proceeded nonetheless, and on 5 December 1995 the United States once again announced a new step in the process. During a conference in Brussels, Secretary of State Christopher specified the procedures that prospective members would have to follow if they were to join NATO. First, there would be a series of meetings between NATO and applying nations, to inform them of their new responsibilities and obligations. These meetings would also provide NATO with the opportunity to evaluate the state of readiness of applying nations, in order to avoid creating a two-tiered alliance.[67]

By the beginning of 1996 the Clinton administration was approaching the congressional goal of identifying specific countries that the

United States would endorse as potential NATO members. As the momentum for the identification of the new members grew, so too did the parallel work on new institutional links with Russia. The presidential elections of 1996 were approaching, and NATO enlargement was presented as promoting stability in Europe and as a powerful tool for spreading democracy and advocating the merits of a market economy. NATO enlargement also reflected a strong U.S. leadership role in Europe and the strategic importance of NATO as a tool for American influence in that part of the world.[68] During the same year, the Congressional drive to identify the new NATO members reached a climax. House and Senate members were feeling the pressure of various ethnic constituency groups who were lobbying for their native countries. In July 1996 the House and Senate adopted the NATO Enlargement Facilitation Act of 1996. This bill again stated that Poland, Hungary, and the Czech Republic were the front-runners for NATO membership and provided for substantial aid to facilitate the enlargement process. The bill also stated that the first wave of enlargement should not be the last.[69] Applauding such strong bipartisan support, in September of the same year President Clinton asked NATO to hold a summit in 1997 where the new members would be finally identified. Later that fall, Clinton also announced that the new member states would become full-fledged NATO members as of 1999.[70]

Again, this course was accompanied by an ongoing dialogue with Moscow. After the Russian foreign minister, Yevgeny Primakov, met with NATO to discuss the basis for a renewed dialogue between Moscow and the alliance, Secretary of Defense William Perry brought forward a new program for cooperation between NATO and Russia. It would include a permanent liaison between the alliance and Moscow, consultations for the extension of IFOR, Russian participation in the planning of joint multilateral task forces, a crisis consultation cell, and a precise timetable for military meetings between NATO and Russia.[71] Anticipating a breakthrough with Russia, Secretary of State Christopher declared at a North Atlantic Council meeting in December 1996 that the candidates for 1999 would be announced at the Madrid Summit of 1997. From that point on, the United States, rather than NATO, would be responsible for appeasing and reassuring Russia, and bilateral dialogue would continue until the summit.

In March 1997, during bilateral talks in Helsinki Clinton and Yeltsin agreed to disagree on NATO enlargement, but they agreed nonetheless to do their best to manage this unsatisfactory situation. While the United States kept pushing for a special NATO-Russia charter to help manage relations and to create a special forum for talks, Russia insisted that out-of-area NATO missions should be controlled either by the OSCE or by the UN, two organizations in which Russia had substantially more weight.[72] Finally, after months of negotiation, Russia and NATO signed an agreement paving the way for NATO enlargement. The Founding Act on Mutual Relations, Cooperation, and Security between the Russian Federation and NATO was signed on 27 May 1997. This agreement fully details the objectives and mechanism of joint consultation, cooperation, decision making, and action between Russia and NATO. For the United States, the Founding Act represented, as well, a new channel for managing Russian relations. The Founding Act was more than just another agreement: it achieved an important policy objective linked to and allowing for NATO enlargement.[73] The Madrid decision endorsed the preferences that the United States had had from the start, with Poland, Hungary, and the Czech Republic being considered for 1999. Despite other Allied preferences, the U.S. preponderance in the alliance imposed a consensus regarding the three states. With surprisingly little debate over NATO enlargement, the U.S. Senate and House approved the proposed Madrid wave of enlargement in March and April 1998. Bipartisan support for NATO enlargement, as well as the shared perspective of the legislative and executive branches of government, not only guaranteed the first wave of NATO enlargement but also allowed for strong U.S. involvement and leadership in the alliance throughout all the different phases of the process.

Explaining U.S. Behaviour towards NATO Enlargement

Like the post-Dayton Bosnian case, NATO enlargement supports our explanatory model. The actions of the United States clearly respected the tenets of defensive realism. Maintaining and expanding a successful defensive military alliance contributes to general security and stability without unnecessarily provoking states who are not part of this alliance. In this case, extreme measures (i.e., direct bilateral negotiations) were undertaken to manage Russia. Also, NATO was clearly part of the institutional network surrounding the hegemonic power and was deemed a valuable asset that provided vital links between the United States and its traditional allies. NATO was more than just a military alliance; it represented the prototypical ISI, where opportunities to have a voice and co-binding between great powers take place. Let us analyze the various parts of our hypothesis against this second case study.

We can identify several reasons for the high level of American involvement in NATO enlargement. The first is the institution itself and its value in the context of American foreign policy. NATO was touted as the international security institution most responsible for finally ending the Cold War. Through systematic and organized cooperation and coordination with the Allies, NATO successfully held back Soviet influence in Western Europe during the Cold War. It was a strong symbol of Western values and transatlantic unity. With the end of the Cold War, NATO's purpose had been put into question, but unexpected requests for membership by the new Eastern European democracies gave it a new lease on life, and Washington seized the opportunity to reenergize and redirect the alliance so that it could remain a bastion of Western civilization. No ISI fits American foreign policy quite as well as NATO. Based on common values, defensive and nonoffensive aims, cost-sharing, and a traditional openness that welcomes new members in appropriate situations, NATO is a perfect symbol and tool for maintaining what we have described as American open, or penetrated, hegemony. It was thus more than just the personal appeal of Havel and Walesa or the needs of the reborn Eastern European democracies that dictated America's course in this case; a profound historical and normative link with the ISI also influenced that course.

The strategic timing of enlargement also played a role. Following the tenets of defensive realism, the United States pursued an essentially defensive aim (since NATO was still a defensive military alliance) to enlarge NATO. In the security void and uncertainty created by the Soviet withdrawal from Eastern Europe, the United States used what was deemed the most appropriate tool to fill this void and stabilize a historically critical region for Europe. American interests in Europe were still undeniable, and because of its structure of command and because of the fact that European members depend on a strong American presence, NATO was still the best vehicle for American intervention in Europe. No other ISI (not the OSCE and certainly not the UN) offered quite as much leeway for American action. This "employment" of an ISI to attain certain specific American goals (e.g., stability in Europe, new members in the alliance to further tilt the odds in favour of the American position, and the spread of democracy and liberal values outside Western Europe and North America) would certainly appeal to a realist interpretation of how international institutions and states interact.

But the fact that the Americans operated through an ISI, rather than merely offering unilateral security guarantees to the applying member states, indicates that the web of international institutions woven by the American superpower was more than just a tool; it also dictated U.S. action. This is a direct reference to structural liberalism. By fostering the growth of institutions that are favourable to U.S. interests but that nevertheless allow for debate and provide other countries with opportunities to have a voice, Washington only solidifies the international structure surrounding it.

In this case the United States demonstrated strategic restraint through its commitment to NATO procedures and a consensual framework. By supporting NATO enlargement, it illustrated its ongoing commitment to the Atlantic alliance and the viability of NATO in the post–Cold War era. This commitment was a sign of long-term cooperation with America's European allies and an invitation to the new NATO members to join and participate in the Western order. Clearly the United States had its preferences with regard to which East European nations would be part of the first wave of enlargement, and it did not hesitate to let these preferences show in its discussions with other alliance members, but it did allow a discussion to take place. It voluntarily submitted itself to the selection negotiations at Madrid and reached a compromise with the Allies. Had it not done so and had it tried to override the decision-making process, no solution could have been found, since NATO operates and acts only on a consensual basis. Therefore, all the decisions, gestures, and actions of NATO are a constant reminder of the constitutional settlement the United States accepted when it founded and joined that organization. By bargaining and discussing options with alliance members, instead of pounding its fist on the meeting table, the United States showed constant strategic restraint.

Finally, on a note that is somewhat different from our explanatory model but not contradictory to it, U.S. action in this case was made possible because of what was ultimately strong bipartisan support for NATO enlargement. Although this support resulted from tremendous efforts on the part of the executive branch, lobbyists, nongovernmental associations, and the applying member states themselves, NATO enlargement never really created the national debate that one might have expected over such a sensitive issue, because American public opinion was basically behind the project. When it is, foreign policy is much easier to elaborate and implement. We believe that in this case a free reign created the necessary synergy between the various branches of government and allowed for a prepared and initiative-seizing American presence inside the alliance. It is no surprise that most breakthroughs in this case came from the United States rather than other members. It is true that the sheer political, diplomatic, economic, and military weight of the United States inside the alliance can explain this result, but we believe that having a focused agenda gave the Americans very compelling arguments that helped convince other alliance members.

Both post-Dayton Bosnia and NATO enlargement seem to coincide with the hypothesis we have constructed. In both cases, American behaviour within the ISIS was consistent with what a combination of defensive realism and structural liberalism would suggest. Domestic support for the U.S. initiatives must also be factored into our explanation in both cases (although generally less so in the case of post-Dayton Bosnia). Our next case is not quite as conclusive, but it deserves to be analyzed in any attempt to understand why American behaviour towards the UN is not as consistent as defensive realism and structural liberalism would lead us to believe.

United Nations Security Council Reform

The end of the Cold War brought renewed faith in the United Nations and in the potential for an effective collective security system. After years of quarrelling, it now seemed possible for the great powers of the Security Council to reach agreements and resolutions without getting bogged down in unnecessary procedures and unconsidered use of their veto powers. The actions of the United States were not an exception to this pattern of action. The Gulf War of 1991 had underlined the importance of the United Nations for American interests, both as a tool and as a forum in which to bring legitimacy to U.S. interventionism abroad.

With the success of the Gulf War resolutions and of peacekeeping missions around the world (Cambodia and Mozambique were often mentioned), reform of the Security Council was now deemed possible and necessary, in view of the important changes in the international system. In our third case study we examine the American attitude towards this reform project. An important variation can be observed in U.S. behaviour towards the project. Initially, it made major efforts to consolidate the council's authority and to empower it to create an efficient collective security tool. The late years of the administration of George Bush senior and the early years of the Clinton administration reflect this. However, with Clinton's second mandate, the United States became much more critical of the Security Council's possibilities and of the United Nations' impact on world affairs in general. We believe that in this case far more than in any other domestic pressures and domestic political considerations greatly influenced America's attitude towards the United Nations and its behaviour in this ISI. United Nations action was now deemed concurrent with, not complementary to, U.S. preferences in terms of institutional security conduct. We can identify three distinct phases of American behaviour.

Jumping In: Active Multilateralism and the Pursuit of Collective Security.
The late years of the Bush administration were generally favourable to
the United Nations and other multilateral institutions. As part of the
president's New World Order, international institutions provided an
opportunity for the United States to exert leadership without having to
bear the costs unilaterally. The resolutions surrounding the 1991 Gulf
War support this fact. Though its attitude was generally favourable
towards the United Nations, the Bush administration was prudent
nonetheless. No important reforms or policy overhauls were envisioned or deemed necessary. Although it favoured a Security Council
on which Japan and Germany could be permanently seated, it advised
these nations to display caution in their bids for permanent seats.
Opening the door of reform could lead to unwanted and substantial
institutional modifications.[74] The United Nations Security Council
should remain a forum of discussion for great powers where international security action would be debated and undertaken in a concentrated fashion. Hence, no major breakthroughs were apparent in Security Council reform at that point.[75]

In 1992 the publication of Secretary General Boutros-Ghali's
Agenda for Peace report, which was considered a blueprint for international peace action and collective security around the world, had
some impact in the last year of Bush's administration. Bush was initially in favour of establishing more credible international peace operations, even if the administration was against a permanent rapid-reac-
tion force that would have this effect.[76]

If Bush was prudent about UN Security Council reform, Clinton was
anything but cautious. The newly elected president clearly favoured
giving Japan and Germany permanent seats on the Security Council,
without specifying whether they would also give veto rights to the two
economic juggernauts. Permanent seats would bind the two nations to
international security issues, but for the Clinton administration, any
council reform would have to respect economic and political realities.
Actual members should not be affected by reform, but the United
States wished to expand the Security Council by adding a limited
number of new seats. What was at stake for the United States was not
necessarily a more efficient Security Council or a more transparent one
but an attempt to avoid ill-advised reforms that would hinder normal
Security Council proceedings.[77]

For the Clinton administration, humanitarian operations were
directly linked to American interests and fundamental values. By
expressing its desire to make the Security Council a stronger tool for
peace, the Clinton administration was giving its support to assertive
multilateralism, collective security, and preventive diplomacy.[78] A pres-

idential directive, PRD-13, was thus promulgated to lend support to this new course of action. It allowed U.S. troops to serve under UN command in peace operations. Although the directive was widely supported throughout the administration, the official presidential signing was deferred for some time.[79] This was the first indication of a change in Clinton policy. In theory, the United States was certainly in favour of a more active United Nations, but when it came to lending American personnel and material, U.S. behaviour was evidently more prudent.

Second Thoughts: Multilateralism Reconsidered. The American experience in Somalia was a major setback for U.S.-UN relations and a disaster for the Clinton administration's peace operations policy. After the United States military had suffered personnel losses in August and September of 1993, the U.S. Congress was stirred up by the failure of the administration's first peace operations and seized the opportunity to question the costs and command structure of peace operations in general. Confronted by growing criticism, the Clinton administration deferred PRD-13 and slowly proceeded to change course with regard to the United Nations. Addressing the General Assembly, Clinton warned that U.S. troops would not be sent in to help with international peace operations if the United Nations did not become more discriminating and judicious about the type of operation it wanted to get involved in. In this speech Clinton set up several criteria for U.S. involvement in peace operations (Clinton was referring especially to Bosnia): clear political objectives, clear military objectives, clear financial responsibilities, the possibility of NATO command, early U.S. withdrawal if deemed necessary, and, finally, congressional approval.[80]

The loss of eighteen American soldiers in October 1993 only intensified congressional pressure on the Clinton administration.[81] It did not lose time and responded with presidential directive PDD-25, Policy on Reforming Multilateral Peace Operations. Signed on 5 May 1994, it called for important reforms and strongly suggested correcting past mistakes. Far from widening the American capabilities, it reflected the Pentagon's growing displeasure with peace operations. The U.S. military was far from convinced that such operations were useful. PDD-25 also indicated a reduction in U.S. financial contributions for peace operations and completely left out the Rapid Reaction Force. U.S. peace operations had suffered a blow similar to that of the mission in Lebanon in the early 1980s, and the administration was now showing signs of withdrawal. The tide had shifted in U.S.-UN relations, and matters would only get worse.

In many respects, the U.S. attitude towards the UN in 1993 coincided with an important policy change for the Clinton administration. During that period, foreign policy in general shifted from multilateralism and collective security ideals to democratic enlargement and engagement around the world. Spreading political and economic liberalization around the world better served American ideals and interests. With enlargement and engagement U.S. power would be much more assertive: the success of the policy depended on U.S. leadership. Now both multilateralism and unilateralism were considered valid strategies to achieve the objectives of enlargement and engagement.[82] Recourse to the United Nations would now be subject to tight criteria.[83]

Opting Out: United Nations Marginalized. The election of a Republican majority in Congress in November 1994 brought a new generation of representatives bent on reigning in big government. Focused mainly on domestic issues, their approach to foreign affairs was mostly unilateral. International aid programs were attacked, as was U.S. participation in peace operations and financial contributions to the UN. A suspicion of the UN was reflected in the Peace Powers Act, which severely limited presidential options to put U.S. troops under UN command and imposed reductions on U.S. contributions to the United Nations.[84] This act was presented by Senator Bob Dole in January 1995 and could be considered a sign of things to come in the 1996 presidential elections, when Dole ran against Clinton. The UN had become the Republicans' favourite target, which limited the Clinton administration's options if it did not want to provide the Republicans with an election weak spot. It too would now have to take a harder stance towards the UN and marginalize it little by little.

Reform was now the key word for the Clinton administration. If the UN wanted U.S. cooperation in its various endeavours, it had to reduce its bureaucracy and limit financial waste. Secretary of State Christopher declared that only with important reforms would the American people support the UN.[85] Increasingly, U.S. security demands for the UN were aligned with its own security issues and national interests: nuclear proliferation, the international traffic in drugs, environmental issues, and terrorism. This was a far cry from Boutros-Ghali's Agenda for Peace; again, this change of posture was mostly due to congressional influence.[86]

Clinton did not challenge Congress on its UN policy in 1996 and 1997. The UN secretary general would be another victim of domestic quarrels. As mentioned in his memoirs, Boutros-Ghali had become the symbol of all that was bad in the UN (overpowering U.S. government officials, independence from the American superpower, and sloppy financial and bureaucratic administration). During 1996 Boutros-Ghali was ridiculed several times by Republican presidential candidate Robert Dole. The secretary general would have to retire if reforms were to be accomplished. Efforts were also made by Madeleine Albright and Warren Christopher to ease Boutros-Ghali out of his position, to avoid providing the Republicans with political ammunition during the campaign. In March 1996, despite significant pressure from the world community, President Clinton decided to use the American veto on the Security Council to block the reelection of Boutros-Ghali. A compromise was reached with the election of another African, Kofi Annan, which enabled Africa to save face. An African secretary general would serve for two consecutive mandates, as had most secretaries in the past, while the u.s. would dispose of (in its eyes) a troublesome Boutros-Ghali.[87] The UN was increasingly less important in u.s. foreign policy and was instead being identified as a tool of American interests. The Clinton administration was following to the letter the congressional view that past UN dues would not be paid unless reforms were seriously under way.[88]

As time went by, more and more conditions were presented by the United States for reform of the Security Council: Japan and Germany had to become permanent members in any reform plan, and the council would be limited to twenty or twenty-one members, so that it would be efficient.[89] In July 1997 the United States decided unilaterally that only three developing countries would become permanent members of the Security Council. But because there was no precise indication of how these countries were to be chosen, the international community, which resented Washington's unilateral stance, was further infuriated. The United States was also unilaterally creating its own criteria for future permanent members: they would have to subscribe to nuclear nonproliferation treaties, and they would have to liberalize trade.[90] Even the Japanese and German seats were conditional on increased financial contributions to the UN.[91]

The veto issue for new members was completely ignored by u.s. representatives. No actual veto holder would be affected by reform and the veto right would not be limited to chapter 7 articles, as a nonaligned representative had suggested. Veto issues were, according to the United States, completely separate from enlargement issues and should be dealt with at another time.[92] The American superpower was now putting its weight behind this sensitive issue. Multilateralism had clearly been left behind.

Explaining U.S. Behaviour towards the UN

Our model seems to be contradicted by U.S. behaviour towards UN Security Council reform and UN reform in general. The United States clearly failed to support the UN and acted against what could be established as a long-term national interest in seeing the UN maintained and sustained as a viable ISI. In this case the hegemonic power used its considerable weight to sideline reform, and because it could afford to do so, it ignored the UN at a very critical period of its existence. We believe that because the UN is a global ISI and does not specifically revolve around the hegemonic power, it is not considered to be crucial or dominant by the United States, especially in the post–Cold War environment.

As we have seen, U.S. behaviour towards the UN evolved significantly under the Clinton administration. From a multilateral discourse surrounding all UN activities to the hard realist leadership exerted in the last few years, U.S. policy went from high ideals to the use and control of the UN. As the second Clinton mandate evolved, a conclusion was reached: a strong UN Security Council limited U.S. leadership. How does this conclusion fit with our explanatory model and hypothesis?

We believe that in an international organisation where American leadership is not as strong (compared to NATO, for example), the attention and interest of the United States will be lacking. This generalisation is consistent with our model with regard to the energy the superpower will expend on an organisation that will support its hegemonic status and the liberal structure surrounding it. Perhaps the U.S. government feels that the General Assembly is systematically opposed to the United States, and perhaps it thus sees the UN more as an obstacle, a rival institution, than as an international facilitator for security issues. We agree with Edward C. Luck that this view is a mistake, since the UN has never been more receptive to American and liberal values.[93] It would seem that in taking a hard line towards the UN and Security Council reform, the United States is wasting a unique opportunity to mold the organization according to its preferred norms and values. Therefore, U.S. behaviour in this case does not conform to our explanatory model. If it did, the United States would not have let domestic politics affect its relationship with the UN. Rather, it would have seized the moment and transformed the UN along structural-liberal lines (or at the least, it would have encouraged any reform that maintained U.S. status while engaging other nations). But instead, the United States preferred a strong unilateral stance, to satisfy internal pressures. It chose to strong-arm the UN into accepting its propositions and systematically opposed any project for reform that went against an ill-defined American national interest. Even if a solution for Security Council reform has still not been identified, Richard Holbrooke, currently the American ambassador to the United Nations, has softened the u.s. position and is prepared to drop his country's insistence that the limit of any expansion to the council should be twenty or twenty-one seats, without suggesting an upper number.[94]

Clearly, this case study shows how domestic issues can muddle an explanatory foreign policy model. Had it not been for the 1994 congressional elections and the 1996 presidential elections, u.s. behaviour towards the United Nations would have been dramatically different. During the internal power struggle in these elections, the United Nations became an easy target for both parties. Although the American people were generally indifferent (but certainly not hostile) to the UN, their indifference did not stop both the Republicans and the Clinton administration from firing red-hot bullets at the UN. Knowing that they would pay only a negligible political price at home made doing so all the more tempting.

Thus, this case study demonstrates certain limits to our explanatory model. To fully explain American institutional behaviour (or lack thereof), we need additional theories that consider the influence of domestic factors. In order to interpret u.s. conduct, we must add to our main hypothesis the contrary hypothesis of neoclassical realism.

CONCLUSION

Two broad conclusions may be drawn from the test of our explanatory model on all three cases. First, structural liberalism works best with Western international institutions and not as well with global institutions, such as the UN. Western ISIs are centred around the United States and have evolved in tandem with hegemonic power. For example, the United States was present at the inception of NATO and throughout its critical development stages. We can safely argue that no other state has had as much impact on this ISI, hence its overwhelming weight inside the alliance. The same can be said of post-Dayton Bosnia, which is closely linked to NATO, but also to the European security systems in general. The United States tried to act as the architect of security after the First World War and failed miserably, but it finally succeeded following the Second World War with the creation of NATO and the Marshall Plan and with the backing of stronger European regional integration through all its different stages, from the Steel and Coal Union of the 1950s to the Maastricht Treaty of the 1990s. The Cold War certainly fostered closer ties with Western ISIs, and the end of the

Cold War probably facilitated the subsequent transition. Nevertheless, the networks created between the hegemonic power and Western ISIS are certainly more efficient than global ones such as the United Nations.

In this case as well, the Cold War had an impact on U.S.-UN relations. Having been an important founding member in 1946, the United States more or less abandoned authentic UN participation during the Cold War. Without analyzing all the historical cases, a certain pattern of "usefulness" emerges when one looks at the U.S.-UN relation during the Cold War. The United States participated vigorously if and when the UN could help undermine America's Soviet adversary and further its own aims, but certainly less so when it could not. This pattern of behaviour has left a strong imprint on U.S. foreign policy. Although the Bush administration and the Clinton administration in its early years showed genuine interest and goodwill in UN reform, this interest dramatically decreased when UN actions were deemed inefficient and unpopular by the U.S. media and by members of Congress. From the Somalia fiasco to the Bosnian nightmare, the U.S. relation with the UN grew more and more distant as it moved outside the networks of relations that were deemed essential for maintaining global stability and the hegemonic power's central position in world affairs.

But as the UN case clearly illustrates, our second conclusion takes into account the ever-present tensions between domestic players in the United States and its foreign policy, even with respect to ISIS. The U.S. foreign policy establishment is a complex entity that encompasses a wide range of players: the executive branch, Congress, the media, and even academics and powerful private personalities. Generating a "national interest" is hard enough for the United States but acting accordingly is even harder. When the domestic actors are of the same mind on certain issues, then U.S. action is generally coherent and efficient. When they are not, U.S. foreign policy seems dislocated and uneven, as was the case with UN Security Council reform and UN reform in general. Most U.S. foreign policy players recognize the overall importance of the UN to U.S. interests and international stability, but few agree on specific U.S. action to support and sustain UN activities. This disunity translated directly into the troubled U.S.-UN relation in the post–Cold War era. Lacking focus and specific objectives, U.S. policy towards the UN floundered. The same cannot be said, however, with regard to NATO enlargement and post-Dayton Bosnia. With NATO enlargement, the Clinton administration managed to create a policy that rallied the most important domestic players, even if it had to adopt a two-track approach, one with new NATO members and another with Russia. Congress actively supported (and sometimes even pushed) the Clinton administration while the media and public opinion generally favoured NATO enlargement and did not oppose implementation of the Clinton policy. Although Congress was not as cooperative in the post-Dayton Bosnian case, it did not oppose the administration on the ultimate outcome. Thus, the three case studies clearly show that u.s. foreign policy is much more consistent when it has the support of domestic players. This pattern can also be observed in many other Western democracies, but it is exacerbated in the United States in a way that is unmatched anywhere else.

The influence of domestic players clearly supports the hypothesis of neoclassical realism and at the same time strengthens the explanatory power of defensive realism and structural liberalism in combination. Gideon Rose best describes what neoclassical realism stands for:

It explicitly incorporates both external and internal variables, updating and systematizing certain insight drawn from classical realist thought. Its adherents argue that the scope and ambition of a country's foreign policy is driven first and foremost by its place in the international system and specifically by its relative power capabilities ... They argue further, however, that the impact of such power capabilities on foreign policy is indirect and complex, because systemic pressures must be translated through intervening variables at the unit level.[95]

The relations that bind states with ISIs are not free of these unit-level constraints. Along with our main hypothesis, which combines defensive realism and structural liberalism, this neoclassical explanation underlines the importance of the context within which foreign policy projects and endeavours are envisioned, formulated, and implemented. Domestic issues will often not affect state behaviour with ISIs, since that behaviour is usually bound by very clear and precise rules and regulations. However, when state actions do not correspond to normal institutional behaviour, one must not overlook the different unit-level characteristics that might affect institutional relations. So the famous "black box" is not fully opened in this case, but it is carefully examined, since all states are not alike in their appearances and their building materials. To deny this specificity in the making of u.s. foreign policy would be a fatal mistake in the study of great power-ISI interaction.

We believe that the model created with the combination of defensive realism and structural liberalism allows us to better understand its relation with ISIs. Although the UN case does not fully comply with our suggested model, we believe that exceptional internal pressures were responsible for the distortions in this particular case; they do not seem to be a common, recurring phenomenon with other ISIS. The United States will continue to espouse multilateralism as a virtue and will constantly face the temptation to use multilateral institutions as a tool to achieve the goals of its own national interest. Unlike other states, by virtue of its own power the United States can and will continue to override, and sometimes even contradict, the institutions it helped to create, and it will act unilaterally.[96] What needs to be understood is how and why the United States will choose one course or the other and act either in concert with or without ISIS. The model we propose offers a solution to these questions. It cannot fully explain all cases (no model can presume to do so), but we believe it generates a proper lens through which to view U.S.-ISI relations and offers many research possibilities.

Failing to Join the West: Russian Institutional Security Strategy during the Yeltsin Years

JEAN-PIERRE LAVOIE
AND JACQUES LÉVESQUE

The close of the twentieth century was marked by the accelerated fall of the Soviet empire and the end of the struggle between two opposing sociopolitical systems. This bipolar confrontation had reverberated upon the entire world and had warranted the priorities that were accorded to the balance of forces, as well as to the balance of power. Consequently, the shelving of the East-West division put an end to a dynamic that had endured since the end of the First World War.[1] The USSR (and then Russia), as a power now in decline and seeking its own road to democracy, would henceforth have to forego risky military adventures. Preventive wars,[2] whose goal is to maintain or, indeed, the regain great power status, were now out of the question.[2] The only remaining option for the USSR was to come to an accommodation with yesterday's enemies. This accommodation has taken some unique twists. The present study will focus on one aspect of Soviet/Russian accommodation: institutional security policy.

Soviet/Russian accommodation in its institutional form has followed a rather interesting trajectory. The Soviet and Russian leaders have remained conscious of their relative position in the international arena and of the tendencies that might affect it. Mikhail Gorbachev evaluated the ever-widening economic and political gap between the capitalist West and the USSR. His conclusions led him to attempt, by means of a strategy of bandwagoning with the Western powers, to capitalize as much as possible on past gains, in order to maintain the position of the Soviet Union on the international chessboard.[3] He hoped with the same stroke to spur these powers to aid him in his attempt to institute the internal economic reforms that were necessary for the survival of the socialist system. Developing his new internationalist and profoundly humanistic ideas within a limited circle of reformers, he hoped to synthesize them with the principles of behaviour promoted by the West.[4] Gorbachev thought that the United States and the Western powers would be prepared to define the new norms of international behaviour in collaboration with the Soviet Union. To a large extent, he was following a logic similar to that of his idea of a Common Home, advocating a hybrid model founded upon the convergence of humanist and Western ideas.[5]

Under Boris Yeltsin, Russia continued its attempt to westernize by means of a program of identity construction. Responsibility for this program was entrusted primarily to Andrey Kozyrev and to several liberal-reformist practitioners of shock therapy. Russia was thus ready to develop expectations and policies compatible with those of the West, as well as to assume roles that would complement those of the Western powers. The liberals under Kozyrev felt that it was possible to restructure the international order together with the Western powers in a manner that would provide Russia with a leading institutionalist role and that would simultaneously allow it to maintain its great power status. By December 1992, however, Russia was already showing signs of dissatisfaction with initial Western reactions.

Kozyrev's fervent hope had been to make Russia a strategic ally of the Western powers, but despite extensive privatization and the establishment of the first market institutions in Russia in 1992, the Western powers maintained a cautious attitude towards Russian institutional expectations. Political and ideological divisions within the Russian elites, as well as a lukewarm attitude (to say the least) to the program of shock therapy, were often invoked as evidence of the problems of Russian democratization. Moreover, the Yeltsin government's powerlessness in the face of the rise of a careerist and, hence, untrustworthy oligarchy clearly weighed against integrating Russia into the Western defence and security networks. At best, the Western powers seemed to be interested in constructing institutional channels to support Russian enthusiasm for an extensive series of liberal and capitalist reforms. But with the proposal to enlarge NATO, which was placed on the agenda beginning in 1994, it became clear that Kozyrev's institutionalist orientation would not produce any tangible results and was thus dismissed sine die.[6]

Under Yevgeny Primakov, Russia adopted an unquestionably more skeptical attitude towards institutionalism. Primakov and the statists considered participation in security institutions as the sine qua non of Russian maintenance of great power status. But the Russian statists, in contrast to the liberals, did not believe that the international rules were neutral and balanced enough to permit the country to advance its own security preferences. Russia's geopolitical interests did not converge with those of the Western powers. Reinforcing the viewpoint of the statists, the *derzhavniki* and the nationalists held that institutional participation would place Russia in subordinate roles.[7] This profound skepticism was part and parcel of Primakov's thesis of nascent multipolarity: institutional cooperation would henceforth be dealt with according to the logic of constructing a multipolar world. For Primakov, multipolarity was more a principle than an emerging reality. It would ensure the preservation of Russia's great power status while allowing the country to forge a new Eurasian economic space in cooperation with the newly independent states.[8] It was hence imperative that security institutions promote multipolarity. But this goal implied a policy of limited cooperation, as opposed to a process of identification in which the Western powers and Russia would devise a common security identity.

RUSSIA'S MAIN STRATEGY
TOWARDS INTERNATIONAL SECURITY INSTITUTIONS

Despite all the factors just discussed and despite the ascendance of the statist tendency, the perception that it was necessary to utilize the security institutions for multiform activities did not disappear. Accurately estimating that it did not possess the means to actively oppose NATO's eventual enlargement, Russia continued to demonstrate its interest in cooperating with the Western powers, as evidenced by its participation in NATO's post-conflict operations in Bosnia-Herzegovina. But this institutional orientation does not seem to have been informed by consistency in its objectives. During the Yeltsin years, Moscow wavered between two divergent positions, seeking to become integrated within the Western institutional security and defence networks while simultaneously maintaining a certain skepticism towards the results of its participation within them. Consequently, Russia was unable to define for itself a clear role within the international security institutions, since it failed to devote the required energies in the appropriate directions. For example, its insistence on developing a Eurasian regional security system under the aegis of the Commonwealth of Independent States (CIS) was not entirely consonant with the notion of full collaboration with the Western states and their security institutions. Indeed, the construction of the CIS as a Eurasian security institution did not seem to be compatible with the notion of developing multiform institutional relationships with the Western powers.

The Western powers pursued a minimalist policy. They were willing to concede that Russia did indeed possess certain foreign interests in its "near abroad" that it must protect,[9] but they refrained from translating this recognition into active support for a precise program.[10] They expressed reservations, indeed even frank disagreement, with such a project, citing the desire of many Eurasian states to determine the instruments and guarantees of their respective national securities on their own. In seeking to legitimize its activities in its near abroad, and consequently to legitimize the CIS as a security institution within the system of Eurasian states, Russia encountered stiff resistance. On the one hand, the Eurasian states were reluctant to collaborate with Russia for fear of slipping into an asymmetrical relationship. On the other hand, the Western powers, who were committed to preserving the sovereignty and independence of these new states, did not want to support an institutional project that risked resurrecting the Soviet Union in a new guise.

Nevertheless, for the sake of their own security, the great Western powers had to guarantee the maintenance of a certain degree of order in the region. However, they were not prepared to invest, either at the multilateral or bilateral level, the military resources necessary to maintain that order. Other than Russia, they could see no nearby state that could organize and stabilize the region. They furthermore felt that a stabilizing initiative on the part of one of them could lead to an escalation of conflict in this historically explosive territory. Despite everything, Russia therefore appeared to be the sole potential guarantor of Eurasian order.[11]

Paradoxically, Russia found itself somewhat isolated, especially because it continued to insist upon integrating and controlling its near abroad and its "natural sphere of influence."[12] Russia became a contested state, and "in certain parts of what had once been its empire, no more than one player among all the others."[13] The example of Uzbekistan, which in February of 1999 decided to break the security pact that linked it to the CIS, is an excellent reflection of the loss of Russian influence in central Asia.[14] However, as the Yeltsin government was approaching its demise, the Russians were in the process of trying to establish a more active presence in the regions of the former Soviet Union. This presence did not involve a sustained effort to establish the CIS as the organizational instrument of concerted action and intervention in the region: On the contrary, this period witnessed a clear Russian tendency to develop bilateral relations, even at the expense of international security organizations such as the CIS and the OSCE.[15]

Nor was this the only instance of preferential incompatibility. Moscow proved unable to decide upon the relative importance of the four most crucial security institutions – the Security Council, NATO, the Organization for Security and Cooperation in Europe (OSCE), and the CIS – Kozyrev expressed only a vague preference in this regard.[16] Russia pursued a policy towards all four that could only be described as ambivalent. By way of example, in the case of the OSCE and NATO, a more prudent institutional policy informed by a more vigorous program of intervention at the OSCE might have complicated the designs of the Americans and other Western powers for enlarging NATO towards the East. Had the Russians adopted such a policy, even an expanded NATO would have found it more difficult to legitimize its institutional ambitions. The Euro-Atlantic Partnership Council (EAPC), which to a large extent paralleled the OSCE, would thus have been obliged to develop roles that were complementary, as opposed to superior, to it. Despite all of the hopes placed upon the OSCE, the Russian government was not able to define a clear mission for it – in fact, it did not even want to.[17] Instead, Moscow's discourse regarding the powers it was prepared to accord the organization remained, to say the least, ambivalent. Because of its failure to clearly define its institutional security priorities, Russia could not pursue a systematic institutional strategy with any degree of determination. Nor was it able to advance its vision of institutional reciprocity with its Western interlocutors. The net result was that NATO emerged as the predominant institution,[18] with Russia on the outside of the organization and at risk of becoming what Jack Snyder has called a "geopolitical backwater."[19]

A similar argument may be formulated with respect to the United Nations Security Council. Here again, Russia pursued a policy of ambivalence. As we shall see (in our second case), at first the Security Council represented a means of safeguarding Russia's international status. It also served as a source of legitimization of the roles Russia was seeking to play in its near abroad. However, as a result of Russian strategic propensities, the council became a means of rigorously identifying the security missions of the Western powers that most likely exceeded their strict collective defence needs. The war in Kosovo confirmed Russia's apprehensions: the Western alliance did not hesitate to bypass the Security Council when it appeared necessary to do so in order to reach its international political objectives. Instead of pursuing an extended program of reinforcing the Council, with all that this implies in terms of negotiations and alliances within that security institution, Russia elected to play a fundamentally conservative, wait-and-see role.

Explanatory Objectives

Our study thus reaches two principle conclusions. The first is that Russian institutionalism was a failure. As soon as it made its appearance on the international scene, Russia clearly expressed its intention of joining the ranks of the Western powers as quickly as possible, to the point of offering its allegiance to the American leadership.[20] In many respects, Russia would have preferred to follow the German path, anchoring its own security to Western institutions and playing an active role in weaving the multiform security links being sponsored by the West. But this anchorage implied that several important conditions would be met. On the one hand, Russia sought the support of the Western powers for its effort to remodel institutional relationships within the new Eurasian states system. On the other hand, Russia expected to play a crucial, if not decisive, role in reshaping Western security identity. However, Russia's desire for institutional reciprocity with the West remained unrequited.

The enlargement of NATO indubitably represents the failure of Russia's quest for integration into the Western family. Our second conclusion is that in the long run Russia was obliged to assign a more modest objective to its institutionalist efforts. Not as powerful as the former USSR, Russia feared losing the international status conceded to it by its peers upon the dissolution of the Soviet Union. Well before NATO's enlargement, Moscow realized that the Western powers would not offer it the opportunity to join their exclusive club. Hence it fell back upon its traditional realist reflexes. Essentially under the foreign policy leadership of the statists, Russia adopted a markedly skeptical attitude towards the international institutions, an attitude that was incorporated in a limited institutional strategy involving the preservation and promotion of Russia's international status within the international security organizations while awaiting the resurgence of its capabilities and the emergence of new powers.

EXPLAINING RUSSIAN INSTITUTIONAL SECURITY STRATEGY

Each theoretical approach that we will discuss further in this chapter cannot by itself explain the complexity of Russian institutional security behaviour. In the present case, Russian institutionalism failed because Russia did not manage to establish institutional mechanisms of cooperation with the Western powers and did not participate in the elaboration of new rules dealing specifically with current problems of international security. Russia was consequently unable to develop expectations compatible with those of the West and to define roles that it could play within the security institutions. This failure also ended in Russia's inability to establish reciprocity with the Western powers.

According to the institutionalist approach, this failure can be explained by the fact that both Russia and the Western powers (perhaps simultaneously) found the transaction costs of cooperation prohibitive and therefore preferred not to develop relationships of reciprocity. As was the case in Russia's dealings with NATO, relations with the Western powers were limited to simple acts of coordinating security policy. This was not the first choice of the Russian institutionalists.

The different institutionalist theories that have been applied in various empirical studies suggest few obstacles for an actor that is prepared to exchange information regarding its intentions, preferences, and behavioural standards when seeking to propose new roles and develop new expectations with its peers. But quite the opposite was true for Russia and the Western powers. The challenge that the institutionalist approach therefore faces is to explain the failure of reciprocity despite the efforts undertaken by a state that followed almost all the precepts of institutionalist theory. It is known that the institutionalist approach has not proven to be very enlightening about institutionalist failures.[21] The present study attempts to clarify the circumstances of the Russian institutional failure.

It must be said, however, that the liberal institutionalist approach cannot by itself provide a complete explanation, because the Russians failed, in part, for reasons that are external to issues of institutional security interaction. We must therefore use two other recognized theoretical approaches: neoclassical realism and constructivism. Neoclassical realist analysis perceives the Soviet/Russian leaders as being aware of the decline, indeed the free fall, of Soviet/Russian power.[22] Their first reaction was to reduce the pernicious effects of the relative decline in Russia's position in the international power-distribution system.[23] Russia had inherited a status that was still universally recognized by the great powers. Its dilemma, viewed from a neoclassical realist perspective, was to hold on to this status while it reconstructed those capabilities that corresponded to the maintenance of such a position in the international community.

As explained by the neoclassical realist school, not all states possess the same strengths or capabilities. Consequently, few are able to ensure their own survival. They are, in fact, sensitive to their relative position within the international system and to the trends that may affect it, and hence most states desire some form of cooperation. They can try to counteract threats by means of power relationships with other states (balancing). Alternatively, they can do so by aligning their policies to those of more powerful states (bandwagoning), but at the risk of losing a significant measure of autonomy.[24] In short, according to some neo-classical realists, systemic characteristics and environmental factors restrain choices and predispose states towards certain models of behaviour, but they determine nothing.

This school of thought allows for a better understanding of Russia's behaviour with respect to the reform of the UN Security Council after 1993 and the enlargement of NATO to the East, and it helps to clarify Russia's ever-increasing geopolitical isolation. Realizing that the major powers were not interested in having Russia competing with them on the international stage, Moscow gradually returned to its preferred zone of influence: Eurasia.

According to neoclassical realism, security institutions are no more than settings where major powers reach agreements on how to balance their interests and determine the modalities of international governance. It is the international status of a major power that allows it to participate in the decision-making process leading to the adoption of these modalities. Consequently, it is understandable why for Russia it was of greater importance to preserve its status than to achieve reciprocity with the Western powers. Indeed, loss of status would also signify for Russia that it would have to renounce any hope of favourably negotiating reciprocity with its Western peers. The security organizations proved to be instruments of leverage that were used to control gains and losses in status based on capabilities or powers recovered or lost. Thus, the CIS was designed first and foremost to keep in check destabilizing undercurrents in Eurasia. But it was also supposed to act as a power lever in the construction of a security institution in its geopolitical space.

Through the security institutions, Russia was able to do no more than play a defensive game, but a game that was interspersed, however, with some offensive sorties. For example, Moscow censured the enlargement of NATO, but it was unable to do anything tangible about it because it lacked the means to exercise power. In their heart of hearts, the Russian liberal and statist strategists knew that enlargement did not in and of itself constitute a threat. It entailed nothing more than encouraging certain destabilizing effects in a Eurasia that a state apparatus weakened by corruption and by the inability to construct new political, social, and economic institutions found difficult to control. But, having suffered institutional setbacks, Russia intensified its criticism of the international political objectives of the Western powers.

Russia declared that it would oppose enlargement by means of geopolitical countermeasures. It pursued a Sino-Russian strategic partnership, but this strategy did not produce institutional security mechanisms: neither Beijing nor Moscow put forth an institutional security program that was accompanied by a rigorous timetable. It seems that in its international endeavours the Russian leadership was following a realist approach almost to a tee, as was evidenced by Primakov's promotion of the multipolarity. Perhaps the constructivists are correct in suggesting that the realist prejudice of the Russians in fact predisposed them to fail in their institutionalist enterprise.

Constructivists would attribute the failure to Moscow's inability to show the major Western powers that it deserved their confidence and should be invited to participate in the reconstruction of its security identity.[25] Having helped bring about the demise of the Soviet Union, Russia expected to play a full role in the reconstruction of the cohesion of the major Western powers. Beginning with Gorbachev, the Soviet Union began a complete recasting of its security identity. As the Gulf crisis of 1990–91 showed, one of Gorbachev's objectives was indeed to demonstrate to the West how far the USSR had progressed in reshaping its international ideas and how far it had moved in the direction of linking itself to Western identity.

Russia's hopes of joining the Western group were not mere flights of fancy. The Western powers no longer considered Russia to be a threat. They determined that security-related cooperation with Russia in certain instances was both possible and necessary. Nevertheless, they remained ambivalent with respect to the effects of a Russian presence on the cohesion of their own group. Some Western institutional architects thought that Russia, itself in search of its own identity, represented a risk to the reconstruction of the Western security identity. The Western elites ruled out the integration of Russia into their group because of the inherent instability of the Russian elites, of which a considerable proportion did not appear to be committed to the construction of a state founded upon the rule of law. The social construction of Western security identity presented its own problems, and Russia lacked the prerequisite conditions to participate in the process of its reconfiguration within the institutional networks.

A TRILATERAL MODEL

The trilateral model that we shall use is not simply a compilation of the three approaches discussed in the previous section. In fact, the analysis of institutional security behaviour follows a certain sequence, and each approach has its complementary role within it. Our present goal is not so much to favour one approach at the expense of another as to use the robust elements of each to maximize our understanding of the logic of Russia's institutional behaviour. To a large extent, the constructivist argument proposed is similar in its theoretical implications to the institutionalist approach, but it should be positioned farther down the line in the analysis.

With the collapse of the Soviet Union and the end of the Cold War, the Western powers no longer considered Russia to be a threat. But they were reluctant to admit it to their group when the West itself was reconstructing its own security identity: Russia might prove injurious to the process. Moreover, it is essential to remember that the cohesion of the Western group was not invulnerable. Now that the Soviet menace had disappeared and had been replaced by a collection of risks that were difficult to identify, several areas of dispute came to the fore. The Western powers were therefore not willing to complicate the process of renewing their identity by taking in a Russia that was itself in search of an identity.

As we shall endeavour to emphasize in our discussion of NATO enlargement, institutionalist analysis fixes responsibility for the failure to establish reciprocity between Russia and the Western powers on this Western reluctance to integrate Russia into the process of social identification. But should this reluctance and the fate reserved for the mechanisms of cooperation lead us to infer that the exclusion of Russia from the Western group doomed institutional interactions from the outset? We think not. Positive results might just as easily have emerged from such interactions, and, therefore, Russian success in the mechanisms of reciprocity might in fact have facilitated its entry into the process of Western social identification.

At what point in our analysis, then, should we introduce neoclassical realism? Up the line or down the line from the two previous approaches? From the perspective of the Russian leadership, the neoclassical realist approach stands at the beginning of the analysis of international security behaviour. It was, after all, the perception of declining Russian power in the international system that led this leadership to seek unlimited cooperation with the Western powers – to the extent that Moscow was willing to accept American leadership. But it must be emphasized here that Russia's initial reaction was not to resort to the game of realpolitik. It did not rush headlong into an attempt to create a united international front against Western hegemonism.

Russia's first reaction was to board the moving Western train and, as a consequence, to speed towards Western institutions. It was not the appearance of a new national identity under Gorbachev – an identity that was not the product of a sociopolitical transformation of civil society but rather the work of a limited group of capable leaders – that seems to have caused the institutional security behaviour. Nor, moreover, was it the lack of institutional dexterity on the part of the Russian leadership or the functioning of the security institutions themselves. It was, rather, the perception that the Soviet state had to undergo a complete renewal in order to meet the new social and economic challenges, that led Gorbachev to advocate the construction of new international norms, in collaboration with the West. And it was this same perception that persuaded the Yeltsin government to differentiate or, at least, to substantially moderate its institutional security policy when it realized that the Western powers were disinclined to accept Russia within their inner circle.

CASE STUDIES

Soviet Diplomacy during the Gulf Crisis

At the onset of the Gulf crisis in 1990, the Soviet Union could not side with Iraq without compromising not only its relationship with the United States but also the entire direction of its new foreign policy. As a permanent member of the United Nations Security Council it could clearly support UN action to liberate Kuwait while avoiding any military commitment and while preventing, if possible, the deployment of other troops under the auspices of the UN. Ideally, the USSR would have preferred the UN to obtain an Iraqi withdrawal without resorting to military force. This step could conceivably have removed the risk of revealing to the entire world the degree to which it lagged militarily behind the United States and the members of the new coalition. Moreover, the Soviet Union wanted to avoid any perception that its strategy of bandwagoning behind the major powers called into question its involvement in the Middle East. It also wanted to avoid a de facto acceptance of its own international decline. The Gulf War provided the Soviet leaders the opportunity that they had been hoping for to promote the rules they had already been advocating for several years.

The USSR seemed, moreover, to be tempted to take advantage of the crisis to put a fresh shine to its new foreign policy, which was largely oriented towards reinforcing the UN and its role. As a permanent member of the Security Council, the Soviet Union, would henceforth subsist on the ability of the United Nations to resolve conflicts through solid international consultation. The Gulf conflict would allow Russia to effect the transition from a disappearing bipolar order to a new system of collective security defended by the UN. The crisis also clarified the extent to which the Soviet leaders understood their relative weakness on both the national and the international level. This weakness led them to do all they could to augment the role of the UN Security Council as a means of limiting, as much as possible, the power of the United States. Moreover, the policy of concerted action with the United States and its allies within the framework of the UN remained in complete conformity with the "new political thinking" of Gorbachev and was in no way injurious to immediate Soviet interests (its need of Western aid for its reforms, the necessity of dealing with internal political instability, and so forth).

Finally, when the Soviet Union realized that, despite its best efforts, the American agenda at the UN Security Council had prevailed – and what is more, military intervention under U.S. command was inevitable, a different option came to the fore: remaining neutral in the hope of presenting the image of itself as a mediating power that was able to contribute decisively to the resolution of major conflicts.[26] The USSR thus managed to avoid alienating Iraq, all the while sidestepping criticism on the part of the international community.[27] It continued to waver between the willingness to participate in the Washington-led coalition and a desire to distance itself from it, so as to better play the role of intermediary, searching for a peaceful resolution of the conflict. For that matter, Soviet diplomats attempted until February 1991 to negotiate a peace plan; however, their persistence in trying to resolve the conflict through diplomatic means at times appeared suspect to American eyes.

Some countries, such as France, which had on 26 August signed a common declaration with the USSR, viewed these attempts in a favourable light. President Mitterand even stated, during a private conversation with Yevgeny Primakov, that it would be desirable for France and the Soviet Union, two permanent members of the Security Council, to harmonize their positions on this issue.[28] This gesture represented an attempt to "play the coalition card" within the Security Council in order to reverse the current trend and restore to it a genuine political and strategic role. However, this attempt at "balancing" quickly failed.[29] Great Britain, the United States, and France remained united. After the hostilities began, the Soviets found themselves isolated in proposing a peace plan.

For their part, the Americans clearly expressed a desire to have the Soviets play a part in the resolution of this crisis. Their goal was to limit the impression that the United States was acting hegemonically. It was completely to President Bush's advantage to establish an impression of strict cooperation with Gorbachev. On one hand, this strategy allowed him to maintain a firm grip on international affairs, and on the other hand, it helped his opposite number uphold the image in Soviet public opinion that the country was still a great power. This behaviour also helped the United States exert pressure on China, which had been politically isolated since the repression of Tiananmen Square and which had threatened to use its veto in order to avoid becoming involved in the conflict. (A compromise was reached on 19 November 1990.) The American representatives thereby avoided the emergence of any alliance, however circumstantial, between China and the USSR.

A "summit" meeting in Helsinki between Bush and Gorbachev in September 1990 fostered the impression that the USSR remained an indispensable interlocutor of the United States. Gorbachev took advantage of this meeting to insist that the Soviet Union should remain an essential player on the international stage. Nevertheless, the general behaviour of the Soviet leaders suggests some realism on their part regarding the actual balance of power in world politics. Their strategy was to capitalize as much as possible politically on the influence the USSR continued to derive from its position as a permanent member of the United Nations Security Council and to collaborate with the Americans.

This strategy of bandwagoning resulted from specific conditions linked to *perestroyka*. The leaders feared any isolation of their country. To withdraw solidarity from the great powers would jeopardize important elements related to their new policies, such as arms control and the maintenance of order in Europe and the world. Moreover, for economic reasons the USSR could not turn its back on the Western countries, whose aid seemed an essential buttress for the program of reforms.[30] The leadership was all too well aware that the success of these reforms depended to a large degree upon weaving durable new links with the West.

During this conflict, the Soviet Union seemed to demonstrate that it was nothing more than a prisoner of the dynamics and constraints of its own international political "agenda." The core of the idea of partnership with the West, itself tied to the spirit of the "new thinking," governed all Soviet reactions. Gorbachev nevertheless favoured this approach, hoping to at least give his country a new international mission, this time one that was based on the defence of international law and the establishment of common norms in matters of international relations. This strategy was meant to compensate for the decline in the position of USSR in the global balance of power, while providing it with some of the political capital required to resolve its raging internal crises.

The speeches of the principal leaders clearly testify to a radical change in Soviet foreign policy from what it was during the Cold War. Thus, Eduard Shevardnadze, speaking in support of UN efforts to resolve the crisis in Iraq, stated, "Iraq's aggression against Kuwait and the subsequent annexation of this state are flagrant violations of the fundamental norms governing international relations and of the most fundamental principles of the constitution of our organization, the Charter of the United Nations."[31]

From then on the United Nations and the norms governing it became the point of reference upon which the USSR based its foreign policy. Meanwhile, the government was facing an important internal crisis. Separatist movements in the outer republics were growing stronger, and the Baltic States were demanding their independence. A bloody repression in Vilnius, in Lithuania, on 13 January 1991 and in Riga, in Latvia, on 20 January 1991 rendered rather vulnerable a government that during the entire crisis was trying to present itself as "a state that respects human rights and conforms to the norms of international law."[32]

Reaction to the rise of nationalism in the USSR became fundamental to the very survival of the Soviet Union. Furthermore, the "new political thinking" that Gorbachev and Shevardnadze had been advancing since 1986 and the major reconciliation with the United States were hardly appreciated by important segments of the military establishment. It became increasingly difficult to bury this grumbling after the summer of 1990, when Gorbachev agreed to a united Germany joining the ranks of NATO. The Gulf War provided the ideal opportunity to unite the opposition forces.[33] Moreover, this crisis demonstrated the difficulty of instituting a collective form of security within a heterogeneous system and signaled the failure of Gorbachev's "new thinking."

As the conflict wore on, these internal pressures resulted in the members of the government who favoured a clear partnership with the West losing influence to more conservative elements. In addition, Gorbachev was trying to act on two fronts at the same time: directly negotiating with Hussein (Primakov) while simultaneously bandwagoning, wholly collaborating with the United Nations coalition (Shevardnadze). The Soviet Foreign minister, Eduard Shevardnadze, was one of those to lose influence, and on 20 December 1990 he submitted his resignation. These strategic setbacks led the Soviet leadership to acknowledge the limits of collective security and of their influence within the UN Security Council and to acknowledge also their inability to secure allies among the great powers.

Shevardnadze's successor as head of Foreign Affairs, Alexander A. Bessmertnykh, continued to defend what had been the major principles of Soviet policy since the beginning of the Gulf crisis and did not call into question support for the coalition. Within the country, changes were becoming more apparent. Reformers such as Yakovlev, Bakatin, Petrakov, and Shatalin were replaced or left, giving way to more conservative members such as Ivachko, Yanayev, and Pavlov. These changes attested to the growing influence of a more conservative wing within the political class.

We have thus far observed how, throughout this conflict, the Soviet leaders expressed a clear desire to confer upon the UN its due power. They stressed, among other things, that since its formation the UN Security Council had not resorted to using its Military Staff Committee when important crises occurred. And they most assuredly desired to limit the power of the American military leadership, as the Soviet minister of foreign affairs made explicit on 9 August 1990, stating that "speaking concretely, we believe that the Security Council should now take responsibility for bringing to a conclusion [the problem of Kuwait]. We are at the same time prepared to initiate consultations within the framework of the Security Council Military Staff Committee, which, by virtue of the UN Charter, can fulfil very important functions."[34] At the UN rostrum Shevardnadze added, "First and foremost, [the Security Council] must launch initiatives likely to accelerate the work of the Military Staff Committee and must study the practical aspects of placing national contingents of troops under the command of the Security Council."[35]

From August to December 1990, the Soviet Union voted in favour of the twelve resolutions of the UN Security Council, from the request for "immediate and unconditional withdrawal" from Kuwait (Resolution 660) to the authorization to "resort to force against Iraq" (Resolution 678). The USSR tried everything to avoid recourse to force. Nevertheless, the Soviet desire to defend the rules of international law and breathe new life into the United Nations indirectly provided the United States with the legitimacy it needed for armed retaliation. The Soviet Union would have done anything to avoid (or to give the impression of wanting to avoid) a confrontation on the ground, without however officially dissociating itself from the ultimate goal of the allies: the liberation of Kuwait.

We have seen how the UN Security Council was one of the last forums where the USSR could still be perceived as a great world power. Nevertheless, we must emphasize that the Soviets failed in their attempt to have the UN intervene directly to avoid a confrontation. When it finally became clear that such a confrontation was inevitable, the USSR was neither able to see to it that the Security Council would act directly, using its own means, or that it would carry its intercession with Iraq through to fruition. This brief episode clearly demonstrates the new balance of power and influence within the UN, as well as the inability of the Soviet Union to create alliances within the Security Council.

The Reform of the UN Security Council

As we have seen, the Gulf crisis reinforced the idea, already present in Soviet discourse, that the Security Council of the United Nations should be reformed to give it a new role in the resolution of disputes. Indeed, there was a clear continuity between the Soviet leadership and their Russian successors in this matter. The new government merely pursued the work of its predecessor and hoped that the reforms undertaken at the UN since 1990 would lead to the establishment of a system of collective security under the aegis of the Security Council, of which Russia was a member.

These attempts to reform the Council and to enlarge its powers to intervene in the different regions of the globe eloquently illustrate the new Russian approach to international security.[36] Beginning in 1993 it would subsequently be linked to the quest for consolidation of a Russian sphere of influence.[37] At the same time, it became apparent that a certain disillusionment had set in with respect to the idea of a true partnership with the West. On the one hand, Russia continued to maintain good relations with the West, expecting in return (as in the Gorbachev era) its direct (state-to-state) or indirect (through the IMF, the World Bank, and so on) financial aid, which was essential for the transition to a market economy and participation in the G8. On the other hand, it maximized the power conferred upon it as a permanent member of the Security Council, in order to orient UN reform in a way that would safeguard its own precious and fragile assets. The legitimacy of the international security institutions was now more than ever useful for Russia as a means of attempting to sanction its own policies and its peacekeeping interventions in the region of the Commonwealth of Independent States (CIS).

Russia remained opposed to any structural reform that would strengthen the General Assembly at the expense of the Security Council. The Russian leaders accepted a possible enlargement of the Security Council but maintained that the power of the five permanent members (for example, their veto power) should, as a quid pro quo, remain the same.[38] Since the Security Council was one of the last vestiges of the Soviet era to still provide Russia with some influence in international affairs, Moscow insisted that any reform of the division of powers within the United Nations must go through the Security

Council and receive the unanimous consent of its five permanent members. The Russian leaders wished to maintain an influence – indeed, a decisive influence – on the great European and international questions.

Expanding the Security Council remained foreseeable and even desirable as a means of reflecting the current reality. For its part, Russia suggested increasing the number of permanent and nonpermanent members to twenty and considered Japan and Germany to be important candidates for inclusion in a renewed council.[39] These two new permanent members would not, however, enjoy the power of veto. Moscow furthermore stipulated that enlargement should not be limited to these two countries and that it would be prepared to support the inclusion into the Security Council of one country each from Asia, Africa, and Latin America. This position seemed to confirm Russia's desire to limit the leadership of the United States and its allies, to reinforce the role of the five members of the Security Council possessing veto power, and to offer an important platform to countries that might eventually be part of future alliances.

During its first two years, the Russian Federation continued the work begun earlier by the Gorbachev-Shevardnadze duo with respect to the UN and its power to intervene in regional disputes. President Yeltsin's speech to the Security Council in January 1992 sums up nicely the position of the new federation with regard to the UN and the reinforcement of collective security under its aegis. He emphasized the importance of providing this international institution with all the tools necessary to actively resolve the important problems emerging throughout the world. The Russian leadership benefited from the end of the Cold War: it could use the great visibility of regional conflicts and the important place they were accorded on the agendas of the great powers to try to equip the Security Council with a new role. To this end it proposed the introduction of a "rapid intervention apparatus that would enable the United Nations to intervene in armed conflicts and the endowment of the UN with new institutions that would allow it to intervene in economic and social processes on a global scale."[40]

This idea had been floated previously, in November 1990 during the Gulf crisis. At that time, Nikolai Smirnov, representing the USSR at the United Nations General Assembly, proposed the creation of a reserve composed of armed forces and military observers "that would enable [the UN], facing a crisis situation, to rapidly and at minimal cost activate the necessary forces."[41] According to the Soviets, it was time "to have the permanent members of the Security Council participate more actively in peacekeeping operations."[42]

For the new Russian government, the end of the bipolar world and the multiplication of regional conflicts were forcing the major powers to seek long-term global solutions. If they were to resolve future conflicts, they felt, the Cold War must give way to concerted action by the great powers within the Security Council of the United Nations. The government wished to at last capitalize on the various efforts to achieve political reconciliation, including outright concessions, that had been carried out since Gorbachev. Now that Russia had demonstrated that it shared the same political and economic values as the great Western powers, there should be no obstacle to establishing a system ready to defend these same values.[43] Thus, Kozyrev, the foreign minister, asserted in 1992 that "For the first time in history, there exists an unprecedented opportunity to put into practice the principles proclaimed by the United Nations ... The world is not one of pax sovietica, of pax americana, of pax islamica or of any monopolistic system. It is one of multipolar unity in diversity."[44]

This support for UN peacekeeping and conflict-resolution was one of the major elements of the new Russian foreign policy and seemed to guide the Russian position on Security Council reform. In this sense, Yeltsin continued the work of his predecessor Gorbachev, who at the end of 1988 had called into question the UN's mission as it was being applied to its "global security project."

The Russian leaders hoped that in the course of settling conflicts on the territory of the CIS, formal collaboration between the United Nations and the Commonwealth of Independent States would develop in the near future. They hoped, moreover, that this collaboration would legitimize the CIS and the preponderant role played by Russia therein.[45] Furthermore, this support for the regionalization of conflict resolution was linked to a new discourse with respect to Russia's sphere of influence in its near abroad.

The great powers dominate international security institutions such as the UN and use them to serve their own interests of state. Here we have a good example of a great power defining the conditions of international security in a way that eventually provided it with some leeway in its interpretation of the charter of the United Nations.

This discourse reveals the shift in Russian foreign policy starting in 1993. Different Russian political circles chastised the government for sacrificing too much in the name of reconciliation with the West, at the expense of geopolitical interests and the country's Eurasian vocation. This struggle between the universalist Westernists and the partisans of rebalancing Russian foreign policy in the direction of the country's near abroad (the so-called Eurasianist approach) came to increasingly favour the latter tendency.

During the summer of 1992 Yevgeny Ambartsumov, president of the International Affairs Commission of the Russian Supreme Soviet, presented a report to the Ministry of Foreign Affairs. His recommendations included the notion that "as the internationally recognized heir of the Soviet Union, Russia must base its foreign policy on a doctrine that proclaims the geopolitical space of the former USSR as a sphere of its vital interest (as Latin America was, under the U.S.'s Monroe Doctrine), and it must obtain from the international community the understanding and acknowledgement of its fundamental interests in that space."[46] At the same time, Kozyrev, who had been the most enthusiastic and optimistic of Westernists, was subjected to the wrath of the parliamenty majority, under the leadership of Ruslan Khasbulatov, for his policy of accommodation with the United States.

Because of these pressures, political discourse at the government level tended to change after 1993. It seemed that internal tensions pushed Moscow all the more to insist internationally that Russia should be able to maintain a grip in its own sphere of influence. The government justified its position by invoking reasons of security and the defence of Russian minorities in the former Soviet Union, but behind this rationalization lay a hidden desire for the consolidation of power, with a view to limiting the influence of the Western powers in the region and regaining the prestige of a major global power.[47]

As of February 1993, President Yeltsin himself took up some important elements of the Ambartsumov report and clearly stated, at a meeting of the Civic Union, that "the time has come for the authorized international organizations, including the United Nations, to confer upon Russia a special mandate as guarantor of peace and stability in this region."[48] Despite the rather considerable internal pressures, Yeltsin succeeded in keeping the Westernist Kozyrev in his post as foreign affairs minister. Nevertheless, on 26 January 1993 Yeltsin stripped him of the responsibility for coordinating foreign policy, transferring it to the Russian Security Council.[49] This move demonstrated the current balance of power in Russia. Moreover, this tendency, which was favourable to the centrists, became even more marked after the dissolution of Parliament in September 1993, and it revitalized the role of the military.

The military doctrine set out in November 1993 accurately reflected the latitude claimed by the Russian government for its actions in the region.[50] In this document, Moscow clearly articulated its intention to station its armed forces in the region of the CIS. It should be noted, on the other hand, that the government emphasized that intervention must take place within the framework of bilateral or multilateral agreements, which suggests that the international institutions were still part of the Russian plan.

The political support for the type of behaviour already exhibited by the military in certain regions gave rise to concerns in the near abroad that were particularly discernable in the Baltic states, Belarus, Ukraine, and Moldavia. On the other hand, it is important to emphasize that certain Central Asian leaders looked favourably upon the establishment of close relationships with Russia, because they felt that it would guarantee them some stability in matters of security.[51] Some analysts saw in these developments the beginning of a new global security dynamic according to which Russia would be confined to its territory, while "global issues" and other regional conflicts would fall under American authority.[52]

The Eastward Expansion of NATO

Even though in 1992, during its brief phase of pursuing an unconditionally Westernist foreign policy, Moscow created an impression that it felt otherwise, the Russian leaders categorically opposed the enlargement of NATO towards the East when the issue came to the fore of the international agenda in 1993.[53] Just as Gorbachev had done when he opposed the inclusion in NATO of a unified Federal Republic of Germany, they claimed that this international security institution was now obsolete. According to Moscow, it was a symbol of the Cold War and a bipolar world, and as such it had no raison d'être in this period of cooperation between the two superpowers. Despite Moscow's opposition, which was buttressed by Russia's presence in the international security institutions and the prestige it had inherited from the defunct Soviet Union, the Americans persisted in their efforts to expand NATO eastward. Consequently, unable to obtain the demise of NATO and its replacement by a new European security architecture in which their state would have its place, the Soviets and then the Russians demanded that the Atlantic Alliance be subordinated to the Conference on Security and Cooperation in Europe (CSCE, subsequently the Organisation for Security and Cooperation in Europe, or OSCE). Conscious of their loss of influence on the European and international stages, the Soviet and then the Russian leadership attempted to preserve a major formal institutional role in matters of European security. Their success in this respect would also have served the purpose of limiting American influence.

But, having failed to succeed in this regard, Gorbachev and then Yeltsin were left with an ultimate fallback position, namely, to insist that the USSR and then Russia itself become members of NATO, which latter would then become a new, pan-European cooperative security structure in which their country would have its place. The Russian leadership surely viewed this scenario as a good way to convert NATO into a new body devoid of its original legitimacy. It should be noted, however, that no formal request was ever made to this effect. The leaders surely understood that their request would inevitably be refused by the Americans and would only serve to legitimize the process of enlargement.

After much hesitation, on 22 July 1994 the Russian government decided to join the Partnership for Peace (PFP). However, as a permanent member of the UN Security Council and a recognized nuclear power, the Russian government demanded that their country be granted a special status. After a delay of over ten months, a separate program for bilateral cooperation between NATO and Russia was finally signed. The delay can be attributed to the repeatedly-expressed Russian dissatisfaction with two important decisions reached at the January 1994 NATO summit: NATO's intention to eventually welcome Eastern European countries into the organization and NATO's reorganization to support its new strategy, which was centred on conflict prevention.[54] As noted by Yuri Rubinski, "these decisions were at the origin of the worst confidence crisis between Russia and the West since the end of the Cold War."[55]

Russia refused to lag behind this process. It spared no effort to increase the number of participants in the CSCE, which was in turn institutionalized to become the OSCE, to fifty-five members.[56] Despite all the hopes resting on the OSCE, the Russian government was unable or, in truth, unwilling, to define for it a clear mission and maintained an ambivalent discourse with respect to the powers it was prepared to grant it.[57]

In January 1996 Yevgeny Primakov took over as head of the Ministry of Foreign Affairs. Faced with the impossibility of forging a real strategic partnership with the United States and having a somewhat significant influence on its policy, Primakov quickly distinguished himself by adopting a more critical stance towards the United States and by prioritizing new relations with the Commonwealth of Independent States (CIS) and a heightened rapprochement with various Asian countries. This strategic fallback position, an attempt to modify the balance of power through alliances, shaped the new trend in Russian foreign policy. Concurrently, Russia continued to promote the notion that the ideal alternative to NATO enlargement was "the transformation of the Organization for Security and Cooperation in Europe (OSCE) into a central element of European security architecture."[58]

By means of this alternative, Russia hoped to see a truly pan-European security system established within which it would be a full partner. Consequently, Moscow constantly opposed, often vehemently, any eastward enlargement of NATO that would leave it excluded. Thus, speaking at the General Assembly of the United Nations on 24 September 1996, Primakov stated that "We must be careful not to replace the old fronts of opposing blocs with new lines of division. This is precisely why we accept neither the idea that NATO's military infrastructure should be expanded into the domain of the ex-Warsaw Pact nor the attempts to make this alliance the axis of a new European system."[59] Moscow was reacting to an offensive on the part of the Western countries (in truth, the United States) that, by enlarging NATO, seemed to be choosing to pursue a balance of power rather than cooperation with Russia. The American post–Cold War leaders (Bush and Clinton) clearly expressed their desire to maintain an upper hand in this international security institution and thereby consolidate their position as the sole superpower, able to limit any other power that might prove to represent a direct or indirect threat to them.

History has repeatedly demonstrated that if Russia is to establish a security system that will counter external threats, it must always begin with control of the country's immediate periphery. Russia therefore placed greater emphasis on the "primary circle" of its security interests: its own federation and its near abroad. With this attitude Russia itself impeded the work of the OSCE in the region of the CIS. The Chechnyan conflict remains a good example of the lack of coherence in Russian policy towards this security organization. While praising its merits, Russia had difficulty accepting the OSCE's participation in the resolution of conflicts within its own region. Therein lies the paradox: on the one hand, Moscow preferred to replace the U.S.-dominated NATO with the OSCE, thereby reducing the relative clout of the Americans. On the other hand, Moscow seemed to hesitate to accord this security organization real powers, for fear of being consequently undercut by its intrusion into Russia's zone of influence. Moreover, the OSCE was liable to become a protective shield over Russia's near abroad that would considerably limit its ambitions. As a result, the Russian government became increasingly tempted to establish its own operational contingents around the CIS.

Russia's inclination was to rely on a collective security founded upon a CIS that it would itself control. Moscow, moreover, (very presumptuously) threatened to transform the CIS into a military alliance in the event that NATO expanded.[60] NATO subsequently voiced a willingness to "accompany" the countries of the former Soviet Union in their relations with Russia (while remaining silent with respect to their integration into the organization).[61] This could behaviour only irritate and worry Moscow and stimulate anti-NATO reflexes within Russian political circles. Since this time, Russia has increasingly tended to sidestep the CIS in favour of bilateral agreements and direct military intervention. Russia's security interests have taken priority over any military agreements with its neighbours, and its interventions have in no way respected the UN's rules of international law, which it had formerly seen so fit to praise.

For various reasons that are specific to each Russian political milieu, opposition to NATO's enlargement became the object of an almost total consensus in Moscow.[62] The nationalists and the communists worried first and foremost about its strategic and geopolitical implications. For the liberals and Westernists, it was the marginalization of Russia in relation to a NATO that was apt to become the main security organization in Europe that they found troubling.[63] Their bitterness was particularly strong, to the degree that they considered themselves to have contributed to the peaceful withdrawal of the Soviet Union from Eastern Europe in 1989 and to have subsequently favoured the dissolution of the USSR – all so that Russia might at last (according to the terms employed in 1991–92) rejoin the "ranks of the civilized world" and become full partners therein.[64] They believed that they deserved a greater return on their investment and that the enlargement of NATO served only to discredit their policy in the face of their opponents.

The Bosnian crisis, in particular, exemplified the new tendency taking shape in matters of collective security.[65] By giving NATO some powers of intervention in the region, the United Nations accorded it the specific role of sole guarantor of international order. Consequently, the American political elite abandoned the very notion of a broadened role for the UN, an idea they had considered immediately after the end of the Cold War. This crisis also demonstrated that Russia was no longer a heavyweight player on the Old Continent and that, even in the case of several truly important interventions, the Americans hardly consulted Moscow at all. In addition, NATO concurrently developed a tendency to act alone, without taking into consideration decisions made at the UN Security Council.[66] Despite numerous attempts to change this practice, the Russians found themselves increasingly brushed aside. President Yeltsin and his team could not ignore this strong tendency, which led them to adopt ever-stronger positions regarding a NATO enlargement which, under these conditions, could not help but further marginalize Russia in European affairs.

Although it continued to oppose NATO's enlargement, Russia was aware that it lacked the means to block it, and so Moscow attempted to use what little political influence it still had to extract some concessions from the United States as compensation. These concessions were set down in the Founding Act, signed by NATO and Russia in 1997.[67] It would be difficult to contest the idea that what Russia finally received reflected its new position on the global chessboard. The Russian expectations, it must be said, had been very broad. Moscow had wanted to transform NATO from a strategic alliance into a security forum. To continue exercising some control over the European region, Russia had proposed a seventeen–state (sixteen plus one) mechanism, a decision-making council that would deliberate upon future questions of European security.[68]

Moreover, having utterly failed to improve its strength relative to the great Western powers, Russia found itself isolated within the CIS with respect to the question of enlarging NATO to the East. Rather accurately illustrating the downfall of Russian regional policy, Moscow was unable to rally the CIS member states to oppose NATO enlargement and thereby make the Americans abandon this project. Significant differences prevented the emergence of a common stance: "The Ukraine, Georgia, Azerbaijan, Uzbekistan, Turkmenistan and Moldavia determined that this enlargement would not threaten their national interests; they felt on the contrary that these would be improved by reinforcing their cooperation with the Atlantic Alliance."[69]

The changes that took place at Russia's southern border worried the country's leaders. At that time Georgia, Ukraine, Azerbaijan, Moldavia, and, lastly, Uzbekistan created a new organization, the GUUAM (the acronym is formed with the first letters of the countries involved).[70] They appeared to be distancing themselves significantly from the CIS. Russia found itself increasingly isolated within the very region to which it had laid claim. To this development we can add the creation of the Black Sea Economic Cooperation Zone (in February 1992) and the Economic Cooperation Organization, which brought together Iran, Turkey, Pakistan, the central Asian states, and Azerbaijan.[71]

CONCLUSION

Our three cases clearly demonstrate, in short, that after the end of the Cold War, Russia, just like the USSR in 1991, lacked the political and military power to initiate significant diplomatic manoeuvres and to assert itself vis-à-vis the United States. The Russian leadership, moreover, seemed to adopt a realistic practice when intervening on the world diplomatic stage. The leaders were sensitive to the problems that were ravaging their country and limiting their ability to pressure other states. Since the Gorbachev era, the leadership had realized that they could not dramatically influence the course of events. In this sense, the place of Russia within the international security organizations (the UN, the OSCE, and so on) became more than ever invested with capital importance.

The Gulf War signified a new era. As described so well by Lucien Poirier, "Everything happened as if the Gulf conflict had as its historic function to bring forth the incontrovertibly clear emergence of the new order, an order that was until then indiscernible, but which was now maturing within the chaos."[72] The transition that some observers had so dreamed of, that is, from a bipolar world to a multipolar world dominated by international institutions of collective security, never took place. The tendency since 1991 has been towards unipolarity focused upon the great power that was America, a power that excelled at using its own position within NATO to isolate Russia more and more. Itself formerly a superpower, Russia was now confined to the role of gendarme within its immediate periphery, but it found even this task difficult to fulfil.

The Gulf crisis did not permit the Soviet Union to bring about the passage from a disappearing bipolar world to a new system of collective security defended by the UN. The Americans, for strategic reasons, demonstrated a clearly expressed desire to involve the USSR in this crisis and its resolution, but at the same time kept almost total control over the unfolding of the process. Gorbachev's strategy during this crisis of partnership with the West was a failure. In addition to failing to give his country a new, higher-profile international reputation, this brief episode demonstrated the relative weakness of the Soviet Union and its inability to influence conflict resolution in the world.

Concerted action with the West, as developed by Gorbachev, was to have helped him solve the USSR's own problems by procuring direct aid from the West. As was the case with German reunification, the Soviet Union obtained little in return for its numerous concessions to Western wishes. In spite of this failure (and, in truth, in spite of itself), the Soviet Union continued to pursue this course of action. Gorbachev persisted because he hoped to at least give his state a new international mission founded upon the defence of international law and the establishment of common norms with respect to international relations.

The UN Security Council was one of the last forums where the Soviet Union could still be perceived and treated as a great power. Even though the Gulf crisis did not allow the Soviet Union to make the Security Council the decision-making body par excellence for the conflict resolution, it did enable it, by means of numerous diplomatic interventions, to raise a debate about this body's role in the resolution of regional conflicts.

After the Gulf War, the Soviet Union (and then Russia) came to favour broadening the interventionist powers of the UN and the OSCE at the expense of that of NATO. The goal was to turn the former organizations into the new collective security structures. They could then have given Russia a position of choice in the resolution of conflicts in Europe and in the world at large.[73]

The UN Security Council was thus "considered by Russian diplomacy to be a primary vehicle of multipolarity as well as the establishment of preferential tactical or strategic relationships" with other powers.[74] The Russian leadership saw in multipolarity a means to advantageously position their country in the new, emerging power configuration. Promoted as a means of mitigating the relative weakness of the new Russian state, the limits of multipolarity quickly became apparent. It would benefit Russia only when specific conditions came together, for example, when there were divergences between the Western powers and a UN action took place or the Russians had the power to influence the actors in a particular crisis situation. However, such conditions would rarely occur, since the Western powers remained united around the American superpower.

The Kosovo crisis led the Russian leadership to believe that NATO was going to play a preponderant role in the resolution of conflicts in the world, at the expense of the UN and the OSCE.[75] Conceivably feeling pushed back towards the East by the enlargement of NATO, the Russian government wished to consolidate its influence, and indeed its power, in its "primary circle" of security. To do this, it attempted to obtain international legitimacy through the UN. Moreover, the reforms it proposed for this institution went in this direction: Russia wished to be given the role of guarantor of order in Eurasia.

The enlargement of NATO signified the failure of Russian institutionalism and its quest for reciprocity with the West. This episode clearly demonstrated that Russia was investing less effort than the USSR had invested in the defence of its strategic interests. The Russian leaders considered, and rightly so, that Russia had lost too much power to allow it to get involved in risky diplomatic adventures. They very likely feared that Russia would lose the status it had inherited from the defunct Soviet Union.

In summary, despite a very different economic and political system, certain elements in the pre-1993 Russian Federation were holdovers from the Gorbachev era. We have discussed Russia's desire to curb instability within the near abroad, in order to limit its own internal instabilities. The government attempted by all available means to avoid neighbouring regional powers such as Turkey, Iran, Afghanistan, or the Caucasian States gaining influence, at Russia's expense, on the countries in Russia's zone of influence.[76] Moreover, these successive governments in Moscow did everything to avoid Western interference and to perpetuate relations of economic exchange dependent on and favouring Russia's economic prosperity. Russia's very considerable military and economic superiority over the countries in its periphery favoured the attainment of these objectives. Moscow's strategy for the former Soviet Union consisted therefore of threatening the use of force in order to increase Russia's influence at the international level and banking on the dependence of the peripheral states in order to obtain concessions favourable to Russia's economic, political, and security interests. It also consisted of structuring regional cooperation in a way that would establish Russian leadership and to consolidate Russia's power within the regional organizations.[77]

Russia's exclusion from NATO, furthermore, created a problem of legitimacy for it in the region. The eastward expansion of NATO thereafter became a threat, because of the strong attraction it held for the countries of Russia's near abroad. These countries, seduced by Western models of economic and political development and worried about the prospect of rediscovering themselves under Russia's "protective" wing, were already cooling their heels waiting to join NATO. Consequently, NATO seemed to "rival" the CIS, exerting a direct pressure on a Russia anxious to maintain its grip on the region.

Finally, despite many declarations to the contrary and despite the hopes of numerous liberal institutionalists, we believe that the West did not help Russia in any consequential way with the democratization of its political system. Witness the West's support for Boris Yeltsin's 1993 constitutional coup and for rapid and brutal economic reforms that did not take into account the economic and social reality, among other things. Moreover, even though Russia was frequently consulted, its fundamental interests were not taken into consideration in the decisions that influenced the world order. While leaving it with the weight of responsibility for the nuclear and geographical heritage of the Soviet Union, the Western powers made the most important decisions involving the future of the world order in a manner that went against Moscow's position.

After the Gulf War episode, the Soviet Union and then Russia were not invited to participate in the establishment of common guideposts. To be sure, pressure was constantly exerted upon Russia to agree to bend some aspects of its foreign policy, but this pressure was seldom accompanied by significant military or economic incentives. Western financial support, offered through international financial institutions such as the IMF, essentially only encouraged the opening of the Russian market to foreign products. In the eastward enlargement of NATO, not only did the major powers, led by the United States, refuse to allow Russia to play the role of a major power, but they also isolated Moscow throughout the process. This process of strategic expansion into Russia's old stomping ground was already well locked in when

Moscow's "agreement" came along and did nothing but add to its legitimacy.

Nor did the great powers act in a way that would strengthen democratic international institutions such as the United Nations, so as to better integrate Russia within the select group of international decision makers and provide the UN with "an independent force within the international system."[78] They did encourage economic shock therapy – very often at the expense of respect for democracy. And they did nothing to help Russia secure its region and maintain an integrated economic system that could have served as a starting point for peace. On the contrary, the IMF offered a program that proposed the abolition of the ruble zone, which would have had a considerabe effect on trade between the republics of the former Soviet Union. (Owing to the extreme economic dependence inherited from the Soviet planned economy, this measure would have had a great impact.)[79] The IMF even went as far as offering technical assistance and funding to encourage the newly independent states to mint their own currency and establish their own central banks.

CHAPTER THREE

France: International Security Institutions as an Alternative to Power Politics

ALEX MACLEOD AND HÉLÈNE VIAU

In the eyes of many observers France has for long stood out as the quintessential realist state.[1] We argue in this chapter that this traditional view of the country's international behaviour does not offer a satisfactory explanation of how and why France uses international institutions to resolve international security problems in the post–Cold War era. We also contend that neoliberal institutionalism, which shares so many realist premises, also falls far short of providing a convincing account of the French approach to international security, despite its initial promises. Contructivist approaches offer a more promising way of looking at this question. We use three recent, but very different, cases – the debate over the reform of the UN, the conflict in Kosovo, and the fight against international terrorism – to show that the recourse to international institutions has become a vital part of French security policy and goes well beyond the traditional realist and institutionalist views based on maximization of power, and their debates over the nature and the true extent of cooperation between international actors.

THE LIMITS OF REALISM
AND NEOLIBERAL INSTITUTIONALISM

At first blush there would seem to be a lot of evidence to support the realist interpretation of French foreign and security policy, even after the end of the Cold War. At least since François Mitterrand became president in 1981, there have been few discernible differences between successive governments, whatever their political colour. Though there may often be a debate over foreign and security policy among French intellectuals, governments can usually depend on solid support for it from public opinion. Thus, it would be easy to claim that France fits all the criteria for consideration as a "unitary actor." As for being "rational," few would dispute the fact that France aggressively pursues its national interest, and given the importance it has always jealously attached to its international status and to its influence, this national interest is clearly linked with a concept of power. In the words of a recent analysis of French foreign policy, France developed a strong sense of national interest, and it "so firmly believed this to be a universal norm that it assumed any state that claimed to be acting for 'higher' motivations was being hypocritical."[2]

Realism would then explain the country's participation in international security institutions essentially in terms of its quest to regain and maintain its great power status within the international system. From the realist perspective, international institutions have not lived up to French expectations. As a reflection of the distribution of power within the international system, they have forced France to conform to the objectives defined by the great powers, especially the United States, rather than allowing it to affirm its own particular role. The end of the Cold War, with the reinforcement of the American position and the rise of Germany as a potential threat to its position as a European leader, has tended to aggravate this situation. International institutions have become a further constraint on the freedom of France to make its own foreign policy.[3]

Not all realists agree with such a stark view, however. According to one popular view among French observers, international institutions act as a "multiplier of its power" that helps it achieve national goals.[4] Others, like Marie-Christine Kessler, are less charitable, claiming that the French presence in the world's leading decision-making bodies does nothing more than allow France's political leaders "to believe that the country's global influence is not linked to its available financial and economic resources."[5]

Yet French policymakers have acted as if institutions do matter. They have played a major part in pushing for further integration within the European Union (EU) and have taken concrete steps, along with Britain, to devise a truly European defence policy. At no time since the end of the Cold War has France shown any hint of wishing to face a major international security problem outside an institutional framework. Moreover, it has played a leading role in seeking to reform the international institutions to which it belongs. Realism cannot adequately explain such behaviour, unless the concept of national interest is defined so broadly that it loses its traditional realist meaning or unless, of course, it can be shown that, like Molière's Monsieur Jourdain in *Le Bourgeois gentilhomme*, French decision makers have simply been practising realism all along, without knowing it.

Neoliberal institutionalists would reject the realist view that France has become subordinate to the great powers within international institutions and has lost its capacity to make its own foreign policy. In other words, they would claim not only that institutions lead to more equal relations between states but also that institutionalized multilateralism is the object of management and negotiation, not something that is imposed on states. Though institutionalists would argue that institutions do count and do influence state strategies and behaviours, they share with realists the view that national interests are permanent and can usually be reduced to the idea of maximizing power within the international system. Neither school examines to any great extent how institutions may affect such variables as the definition of national identity or domestic policy debates, which play such an important role in formulating national interests. Where the two do differ is over the degree of cooperation within the international system, expressed in terms of relative versus absolute gains, and in the institutionalists' belief that institutions contribute positively and decisively to that cooperation.[6] But in both cases, it is a question of cooperation within a basically anarchical international system.

Realism and neoliberal institutionalism make too many simplistic assumptions about state behaviours and leave too many questions unanswered to provide a satisfactory framework for explaining France's recourse to international security institutions in the post–Cold War era. They say little or nothing not only about how institutions influence the decision to work or not to work within institutions to solve international security problems but also about perceptions of how the international system does and should function, of relations between the actors of the system, and even of the very nature of the system itself.

FRENCH INSTITUTIONAL BEHAVIOUR
IN A CONSTRUCTIVIST THEORETICAL FRAMEWORK

According to the contructivist perspective, national interests cannot be simply accepted as a given. They evolve, they are often redefined, and they cannot be limited to material interests, as traditional realists seem to believe, or to a purely military conception of security. In deliberate opposition to the traditional realist view, Martha Finnemore puts the constructivist case in the following terms: "states' redefinition of interests are often not the result of external threats or demands by domestic groups. Rather, they are shaped by internationally shared norms and values that structure and give meaning to international political life."[7] As Jeffrey Checkel has pointed out, constructivists do not have a monopoly over norms and their importance in international relations. However, both realists and institutionalists tend to see them as part of the superstructure of international relations, with little "causal force" in the case of the former and as instruments of regulation in the case of the latter. Constructivists, on the other hand, view them as "collective understandings that make behavioral claims on actors."[8]

It is not always clear to what extent and how these norms, defined here as established standards of behaviour, become part of a state's national interests. Some states may not appear to pay much more than lip service to such norms as human rights and democracy, but the fact that they are sensitive to such issues, even if only to reinterpret them in a way that allows them to claim they are upholding them, indicates that they can no longer ignore them. States that deliberately set out to violate them or to cast them aside can usually expect to find themselves generally isolated or at least shunned by the major powers and to feel the weight of pressures such as sanctions. However, constructivists go no further than to claim that these norms create an environment that is conducive to orienting states' actions in one direction rather than another. They cannot ensure that states will necessarily behave in a particular way.

Constructivists insist on identity as intrinsic to the shaping of national interests. They do not, of course, reject the role played by material interests in this process, but even the importance of material interests to a definition of the national interest may be largely a function of popular and elite perceptions and culture. National identity is made up of generally shared ("intersubjective") values, views of what the state represents for its members and for the outside world, the roles that this state does or should assume in the international system, the way the members of this state think that others view them, and the status or the place in world politics they feel belongs to their country. It will help decision makers to prioritize certain objectives that, in turn, will become national interests. Having said that, it must be emphasized that identity does not determine interests. In all cases, identity is "socially constructed," that is, it is neither immutable nor an intrinsic given, and it can therefore evolve and contribute to changes in foreign policy. Thus, a crisis of national identity may well be translated into a crisis of foreign policy while a state seeks to redefine its place in the international system, perhaps as the result of exogenous forces or of internal upheavals.

Finally, constructivists make a close connection between norms and identity, since, in the view of one group of authors, norms either define ("constitute") identities in the first place (generating expectations about the proper portfolio of identities for a given context) or prescribe ("regulate") behaviors for already constituted identities (generating expectations about how those identities will shape behavior in varying circumstances). Taken together, then, norms establish expectations about who the actors will be in a particular environment and about how these actors will behave.[9]

As this quotation suggests, there is an important distinction between constitutive and regulative norms. However, although the norms that concern us most here contribute to constituting French identities, it needs to be emphasized that regulative norms also affect identities, since they act as parameters within which constitutive norms operate and often themselves become constitutive norms as states internalize them.

In collective action the cost of cooperation must be considered, along with the issue of formulating new definitions of self, or in other words, of defining national identity.[10] For constructivists, states and their environment are intertwined, since they form part of an "intersubjective structure" that, as Alexander Wendt has put it, is composed of "shared understandings, expectations, and social knowledge embedded in international institutions and threat complexes, in terms of which states define (some of) their identities and interests."[11] Thus, international institutions and state identities can influence each other through norms that may either define identities or prescribe and regulate behaviours associated with already existing identities.

Institutions do not just change the strategies used by states to pursue their interests, but they also affect the actual formation of these interests. Whereas neoliberal institutionalists study norms or institutional rules to see whether they influence how states pursue particular interests, constructivists tend to look at norms within the general process of building and legitimizing state interests, which then shape state strategies. At the same time, state identities act upon interstate normative structures such as international institutions,[12] which themselves "also express identities."[13] It will be claimed here that institutions and norm-building through institutions are now at the heart of French national identity. It is through its active role in international institutions that France places much of its claim to its *rang*, or status as an important power. In particular, it has attempted to place itself among the "norm entrepreneurs" of the world, a concept that has been defined as "an individual or an organization that sets out to change the behavior of others."[14] For example, thanks to the leading role played by the Franco-German tandem in developing European integration from the very beginning, France has obviously had the opportunity to act as a norm entrepreneur within the European Union. On the other hand, despite its role in drafting the UN Charter of Human Rights in 1948, the aloofness of France from the United Nations tended in the past to make the role of norm entrepreneur more difficult to play in that institution. However, the end of the Cold War and the easing of tensions between the two main protagonists of that era within the Security Council have broadened the scope for taking on the task of norm entrepreneur by a lesser state that is bent on influencing the course of international affairs.

Through international institutions, French identity in the post–Cold War has been changing and has either modified traditional interests or created new ones. First among these interests is the need to maintain French influence and, in particular, its status as a major international player, its *rang*, without which France would soon find itself on the sidelines. In the second place, it aims for a world where politics takes place through multilateral institutions and where decisions involving international peace and security must be clearly authorized by these institutions.[15] Third, this new emphasis on multilateralism has brought changes to the practice of one of the central values, or interests, of traditional Gaullist foreign policy, that of national independence, or, more strictly, of stretching the frontiers of the autonomy of French foreign policy. Reference is still made to this value, but the practice of French policy in the EU and the UN would appear to indicate a shift toward exercising influence through such institutions and toward not acting alone. In other words, France accepts the constraints of institutions, and it will use all the means at its disposal to assert its position and to bring others around to its position; but it also tacitly agrees that it cannot act independently of these bodies. Fourth, in keeping with its role as a norm entrepreneur, those norms which it has convinced others to adopt will act as a constant point of reference both for its own conduct and for that of other states. Finally, France must defend the various components of its identity and ensure that they are recognized by the other major powers, in particular, the United States.

The process just outlined suggests a model of French institutional behaviour in which a two-stage sequence of environment-state and state-environment relations takes place. In the first stage, there is a tendency to resist the demands for any changes in norms coming from the international environment and to cling to traditional identities and norms. As the new situation imposes itself, the environment will exercise an ever-increasing influence, forcing a response to its pressures through some form of adaptation, which will usually include accepting new norms. During the second stage, French decision makers will adopt a more proactive stance, as they assume the role of norm entrepreneurs.

These two stages have tended to become superimposed. In the new conditions after the Cold War, France has had come to terms with changes in its international environment, such as German reunification and the end of bipolarity, that have affected its identity both at the regional and global level and have in turn influenced its interests and its behaviour.[16] Having gone through this process of adaptation and reassessment, it has itself become an agent for change in the international system by diffusing the norms that have become an integral part of its identity. Hence, we will see that two sets of norms have guided France's institutional conduct. On the one hand, there are the traditional principles (stage 1), such as sovereignty and national autonomy, that belong to the notion of a France as a world power and that favour intergovernmental institutions. On the other, newer norms (stage 2) like liberal democracy, human rights, and the market economy (the EU's "Copenhagen criteria") have led this country to propose the concept of the "right of humanitarian interference" as a security interest and to push for more efficient peacekeeping missions.[17] Both these ideas would have been anathema to General de Gaulle and his conception of the national interest.

CASE STUDIES

Reform of the UN Security Council

In the post–Cold War world, the United Nations has become the focal point of French foreign and security policy.[18] In particular, France's position as a permanent member of the UN Security Council (UNSC) has always been cited as one of its main claims to its status as a global power. Any move to change the composition or the functioning of this body would therefore represent a direct challenge to the traditional French identity and norms and to France's perceptions of its interests. By the same token, acceptance of substantial reform in this area would also signal that some profound changes were taking place in these three components of France's institutional behaviour.

The evolution of French thinking on United Nations reform, which meant above all altering the UNSC, has very closely followed the steps outlined in our two-stage model. The French authorities began by resisting calls for change within the UN and vigorously defended the status quo. Over time, they began to backtrack on their initial refusal to acknowledge the consequences of changes in the international environment and to seriously reconsider demands from some states for Security Council reform.

France encountered the question of transforming the UN Security Council well before the program for reform was officially launched in September 1993. As early as September 1990 the then Soviet Union proposed that a united Germany should get a permanent UNSC seat. Italian prime minister Giulio Andreotti followed up this suggestion with the idea that Britain and France should yield their seats to the then European Community and to Japan. As could be expected, France reacted strongly against these proposals on the grounds that there was no reason to change the UNSC membership, since it rested on an irreversible historical situation. The French government then embarked on a campaign to defend its position in the UN, which had for so long been a vital source of its international influence.[18] In an attempt to counter calls for reform, President Mitterrand initiated a G7 summit, held in January 1992, at which he put forward several proposals to strengthen UN peacekeeping missions, in which France would play a leading role.

Clearly, this behaviour belongs to the first stage of our two-stage model, since the state was reacting to its environment. In doing so, France insisted on the norms that were most closely associated with its traditional perception of its identity: sovereignty, national autonomy, prestige, and its "civilizing mission."[20] However, even at this stage, a state may well feel itself being influenced by the emerging norms of the international environment, as it becomes "socialized to accept new norms, values, and perceptions of interests by international organizations."[21] Thus, over the next two years France began ever so slowly to soften its position on UN reform, especially when Japan and Germany publicly called for UNSC reform in the summer of 1992. As yet, this meant no more than agreeing to talk about this "problem [which] is being raised by several countries."[22] It did not indicate that France had suddenly accepted the idea of a change in membership of the Security Council. On the contrary, it took of advantage of this apparent opening to explain its opposition to any enlargement of the Council, using the old maxim that "if it ain't broke, why fix it?"

By the summer of 1993, with the U.S. announcing its official support for a permanent Security Council seat for both Germany and Japan, this position had become less and less tenable. French politicians and diplomats began to talk of how the world had changed and to say that the council should take this into account in any plan for reform. The changes included recognizing that Japan and Germany were now democracies and had become an important part of the international system. This reversal of French policy cannot be adequately explained by realist theories. By accepting, even with conditions, the very principle of changing the composition of the UNSC, France was accepting the possibility of diluting, not maximizing, its international power and influence, at least in the traditional realist sense of these terms.

As France slowly adapted to the idea of the need for UN reform, the second stage of the sequence began to superimpose itself on the first one.

The country then decided to influence the emerging institutional environment itself, setting itself up as an agent for change of the UNSC. It took advantage of the logic for renewal of the Security Council to influence the normative structures of the UN by disseminating norms originating from its own evolving sense of identity and worldview. Thus, the norms of human rights, legality, and solidarity, which were superimposed on the norms underlying the French position adopted during the first stage (including sovereignty and prestige) lie behind French proposals for UNSC reform and French behaviour toward this institution.

During this second stage, French policymakers attempted to influence how changes were made in the composition of the UNSC by subjecting them to five conditions, all of which coincided with particular French identities, norms, and interests.[23] These included the following:

1 No present member should be forced to give up its seat. Stage 1: France clings to traditional identities and norms; and sees itself as a medium-sized power with global interests, with prestige; it wishes to maintain France's international status and promote its international influence.
2 Permanent members must not lose their veto rights. Stage 1: French behaviour is guided by the republican tradition, sovereignty and national autonomy, and inter-governmental institutions.
3 Only states that represent a certain weight, notably in economic development, should be admitted to the UNSC. Stage 1: France acts as a medium-sized power with global interests and prestige; it wishes to maintain France's international status and promote its international influence.
4 There must be equitable representation of all regions. Stage 2: France becomes an agent for change by diffusing norms that are an integral part of its identity as a democratic state, based on the rule of law; it promotes international cooperation, multipolarity.
5 The new members of the UNSC must agree to participate fully in UN-sanctioned peacekeeping operations. Stage 2: As a democratic state based on the rule of law France is a norm entrepreneur promoting human rights and legality, humanitarian intervention, peacekeeping, and upholding the authority of the UNSC. It is acting through international institutions, promoting internationally created norms.

Finally, in September 1997 Foreign Minister Hubert Védrine declared that France considered the Razali report to be a good basis for discussion of UNSC reform. However, France would not propose any concrete changes, though Védrine did specify that France would not agree to give up its veto power.[24]

During this second stage, French policymakers also sought to link reform of the UNSC with changes in the broader normative structures of the UN. They claimed that only global UN reform could favour development of a multipolar world, and hence a stronger system of international law. Consequently, although they accepted UNSC restructuring, they considered it more relevant to improve the framework of peacekeeping missions and increase the UN's general efficiency first. Their plans included reviewing how the UN was financed. The review would provide the basis for reform of the secretary-general's office, which, it was felt, should have more resources for peacekeeping missions.

The French insistence on tying changes in the UNSC to peacekeeping operations shows how the two sequences of France's institutional conduct are superimposed. On the one hand, French contributions to peacekeeping operations help to legitimize the country's seat in the UNSC. On the other, by meeting the norms of human rights and international solidarity and the interest of humanitarian intervention, they promote the norms and interests inherent in the French identity and influence the normative structure of the Council. Within the second stage, France has tried to establish a new rule, which states that it is the duty of every permanent member of the UNSC to participate in peacekeeping missions, an idea that was totally proscribed during the Cold War. In other words, the more the UN affirms its international role through its efficiency, the more peacekeeping missions are likely to succeed and the more the French objective of a multipolar world more respectful of humanitarian norms will be realized. Thus France's identity as a great power will be enhanced and its influence and universal roles will be legitimized.

The two-stage model as it applies to reform of the UNSC shows that the relationship between identities, norms, and interests is forever shifting, but that the old is not simply jettisoned to make room for the new. The Security Council continues to be an indicator of France's international status and an instrument through which it can exercise its influence. For example, the French have responded to demands for greater transparency and more democracy in the way the Council works with little more than an offer of some public debates, but "without renouncing the practice of informal consultations," clearly showing that the old thinking has by no means disappeared.[25] Yet France has also moved not only on the question of the composition of the UNSC but also on creating or reinforcing the norms it feels this body should represent, which include formulating and enforcing international law and direct involvement in peacekeeping operations. As we will see in the next section, the Council has now become, in French eyes, a vital source of the legitimization and implementation of the norms that have become part of the post–Cold War world.

The War in Kosovo

The break-up of the federal Yugoslav state and the ensuing instability it provoked in the Balkans presented France's emerging policy of security through institutions with its most important test since the end of the Cold War. In the first place, it brought into play both its traditional and its new international norms. Second, it involved all the major international security institutions to which it belonged – NATO, the UN, the EU, the West European Union (WEU), the G7, and the Organisation for Security and Cooperation in Europe (OSCE). Finally, it spawned a new security institution, the Contact Group, composed of the main players in the security of the Balkans, the U.S., Russia, Germany, Great Britain, Italy, and France.

In accordance with our two-stage model, the first French reactions to threats of secession and to ethnic tensions in Yugoslavia tended to reflect difficulties with coming to terms with a novel situation. Calls to maintain the integrity of the Yugoslav state, a clear allusion to the French notions of the "one and indivisible Republic" (with its emphasis on territorial and political unity) and of the "republican model" of social integration (with its refusal of any ethnic differences between citizens), remained unanswered. As for a "European" solution, it proved totally impossible. Just as it was to do on the issue of UN reform, the French state found itself compelled to respond to pressures from its immediate international environment and to accept new identities and review its norms and interests. It had to update its conception of security to include the notion of "strategic interests," which involved maintaining peace on the European continent.[26] It was forced to rethink the whole notion of peacemaking, which was becoming closer and closer to the practice of peace enforcement. It also had to come to terms with reconciling the demands of NATO with its belief in the UN.[27]

Well before NATO launched its first air raids against the former Yugoslavia on 24 March 1999, involvement there had forced France to enter the second stage of the change in its institutional behaviour. The new war would provide further opportunities to develop and define the identities, norms, and interests underlying this conduct. In particular, it was better equipped to advance two of the most important interests associated with this second stage: reinforcing the EU's international influence and defending the authority of the UNSC. The conflict also gave further impetus to the norm of humanitarian intervention. Nevertheless, as we will show, France had not renounced the historical values that belonged to stage one.

From the very beginning of the military operations against the former Yugoslavia, France identified the norms that motivated it. French leaders talked about a battle for a certain conception of Europe

and European values,[28] for human rights,[29] even for European civilization.[30] Or, more simply, they talked about a defence of European security and regional stability.[31] However, from the French point of view it
was also necessary to justify both the legality and the legitimacy of this
action against a sovereign state with specific references to the three
UNSC resolutions on Kosovo that had been adopted in 1998 (1160,
1199, and 1203) and to defend recourse to NATO as the only possible
response to an urgent situation: the intervention of NATO was necessary
because the Security Council was, as yet, in no position to play its role
of maintaining peace and international security.[32]

Throughout the whole conflict in Kosovo France felt decidedly
uncomfortable with the decision to bypass the UN, and it took great
pains to insist that NATO's intervention represented an exception that
under no circumstances could constitute a precedent and that UN sanction for any final settlement was absolutely indispensable. It dismissed
the first charge made by domestic critics of the conflict, especially on
the left, that the government was simply bowing to American pressure,
by insisting that NATO could act only with the support of all nineteen
UNSC members and by declaring publicly that France had used its influence to control both the military actions and the general strategy of
that organization. In doing so, French leaders confirmed their
country's traditional policy toward NATO – namely, solidarity in a
period of crisis – with full participation at the military level, while at
the same time maintaining their country's right to autonomy by insisting on its veto power.[33]

The Washington Summit celebrating NATO's fiftieth anniversary in
late April 1999 provided France with an excellent opportunity to set
out its own views of the direction NATO should take. According to a
Ministry of Foreign Affairs spokeswoman, France achieved four objectives in Washington: a clear definition of the geographical limits of
NATO's military activities; recognition and acceptance by NATO of the
notion of European defence; preservation of an open door to future
enlargement, especially for Rumania and Slovenia; and reaffirmation of
NATO's respect for the UN Charter and the role of the Security Council,
in particular in peacekeeping operations.[34] Despite these claims, French
success in Washington was certainly overstated, but the claims do indicate the depth of France's desire to convince public opinion that continued participation in NATO in no way jeopardized that country's
autonomy within an organization with which it had had a difficul relationship since the days of General de Gaulle.[35] But they also suggest that
France could not really conceive of European security without NATO,
even if it sought to limit the extent and the scope of its activities.

If the urgency of the situation demanded military intervention by

NATO, there could be no question of circumventing authorization from the Security Council. Throughout the crisis France clashed directly with the United States over this issue. In the words of Prime Minister Jospin, early in the conflict, the UN had to regain its role and play "a central [part] in the search for a settlement."[36] United Nations approval for NATO's actions and the need for the Security Council to take responsibility for the final settlement and peacekeeping within Kosovo became recurring themes of French policy.

President Chirac revealed the extent of differences over these issues during the Washington NATO Summit. In a press conference he talked of French disagreement with the position of some of "our allies and notably our American friends" who advocated freeing NATO from UN authority.[37] In his view such a dispensation could lead to others and would be tantamount to "accepting or imposing the law of the strongest." This was not just a quarrel about the conduct of this particular conflict. In the French view, it was the "whole international order put in place after the Second World War which was being questioned in this discussion. It was also our vision of the world which was in some ways being discussed, even threatened." After the conflict, the French president felt he could declare that French diplomacy had scored a decisive victory by ensuring that the UN had been present from the very beginning and had found again "the role and the place it must have in a world organized with a rule of international law."[38]

The French "vision of the world" included reserving an important place for Russia in European security. French policymakers insisted frequently on the impossibility of obtaining any meaningful solution to the conflict with Yugoslavia without Russian involvement. This claim was undoubtedly true, but keeping Russia within the peace-making process also promoted two important French interests: the emergence of a multipolar international system and the affirmation of the ultimate authority of the UNSC, which depended on Russian cooperation. The rather nebulous G8 provided the necessary forum in which agreement could be reached between the major industrial powers and, more specifically, between four of the five permanent members of the UNSC. A document adopted by the G8 on 6 May 1999 became the basis for the UNSC resolution on a settlement that was voted on a month later. The French congratulated themselves on having played a major part with Russia in bringing about this result and on having obtained a meeting that "not everyone desired."[39]

While France pushed hard for a prominent role for the UN in the conflict, it was not the only organization that it sought to promote. It also saw this war as an opportunity to assert the international influence of the European Union, thereby confirming the French identity as political leader of the EU. The conditions for greater EU participation were certainly much more favourable than in the war in Bosnia, from which it had been effectively excluded. In the first place, with three new members, all traditionally neutral, and at least four states from Eastern Europe who had been promised early accession, the EU had strengthened its claim as the main representative for post–Cold War Europe. Second, France had begun to clarify its relationship with NATO and had succeeded in getting recognition of the concept of a European defence and security identity, even if its actual content remained vague. Third, Britain had elected a much more pro-European government, with a huge parliamentary majority, which, by signing a joint defence agreement with France in Saint-Malo in December 1998, had at least expressed its wish for closer defence ties between Europeans through the EU. Finally, the EU had adopted the Treaty of Amsterdam in June 1997, which specifically referred to progress towards a common defence policy and which came officially into force on May 1 1999.

At all stages of the conflict in Kosovo French leaders stressed the need for the EU to play a full role. According to Foreign Minister Védrine, this meant that it should act as a "designer and a leader" and not just as a "counter for distributing subsidies for reconstruction."[40] France attempted to translate these sentiments into a series of immediate, medium- and long-term policies. In the short run, the allies agreed that one of the most important measures for hastening the conclusion of the conflict would be to use oil sanctions against Yugoslavia. French policymakers argued, successfully, that there was no legal basis for an oil blockade within the NATO framework. Moreover, they claimed that the type of embargo envisioned by certain NATO members, which would have involved boarding ships from third-party countries and blocking access to the ports of Montenegro, constituted an act of war and, as such, needed authorization from the UNSC. In mid-April, at a meeting of the European Council, the EU's supreme decision-making body, France proposed, and obtained unanimous support for, a policy of oil sanctions against Yugoslavia that was binding on all EU members and that called for associate EU members to respect it. After some wrangling at the Washington Summit, NATO also agreed to abide by the same policy.

As a medium-term measure, France advocated that the EU should assume full responsibility for civil administration over Kosovo once a settlement had been achieved. However, even before the conflict was over, it had began to soften its position on that issue. Foreign Minister Védrine acknowledged that the decision was up to the UNSC, adding that the EU was "in a way a candidate for this mission in liaison with the OSCE."[41] As for NATO, France was determined to limit it to a strictly military role and to see that it played absolutely no part in running civil affairs. Though France gained unanimous EU support for its position, it had to bow to the decision to create a UN-administered Kosovo. However, it did not give up the fight entirely and called for the administration to be headed by an EU personality. While struggling to affirm European influence, President Chirac did not overlook the more traditional French interest of preserving his country's international prestige: he lobbied for the post to be filled by his country's own candidate, Health Minister Bernard Kouchner.[42]

At the behest of Germany, which presided over the Union at the time, the EU put forward its principal plan for ensuring long-term security in the Balkans, the Stability Pact for South-East Europe. The debate around this ambitious idea throws some light on the French view of the EU. Publicly, the government welcomed this plan but tried at the same time to play down its real importance. The official Ministry of Foreign Affairs spokeswoman explained that it was not really a plan but, rather, consisted of some "German ideas" that President Chirac had already suggested were interesting and could be useful but "largely covered the ideas of other allies."[43] As for Foreign Minister Védrine, he damned the project with faint praise, calling it a "good working basis for a great European Union policy."[44] As Védrine pointed out, this proposal simply picked up on the Stability Pact for Central Europe already put forward by France in 1993 and adopted by the OSCE in 1994.[45]

As if this threat to a fundamental French identity, that of the political leader of the EU, did not suffice, France also considered that it endangered one of its fundamental interests. The Germans, backed by other members, including the British, had used this opportunity to raise an issue that had by no means been settled, that of further enlargement of the EU to include the Balkan states and others from Eastern Europe. Such a plan would obviously postpone indefinitely French aims for a more integrated European Union. As one French diplomat expressed it, "Either Germany has partly abandoned the shape of Europe for which it has worked for forty years, or it wants to reshape it differently."[46] Despite these objections, France had no choice but to accept a plan that obviously enjoyed wide international support.

French policymakers saw a more positive future for one of their most cherished projects for the European Union, a truly European defence policy. As we have seen, they considered that recognition of efforts to build a European defence and security policy was one of the most significant gains from the NATO summit in Washington. They also acknowledged that the Kosovo conflict had revealed the very real weaknesses of a united European defence policy. However, they saw positive signs pointing toward new thinking on the topic. In December

1998 French and British leaders met at St-Malo and came to an agreement on the future European Security and Defence Policy, which heralded a radical change in the British attitude, even though NATO still remained a very important part of European military security in that document. The operations in Kosovo underlined how indispensable the Franco-British axis had become to any meaningful European defence policy. At the very moment when the end of the conflict was in sight, the European Council, meeting in Cologne, adopted the outlines of a common defence and security policy that still had to take concrete form. Despite President Chirac's claim that it was "an important moment in the construction of a European defence identity,"[47] the more cautious foreign minister, Hubert Védrine, warned that there was still a long way to go and that there was no reason to think that either a European defence policy or a common European foreign policy would emerge "fully armed" from the Kosovo crisis.[48] He also noted that the conflict had clearly demonstrated that only NATO possessed the military means for a large-scale operation.[49] Finally, in accordance with the French view of how security institutions should operate, Defence Minister Alain Richard declared that the decision taken in Cologne had reiterated that a European defence policy was an intergovernmental one, thereby preserving an interest linked to the country's Republican tradition.[50]

In accordance with its historical state objectives, at every stage of the conflict France attempted to exert its influence within the institutions involved and took full advantage of its potential veto power. Not only did French decision makers insist on seeking general UN authority for the operation as soon as possible (which meant including Russia) and on giving the EU a leading role, they also attempted to impose France's humanitarian norms on NATO. President Chirac boasted after the conflict that "there was not one single target which was not agreed upon by France beforehand."[51] Throughout the conflict, public statements by government leaders and official spokespersons confirmed that France had intervened within the Alliance to halt attacks on Yugoslav civil installations (in particular the bridges of Belgrade), to steer air raids toward attacks on Yugoslav forces deployed in Kosovo itself, to spare Montenegro as much as possible, and to prevent NATO from proceeding to stage three of its operations, which would have meant intensifying and extending air raids.[52] Prime Minister Jospin also explained to his government colleagues that NATO's five conditions for ending its operations were based on "French proposals."[53]

However much French decision makers might celebrate this collective victory over Yugoslavia and proclaim that it would not have been possible without the intervention of international security institutions, they were forced to admit not only that European security still depended on a continued U.S. presence but also that the EU's contribution left much to be desired. As Foreign Minister Védrine freely acknowledged to journalists, Europe's preponderant role in solving the crisis was due above all to the coordination between "the four great European diplomacies," and not to "Europe as such, as the European Union."[54] Clearly, French foreign policy in general, and its European security policy in particular, found itself caught between the claims of its first-stage identities, norms, and interests and the post–Cold War evolution toward those of stage two, which implied international security through collective action within institutions, in place of a traditional national defence policy.

The Fight against Terrorism

Although the question of terrorism on French territory hit the headlines with a series of bombings in 1995–96, in fact the question of terrorism occupied an important place among French security concerns throughout the nineties. It raised two issues that France sought to deal with through international institutions: how to tackle the causes of terrorism and how to counter it as a threat against national security. As in the former Yugoslavia, France looked first for a European solution through the EU before calling on bodies with a wider geographical mandate, in this case the G7/G8.

European-wide cooperation over terrorism was not a product of the end of the Cold War. Already in 1976 members of the then European Community had formed the informal Trevi Group to foster cooperation on law-and-order issues, especially terrorism. These issues were later incorporated into the justice and home affairs provisions of the Maastricht Treaty. Despite the existence of cooperation mechanisms to fight terrorism, consensus on this issue was by no means easy to achieve. So it is not surprising that, though France tended to respond to international terrorism in the nineties with measures that belong to stage 2 of our model, behaving in a way that was consistent with the phenomenon of superimposition, it proved somewhat reluctant to completely abandon traditional stage-1 policies based on the norm of national sovereignty. In particular, when the first terrorist attacks took place in Paris in the late summer of 1995, the government invoked the Vigipirate plan, which was originally adopted in 1978 to give the state greater powers over civil liberties to fight terrorism, and suspended the freedom of movement between borders set out in the EU's Schengen Agreement, which had only just come into force.[55] The French attempted first of all to deal with terrorism through a series of bilateral operations with their

European partners. They agreed only in 1995 to implement the 1991 convention creating Europol, a system for exchanging information on criminal activities that had been fiercely resisted by some members of the government on the grounds that it involved too much integration of police and judicial affairs. Terrorism was supposed to become part of the Europol mandate two years later, though this did not actually happen until 1999, which indicated how reluctant France was to abandon an important manifestation of national sovereignty.

Clearly, recourse to an institutional solution to the terrorist threat belonged initially to stage 1 of our model, for at least two reasons. In the first place, the Trevi Group and its successor Europol represented a strictly intergovernmental approach to the question. They were therefore totally compatible with the norms of national autonomy and sovereignty, which were linked, in turn, with the Republican tradition. Second, there was little hint of the norms of international cooperation, of liberal democratic values, of an interest in political dialogue, of development aid, or of promoting the EU's international influence, which were to pervade the French approach to terrorism as it evolved throughout the nineties.

The French authorities thought that reactions in the Arab world to the Gulf War would lead to terrorist attacks, but in fact events in Algeria were to spark the worst spate of bombings to take place on French soil since the mid-eighties. France had upset Muslim radicals by supporting the Algerian regime's decision to cancel the second round of legislative elections in December 1991, which would undoubtedly have favoured the party supported by Islamic militants. As terrorist attacks and assassinations against French nationals began to increase in Algeria, the French government decided to ignore appeals from Muslim fundamentalists to stay out of Algerian affairs and to back up its support for the regime with aid and loans that were intended, in the words of Foreign Minister Juppé, to "facilitate and encourage the political dialogue" within the Algerian state and to " help it to overcome economic difficulties."[56]

In November 1994 the French public discovered the extent of the terrorist threat. The ministry of the Interior announced that it had broken up a group belonging to the Algerian terrorist organization Armed Islamic Group (GIA). News spread that several clandestine Islamic networks existed in France that had declared this country as one of their prime targets. It was also reported that these groups could have connections with Morocco, Turkey, Egypt, Afghanistan, Iran, and perhaps even Pakistan.[57] The wave of attacks against trains and the Paris subway launched in the summer of 1995 appeared to confirm the public's worst fears. The fight against terrorism quickly jumped to the top of the French security agenda.

Though it enjoyed a special relationship with Algeria and the other North African states, a traditional sphere of French influence, Paris did not wish to carry out a policy of terrorist prevention on its own. It also attempted, with some success, to rally the European Union around its strategy of using economic development to ensure stability within this region.[58] With the other two main Mediterranean members of the EU, Italy and Spain, France organized a Euro-Mediterranean conference, which was held in Barcelona in November 1995, shortly after the first wave of terrorist attacks in France, and which was intended to launch a long-planned Euro-Mediterranean partnership, as part of a general French-inspired EU strategy for maintaining political stability in the whole Mediterranean basin.

In early 1996 France began to widen its fight against terrorism with an offer to help the Israeli and Palestinian authorities to combat this phenomenon in all its forms. To this end, it joined other EU members, the United States, Russia, and some twenty other states at a summit meeting on international terrorism that was suggested by Yasser Arafat and held in the Egyptian town of Sharm el-Sheik in March 1996. France, which till then had expressed scepticism about the usefulness of such broadly based summits, assumed its identity of norm entrepreneur in opposition to the American antiterrorist strategy, which was based essentially on the concepts of repression and retaliation. The conference adopted a document that included most of the measures France had put forward when EU foreign ministers met informally in Palermo to prepare for the Sharm el-Sheik summit. In particular, it announced that the economic development of the Palestinian territories remained the best defence against terrorism.

French influence over the international norms to be invoked against terrorism was felt most strongly in the G7/G8. The issue was brought up at this institution's annual summit in Lyon, which was held just three months after Sharm el-Sheik and which opened only hours after a terrorist attack against the U.S. forces base in Dhahran, in Saudi Arabia. The Lyon summit adopted a unanimous declaration on terrorism. The French then proposed that G7/G8 foreign ministers and ministers involved in fighting terrorism should meet a few weeks later in Paris to examine ways of reinforcing antiterrorist measures.

This conference underscored differences between European and U.S. antiterrorist norms and strategies. The Americans called for the creation of an international organisation specifically to combat terrorism, a proposal that the Europeans strongly rejected. Washington wanted to draw up a black list of "rogue" states, states that were accused of supporting terrorism and were liable to sanctions and that would be totally isolated from the international community. The Europeans refused such a policy in favour of a "critical dialogue" with these suspects. The French delegation was particularly forceful in denouncing what it saw as an old-fashioned approach that presumed that terrorism was fomented only by states, whereas, according to Foreign Minster Hervé Charrette, terrorism was now above all "the affair of small or not-so-small groups supported by networks, which use extremely diverse methods throughout the world."[59] In spite of these deep divergences, the meeting approved a final text that announced several concrete measures against terrorism. The measures were based on an "agreement on the need to seek solutions which take into account all those conditions likely to ensure a long-lasting settlement of unresolved conflicts and to take care of the factors which risk favouring the development of terrorism."[60]

The final text represents without doubt a win for the European position. With the European emphasis on going beyond punishment in order to act upon the socioeconomic, political, and cultural conditions that foster the emergence of terrorism, it goes directly against the American view. The French delegation took pains to point out that not only did this text omit any reference to sanctions, but it also made it clear it was not a "document of threats against any other country."[61] The results of this conference illustrate once again the complexities of the relationship between the two stages of French interest formation. On the one hand, the French expressed the emerging stage-2 norms of liberal democratic values and international cooperation that are associated with the identity of a democratic state based on the rule of law. On the other hand, they continued to hold onto the norm of national autonomy belonging to the Republican tradition by reminding the other participants of the need for each country to retain some room for manoeuvre in its choice of methods for dealing with terrorism and especially to retain the freedom to make contacts with other states.

On the issue of terrorism, France has had some success in becoming a norm entrepreneur. Differences between Europeans and Americans over terrorism have tended to be reduced, though, as u.s. policy since the events of September 11, 2001, reminds us, punishment and retaliation remain an important part of the American arsenal against all forms of terrorism. Before the assault against the Twin Towers, there had been signs the European approach had made some inroads into u.s. thinking. American terrorism specialist Bruce Hoffman admitted as much, when he wrote that "although it has become fashionable [in the United States] to dismiss Europe's approach toward terrorism as counterproductive, there is reason to believe the European way of doing things might yield more effective results in the long run."[62] But obviously, the u.s. approach to the issue clearly predominates once again. France has had little choice but to follow the American lead, despite some qualms – which are shared by its European partners – about how the United States has dealt with the question of the status of al-Qaeda and Taliban prisoners held in the American naval base in Guantanamo. At the same time, if the French have felt the need to show complete solidarity with the United States on the immediate solution to the situation in Afghanistan and the fight against Osama Ben Laden (as President Chirac made very clear in his 2002 New Year's message to the diplomatic corps) little has changed fundamentally in the French view of the need for a different long-term strategy:

Analyzing the events of September 11 also means reflecting on the gap between the almost unanimous condemnation of the attacks by governments and the reactions of certain peoples ... We must be attentive to these reactions from these peoples, as we should be to the size of those movements protesting against globalization ... Whilst we reject intellectual confusion and sometimes summary analyses, we must not be blind or deaf ...We must settle those conflicts whose permanency can only create frustrations and excesses. We must take into account the anguish and distress of these peoples. We must not leave them without any hope of development, without hope for peace with dignity.[63]

CONCLUSION

The three cases presented in this chapter deal with very different aspects of French security policy, but they all point in the same direction. Action through international institutions has provided an alternative to traditional power politics for a state whose leaders have been obsessed in the past with asserting their country's right to the status of a global power and insisting on defending sovereignty and national autonomy. It has been argued here that neither realist nor neoliberal institutionalist approaches can adequately account for this change in French international behaviour, because their terms of reference are too narrow. The insights of constructivism, in particular insights concerning the role identities and norms play in defining interests, are necessary to complete the picture. It is in this sense that we have talked of an alternative to, and not of a substitute for, the practice of power politics.

Constructivism does not deny that states may and do pursue national interests and may behave more in accordance with the precepts of Machiavelli and Clausewitz than those of Kant. Constructivism is not a form of idealism. It simply challenges the realist tendency to view national interests as constituting a more or less permanent value based on material factors, and it challenges the notion that states are motivated above all by maximizing their power or ensuring their survival in a fundamentally hostile and anarchical international system.[64] It argues, rather, that analyzing national identity and norms, both as a guide for a state's own international behaviour and as a source of the definition of national interests, yields a far better understanding of how states conduct themselves and why.

Altering national identities is a very slow process that can be accelerated by profound changes in a state's external environment. In most situations where identities go through some sort of transformation, many of the features of past identities continue to assert themselves and to live side by side with the new: the old and the new are superimposed. Superimposition results from a two-stage sequence in which states first resist pressures for change coming from the environment and then attempt to act upon the system by promoting new norms associated with newly acquired identities. This model does not, of course, apply to all states, but it would appear to describe the process through which states that have any claim to wide international influence are likely to pass under similar conditions.

No one can deny that the end of the Cold War was a shock for France and initiated a national identity crisis that, in turn, put into question both the objectives and the means of foreign and security policy. As each of our cases shows, France found it difficult to acknowledge that changes in its circumstances forced reassessment of its national identity. It resisted change but finally gave way to accepting new identities that were grafted onto identities that had existed until then in more or less the same form as they had when they were enunciated by General de Gaulle in the late fifties and early sixties.

But identities do not evolve in a vacuum. On the one hand, they are affected by the external environment, which includes the prevailing international norms that regulate international behaviour. On the other, they go through a process of producing new norms, which, the country's leaders proclaim, will not only orient their future conduct in the international system but will also influence the principles underlying the operation of the system itself. In other words, these constitutive norms will also take on regulative characteristics. In this way France will have contributed to transforming the international system. This particular example illustrates the close relationship between norms, identity, and the definition of national interests.

In the post–Cold War era, French policymakers have made it clear that they consider institutions have become the major place where international relations take place. This view is totally consistent with the neoliberal institutionalist interpretation. However, we have argued here that institutions do not simply constitute a vital instrument of international cooperation but also make up part of the French national identity, in the sense that none of the interests linked to stage-2 identities and norms can be pursued outside an institutional framework.

Becoming a "Normal" Actor in World Affairs: German Foreign Policy and International Security Institutions since Unification

JOEY CLOUTIER, BENOÎT LEMAY,
AND PAUL LÉTOURNEAU

In the days following German unification, some observers predicted that Germany would return to its old ways, with policies defined by terms such as *Schaukelpolitik* (the policy of fluctuating between the East and the West) and *Machtpolitik*, and that it would seek to dominate Europe. Others suggested that Germany would follow its traditional policy of restraint, marked by multilateralism and noninterventionism, as it had done since the beginning of the Cold War. Neither of these two predictions was right. Quite to the contrary, in the last decade, Germany has sought to "normalize" its foreign policy, by becoming more involved in international institutions and participating in peacekeeping missions outside NATO's area of responsability.

Considering the evolution of German foreign policy since the end of the Cold War, one has to ask what could explain this behaviour. Was it the result of changes in the structures of the international system since the fall of the Berlin Wall or the result of choices made by the political elite? Did other internal or external factors influence Germany's institutional security behaviour? These questions concerning German diplomacy over the last decade form the basis of this chapter on Germany's institutional behaviour since 1989.[1]

We will begin by putting forward a theoretical argument about the strategic logic that has been followed by Germany. The resulting theoretical framework will then be applied to three historical cases: German unification, German participation in United Nations operations in Somalia, and the reform of the United Nations Security Council.

EXPLAINING GERMANY'S INSTITUTIONAL CONDUCT

Germany's institutional conduct with respect to security can be explained by two overriding considerations: its need to reassure its neighbours of its intentions – which means that it had to be predictable and a reliable partner and that it had to be perceived by the international community as having been rehabilitated – and its desire to play a more important role on the international scene by attempting to increase its status and to reinforce its position in international security institutions. The end of the Cold War has meant that, to a certain extent, the Federal Republic's foreign and security policy has been "normalized." As we use it here, "normalization" refers to a process that leads Germany to regain complete control over its foreign policy. Germany's normalization coincides with the arrival, in 1992, of a new generation of diplomats and civil servants in Departments of Foreign Affairs and Defence, as well as with the emergence of new political leaders such as Foreign Minister Klaus Kinkel of the Free Democratic Party (FDP) and Defence Minister Volker Rühe of the Christian Democratic Union (CDU). The normalization process went even faster after the 1998 fall elections, with the arrival of their younger social-democrat and green successors, Chancellor Gerhard Schröder and Foreign Minister Joschka Fisher. Germany intends to defend its interests in the same way that other powers do, which implies active participation on the international scene.

Nevertheless, the transition from being seen as a "subject" to becoming an "actor" does necessarily reflect a fundamental change in behaviour. If anything, it may simply indicate for a shift towards an institutional policy that is more explicitly focused on strengthening Germany's role as a leader by openly promoting its interests. The term "subject" refers to Cold War Germany, a power that had not enjoyed complete sovereignty since the end of World War II: the four victors of that war had kept residual powers in the areas of foreign and security policy. But through unification, Germany became an "actor": it took on its international obligations and assumed its place as a normal and sovereign power. In other words, the "new" German foreign and defence policy is consistent with the policy followed during the Cold War. While Germany has fully capitalized on its status as a sovereign state with different economic and geostrategic advantages and a new international context, the same variables that prevailed during the

Cold War are still relevant. In the case of Germany's participation in peacekeeping operations, the foreign- and security-policy-making elites have taken various criteria into account.[2] These include a clear international mandate for the United Nations; maximum involvement in the decision-making process; a mission clearly based on conflict resolution; and German involvement alongside its NATO and WEU allies. In addition, if Germany is to participate, there should be a direct threat to Germany or to the European or the international community.[3] Furthermore, each UN mission requested is to be treated individually before any decision is made about German involvement.

Political culture is a key variable in German foreign policy. Since the end of World War II, the country's political culture has been forged by the lessons learned from Germany's past, especially from the horrors of National Socialism and from the Cold War. This deeply rooted political culture is pacifist and antimilitarist, and Germans understand the potentially disastrous consequences of an expansionist foreign policy based of the use of force. The debate surrounding the deployment of German troops during the Gulf War pitted the different political parties against each other, and ultimately, the constitutionality of German troop deployments had to be ruled upon by the Federal Court in July 1994.[4] Given these circumstances, any return by Germany to its old ways is difficult to imagine.

The political elites have assimilated the values and norms of the current political culture, which has guided the elaboration of foreign and security policy since 1945. German policy toward international institutions reflects the Constitution of the Federal Republic, which has entrenched respect for international law over national law.[5] One can, therefore, understand the importance placed on institutions such as NATO, the Conference on Security and Coperation in Europe (CSCE, now the Organisation for Security and Cooperation in Europe, or OSCE), and the European Community by the rulers of West Germany during the Cold War. The Federal Republic of Germany found itself in a unique position after World War II. Operating in a bipolar international system, this semisovereign state, divided by and dependent on the great Western powers for its security, had to work almost entirely through international institutions to promote its foreign policy interests. Therefore, with time, these institutions not only became a forum for cooperation and promoting Germany's political and economic interests but also provided a normative framework for its foreign policy.[6] Political elites have a significant influence on public opinion through articles, interviews, or speeches. Thus, in a continuing process of political and civic education, Chancellor Kohl and Foreign Ministers

Genscher and Kinkel, as well as Defence Ministers Stoltenberg and Rühe, succeeded in making their plans acceptable, while respecting the broad principles of the postwar political culture.

International pressures on the Federal Republic of Germany must also be considered. While Germany must reassure its neighbours about its intentions, they, paradoxically, want to see it more actively involved in international affairs.[7] The traditional culture of restraint is no longer acceptable. The crisis in the Persian Gulf and then the Gulf War were the catalysts for this change. This conflict forced Germany to adapt and define its foreign policy priorities more openly in the post–Cold War era.[8] American pressure was also important: Washington, realizing that the Federal Republic of Germany was of fundamental importance both to European integration and the perpetuation of NATO, had already proposed that Bonn should join in becoming a "partner in leadership."[9] The partnership left no doubt that the Germans had now replaced the British as the key American ally in Europe.[10] After unification, the end of the Cold War, and the arrival of Bill Clinton in the White House, the pressure on Germany increased. In July 1994, the U.S. President declared, "I do not see how Germany, the third biggest economic nation in the world, can escape a leadership role ... it has no other choice ... Germany cannot withdraw from its responsibility."[11] Earlier that year, the U.S. Senate had adopted a resolution that called upon Germany to participate fully in international peacekeeping efforts.[12] UN Secretary General, Boutros Boutros-Ghali, during a visit to Bonn in January 1993, had also declared that without German involvement the UN would not be able to fulfill its international obligations.[13]

Over the last decade of the twentieth century, three events defined Germany's new position on the international scene and set the guiding principles of German interactions with international security institutions. Unification in 1990 laid the foundations for a progressive normalization of its foreign policy. German involvement in the military side of the UN operation in Somalia (1992–94) provided a concrete example of its ability both to assume its international responsibilities and to legitimize the role it has gained in the UN. The request for a permanent seat on the UN Security Council, now a main objective of its foreign policy, reflected Germany's true status in Europe.

GERMAN UNIFICATION: A EUROPEAN GERMANY, NOT A GERMAN-DOMINATED EUROPE

In the case of German unification, which illustrates how security interactions have been regulated, the internationalist approach highlights the importance for West German decision makers during the Cold War of international institutions such as NATO, the European Community, and the CSCE. After World War II the Federal Republic of Germany found itself in a unique position that explains the favourable attitude of the leadership in Bonn toward international institutions. Divided and semisovereign but dependent on the Western powers for its security in a bipolar system, West Germany turned to international organizations to promote its foreign policy interests.[14]

Germany continued its Cold War policy toward institutions and used them during unification to defend its national interests and reduce the uncertainties about its intentions. Because of its past, which had been shaped by the Wilhelmian and Hitler eras and which had been marked by a policy of military might and expansionism, Germany had to reassure its neighbours that, once reunified, it would not pose a threat to their security. To do this, the Federal Republic of Germany had to emphasize its strong commitment to the international institutions to which it belonged.

Chancellor Helmut Kohl and his Foreign Minister Hans-Dietrich Genscher became the spokesmen for European integration and suggested speeding up the process by focusing on an economic, monetary, and political union of the members of the European Community. Aside from the development of East-West cooperation on an economic and political level, Kohl and Genscher also supported strengthening the structures of the CSCE so that it could play a larger role in Europe, while creating a legitimate foundation for a continuing role for the USSR in Europe after its withdrawal from East Germany. The creation of the CSCE was seen as a security policy analogous to Soviet leader Mikhail Gorbachev's "European Common House." The West German government also insisted on redefining NATO, to make it an instrument of cooperation with the East and no longer one of confrontation, and on reducing the German armed forces in the context of negotiations on the Conventional Armed Forces Reduction in Europe (CFE). By promoting such policies, the Bonn government made it clear that its objective was to help Gorbachev convince the members of his government to accept the involvement of a unified Germany in a Western military alliance.[15]

By standing firm on the issue of a unified Germany's involvement both in NATO and the European Community, Chancellor Kohl succeeded in reassuring his Western allies, especially the United States, Britain, and France, of Germany's ties to the Western alliance and it consequently gained their support for unification. The chancellor also put Soviet concerns to rest by presenting himself as a supporter of a broader role for the CSCE. Beyond wanting to reassure its Western allies and the USSR in order to legitimize the unification process at the European level, the government in Bonn sought to garner public support for unification in both West and East Germany by emphasizing international institutions during its negotiations on unification, thereby weakening the opposition of German intellectuals and politicians. Through this institutional policy, the Federal Republic sought to prove to its European neighbours and its own population that it no longer had any ambition to become a great military power that would pose a threat to European security.[16]

If a unified Germany's commitment to the Western alliance was a condition sine qua non for American, British, and French support for unification, it also linked West Germany's policies to Western international institutions. The Bonn government was promoting European integration and suggesting a redefinition of NATO's role and the strengthening of the CSCE, not only to facilitate the acceptance of the involvement of a unified Germany in the Atlantic alliance but also because its members believed in the virtues and advantages that these reforms would offer Europe.[17]

Shortly after the fall of the Berlin Wall, on 9 November 1989, the Bonn government made many declarations about the German right to self-determination, as laid down in the 1975 Helsinki Agreement, which has been negotiated through the CSCE. At the end of November 1989, Chancellor Kohl presented a ten-point program for a confederal structure between the two German states, as a step toward an inevitable unification in a federal state. The program provided a crucial role for international organizations in negotiations on unification. It recommended opening the European Community to East Germany and any other East European countries wishing to engage in liberal democratic reforms. It also advocated broadening the role of the CSCE and called for further East-West cooperation and real progress in negotiations on disarmament and arms control in Europe.[18]

References to the rules, principles, and values of these institutions served as a basis for the claims of the Federal Republic but also for all states involved in the negotiations. International organizations played an important role in the unification process by serving as references in bilateral and multilateral negotiations. During the negotiations, the West Germans and the Americans were able to persuade the Soviets to accept the principles of the CSCE, as defined in the Helsinki Agreement of 1975. If Gorbachev's support for unification recognized Germany's right to self-determination, his support for a unified Germany's involvement in NATO acknowledged, according to him, a state's right to choose freely the alliance it wants to join.[19]

The institutionalist argument shows that German unification could not have happened without the consent of several states and international institutions, notably the four victorious powers of World War II and the European Community. This can be explained as the result of the residual powers that had been granted to the United States, the United Kingdom, France, and the USSR since Germany's surrender in 1945 and of the integration of the two German states into the Western military, political, and economic alliances: both were consequences of the Cold War and the division of the European continent between two blocs.[20]

Germany also recognized that the four meetings that served as the framework for negotiations on unification between the two German states and the four victors over Hitler's Germany ("2+4") turned out to provide a flexible method for solving the complex questions relating to sovereignty, the status of the alliance, and the territorial borders of a unified Germany. However, in the area of defence the unification process was defined by the international institutions to which the Federal Republic of Germany belonged.[21]

In essence, according to institutionalists, the way in which the Bonn government reacted after the Cold War was significantly influenced by the existence of international institutions and the belief in their intrinsic values. However, even though these institutions shaped the expectations of the West German political leaders, they were also used to achieve the latter's own goals.

On a classical realist approach it could be argued that German unification happened after an intensive session of bilateral and multilateral negotiations that succeeded because of a group of exceptional leaders – exceptional as much for their qualities as statesmen as for their ability to cooperate. Most notably, the political leaders of the Federal Republic of Germany and the USSR enjoyed a long-standing relationship that allowed them to develop close personal ties, even friendship.[22] Stephen F. Szabo makes this argument when he claims that the crucial decisions and the most important agreements about German unification were the work of eleven men from three countries: the heads of state and diplomats from the Federal Republic of Germany, the United States and the USSR; those of France, Great Britain, and East Germany played only a secondary role in negotiations.[23]

Exemplifying the classical realist view, Elizabeth Pond maintains that the administration of George Bush senior played a decisive, central role in the events that led to unification and that the result would have been significantly different had Washington not done so. The United

States also reversed initial British and French opposition and convinced the Soviet Union that it could support German unification while preserving its dignity and avoiding isolation.[24]

Once the principle of unification had been accepted by the major powers, the Bonn government had to place the process of unification within the context of the European integration and development of the CSCE if it was to reinforce the legitimacy of German unity in Europe. Moreover, Germany committed itself to remaining within NATO after reunification, thereby guaranteeing the continuity of the alliance and the U.S. presence, while simultaneously reassuring the Western European – and even those in Eastern Europe – that Germany did not pose a threat. The U.S. presence within the Atlantic Alliance provided a counterweight to German power in Europe. The Genscher Plan, proposed by the then foreign minister, Hans-Dietrich Genscher, in early 1990, was aimed at assuaging Soviet security concerns by declaring that NATO would not expand eastwards. It was based on the "2+4" treaty on security policy after German unification and on a redefinition of the purpose of the alliance. It convinced Gorbachev that the participation of a unified Germany in NATO was in the interest of all European countries dedicated to peace and stability.[25]

Classical realists insist that American and West German decision makers shared the opinion that the USSR should not be isolated or humiliated during the "2+4" negotiations on German unification. They did not forget the consequences of the Treaty of Versailles for Germany. It was therefore important that the Soviets should not think that with unification they had lost the Cold War. Bonn and Washington consequently sought to reassure Gorbachev that his country would be treated with dignity as a full-fledged member of Europe during and after unification. Since it was to everyone's benefit that the progressive collapse of the Soviet bloc in Eastern Europe be managed in a way that favoured the emergence of a new security order on the European continent, unification could not be seen as harming the security interests of the USSR. Instead, they had to be taken into consideration during unification in order to guarantee that the new European security order would not be put in doubt.[26] The Genscher Plan and the redefinition of NATO's mission in Europe convinced the Kremlin leadership that a unified Germany within NATO and the framework of the CSCE and the European Community would be a better partner than a neutral Germany – especially for the USSR and especially for maintaining peace and security in Europe.[27]

The neorealist approach has based its argument on the fact that German-Soviet bilateral negotiations were the most important, since they sealed unification. These negotiations were conducted outside the framework of the "2+4." It was during a meeting with Kohl in Moscow on 10 February 1990 that Gorbachev gave his official support for unification and it was during a meeting in the Caucasus with the West German Chancellor in mid-July 1990 that the Soviet leadership accepted the principle of a unified Germany within the Atlantic Alliance. According to Timothy Garton Ash, a prime exponent of the neorealist approach, the agreement on German unification was a product of the participants in the "2+4" negotiations most importantly the Federal Republic of Germany, the USSR and the United States – the three big players at the end of the Cold war.[28] The main agreement reached in the Caucasus was the fruit of bilateral negotiations between Bonn and Moscow. These recurring bilateral German-Soviet negotiations played a greater defining role than the rest. By coming to the financial aid of Gorbachev on three separate occasions (in January, May, and September 1990) in a desperate effort to modernize the USSR, the Federal Republic strengthened the chances of German unification. However, Ash notes that this behaviour "was also a very long way from the new, post-national, multilateral style of international relations, which the Federal Republic publicly preached and which went by the name of 'Helsinki'. In style and content this was a great power deal. As Gorbachev himself remarked at the concluding press conference, 'We [have] acted in the spirit of the well-known German expression Realpolitik.'"[29]

For Garton Ash, the negotiation of German unification recalled the Crimean conference that was held forty-five years earlier: it was a "Yalta to undo Yalta." Even though it was peacetime diplomacy, "it was still élite, great-power diplomacy, the few deciding about the many."[30] Far from turning to multilateral negotiations within various international institutions, the Federal Republic was content to conduct traditional great power diplomacy. "This was Realpolitik in a highly civilised form, with the telephone and the cheque book instead of blood and iron; but it was Realpolitik all the same."[31]

None of the theories just described seem to encompass all the independent variables in our hypothesis about the behaviour of Germany towards international institutions. Since our variables are not exclusive to any of these theories, we must therefore examine the bulk of their arguments, while offering a nuanced critique of their interpretations, in order to reorganize all our independent variables.

In essence, our theoretical model claims that the Federal Republic of Germany turned to international security institutions partly to reassure its neighbours and domestic public opinion and partly to fulfill national objectives on the issue of German unification. The main independent variables of our theoretical model are the following: the role of West German political elite, the institutional political culture that the Germans forged during the Cold War, their belief in the intrinsic values of international institutions, the lessons they learnt from their past, and their awareness that their foreign policy must be set within a multilateral framework.

The case of unification conceals one specific variable that is highlighted by neorealists and, to a lesser extent, by classical realists, but not by institutionalists, to explain Germany's behaviour toward international institutions: the significant changes in the structures of the international system that came about with the end of the Cold War and German unification. The end of the Cold War caused a major disturbance in the international European system by bringing an end to the bipolar order of the postwar era, which had rested on the division of the European continent and the German nation into two antagonistic blocs at the political, military, economic, ideological, and social levels. Germany benefited the most from this transformation, since it allowed it to regain its political sovereignty and, consequently, its status as an independent international "actor" and not a simple "subject." With the Cold War now over and with the gradual collapse of the Communist Bloc in Eastern Europe and the impending dissolution of the Warsaw Pact and the Soviet Union, a unified Germany could become more independent of the Western powers. It could maintain its own security and affirm itself as autonomous from the two main military powers, the United States and the USSR. The end of the bipolar system on the European continent and German unification marked the return of Germany as a major actor in Europe.

But the transition from subject to actor did not fundamentally change Germany's behaviour toward international organizations: if anything, it focused it more explicitly on an institutional policy that sought to heighten its status on the international scene. This policy should not be interpreted as an attempt to increase Germany's national power. Rather, the goal was to acquire greater responsibilities at the international level.[32]

The institutionalist approach underscores the role played by the German institutional political culture that was forged during the Cold War. It explains this political culture as one that was based on the unique position that the Federal Republic found itself in after World War II. Semisovereign, divided, and dependent on the great Western powers for its security, Germany had to rely entirely upon international institutions to promote its national interests. Continuing the institutional policies of the Cold War, the Federal Republic resorted to international organizations to defend its national interests during unification; Bonn's reactions were determined by the existence of international institutions and a belief in their intrinsic values.[33] This perspective explains the German desire to reform NATO, pursue European integration, and strengthen the structures of the CSCE. Even though these institutions shaped the expectations of the West German leadership, they were, nevertheless, used to further German interests and achieve German goals.

Institutionalist and classical realist approaches add another goal to the institutional policies pursued by the Bonn leadership during unification and establish another independent variable used in our explanatory model: that of reducing uncertainties with respect to their intentions. Germany had to reassure its neighbours that, once reunified, it would not seek hegemony over the European continent and it also had to reassure domestic public opinion that Germany would remain a good international citizen after unification.[34]

To this end, the Federal Republic never wavered in its commitment to international institutions such as NATO, the European Community, and the CSCE. Germany's political leaders knew full well that their country had more to lose by going it alone – which would mean maintaining a unilateral foreign policy – than it would if it became involved in the widespread network of security institutions.[35] Within that framework Germany could fulfill its national objectives more easily, while maintaining a greater level of legitimacy, at both the national and the international level.

Even though the institutionalist argument highlights the contributions of bilateral negotiations between the victorious powers and the two German states, either through the "2+4" negotiations or private meetings, it diminishes their importance with respect to international institutions. Unlike neorealists and, to a lesser extent, classical realists, institutionalists seem to ignore the fact that the unification process put the spotlight on the role of the great powers, since without the consent of both superpowers, unification could never have happened.[36]

According to neorealists, it was the bilateral German-Soviet negotiations that were the most important factor, because they secured unification. These negotiations took place outside the "2+4" framework. It was during a meeting with Kohl, in Moscow on 10 February 1990, that Gorbachev gave his official support for unification, and it was during a meeting with the West German chancellor, in mid-July 1990 in the Caucasus, that the Soviet leadership accepted the principle of a unified Germany within the Atlantic Alliance.[37] Since the Allies had maintained residual powers over a divided Germany, it is obvious that the final agreement on unification was made possible by the consent of the countries that took part in the "2+4" discussions, even if it was endorsed afterwards by the international institutions.

As classical realists claim, once the principle of unification was accepted by the great powers, the government in Bonn had to put unification in the context of NATO, European integration, and the development of the CSCE, in order to reinforce the legitimacy of a unified Germany in Europe.[38] By turning to international institutions and referring to their values and principles during the negotiations on unification, the Germans helped to speed up the process. However, international institutions were largely ignored in bilateral negotiations.

Even though negotiations were dominated by great power diplomacy, because the leaders of the "2+4" were put to the fore – notably the leaders of the Federal Republic, the United States, and the USSR, references to the norms, principles, and values promoted by the international security institutions also served as a basis for the claims of the parties involved. This argument is underestimated by neorealists. In fact, one must not forget that Germany's commitment to the Western system of alliances, and in particular to NATO, was a fundamental condition for receiving the agreement and support of the American, British, and French governments for unification.[39] While Germany's firm commitment to NATO and the European Community reassured its Western allies, its commitment to the CSCE reassured the USSR and its East European neighbours.

Another independent variable is the crucial role played by the West German elites during the process of unification, particularly Chancellor Kohl. More than any other political leader, it was Kohl who took advantage of the historic opportunity that the fall of the Berlin Wall and the end of the Cold War gave Germany. On 28 November 1989 he succeeded in hurrying up the unification process by presenting a ten-point program that guaranteed that the evolution of the German question would no longer depend only on the four victors of World War II, especially the USSR, which was concerned about the recent upheavals in Eastern Europe. The chancellor's ten-point program sought to channel the chain of events in East Germany toward a specific objective: the progressive union of the two German states. "The window of opportunity in which it was possible [to get unification] was very limited ... It required a fast tempo," Kohl later stated.[40] The question then arises whether another chancellor would have shown that much initiative during such a crucial time in German history.

Much can be said for Kohl's insistence on maintaining a reunified Germany within NATO when a quarter of West Germans and half of the East Germans favoured adopting a neutral military stance after unification.[41] With the support of Horst Teltschik, his main advisor on matters of security policy, and Gerhard Stoltenberg, his defence minister, Kohl managed to convince Genscher, who was calling for complete demilitarization of the territory of the former East Germany, to expand NATO into the former German Democratic Republic (GDR), but under certain conditions that would be acceptable to the leadership in Moscow, in order to avoid alienating it.[42] Furthermore, friendship between Kohl and Gorbachev facilitated the negotiation of the "2+4" treaty, as is mentioned by classical realists.[43]

Finally, we can add a constructivist element to complete the analysis of German behaviour toward international security institutions throughout the negotiations on unification. This element is the Germans' identification with the multilateral principles of the establishment of international security institutions. Thomas Mann's saying that "we do not want a German Europe, but rather a European Germany," which was repeated many times by German decision makers during unification, especially by Foreign Minister Genscher, highlights the desire to merge, in a balanced way, Germany's and Europe's interests.[44] This desire is an element of the identification with principles that reinforce the identity of a peaceful and "Europe-oriented" Germany.

STEPPING INTO "NORMALITY": THE BUNDESWEHR'S DEPLOYMENT IN SOMALIA (DECEMBER 1992 TO MARCH 1994)

The flight of dictator Mohammed Siad Barre in January 1991 left Somalia without a central government. Clan wars erupted between different groups led by the infamous "warlords" who had seized the arms left over after the end of the Cold War. During this period of anarchy and chaos in August 1992, a famine struck that, according to the International Red Cross, affected more than 4.5 million Somalis to varying degrees.[45] The UN Security Council first reacted by forming UN Operations in Somalia (UNOSOM I: April-December 1992). On 4 December 1992, the Security Council, which proved unable to guarantee the security and effectiveness of humanitarian operations, adopted resolution 794. This resolution authorized UN intervention in Somalia by the United Nations Task Force (UNITAF: December 1992–April 1993), which was under American command.[46] Germany had been taking part in an airlift operation organized to send food to Somalia since August 1992. When the creation of UNITAF was announced, Germany once more supported the UN's decision and declared itself willing to send troops from the Bundeswehr.[47]

Although it has not been studied extensively, participation by German armed forces in the UN deployment to Somalia was the first real international and domestic test for the newly unified country. Germany claimed the right to a permanent seat on the Security Council in 1992, and the ongoing constitutional debate on the matter would be fueled by the deployment of the Bundeswehr outside NATO's area.

Classical realists argue that German participation was a successful test. As an important step on the road to "normalization," it showed that Germany could respond to international pressure, while also taking into account public opinion and the views of its political elite. Two practical reasons pushed Germany into participating in the operation, despite the lack of a domestic consensus. First, there were concerns about how other states would perceive Germany's decreased defence budget following the end of the Cold War. Second, the government also thought Germany should increase its participation in UN operations in order to support its bid for a permanent Security Council seat.[48] For realists, Somalia was a test that could legitimize an eventual leadership position for Germany, which had already made the a priori decision to support the United Nations as the principal institution for maintaining peace and security in the world. The new structure of the international system dictated the behaviour of the big powers, and Germany's leaders saw international security institutions as a forum in which to promote their country's interests and play a leadership role.

The institutionalist perspective emphasizes Germany's reputation in an international system where security institutions provide both collective and individual advantages. Had Germany chosen not to participate in the UN intervention in Somalia, it would have put the UN in danger, as well as the legacy of the Cold War, and it would hve risked progressive isolation. For John S. Duffield, German participation in UNOSOM illustrates both a strong interest in international security institutions and the continuation of the traditional culture of restraint. These two aspects of German policy are also found in the lessons learned from deployment in Somalia and the judgment handed down by the Constitutional Court in July 1994.[49]

The arguments advanced by these two theoretical interpretations – realism and institutionalism – are correct, but they do not go far enough in explaining German foreign and security policy. The participation of German peacekeepers in the UN operation in Somalia within the framework of UNOSOM I and UNOSOM II (1993–95) is particularly interesting for our study. Having followed the path of normalization since unification, the Federal Republic outlined the fundamental principles of its foreign and security policy, based on lessons learned from its first involvement in such an operation. The fact that German inter-

ests were in no way threatened is important. Bonn played the multilateralist and cooperation cards with its allies, while its goal was to take
its place among the great powers so that it could play a role that more
accurately reflected its place in the international system. For Bonn,
Somalia demonstrated its support for international security institutions
and showed the Federal Republic's desire to be a leading actor on the
international stage.

Once the Security Council had authorized Operation Restore Hope,
the federal government committed German troops to the second phase
of the UN mission to Somalia. Chancellor Kohl justified military
deployment as necessary for reconstructing the war-torn country. The
government's position was resolutely institutionalist. Germany was
under pressure from the international community, which had not
accepted its restraint during the Gulf War very well.[50] The federal government used this opportunity to advance the process of normalization
that it had begun since unification. By stressing the humanitarian
aspect of the intervention, the government also wanted to reassure its
population that the Bundeswehr was undertaking a humanitarian
mission in support of the UN. The United Nations operation was in
keeping with the institutional policy it had been following since the
creation of the Federal Republic. It was the result of a decision made
by the Security Council. Its main allies, specifically the United States
and France, were participating in it. Its humanitarian characteristics
corresponded to the values and norms of the German population.

Could Germany have afforded not to participate in the military
deployment in Somalia? No, simply because it was seeking a permanent seat on the Security Council. Participation in the operation was
the "downpayment for the entrance fee" (als erste Rate auf den Ein-
trittspreis).[51] Germany wanted to prove itself willing and capable of
more actively supporting the decisions of the UN (which it believed
should be the central body for maintaining international peace and stability),[52] while taking at the same time a calculated risk of facing opposition from the left and the liberals.[53] The government did not wait for
an answer from the Constitutional Court on the question of the constitutionality of participaion and instead, before a judgment had been
handed down, it included the principle of German troop deployment
outside NATO's territory in the 1994 Defence White Paper.[54]

Deploying personnel from the three branches of the armed forces in
Somalia constituted a precedent in post–Cold War German foreign
policy. The federal government succeeded in "educating" the population as to the duties and responsibilities of Germany, arguing that
Germany had the moral obligation to act in support of UN humanitarian missions. This first deployment was conducted within the

normative framework that existed before unification, in this case under UN auspices, a body that had a central role in the application of German foreign policy.[55] The culture of restraint, which it had followed during the Cold War, was no longer acceptable, and the political leadership in Bonn understood this.[56]

The German involvement in Operation Restore Hope was conducted against a backdrop of virulent constitutional debates. Some observers within the German press questioned the logic of the UN intervention and the participation of German armed forces in the mission.[57] Public opinion, however, had evolved on this issue since the Gulf War. The German people were conscious of the Federal Republic's international standing, but anxious that Bonn should focus on diplomatic and humanitarian roles. In February 1993, 54 percent of respondents to a survey considered it impossible for a country as prestigious and important as Germany to remain on the sidelines of the international system, instead of taking on a more important role. Indeed, 77 percent of respondents were in favour of the Bundeswehr's humanitarian intervention in Somalia.[58] This is yet another case where the political leadership rightly foresaw the evolution of public opinion, which was the product of the progressive normalization of foreign policy and an educational process.

The Federal Republic had little influence on shaping the objectives of the UN operation in Somalia. It remained discreet, contenting itself with integration into the framework of the operation and limiting itself to a role in "logistical support of an area of operations with little combat exposure."[59] The German leadership rightly chose not to play a leading part, preferring to maintain its traditional restraint and thus minimizing the risk of mistakes and a loss of German lives that could have led to confusion over the rules of engagement and a chaotic political and military situation. This "arrangement" between Bonn and the UN served as the basis for German deployment of troops in the Horn of Africa.[60]

In total, Germany's participation in Restore Hope cost more then 500 million marks and involved over 4,000 military personnel.[61] Although the operation resulted in a stalemate for the United Nations and German soldiers were withdrawn in March 1994, it had a lasting effect on Germany, which saw its largest troop deployment on foreign soil since World War II.[62]

The pressures of the international community, which demanded that Germany become more involved in UN operations and show its willingness to assume a larger role within the UN, are variables that appear only in classical realist analyses. Institutionalists claim that the responsibilities to the UN and the German political culture were determining elements in the Somalian case.

These theoretical approaches, however, have not put enough emphasis on the benefits that a multilateral policy brings to the security field. Germany's diplomatic behaviour demonstrated that it was a dependable player dedicated to peace, stability, and security. Germany showed that it had the means to reach its goals. Furthermore, constructivist elements should be added to the variables already listed. The moral obligation to participate in humanitarian operations draws on norms and values that are deeply engrained in the German political culture. Because deployment of the Bundeswehr fitted into the continuing multilateral policy developed during the Cold War, the government received strong public support.

GERMANY'S BID FOR A PERMANENT SEAT IN THE SECURITY COUNCIL (1992–97)

As an international security institution the UN is at the centre of German diplomacy. Since unification and the end of the Cold War, German's political leadership has repeatedly expressed its desire for the UN to become the key to international peace and order. In the eyes of the Federal Republic the UN, and more specifically the Security Council, does not reflect the reality of today's international system and must be reformed.

Classical realism prevails amongst analyses of the case of Security Council reform.[63] That perspective outlines four main reasons why Germany to sought a permanent seat on the Council. First, it wished to influence world events that directly or indirectly affected its national interests. Because of its geostrategic position at the heart of the European continent, on the dividing line between the East and the West, the Federal Republic is dependent on its external environment. Joining the Security Council as a permanent member would increase its own security, as well as that of Europe, which is threatened by the interethnic and intergovernmental struggles of Eastern Europe, particularly in the Balkans.[64]

Financial considerations are also important. Germany is the third largest contributor to the UN budget, behind the United States and Japan and, incidentally, ahead of the other four permanent members of the Council. Germany is "one of the world's largest national economies, with one of the world's leading currencies, a highly industrialized democracy, a high level of technical and scientific knowledge, culture and information, a country that has a very able diplomatic service with experience that extends the world over, a State whose armed forces are modern and unique in the way they are structured and organized along democratic principles, and one of the main

distributors of development aid."[65] Because of its economic and financial strength in Europe a permanent seat for Germany in the Security
Council can only reinforce the effectiveness of the UN, by providing it
more certain and predictable support for this international institution
that cannot balance its financial affairs.[66] Within this context, some
commentators push for the democratic principle of "no taxation
without representation," while others advocate a change in the voting
procedures of the United Nations, linking these to membership fees,
and advancing Germany's case for a permanent seat.[67]

Reform of the Security Council is necessary because its composition
and status reflect the international realities of 1945.[68] The Security
Council no longer reflects the new post–Cold War international order.
Consequently, as Michael Schaefer argues, the addition of new permanent members, such as Japan and Germany, would reflect this new
order and strengthen the legitimacy of the Council.[69]

Germany's claim for a permanent seat on the Security Council is
underpinned by its willingness to play a larger role on the international
stage as a defender of human rights and by its desire to emphasize the
process of political self-rehabilitation that began on the ruins of
Nazism. Permanent membership on the Council is, according to Karl
Kaiser, "the best way to stop Germany from going down a nationalistic path spurred on by its frustration, its absence of participation, even
its exclusion."[70]

While recognizing the legitimacy of the German demand, some commentators doubt that Security Council reforms will occur any time
soon. The support of two-thirds of the General Assembly and each of
the five current permanent members remain important structural obstacles that considerably reduce the chances of any reform.[71] Furthermore,
dissatisfaction is rising amongst Third World countries, which make up
two-thirds of the General Assembly. They denounce the current composition of the Council, which does not reflect the North-South balance
or the regional and cultural diversity of the United Nations. It is, therefore, doubtful that they would allow the addition of a third permanent
member from Europe. Wolfgang Wagner also questions Germany's
ability to assume responsibility for UN operations and argues that in the
present context, restraint could very well lead to progressive international isolation.[72] Gerhard Kümmel is even more pessimistic about the
prospects for successful reform: "In sum, we can anticipate that comprehensive reform of the UN will only take place under extraordinary
circumstances – a situation which seems unlikely to develop."[73]

Germany's behaviour toward Security Council reform shows both its
willingness to play an active role in the new international order and its

conviction that the UN is the key international security institution. Since unification, this conviction has been repeated many times, often as an oath of loyalty, by the German leadership.[74] The arrival in 1992 of new foreign and defence ministers Klaus Kinkel and Volker Rühe,[75] was highly typical of the new Germany's foreign policy style.[76]

On 23 September 1992, Kinkel officially announced to the UN General Assembly Germany's intention to seek a permanent seat on the Security Council.[77] This declaration, which was made barely two years after unification, clearly went against the policy of restraint of the Cold War, which had been represented by Ministers Genscher and Stoltenberg until just a few months before. Some observers feared Germany would be set on a new path of Machtpolitik, when in fact, the German leadership wanted the Federal Republic to assume its responsibility on the international stage within the framework of the UN.

Kinkel's announcement came as a surprise, because Germany had never contributed to peacekeeping operations. Increased responsibility within the UN and on the international stage could only be undertaken on the diplomatic level and could not be based only on the economic and financial importance of Germany. Kinkel repeatedly declared that Germany would have no chance of joining the Security Council as a permanent member if it was not disposed to actively participate in peacekeeping operations.[78]

Moreover, Germany wanted to remove some of the pressure that weighed heavily on its shoulders by shifting the focus of the debates away from the German question to the ability of the international community to meet its challenges. Bonn, therefore, responded favourably to international calls for increased German involvement in the UN's military operations and, in doing so, "challenged" the international community. During this time, the German demand for a permanent seat was no longer the focus of discussions. The process of organizational reform brought to the forefront the claims of the Third World and called into question the way in which the UN functioned as a whole. Having mobilized its diplomats, who worked overtime behind the scenes to rally the necessary two-thirds support of the General Assembly, Minister Kinkel put forward a compromise position. This proposed the election of five new permanent members, including Germany and Japan, as well as four nonpermanent members.[79] The make-up of this select group of permanent members was not limited solely to the nuclear and military powers. In the context of the post–Cold War period, Germany argued that the Security Council would have to make room for new members who, because of their economy and their demography, as well as their position as regional leaders, could no longer be kept out. Failure to do so would deny current international reality.[80]

The proposals were flexible on the question of a veto in the Security Council, but they would not accept the creation of second-class permanent members deprived of veto power. Instead, Germany favoured exclusive use of the veto on questions relating to the use of force. In the eventuality of expansion, Germany would encourage including a revision clause that would allow performance reviews of the permanent members every ten or twenty years.

The UN was concerned about the constitutional wrangling in Germany over deployment of German soldiers to Somalia. The judgment handed down by the Constitutional Court in Karlsruhe in July 1994 rejected the constitutional objections against the deployment of German soldiers outside NATO territory and was, therefore, an important step in legitimizing Bonn's claim to a permanent Security Council seat.[81] The judgment also established a fragile domestic consensus that laid the foundations for future foreign and security policies, as demonstrated by the rise to power of the Red-Green coalition in the autumn of 1998, whose agenda was based on the same policies. The Karlsruhe tribunal confirmed the legality of the principle of participation of German forces in peacekeeping operations, while requiring the Bundestag to be consulted before any deployment:

the Federal Republic of Germany is at liberty to assign German armed forces in operations mounted by the North Atlantic Treaty Organization (NATO) and Western European Union (WEU) to implement resolutions of the Security Council of the United Nations (UN) ...

the Federal Government is required to obtain the Bundestag's explicit approval for each deployment of German armed forces. Such approval must in principle be obtained prior to their deployment.[82]

Germany was admitted to the Security Council as a nonpermanent member in 1994. According to many observers, its record during two years on the Council was good and demonstrated "Bonn's willingness to prove its abilities to manage the responsibilities and powers associated with such a status." [83] Most notable among its accomplishments were initiatives that established an international criminal court to punish crimes committed in the former Yugoslavia and that led to the Security Council adopting resolution 986, which allowed Iraq to export oil in exchange for food and medicine. Furthermore, Germany was actively engaged in a number of regional crises, such as the crisis in Georgia, and the Bundeswehr actively participated in the missions of the Implementation Force (IFOR) and the International Stabilizing

Force (SFOR) in Bosnia-Herzegovina to ensure compliance with the Dayton Accords. [84] Nevertheless, a project led by the Working Group on Security Council Reform has now hit a dead end. German ambassador to the UN Dieter Kastrup recently highlighted the problem: "Our own efforts in this working group to reform the Security Council are widely seen as disappointing. Results seem to have gone no further than when we began our work five years ago. Therefore, it seems to be important first of all to restore the sense of common purpose we have obviously lost."[85]

Since the beginning of the UN reform project German diplomats have sought to ally themselves with developing countries and countries in the nonaligned movement. They have done so by defending the practice of giving permanent and nonpermanent seats on the Security Council to these countries.[86] Recently, Germany joined forces with India in a bid to strengthen its candidacy. Its claim also served as a springboard toward greater normalization, since it provided a way of legitimizing the principles underlying its foreign policy.

To legitimize its request for a seat on the Security Council before public opinion and the international community, Germany seeks to be reassuring. The crux of its argument can be summarized as a firm and clear desire to be more actively involved in international affairs, while not departing from a foreign policy anchored in the network of Western international institutions and dedicated to multilateralism and while remaining conscious of the duties and moral obligations left by Nazism. The German government has attempted to create a consensus, not only within its population but also between all nations, concerning the principles of foreign and security policy that are deeply embedded in its political culture. As has already been shown, restraint confined it to the role of "supplicant," which is unacceptable for both Germany and the international community. The post–Cold War era has left a certain security vacuum, and Germany must pursue the protection of what it sees as its national interests.

The Federal Republic sees an opportunity to increase its security through greater involvement in the decision-making mechanisms of the United Nations, where it can use its influence to defend its interests and the dangers that threaten it. On the one hand, instability in the Balkans created a flood of refugees, the bulk of whom went to Germany and could, hypothetically, threaten its domestic security.[87] Furthermore, Germany is poor in natural resources and is therefore dependent on imports. The reverse is also true: it exports huge amounts of goods, especially to Russia and to the East, where democracy and political stability are still very fragile. Consequently, it must guarantee its access to the natural resources it needs and it must guarantee the stability of its markets. Situated in the heart of Europe, Germany would be directly threatened by any significant political instability at its doors. Conflicts must be kept at bay and security for Europe and Germany must be guaranteed.[88]

Germany made a conscious choice to seek greater involvememnt in UN decsion making, a choice that was conditioned both by the central importance of the UN in making foreign and security policy and by Germany's limited options in the matter. Bonn sought to underscore the importance of Germany's participation in the organization by pointing out that it contributes 8.93 percent of the total organizational budget and by arguing that Germany, as a civilian power, is ready to play an active role within the organization and to participate in UN operations, whether they be humanitarian or military. Furthermore, Germany has always respected its financial obligations toward the organization and, in this way, ensures that it will receive predictable aid. Finally, Germany wants to be even more deeply anchored to the institution, so that, in the words of Karl Kaiser, it can avoid the isolation that led to two world wars in the first half of the last century.[89]

CONCLUSION

A single theoretical approach cannot account for Germany's use of international security institutions in all three cases studied here. To explain German unification and the Bundeswehr's deployment in Somalia, we draw on all four approachs to varying degrees. Security Council reform can, however, be explained with just one approach.

The alarmist predictions of the observers were rapidly proven unfounded following German unification when it pursued its post–World War II institutional policy. Not only does Germany continue to follow its policy of binding itself to the West and its institutions, it has also succeeded in reassuring domestic public opinion and the members of the international community. According to Duffield, "in contrast to ... expectations ... German security policy since unification has been marked by a high degree of continuity and moderation. Far from setting off in adventurous new directions, Germany has exercised considerable restraint and circumspection in its external relations since 1990."[90] On the one hand, Germany has continued to favour a multilateral policy based on the cooperative approaches to security. On the other hand, recourse to nonmilitary means, insofar as the situation allows it, has prevailed in the formulation of security policy. Germany has sought to preserve and has succeeded in preserving both the international institutions that have anchored it and their foundations.[91]

During the Cold War the memories of Auschwitz incited the political and intellectual elite of Germany to maintain a policy of restraint, but the new international context since the collapse of the Soviet bloc, the status of Germany since unification, and pressures from the international community – as well as the evolution of the elite mentalities and public opinion – require a redefinition of the guilt felt at the memory of Auschwitz. From now on Germany is morally obliged to become actively involved in the preservation of international peace and security.

On the road toward normalization of its foreign policy, the Federal Republic has progressively taken on more responsibility, without, however, elbowing out its neighbours. During unification, it confirmed its commitment to international security institutions through its determination not only to remain part of them but also to actively contribute to their development. Somalia was a crucial step. By actively participating in this out-of-area mission, the Federal Republic clearly stated its willingness to implement an assertive foreign policy. This allowed Germany to legitimize its demand for a permanent seat in the Security Council, which would grant it responsibilities that reflected its economic and political weight in Europe. The desire to join the Security Council reflects one of the fundamental objectives of its institutional policy, which seeks to raise its status on the international scene, a necessary step toward defending its interests.

If developing international security organizations was a means to an end for Germany at the beginning of the Cold War, it has now become an end in itself and a crucial element of German foreign policy, which is much different from what it was a few decades ago. The fact that, more often than not, Germany plays the leading role in developing and strengthening these institutions is a great example of the new German policy. Berlin's recourse to them cannot be explained solely as a simple wish to serve its national interests. Quite the contrary, the Federal Republic is aware that in matters of security, everything that benefits its interests benefits Europe's as well, and vice versa. Identifying its national interests with multilateral interests does not necessarily mean that it is pursuing unilateral gains.[92] German policy in the area of security policy is European policy.

Furthermore, Berlin does not seem – not openly at least – to support one international institution at the expense of another, whether it be NATO, the OSCE, or the European Union. It believes that these institutions should be seen as a whole, the result of a policy of multilateral integration.

Given the degree to which institutional policy is embedded within the German political culture, we can predict that this multilateral policy will continue. In fact, the Germans realized long ago that they have more to gain by defending and promoting their interests within international security institutions than by acting unilaterally as a great power, which would risk their isolation and the consequences that would come with it. Moreover, German military participation in the international campaign against terrorism in 2001–2, as part of the U.S.-led operations and the International Security Assistance Force (ISAF) operations, illustrated its will to preserve the foundations of its Western integration policy and clearly showed its determination to remain firmly rooted in the community of Western democracies and its network of international security institutions.

CHAPTER FIVE

Refusing to Play by the Rules? Japan's "Pacifist" Identity, Alliance Politics, and Security Institutions

BRUNO DESJARDINS

The concept of security has developed in many ways since the collapse of the bipolar international system. The end of the Cold War triggered the acceleration of an expansion of this concept beyond the strictly military realm, orienting it towards issues that encompass human security, the promotion of democracy, human rights, and even sustainable development. Since September 11, 2001, no country has underestimated the pressing need to pay greater importance to terrorism and transnational crime and to protect their computer networks against cyberwar threats. During the 1990s, the great powers more commonly had recourse to international institutions and organizations – whatever importance one places on them.

Political discourses and military actions in the 1990s were often imprinted with a liberal flavour, along with an apparent infatuation with multilateralism. The creation of the European Union and the seemingly successful all-around expansion of international institutions probably led international actors to believe that institutionalization was a stable and efficient approach to follow. Nonetheless, one can wonder if it is not premature to conclude that the conditions leading to the emergence of multilateralism and of international institutions can be observed worldwide and whether they are simply the product of circumstances within the Euro-Atlantic region and therefore the result of Western political culture and experience.

It must be noted that the end of the Cold War had more immediate repercussions in Europe than it had in Asia, where its shadow still lingers. Although in Europe the 1990 German reunification represented the final stage of the collapse of the Iron Curtain, in Asia the division of the Korean peninsula still persists and the status of Taiwan remains contentious to this day. Persistent Russo-Japanese difficulties in trying to bring closure to World War II by negotiating a peace treaty are also significant. Moreover, World War II still echoes in the United Nations Charter's "enemy states clauses" that prevent Japan from enjoying all the rights and privileges of member states.

Japan's strategic environment is one in which the major powers coexist and in which multilateral security structures are still a rarity, because bilateralism prevails. If the 1990s have shown the increasing importance of security institutions for Japanese diplomacy, they have simultaneously revealed the cautious reluctance of Japan to step outside the alliance framework when regional security is on the agenda. Even today, and despite its firm support for the United States in the war against terrorism, Japan has resisted direct participation in military operations, even though several U.S. allies fought in Afghanistan and joined the coalition that struck against Iraq. Article 9 of Japan's Peace Constitution and several other legal provisions have been interpreted as constraining Japan from assuming military roles that are not related to homeland defense.[1]

Until the Soviet Union's demise, Japan seldom acted as if military security was a priority; it considered that its alliance with the United States provided it with all the necessary protection. However, this impression dissipated rather brutally when the Gulf War broke out in 1991. Japan realized that its postwar foreign and security policies were being challenged. Increasing international pressure on Japan to be more involved in international security provoked a political crisis and the need for a new debate on defense issues. As a result, and with great reluctance, Japan resolved to participate in security operations beyond the framework of the alliance and under the aegis of the United Nations, as exemplified by the participation of Japanese Self-Defense Forces (SDF) mine-sweeping ships in the Persian Gulf in 1991 and by Japan's unprecedented dispatching of military peacekeepers to Cambodia a year later.[2]

Since then, Japan has influenced the creation of the ASEAN Regional Forum (ARF, 1993), renewed its defense policy, the National Defense Program Outline (NDPO, 1995), reaffirmed its alliance with the United States (1996), and established new guidelines for military cooperation with the United States (1997–99), guidelines that give Japan the responsibility for logistic support for American forces should a regional conflict occur. Thus, Japan has reinforced its alliance while simultaneously enhancing its participation in security institutions. It has also expanded its bilateral security dialogues and exchanges with several countries, including Canada, Australia, and, more recently, India. In so doing, is Japan seeking to increase its strategic independence from the United States in order to play a distinct security role outside the compartmentalization of the alliance? Is this apparent flirtation with multilateralism intended to free it from the strict bilateralism that has characterized its security relations with the United States since 1951? Or, can it be interpreted as an attempt to combine both approaches, and if so, toward what goal?

This chapter seeks to evaluate the importance of international security institutions for Japan's security policy. It does so through an exploratory process that seeks to identify the theoretical approach that can best explain Japanese strategic preferences, without pretending to invalidate or corroborate any particular theory. In what follows, a chronological account of the evolution of Japanese security policies will be provided. These policies will be succinctly analyzed using the realist, neorealist, and neoliberal institutionalist theories and the constructivist paradigm, in order to discern which is best suited to explain Japan's management of security issues. Next, three case studies will examine Japan's behaviour and policy preferences. The first deals with Japan's views and ambitions in respect to the reform of the United Nations' Security Council. The second examines Japanese participation in KEDO (the Korean Energy Development Organization). Finally, the third case investigates Japan's management of the Senkaku Islands territorial dispute involving Japan, China, and Taiwan. The objective here is to identify and explain why Japan chooses to refer issues that concern its national security to international security institutions oor avoids doing so.

JAPANESE COMPREHENSIVE SECURITY
AND ITS GENESIS

Since 1980, Japan has elaborated and set forth a strategy of comprehensive security. This approach was innovative at the time and Japan remains a forerunner on the matter. Its concept of comprehensive security includes three main components: diplomacy, economy, and defense. Until the mid-1980s, the diplomatic and defense dimensions, which had long been neglected, earned for Japan the unenviable image of a political and military dwarf.

The starting point of the so-called debates concerning Japanese security can be traced back to 1946–47, when a constitution dictated, in part, by General MacArthur came into effect. In a tone reminiscent of the Briand-Kellogg Pact, article 9 of the constitution outlawed the use of force as a means to resolve international conflicts and denied Japan the right to rearm itself for that purpose. In 1951, DEMILITARIZED in theory, Japan agreed to an alliance with the United States before having fully regained its sovereignty (which it did in 1952). In 1954, the Self-Defense Forces and the Japanese Defense Agency (JDA) were created. The euphemism inherent in the names of these organizations and the apparent violation of article 9 were justified by the fact that the capabilities of the SDF would be strictly defensive in nature and by the fact that there could be no question of allowing Japan to project the image of a country ready to use its military power to support its foreign policy. The right to self-defense recognized in article 51 of chapter 7 of the United Nations Charter justified this interpretation. The limited role of the SDF was imposed by Japanese parliamentary, or Diet, legislation and resolutions in 1954, and it was further specified in the Basic Policy for National Defense of 1957. This first defense policy – renewed in 1976 and in the National Defense Policy Outline of 1995 – recommended that Japan emphasize the activities of the alliance with the United States, while waiting for the creation of an efficient UN deterrent force, which was provided for in the UN charter.

In the minds of Japanese policymakers the alliance was only a temporary measure that would protect Japan until the UN force could be established. Furthermore, Japan's past alliances, whether with the Axis or with Great Britain, never compelled Japan to adopt any particular security role. Equally revealing is the fact that the first time a Japanese prime minister ever publicly used the term "alliance" to characterize the strategic partnership with the United States was in 1981. The peace and security treaties of 1951 permitted the United States to continue its control of Okinawa, allowed U.S. forces to continue using bases in Japan, and even gave them the right to intervene militarily in Japan in order to safeguard the peace and stability of the Far East.

Officially, Japan thus granted the United Nations the role of guarantor of world peace, while the United States inherited the role of protector, this situation being in complete harmony with the precepts of the Yoshida School, which recommended that Japan adopt a low profile in defense matters. The foreign and security policy of Japan became that of the three "S's" – silent, smiling, and sleeping.[3] In the postwar period and especially after 1956, Japan adopted a rather thoughtless attitude towards defense and a policy of practising what lawyers would call "voluntary blindness." Thus, because of the asymmetrical, nonreciprocal nature of the alliance with the United States, Japan allowed itself to be restricted to a passive and reactive posture.[4]

The implementation of the Japanese comprehensive security policy in 1980 seemed to forecast that Japan would assume a more autonomous defense posture. This impression would be quickly contradicted. The policy took into account the regional context of an American withdrawal, combined with that of a Soviet advance. Iran's Islamic Revolution took place in 1979–80, depriving the United States of a regional foothold, and Afghanistan was invaded by Soviet troops. The USSR also consolidated its Pacific Fleet, convincing the United States to abandon its plans for leaving South Korea. The apparent U.S. retreat made Japan fear that its strategic importance would greatly increase and that it might come under pressure to compensate for this regional retreat, something the Japanese had always resisted.[5] If the concept of comprehensive security took into account the geostrategic environment, it did so only to affirm that Pax Americana was over. Instead of volunteering to help its American ally to reverse the situation by increasing its share of the defense burden, Japan offered to contribute to a new era of global partnership in which it would become a civilian power. This anachronistic concept nevertheless indicated the vision that Japan already had of the only international security role that it intended to play: an economic one.

The fall of the Berlin Wall and the disintegration of the Soviet empire blurred the picture however. The Gulf War and the formation of a coalition to fight that war seemed to testify that peace had become everyone's responsibility. Japan was asked to participate, but it initially rejected this request by invoking constitutional constraints. Japan would have had to break with a defense policy that was limited to the archipelago in order to adopt a collective security approach, even though it had already resisted embracing a collective defense strategy. It might also have been called upon to deploy the SDF abroad, which was prohibited. Indirectly, the United Nations and the United States were insisting on the revocation of the Yoshida strategy and were thus advocating a renunciation of the founding principles of the foreign and security policies that had guided Japan since the 1950s. Japan was being challenged to prove that it truly practised a UN-centred policy, and that it indeed remained a loyal and faithful ally of the United States.[6]

The Gulf War forced the Japanese to question the nature of their postwar pacifism. Did it still consist of "pacifism in one country," withdrawn into itself, or should Japanese pacifism evolve so that it would embrace collective security? Could Japan, now a financial, technological, and industrial power, refuse to play the role devolved to powerful states and continue to follow the Yoshida strategy? Japanese strategic thinking in the 1990s would be influenced mainly by the lessons of the Gulf War and, to a lesser extent, by the end of the Cold War.

REALISM AND JAPANESE DEFENSE

Realists claim that states are the highest authorities in the international system, entities preoccupied with the preservation of their sovereignty and obsessed with ensuring their own survival in an anarchic environment where "all against all" and "everyone for himself" are golden rules. Force is a legitimate part of the state's arsenal within a framework where war itself seems a "natural" activity in the Hobbesian sense.

Classical realism is challenged by Japan's obvious aversion for power politics and the use of military force. Japan's behaviour, which seems one of self-restriction with regard to the means at its disposal, is justified less by factors like power and capabilities and more by the Japanese state's pledge to respect norms that it claims to be unwilling and unable to depart from. Power politics and the use of force have been taboo in postwar Japan.[7] If Japan were officially to take into account the military power of neighbouring states – something it has not done until fairly recently – it would probably have to question its defense doctrine and redefine the SDF's role. This step would be politically hazardous, since it would imply that Japan's involvement in power politics had gone beyond provision for its self-defense and unequivocally ignored the letter and the spirit of the Peace Constitution.[8]

Because Japan allied itself with the United States during the occupation, it becomes difficult to assert that it made a completely free choice to engage in the alliance. Japan, nonetheless, was most certainly informed that the alliance would guarantee it access to the American market and facilitate economic recovery and development. Since Japan possessed no real armed forces or defense policy in 1951, it had hardly any role at all to play within the framework of the alliance. The interesting choices are thus those of 1960 and 1996, when sovereign Japan's wish to reaffirm its alliance – but based on different modalities – was reasserted. The fact that in 1960 and 1970–71, Japan faced social crises and upheavals over alliance and defense issues reveals the extent to which those questions could mobilize people who desired to distance Japan from the stakes of the Cold War. Thus, from a domestic point of view, Japanese behaviour could be analyzed from a realist perspective, since the government could not risk the loss of its electoral support by adopting unpopular defense policies. On the other hand, it is unclear how the quasi-finlandization of Japan in 1951 could serve a superior national interest, unless the state's nominal independence and survival justified the acceptance of political subordination and the loss of a part of its sovereignty. Nothing is less certain.

Japan displays idiosyncratic attitudes towards the military domain, attitudes that are poorly explained by realism. Principles such as the ban on arms exports, the three nonnuclear principles (according to which Japan would never possess or produce nuclear weapons or allow their introduction into the country), and the ceiling of 1 percent of GNP on defense spending are all measures that at first glance seem incompatible with realism.[9] Moreover, the principle of nonexportation of armaments prevents Japan from benefiting from economies of scale, and with its atrophied military production sector, it is subjected to prohibitive costs for its supplies. Exporting weapons, as the great powers do, would solve this problem.

The fact that Japan links its Official Development Assistance (ODA) to the military budgets of benefiting countries, in order to discourage their military spending, demonstrates the antimilitary character of Japan's foreign policy.[10] Japan practises security policies that limit its capabilities and an economic aid policy that limits the militarization of recipient countries. Japan seems, however, to be aware of the limits of this strategic aid policy and of its poor political returns: the ODA has been considerably reduced in 2002.

A NEOREALIST VISION OF SECURITY?

Japan poses a particular challenge to the foundations of neorealism. From the perspective of neorealism the main factor explaining why the units of the international system – states – have a definite, vague or null influence on the structure of the system stems from their aggregate power and the agency of power relations. How must Japanese power be defined in order to evaluate its impact and weight? Surprisingly, in some analyses of security, Japan stands out by its absence,[11] and if it does appear, it is as a middle or minor power. Apparently, the fact that Japan does not possess the offensive or force-projection capabilities that are attributed to the major powers is reason enough to deny it great power status. If the power of a state – alone or allied with other states – determines its influence within the international system, the extent of Japan's power would determine its capacity for action. If Japan is a political and military dwarf, it would be in no position to transform its environment and would instead be constrained and influenced by it.

However, the vast majority of Japanese security analyses focus mainly on the American alliance, transforming the structural perspective by adding the weight of the United States to the balance. The extent of Japan's power is still at issue: Is Japan a major power or not? This question is important, since an answer would allow us to identify the motives leading Japan to ally itself with a major power. To insure its survival or to better protect its interests, a weak state may look for an alliance with a major power, in order to shield it from other states and alliances that may constitute a threat to both itself and the prospective ally. Small powers can also choose to ally themselves with a stronger state that threatens them and against which they would have no hope of offering resistance, either alone or in alliance with other neighbouring states.

The u.s.-Japan alliance was formed at a time when the Japanese state was still managed under the Damocles sword of the authority of the Supreme Commander of the Allied Powers (SCAP). On the Japanese side, membership in the alliance did not follow from a calculation of the forces present or from an analysis of perceived threats as such. In 1951, the alliance benefited the United States: it was intended to facilitate the containment of the USSR and communism in general, while avoiding the re-emergence of Japanese military power – in accordance with the "cork in the bottle" thesis. To the Japanese, on the other hand, domestic, economic, and historical considerations were the main factors justifying alliance with the United States, but those were factors that neorealism tends to ignore. One might wonder whether Japan felt truly threatened by the Soviet Union, considering that in 1956 it studied the possibility of denouncing the alliance treaty with the United States and becoming neutral, in return for a peace treaty and a settlement of the dispute over the Northern Territories. The United States would never have accepted Japanese neutrality; Japan's choices were therefore limited.

Neorealists would argue that Japan opted for the superpower that was the least threatening to it and, furthermore, that would protect it against other hostile powers. The logic of alliance rested, therefore, upon the existence of antagonistic poles. But on what basis would it continue once one of them disappeared? If the Japan of 1951 and 1960 remained weak in comparison to the superpowers and if the power gaps encouraged it to ally, what were its motives in 1996, the date of the latest reaffirmation of the alliance?

Because it has renounced the use of force and because it operates under constitutional restrictions on the nature of the weapons systems its SDF may possess and deploy, Japan has been limiting the development and the range of its political and military power. Japan's military strength and its role are thus better explained reference to the self-limitation of its prerogatives than by the structural and power conditions of the international system.

However, neorealists would never see or acknowledge the contradiction. If they were to take it for granted that Japan's main security goal is regional stability and to assume that the alliance fulfills this goal, then it would appear highly rational for Japan to seek to maintain the status quo in its strategic relationship with the United States. A Japan that is allied with the United States ensures its own survival better than if it defended itself alone. If Japan – which has the second or third most important military budget on the globe, Asia's most powerful air force, and the second most powerful navy of the region (after the u.s. Navy) – were to be considered a great power, the neorealist logic would fall apart, because the alliance could not in that case be explained in terms of the distribution of forces, the balance of power, or threats to Japan. The explanation in fact lies in the allies' desire to pursue their strategic relation: instead of being identified as exogenous, the causes of the survival of the alliance are now endogenous, which neorealism hardly accepts. If Japan evolves in a geostrategic environment without any major threat and if it possesses aggregate power superior to that of its neighbours, does this power not provide Japan with a choice? Is the American nuclear umbrella, along with the forty-seven thousand troops attached to u.s. bases on Japanese soil – particularly in Okinawa, where they have become somewhat of an embarrassment since a rape incident of 1995 – still necessary for Japanese security?

What Japan seems to be missing to be considered a great power is the means to project its forces outside its borders; it lacks offensive capabilities, as well as a nuclear arsenal, which it could endow itself with if it wanted to. Neorealist analyses generally argue that Japan has no need for such forces, since the United States possesses them. This argument then legitimizes Japanese strategic dependency and political subordination. But this dependency is not an immutable fact in the structural equation, even though it is very often taken for granted in most analyses.

What would the end of this dependency imply for Japan? If the alliance fosters stability, its disappearance would result in increased insecurity. With the alliance gone, neorealists would predict the creation, production, and deployment of an independent Japanese nuclear deterrent, heavy bombers, strategic and attack nuclear submarines, and the construction of a stronger blue-water naval force equipped with aircraft carriers. The result of such a drastic change in Japan's military posture would most likely provoke a sharp increase in neighbouring countries' feelings of vulnerability. Japan would heighten tensions and damage overall relations with its neighbours, including the United States, and might trigger a regional arms race. Any massive SDF reinforcement would also further weaken an already fatigued Japanese economy by reorienting considerable financial resources towards a sphere of activity with marginal positive returns. The quest for absolute security would bring absolute insecurity: in playing the neorealist game alone, Japan would actually diminish its chances for survival and would risk suffering losses instead of achieving gains. It played this game from the 1930s until 1945, and it believes it can no longer win.

THE NEOLIBERAL INSTITUTIONALIST TEMPTATION?

Japan proclaims itself a believer in the virtues of democracy, and it advocates the development of market economies as a tool of democratization and as a means to build a prosperous and peaceful international climate.[12] However, the content of its policy speeches varies, depending on the audience; the speeches are more nuanced when they are directed at Asian countries. These discourses sometimes get trapped between a rock and a hard place, since Indonesia, Malaysia, and China, for instance, see them as supporting what they perceive as an American strategy of imposing Western values that denigrate their own values – and, by extension, their authority and state legitimacy.[13] These countries display their skepticism about the pacifying virtues of democracy, the market, and interdependence.[14] The conditions for institutionalization are not as good in Asia as they are in Europe: geography, diverse cultures, different political regimes, and unequal levels of development lend themselves poorly to integration.[15] The Asia Pacific Economic Conference (APEC) and the ARF were the work of small and middle powers. In the two cases, the major powers hesitated, at the beginning, even to sit at the same table.[16] Furthermore, independence is still fairly recent for these Asian countries, which jealously guard their sovereignty. Some Asian capitals fear that international institutions may become the instrument of the hegemonic ambitions of the American, Chinese, or Japanese powers. At the time of its creation in 1967, ASEAN made clear that noninterference in the internal affairs of the member states was a capital rule. Its Regional Forum and APEC both observe this principle.

The absence of North Korea – until 2000 – and of Taiwan from the ARF harms the credibility of the multilateral framework and testifies to the extent to which the common interest remains subordinated to the national interests of the great powers. This partially explains why previous efforts to construct security institutions and expanded alliances have either resulted in failure or experienced only mitigated success: SEATO, for example, has disappeared, and ANZUS has experienced difficulties.

The founders of the ARF loathed the European institutions: for them, the OSCE was a model to avoid.[17] In the existing multilateral Asia-Pacific structures, the search for consensus remains fundamental, and issues that could divide their participants are treated with caution – when they are not suppressed. Asian international institutions do not have any capacity for constraint, in accordance with the wishes of participating states, who do not even want to be known as "members." The processes of Euro-American institutionalization include dimensions of political integration that is facilitated by an economic integration initiated beforehand. But in Asia, only the wish for economic integration is currently being voiced.[18]

Neoliberal institutionalism examines the mechanisms for cooperation and the exchange of information, and it shares its foundations with neorealism. Interstate relations obey an economic logic in which political actions derive from a reckoning of anticipated gains and losses. Even within formal institutions, states retain their sovereign prerogatives. They can always reserve the right to break the rules if they evaluate the resultant costs of noncooperation as less than the costs of cooperation or if the gains resulting from cooperation appear to be less than those resulting from lack of cooperation. The measurement of costs and gains can be facilitated by the existence of formal frameworks – laws, treaties, and conventions. Yet Asia generally resists the idea of formalizing institutional frameworks, preferring not to give them a rigid, codified, or regulated structure.[19] Neoliberal institutionalists rely on the principle that gains produced by cooperation generate a complex dynamic of profitable interdependence, which, by increasing the costs generated by lack of collaboration, makes a return to the strategy of "each for himself" less attractive – if not improbable. This dynamic lessens the effect of power upon institutionalized structures.

The ARF's mandate does not include conflict or dispute resolution. This institution furthers constructive dialogue and political transparency, which are efficient confidence-building measures. Satoh Yukio speaks of "reassuring measures," placing the emphasis on the fact that these confidence-building measures refer to established security problems, while no ARF member dares to clearly identify threats.[20] The ARF remains the product of ASEAN countries' preoccupations with regional rivalry among the great powers, and, consequently, it seeks to encourage transparent dialogue between signatory countries, in order to defuse tensions. But the absence of coercive capabilities does not imply lack of influence. If it remains too early for common political and strategic interests to emerge in Asia, the exchange of views on security by the regional actors is nevertheless expected to reduce the uncertainty that could result from a lack of communication, even if a common vision of security cannot be established.

This goal explains why Japan multiplied the number of its diplomatic initiatives that were aimed at creating and supporting multilateral security frameworks in East Asia and why it encouraged China to join the ARF. Japan's multilateralist order of the day was also intended to make a liar out of history by demonstrating to Asia its wish for cooperation and transparency. A multilateral framework facilitates exchanges, because power relations become more diffuse than in a strictly bilateral context. Inside multilateral institutions, Japan plays a more important role, without giving the impression of wanting to dictate its positions and while concurrently expressing itself in a voice distinct from that of U.S. diplomacy. International security institutions serve as a diplomatic complement and as an alternative to Japan's alliance with the United States, without supplanting or replacing it, however. Although the future of Asian international institutions is uncertain and Japan is skeptical, like a player drawn by an interesting prize, the Japanese prefer to wager, since the only certainty in not betting is the absence of gains. Japan has nothing to win by limiting its participation in multilateral initiatives. Doing so would only communicate to Asia the false impression that Japan is insensitive to Asia's preoccupations and that it is not interested in constructive engagement with China or in defusing regional tensions.

Neoliberal institutionalism gains legitimacy when it analyzes the U.S.-Japan alliance in itself. In this case, the scenarios of breakdown and of continuity take on new dimensions. The durability of the alliance in the post-Soviet environment can be explained by the gains that have been generated by mutual cooperation and by the protection of common interests that are better insured by maintaining it. Interdependency at the commercial and financial levels already favours narrow cooperation between both countries and colours alliance management. This situation is recognized in official U.S. policy papers such as the 1998 United States Strategy for the East Asia–Pacific Region. A breakdown of the alliance would entail political and strategic costs far greater than those generated by its maintenance, which is, indeed, reason enough not to denounce the alliance treaty. On the other hand, it should be emphasized that most of the reasons supporting the continuation of the alliance appear to be less of a military nature than of a political nature.

JAPANESE SECURITY IDENTITY
AND THE CONSTRUCTIVIST PARADIGM

Elements of realism and neoliberal institutionalism partially explain Japan's security behaviour, while neorealism rejects most elements that matter to the Japanese policymakers. These theoretical approaches leave too many questions unanswered, questions that are often worthy of scrutiny. The constructivist paradigm allows for the inclusion of dimensions that are ignored by other approaches but that seem to be most pertinent and relevant for explaining Japanese military security policy-making and management.

Japan's security identity, which is said to be "pacifist," imposes a way of perceiving reality that ignores the balance of power. This perception stems from a pledge not to break with the norms prohibiting the use of force. Article 9 of Japan's Peace Constitution, which defines institutional pacifism, became the main object of dispute and conflict on the Japanese domestic political scene in the 1950s and 1960s. Thus, the "pacifist" norm was not accepted unanimously, even though two variants of it came to be adopted and promoted by opposing sides of the political spectrum, in different ways.

Many factors form the basis of Japanese identity, and they each contribute in their own way to the construction of the "pacifist" identity. First, the question of the evolution of Japan's defense policy during the last decade cannot be separated from the internationalization and globalization of Japanese discourses. Part of the goal of these discourses is, basically, to convince the population of the importance of an increased international role for Japan. But such a role clashes head on with the "recluse mentality" that characterizes Japan.[21] In their political discourse, the Japanese often present the idea that it is the world that requires Japan to be proactive in the international scene, implying that Japan's presence is neither natural nor wished for by Japan itself. The debate over Japan's international role essentially takes the form of questioning the "contribution" expected of Japan, an interesting choice of words, given the circumstances, since it is always possible to contribute without actually deciding or taking the initiative. In fact, Japan's political discourses seem to indicate that it is officially waiting to be assigned a role, since it hesitates to assign one to itself, as most great powers would, particularly with regard to security matters. Obviously, Japanese power lacks new goals and objectives.[22]

The question of internationalization/globalization, combined with that of Japan's contributions, has also caused a renewal of nationalism – of two forms of nationalism, to be more precise.[23] The pacifist identity progressively generated the false pretence that Japan could live in relative political isolation and even benefit from it. The unarmed neutrality advocated by the left and the asymmetrical nature of the alliance helped to erode Japan's need to preoccupy itself with military security issues, and both factors helped to reinforce the impression that Japan could remain cut off from the world's strategic stakes and issues. The calls of internationalization and globalization and the call for Japanese contributions threatened Japan's political isolationism and, indeed, encouraged Japan to come out of its isolation.

These calls breathed new life into two kinds of nationalism in Japan but they also led to a confrontation between the two. One of the two, which might be termed "open and enterprising"(it is still a minority view) aspires to a Japan that asserts itself on the international political and security scenes. The other, which might be termed "inward-looking and defensive" (this is the majority view) compares foreign pressure to a return of the Black Ships and thus to a new forced opening up of Japan to the world, which, supporters of this nationalism believe, would undermine Japanese identity.[24] Japan's international activity, once it crosses the boundaries of the economic and financial realms, seems thus to touch and threaten the essence of the Japanese postwar identity. Many Western observers have been mystified by the nature of this identity, which often appears more ethnic, even racial, than national.[25]

The emphasis placed on identity characteristics that are not closely related to patriotism, for example, illustrates the extent to which the relationship between the state and Japanese identity seems to be avoided or even absent. National symbols such as the flag and the national anthem do not fill the Japanese with feelings of pride and belonging.[26] "Japanese uniqueness theory" seems to separate out the political dimensions of identity. The popularity of discourses on "japaneseness" can be explained precisely by reference to the need to fill the identity void created by the defeat of 1945, when national symbols were dishonoured, and trust in the state shattered.[27]

For the Japanese, Japan's defeat represents a sudden break with their state and their identity. Since the Meiji Restoration of 1868, moral education taught in the schools had forged patriotism. Later, during the 1920s, education became a tool of indoctrination that was at the service of the emperor and of the state. The psychological dimensions of the identification of the Japanese with the emperor should not be underestimated. During the seventy years separating the defeat from the rebirth of imperial Japan, Japanese identity was linked to the emperor and the state. To the Japanese, the existence of the Empire represented proof that their country had become highly civilized and eminently superior to the other nations of East Asia.[28]

The humiliation of defeat should have completely destroyed the feelings of moral superiority and rectitude that stirred imperial Japan. But the American occupation force implemented strategies that alleviated feelings of guilt in the Japanese population. The emperor of Japan retained his throne, and the unlikely rationalization that he had been manipulated by his staff was promoted by SCAP. The emperor escaped the Tokyo tribunal of 1946–48 because no accusations were presented against him. In the same vein, the Japanese people were told that they had been duped by the militarists, that they had been innocent victims of militarism, and were thus to be exempted from any blame.[29] Their conscience eased by this absolution, the Japanese forgot their guilt. In the process, they also began to display a mixture of amnesia and voluntary blindness regarding the reprehensible actions committed in the name of the empire. In any discussion, bringing up topics like the Nanjing massacre or the attack on Pearl Harbor will not be appreciated by most Japanese, even today.[30]

A "victim's complex" was born and was soon to be reinforced by postoccupation revelations surrounding the Hiroshima and Nagasaki nuclear bombings and by the news of several incidents related to H-bomb testing between the years 1952 and 1955.[31] A "nuclear allergy" appeared at practically the same time. The fact that Japan was the only country to have suffered a nuclear attack seemed to confer a new and unique status on it: for the Japanese, the victims of August 1945 had greater historic importance than those, everywhere, who had fallen during the war.

Japan's postwar constitution itself was to become an anchoring point for a new identity. The Constitution of 1889 was replaced by a new one, democratic and pacifist, that would ensure that militarism could not be revived. This constitution would allow for the legitimate return of the left to the political scene, and it extended the right to vote to people who had never been able to express political opinions under the imperial democratic system. Prewar Japanese democracy had limited voting to males alone and suffrage was census-based, so that the vast majority of Japanese did not participate at all in the political life of their country.

Even before article 9 of Japan's Peace Constitution became dear to the Japanese, that constitution was to become the symbol of a new form of freedom and, subsequently, of prosperity and security. Is it then so surprising that among the former Axis members, Japan is still the only one not to have proceeded to revise a constitution that was handed down by the victors?[32]

Article 9 lies at the core of Japan's postwar identity. It is interesting, significant, and perhaps even ironic to observe that the Liberal Democratic Party (LDP) has remained incapable of repealing or amending a "foreign" constitution and that the Japanese electorate, having elected the LDP without interruption for thirty-eight years, systematically rallied itself with the opposing left in defending the supreme law of the country. This unusual situation characterized Japan's domestic politics from 1955 until 1993, when the LDP was momentarily ousted from power.

Last, but not least, the u.s.-Japan alliance itself helped to forge Japan's "pacifist" identity. In postwar Japan, the tie linking the state, society and the armed forces was severed, undermining all attempts at re-establishing confidence in them.[33] Whereas in liberal democracies the armed forces are perceived as the defenders of the state and of its citizens, Japanese democracy was once destroyed by its own military. Regardless of constitutional provisions, the mere presence of American allied forces in Japan gave the impression to many Japanese that they had no need for national armed forces. The u.s. military presence in Japan therefore reinforced the pacifist sentiments.

It is thus possible that Japan manages its security according to parameters that are different from those commonly taken into consideration by the great powers. Its capacity for action is limited by law, by political constraints, and by a society resisting the idea of seeing Japan become once again a "normal country."

Japan's "pacifist" identity is not accepted by many observers outside Japan, and it can even be problematic in the relations Japan maintains with its neighbours. Most of them fully reject the authenticity of Japan's postwar pacifist identity, and they choose to see it through the prism of past fighting experiences between 1894 and 1945. These countries relate themselves to Japan from a different historical reference base and deny the existence of a Japanese identity that is distinct from that of Imperial Japan.[34] East-Asian states feel threatened by Japan today in part because they transfer past images and memories onto their perception of the present. Despite Japan's promises that it will never again become a military power, these states react to it as though it were still a traditional great power.[35] Japan's acquisition of advanced weaponry and its manifestation of autonomy from its American ally continue to be perceived as signs of a revival of militarism. Japan is consequently compelled to explain its defense policy to its neighbours and to periodically reassure them about its peaceful intentions. That a major power feels the need to justify its policies and that its militarization and nationalism are invariably mistaken for militarism and imperialism are revealing about its neighbours' attitudes.

Japan has been reluctant to consider the military dimensions of its situation because of the lessons it has learned from its traumatic history. The adventurism that began with the annexation of the Ryukyu Kingdom in 1878 and ended with nuclear fire and occupation in 1945 provoked a questioning of the nature of power and of the inherent dangers in the use of force. Ruined and devastated by a conflict precipitated by its armed forces, postwar Japan would retain a sharp distrust for all things military.

The period during which it dominated part of Asia casts a shadow on Japan's postwar identity, and the countries that were supposed to be integrated into Japan's Greater Asia Co-Prosperity Sphere do not want this history to be forgotten or trivialized. These different ways of relating to history continue to be one of the main points of friction and contention between Japan and East Asia.[36]

In order to avoid establishing a link between the "old" Imperial Japan and the "new" postwar Japan, in its military security behaviour Japan became both self-restraining and self-censoring.[37] Japanese diplomacy continues to regard with utmost caution the option of using force to achieve political ends – even in a legitimate international framework like the UN. The "pacifist" norm would frame and limit Japanese defense activities by restricting the SDF's sphere of action. Thus, Japan's military doctrines had less to do, until 1995, with geostrategic imperatives than with norms and rules and the conduct they allowed and forbade.

The Japanese prefer to view the SDF as expert at search and rescue operations and as a civil protection force, and they tend not to see it as a true military force, a preference that was strengthened by their support following the Kobe-Hanshin earthquake in 1995 and Mount Osu's eruption in 2000.[38] The nonthreatening image the SDF want to promote is even visible at the Defense Agency's website, where funny manga characters can be seen on the main page.

It is worth mentioning that instead of a defense ministry, Japan has a Defense Agency, whose director-general holds the title of state minister.[39] Civilian control of the military institutions is strengthened by the Defense Agency's "colonization" by members of the influential ministries of Foreign Affairs, Finance, and Economy, Trade, and Industry (METI), which position bureaucrats in the agency in frequent rotation. The Japanese Defense Agency thus finds it difficult to build its own institutional culture and memory. This way of doing things follows from the lessons learned from the prewar era, during which political and bureaucratic power could not prevent the rise of the militarists. The pacifist identity of Japan seems always to influence the management and perception of the domains surrounding its military security and its defense.

JAPAN AND THE SECURITY INSTITUTIONS

United Nations Security Council Reform and Japan: Issues of Justice, Equality, and Prestige

The 1991 Gulf War was the theatre of the first large-scale military operation under the aegis of the UN since the Korean War. Japan came out of it diplomatically weakened, and the conflict proved to be a catalyst for a transformation of its aspirations concerning the UN. Invoking constitutional constraints, Japan did not make a military contribution until the hostilities ended, when it sent a flotilla of minesweepers. This contribution was more than a symbolic gesture, since the SDF was venturing outside the Japanese archipelago, something it had not done officially since 1945. Despite providing U.S.$13 billion, for reconstruction and other nonmilitary activities, Japan was criticized by coalition members for having done too little, too late.

The shame and humiliation it suffered made it urgent to debate its role in security matters that were not related to its immediate defense and questioned the wisdom of its pacifism. But the debate was never wide-ranging enough, and it produced no consensus whatsoever in the political arena. No one wanted to see the SDF in operations causing death either among their own members or among the hypothetical aggressors.

But foreign demands came up against domestic political and institutional constraints. The Japanese Diet twice submitted bills to allow the SDF to participate in UN peace operations. The first bill was defeated and rejected; the defenders of constitutional pacifism prevented its adoption. The second bill – which would be known as the peacekeeping operations (PKO) law – was adopted, allowing for SDF deployment to Cambodia in 1992: Japan had already acted on the major powers' expectations that it would have to assume a greater world security role. Thus, in response to criticisms, Japan did participate in peace missions, but yet forbade its forces from getting involved in missions of the type that NATO conducted in the Balkans – the Implementation Force (IFOR), The International Stabilizing Force (SFOR), and the Kosovo Force (KFOR).

In 1993 Japan identified the UN as a favored means for the international community to create peace. Officially, the Japanese desire to participate in a reformed Security Council had not yet clearly appeared. Speaking before the General Assembly in 1993, Prime Minister Hosokawa departed from his prepared text to assert that Japan was ready to take on its responsibilities within a reformed UN, but the original version of the speech, which had been written by the Ministry of Foreign Affairs had mentioned a reformed Security Council.[40]

This anecdote reveals an important fact: the Ministry of Foreign Affairs recommended more assertive roles and policies than the leaders were ready to see Japan assume. It was not the first time that this ministry had obstructed the government's decisions, nor would it be the last. The question of Japan's role within a reformed UN Security Council divided the political class and proved to be a potential spark that could explode the fragile coalitions that came to power in 1993.

The sensitive issue of military participation in peace operations remained at the heart of their preoccupation with the role of Japan in the UN.

At the fiftieth session of the UN General Assembly in 1995, the minister of foreign affairs, Kono Yohei, drew a portrait of the Japanese position on UN and Security Council reform in which he outlined the position that Japan would never resort to force, which was prohibited by its constitution. Japan would continue to cooperate in the domain of peace operations and improve its contributions in matters of disarmament, nonproliferation, conflict prevention, development, good governance, the environment, and human rights. It asserted a need for reform by highlighting the fact that new powers were now ready to assume responsibilities proportional to their ability. Since 1965, the membership of the UN had increased from 51 to 185 – 189 today – while that of the Security Council had increased from 11 to 15.

Japan proposed several measures that were meant to increase the legitimacy and efficiency of the Security Council: increasing in a limited fashion – to the low twenties – the number of permanent seats, while considering the new powers; improving its representativeness by increasing the number of nonpermanent seats; giving special consideration to underrepresented regions (Asia, Africa, and Latin America); and putting in place better and more transparent work procedures. Japan's position wavered, however, since representatives of the Ministry of Foreign Affairs and Japanese leaders were both attempting to promote their respective visions and probe domestic and international opinion.

Public opinion remained only slightly interested in the issue of a UN reform. A survey conducted by the Prime Minister's Office in 1994 revealed that 18.7 percent of respondents approved of Japan's application to become a permanent member, while 37.3 percent indicated that they agreed with it somewhat.[41] A survey ordered by the Ministry of Foreign Affairs the same year produced different results: 52.9 percent of respondents claimed to support the idea of a permanent seat for Japan, but 41.2 percent of these respondents said they would withdraw their support if becoming a permanent member involved moving beyond constitutional provisions. Even two years after Japanese Blue Helmets had been sent to Cambodia, 38.8 percent still preferred that Japan did not participate in military operations of any kind, including peacekeeping. Only 16.3 percent of respondents approved of a constitutional amendment permitting the SDF to broaden its security role.[42]

In 1996, Ikeda Yukihiko, minister of foreign affairs, indicated in a policy speech at the 136th session of Parliament in 1996 that Japan believed that the priorities of UN reform should be finances first, then reform of the Economic and Social Council (ECOSOC), and then reform of the Security Council. He reiterated the demand for an amendment to the UN Charter to repeal articles 53 and 107 – the "enemy states" clauses.[43] It would be improper for Japan to hold a permanent seat in the most prestigious and powerful institution of the UN when some provisions of the charter still stained its image. Japan devoted more energy to finances and development than to Security Council reform, because these aspects better correspond with its postwar economic identity, which remains uncontested as much inside as outside Japan.

When Prime Minister Murayama Tomichii took power, Japanese efforts at the UN became more timid. A more assertive conduct was demonstrated by his successor, Hashimoto Ryutaro, who reiterated Japan's policy goals at the 1996 summit of the Asia-Europe Meeting (ASEM). He also explained why Japan was interested in becoming a permanent member of the Security Council: for example, Japan would be the only member to have suffered a nuclear attack and the first one not to possess a nuclear arsenal. Hashimoto called for a change in mentality, indicating that if Japan was to cope with post–Cold War realities, the international community also had to try to understand Japan's constitutional constraints, or Japan would not hold a permanent seat. He observed that Japan had to remain true to its Peace Constitution, which did not prevent Japan from participating in conflict prevention and resolution. He cited Japan's efforts to stabilize the Korean peninsula, namely, through the Korean Peninsula Energy Development Organisation (KEDO) and the United Nations Transitional Authority in Cambodia (UNTAC) and through participation in the ASEAN Regional Forum (ARF), to testify to the Japanese role in matters of peacebuilding, confidence-building measures, nuclear disarmament, and the establishment of special UN funds to finance post–Cold War peace operations. Japan did not apparently subscribe to the vision of the great powers that associated its refusal to participate in military operations with political disengagement on its part.

Japan would adjust its position to the Razali Proposition in 1997. This document planned on an expanded Security Council, allowing up to twenty-four members. The number of permanent members (P-5) would double, and seats would be awarded to three representatives of developing states from Africa, Asia, and Latin America and the-Caribbean. Two seats would go to industrialized countries, probably Japan and Germany. The proposition stated that new permanent members would not have the veto that current P-5 members enjoyed, and that P-5 members would be constrained to make use of the veto strictly in matters related to chapter 7 situations, which allow the UN to intervene against states that threaten international security. Japan did not fully endorse the proposition. At the G-7 summit of that year, Japan asserted that all permanent members should have a veto, in order to avoid a difference in status between old and new members. Other declarations were less categorical, though.

A former Japanese ambassador to the UN, Hatano Yoshio, criticized Japan's circumspection and low-key approach to UN reform. The lack of Japanese initiative and the fact that Japan had asserted that it would play the role UN members wished to see it play – within constitutional limits – testified to a passive attitude that was linked to a fear of having to assume greater military responsibilities if it ever was to become a permanent member of the Securty Council. In Hatano's view, only two alternatives presented themselves to Japan: become a "normal state" or become a "handicapped state."[44]

The pacifist identity of Japan, its aversion to force, and its policy of adopting a low profile strategically and politically all clashed with its desire to become a permanent Security Council member. Japan was trapped; it believed itself unable to act as a great power without reviving Asian anxieties, but neither did it ignore the fact that the pursuit of the Yoshida doctrine irritated some of the great powers, who would hesitate to consider it as one of their own. Japan seemed to be waiting to hold a permanent seat – and thus to see its status recognized and legitimated by the international community – before it started acting like a great power.[45] It is as if its political power could not manifest itself without the prior approval of other countries. It will be difficult for Japan to reconcile the Peace Constitution's provisions with the extended security role expected of P-5 members, since while the UN Charter welcomes the possibility of resorting to force in order to resolve conflict (article 42), article 9 of Japan's Peace Constitution formally prohibits it. If Japan seemed to adopt a wait-and-see approach in its UN reform diplomacy, Japanese diplomats actually travelled to many world capitals promoting Japan's candidacy, as well as showing that its checkbook diplomacy did not belong to the past.

Historical liabilities with China and Russia, both permanent members of the Security Council and – if not overtly hostile – reluctant to have Japan as one of their peers, constituted another obstacle. Japan's favoured strategy of insisting on its economic-financial power, in order to raise its international political status, is partially explained by the fact that it was impossible for China and Russia to rival it on this terrain. History also weighed heavily in 1995 when North Korea proposed to the UN General Assembly that the enemy-nation clauses never be repealed from the UN Charter and that the status of Japan as a defeated nation should remain. The North Korean motion was defeated, but China was the sole UN member to abstain from voting. South Korea also hesitates to support Japan, anticipating the diplomatic difficulties of a reunified Korea in an environment where it would be surrounded by great powers holding permanent Security Council seats. History, nationalism, and the realism of East Asian countries all seem to converge to limit the expansion of Japan's international political and security roles.

Some Japanese diplomats denounced Japan's lack of visibility in the UN despite its financial contribution – the second most important capital contribution. The UN budget for 2000 shows that Japan financed 20.573 percent of it, while the combined contributions of Germany, France, Great Britain, and China totalled 23.489 percent of the overall budget. These three P-5 members, together with Germany, provided only 2.916 percent more than Japan alone.[46] A permanent seat for Japan would be fully justified, given its importance in the institution. The denial of this "right" could be perceived in Japan as unjust, discriminatory, and humiliating. The principle of no taxation without representation, which has often been heard since 1992, implies that if Japan does not have a permanent seat, the UN cannot expect it to finance peace operations and other programs unconditionally and forever, since they will continue to be beyond Japan's control.[47] Japan has for a long time avoided being clear on this subject, not wanting to appear egotistical and not desiring to establish a direct link between its financing of the UN and the influence it should possess, but since 1998–99 it has no longer been hiding its dissatisfaction or the fact that this link exists.

Even if it aspires to be rid of its passive and reactive labels, Japan relies upon prudence and the consolidation of its achievements. The issue of UN Security Council reform was overshadowed by the role Japan can play in security matters and by its pacifist identity. As long as Japan is not admitted to the major powers club, it will stand firmly in its traditional role and will support American initiatives. This era may be coming to an end though: the permanent seat coveted by Japan would permit a healthy distancing from the United States, while procuring an insurance policy to ward off the influence of an eventual Chinese superpower, all of which would be supported by the legitimacy bestowed by the international community, which Japan seems to need in order to achieve its political emancipation.[48] That the distancing would be easier with a permanent seat by no means implies that it will take place. However, if veto power escapes Japan, it will be unable to speak out with its own voice, and that might be an important reason why the United States, although it supports Japan's pledge, opposes the idea of granting Japan a veto.

If Japan does not participate in large-scale peace and military operations, it nevertheless occupies a predominant position in the fight
against antipersonnel mines and in the fight for the limitation of
nuclear, conventional, and light arms, where, because of the absence of
the United States, it is better able to establish its leadership.[49]

Kedo: The Acceptance of a Fait Accompli: Safeguarding Alliance Relations

If there is one country that has posed a challenge to Japan's diplomats
since the end of the Cold War, it is the Democratic People's Republic
of Korea (North Korea). Among the issues at stake are the normalization of relations with that country – with which Japan has no diplomatic relations – its nuclear and ballistic programs, and the stabilization of the peninsula, with the ultimate goal of reunification of both
Koreas. KEDO (the Korean Energy Development Organization), created
in 1995, is the sole organization to address the question of nuclear programs, placing Japan in an uncomfortable position.

In 1990 and 1992 Japan endeavoured to put an end to North
Korea's nuclear ambitions, while initiating a dialogue on the normal-
ization of their relations. However, North Korea decided to ignore the
provisions of the Nuclear Non-Proliferation Treaty (NPT) until the
United States removed its nuclear weapons from South Korea. To the
North Koreans, this question did not concern Japan or the International Atomic Energy Agency (IAEA) but South Korea's American ally.
Thus, North Korea rejected Japan – which it considers to be a puppet
and lackey of the United States – as a legitimate interlocutor. The
North Korean nuclear question would be linked to the nuclear dissuasion offered by the United States to South Korea.

In 1992–93, the IAEA inspected many sites, insisting on visiting those
that had been detected by American surveillance satellites. As a result
North Korea threatened to withdraw from the NPT. At the end of 1993,
North Korea proceeded to fire a Nodong-1 ballistic missile into the Sea
of Japan, in an attempt to intimidate its adversaries and show its
resolve to resist foreign pressure.

The United States favoured a diplomatic solution and negotiated an
agreement with North Korea. It agreed that it would never use nuclear
weapons against North Korea, giving more credibility to the February
1992 goal of denuclearising the peninsula, thereby reducing North
Korean fears.[50] After several rounds of negotiation, the Agreed Framework was concluded in 1994, followed by more arrangements. It anticipated that the United States would supply North Korea with two
light-water nuclear reactors (LWR) by 2003, that an international

consortium would be created to finance and develop the project, and that a supply of fifty thousand tons of oil per year would be guaranteed until the first reactor was completed. In exchange, North Korea would have to cease the operation of its existing reactors; it would have to remain a member of the NPT; and it would have to authorize IAEA inspections, as stated in the treaty. Once the LWR construction entered an advanced stage, the IAEA would be allowed to resume its inspections of known sites, and before delivery of the main components of the reactor, North Korea would have to let IAEA inspectors visit each and every site they deemed necessary.

The United States would support the oil costs, while Japan and South Korea were solicited to fund the LWR project, without having been seriously consulted. This caused a problem for Japan, because, since the launch of the Nodong-1 missile, it had linked the question of the nuclear program to that of missile proliferation. If North Korea attacked Japan, conventional warheads aimed at nuclear power plants or chemical or bacterial warheads targeted at urban centers would be devastating. North Korea's missiles represent a clear and present danger to Japan, a danger that is more immediate than its nuclear program. The Agreed Framework of 1994 cut Japan off from negotiations, but it resigned itself to support it even though the agreement was silent on the missiles issue. Prime Minister Murayama pushed for a consortium in which Japan would participate if North Korea bent to all the IAEA demands. Japan would finance 50 percent of the LWR project, for the cause of the nonproliferation of weapons of mass destruction.[51] The Agreed Framework did not call for the inspection of sites that had not been declared by North Korea before construction was advanced, and, because the United States had promised a moratorium on inspections until 1999, Japan had to renounce its policy. It resolved to participate in the American initiative despite its lack of guarantees and reduced demands (compared to the original IAEA requests) and despite the fact that it did not address the missile threat at all.

Aside from Japan's support for the nonproliferation cause, the worrisome proximity of a North Korea equipped with real or potential nuclear capabilities explains its participation in KEDO.[52] An environmental reason was also proposed, since the reactors to be replaced are of the same model as those that exploded in Chernobyl in 1986.

The original structure of KEDO illustrates the differing status of each founding member: the American ambassador is the executive director, and the Korean and Japanese ambassadors have the titles of deputy executive director. Although the United States associates KEDO with a joint effort with its allies, the dynamic remains less trilateral than doubly bilateral, since the dominant position is American, a situation that is justified by the fact that KEDO was an American initiative. The structure is at the same time bilateral and multilateral.[53] Japanese diplomacy candidly admitted that the Americans provided KEDO with its directions. Prime Minister Hashimoto asserted that KEDO's raison d'être was to provide an arena for discussion between the United States and North Korea.[54] North Koreans refuse to consider the role of Japan, recalling that KEDO operates within parameters, plans, and schedules decided by the United States, which clearly demonstrates that Japan is not a leader of the organization and thus should not express itself.[55]

KEDO's first year was eventful. In 1996, the U.S. Congress froze the oil funds that had been promised to North Korea. Japan had to pay the bill. This occurred again in 1997 and in 1998, when cost estimates for the LWR project increased from U.S.$4 billion to U.S.$5.2 billion. The Asian financial crisis and the devaluation of the Won lowered the costs back to U.S.$4.6 billion. Japan's contribution did not falter and was maintained at U.S.$1 billion, despite a 30 percent decrease in the value of the yen.

KEDO hoped to see North Korea adopt a more conciliatory and less hostile attitude towards South Korea, Japan and the United States, since foreign aid that was donated to alleviate famines and epidemics began flowing in and since energy needs were being taken care of. A radical change in behaviour was not observed, however: the destruction of a U.S. OH-58C helicopter in 1994, the incursion into South Korea of a commando in 1996, and a naval skirmish with Japan in 1999 all testify to this. Last but not least, serious naval clashes between both Korea's navies occurred in the Yellow Sea in 1999 and 2002. The events of 1996 brought delays, South Korea having interrupted its participation in KEDO until the North would apologize. South Korea was less demanding in 1999, not wanting to jeopardize its policy of détente with North Korea, the so-called Sunshine Policy it had established in 1998.

Already in 1996 Japan showed itself to be skeptical about the possibility of improving North Korea's attitude. The Geneva negotiations were described as a new Munich, the United States playing the appeasement card in their dealings with North Korea in quite the same way that Great Britain had done with Nazi Germany.[56]

At the end of 1997, Japan confirmed that it would take responsibility for 20 percent of the costs of KEDO: U.S.$1 billion. It would take the form of a loan reimbursable without interest twenty years after the reactors were put into service. This decision represented a policy change, since it had been decided earlier that all contributions would be deducted from any future compensation granted to North Korea. The resumption of normalization talks with North Korea in 1995 brought a separation of these questions. KEDO members were to make their respective contributions official on 31 August 1998, but the event at which they expected to do so was cancelled in reaction to North Korea's test launch of a Taepodong missile.

Japan reacted firmly to the news that a North Korean missile had flown over it and announced its immediate withdrawal from KEDO, the interruption of food aid to North Korea, the ending of chartered flights to that country, and the freezing of normalization efforts. Japan felt that the attitude of North Korea needed to be changed so that it would stop believing that it could always profit from intimidation. It demanded that the United States pressure North Korea to stop its missile program – which was done without any significant results until 2000 – so that any return to KEDO would not be compromised.

The Taepodong incident breathed new life into the theater missile defense (TMD) issue that had been at a virtual standstill since 1994.[57] In the aftermath of the Taepodong launch, the Japanese committed themselves to participate in TMD research more as an act of alliance cooperation than as a result of any careful assessment of the project's strategic value and potential.[58] Some Japanese denounced American carelessness toward North Korea's missile proliferation and development by asserting that the United States, which was well out of the range of the missiles and concerned with sustaining its military-industrial complex, benefitted by stalling on this issue, in order to promote TMD and sell Patriot systems to their allies.[59] Like KEDO, TMD may well represent a way for the United States to dissuade Japan from developing a nuclear deterrent, even in the event that all its neighbours possessed and reinforced their nuclear arsenals.[60] The North Korean nuclear threat, like that of other "rogue states," real or imagined, comes in handy in justifying TMD development without ever questioning the fact that the main goal of a TMD system could very well be the neutralization of the Chinese and Russian nuclear arsenals.[61]

On 21 October 1998, Japan reintegrated itself into KEDO, claiming that the organization provided the most realistic and efficient framework for preventing the development of nuclear weapons in North Korea and that no alternative to KEDO and the Agreed Framework existed.[62] KEDO's executive director asserted that an alternative did exist: that of confrontation or of an increased risk of war in the peninsula.[63] Pressure from America and South Korea, their officials having no desire to endanger the four-party talks in progress with North Korea, initiated this backdown. But Japan came back into the KEDO fold because South Korea opened the door to Japanese participation in an eventual structure for six-party talks.[64] The announcement concerning the talks was made in February 1999 and clearly constituted a form of trade-off to keep Japan in KEDO. This indirect support for the Sunshine Policy was compensated for by the establishment of an emergency line of communication between Japan and South Korea and the resumption of naval exercises. A Trilateral Coordination and Oversight Group was also formed, creating a network of bilateral, trilateral, and multilateral structures centred on North Korea and the United States. Most importantly, Japan's return to KEDO was made possible by a U.S. commitment to bring the missile issue to North Korea's attention, as Japan had repeatedly requested since 1993.[65]

Japan had to support KEDO for several reasons. Participation favoured a faster reconciliation with and between the two Koreas and would help to project a pacific and cooperative image of Japan, which could contribute to the erosion of the powerful negative memories both countries keep alive. KEDO could have constituted the embryo of a multilateral East Asian structure that included Japan. With ASEAN+3 at the end of 1999, Japan participated – with China and South Korea but without the United States – in the creation of a security forum centred on East Asia.[66] The extension of the quadripartite discussions on peace in the Korean peninsula, which included Russia, would constitute a welcome development for Japan, even if it was made possible by a softening of its own policy. The first, informal meeting of the group took place in December 1999. KEDO mostly provided an occasion to reinforce the strength and credibility of the alliance and to avoid tensions, since the Japanese did not always agree with nor share U.S. positions on North Korea but supported them regardless. Japan's refusal to join KEDO would have dangerously undermined the alliance and cast a shadow over its relations with the United States and South Korea. KEDO would have favoured greater integration not only between the United States and its allies but also with China, which plays a major diplomatic role with regard to North Korea and the region. Indirectly, KEDO also provided Japan with an occasion to keep channels open with North Korea, even though bilateral normalization talks remained frozen after the North Korean rebuffs of 1992, 1995, and 1998. Since the winter of 2000, normalization talks have slowly and cautiously resumed, with North Korea seeming to want to make a lie of its "Hermit's Kingdom" label.[67]

KEDO's main goal, however – to stop the North Korean nuclear program – remains to be accomplished. Nevertheless, if KEDO's "secret agenda" is to buy some time in the hope of relaxing tensions with the North Korean regime or if it is to favour inter-Korean exchanges by socializing the North, the objective may already have been partially attained. KEDO nonetheless remains fragile and hopelessly behind schedule, and the North Koreans grow impatient.

KEDO's future as a security institution may therefore be in serious jeopardy. In January 2002, North Korea was identified by the U.S. administration as a member of the "axis of evil" and is thus a potential U.S. target in the anti-terrorist war. Needless to say, KEDO's mission and faith in the Agreed Framework are no longer foundations of U.S. North Korea policy.

The unprecedented visit of a Japanese prime minister to Pyongyang in September 2002 should have been the most significant step toward improving relations with North Korea. Pyongyang finally admitted abducting Japanese nationals, having denied doing so for a decade. This was not to be the only revelation Pyongyang would offer, as its recent admission that its nuclear program has neither been terminated nor frozen has shown. Because of this admission, Japanese diplomacy towards North Korea is back to square one, and ten years of engagement policy have been swept away. Consequently, because KEDO is the main implementation tool of the Agreed Framework, one should expect it to be dismantled, although no KEDO member has yet officially announced this step.

THE SENKAKU ISLANDS DISPUTE: A CLASH OF HISTORY AND NATIONALISMS

The establishment of the U.N. Law of the Sea convention and the delimitation of exclusive economic zones (EEZ) fuelled territorial disputes everywhere. Japan did not escape the turmoil when sovereignty over the Senkaku Islands was firmly contested by China and Taiwan. The islands constitute an important fishing zone and may hold important oil and gas resources. To the Japanese, these islands are the southern part of the Okinawa Archipelago, which became Japanese territory after the annexation of the Ryukyu Kingdom in 1878. The Chinese and Taiwanese asserted that they had been taken as a result of the Sino-Japanese wars of the nineteenth and twentieth centuries and that Japan should have given them back in 1945. Because they were part of Okinawa, the United States took control of them in 1945 and administered them until they were retroceded to Japan in 1972. That same year, Japan and China proceeded to normalize their relations and decided that this territorial issue was to be settled by future generations.

In 1990 the ultranationalist Japanese group Seinensha made its way to the Senkaku Islands in order to repair a lighthouse it had erected there in 1978. Taiwan protested and Taiwanese demonstrators headed towards the contested territory, only to be denied access by Japanese Maritime Security Forces.[68] China sided with Taiwan, and anti-Japanese riots broke out in Hong Kong and Taipei. Only the wish to avoid escalation defused the crisis: Taiwan indicated that it did not support the demonstrators trying to land on the Tiaoyutai Islands (its name for the Senkaku Islands), and China accepted Japan's proposal to settle the question later.

In 1992, China enacted its Law on Territorial Waters and Adjacent Zones. The Diaoyu Islands – the Senkakus – appeared on its list, which was interpreted by Japan as a rejection of the 1990 moratorium. In 1995–96, as the expiry date set by the Law of the Sea Convention drew nearer, China was looking for ways to affirm its sovereignty on contested territories, in order to provide itself with an important EEZ. Thus, in 1995 it fired intermediate missiles near the islands and proceeded to its forty-second nuclear test, drawing the attention of Japan, which put an end to the Official Development Assistance grants to China. The missile crisis of 1996 in the Taiwan Straits did nothing to reassure Japan.

The Seinensha constructed a new lighthouse on the Senkakus in 1996, provoking both China and Taiwan. In response to a journalist who was interested in knowing if the ARF would be brought in on this issue, a Ministry of Foreign Affairs official asserted that there was no need for such a course of action, since Japan did not recognize even the existence of the dispute.[69] Japan, however, tried to involve the United States, and therefore attempted to pull out of the strictly bilateral relationship. Since some of the Senkaku Islands had been used as a shooting range by the U.S. Navy, Japan put forward the idea that the United States already had implicitly recognized Japanese sovereignty over the islands. An agreement with a mysterious Japanese landowner was to be proof of this assertion. The official U.S. position was that it would not interfere in the internal and territorial affairs of China or Japan. Thus the question failed to be treated in a trilateral way. Chinese officials linked Japan's claims to the Senkaku Islands to the spectre of a revival of Japanese militarism, going so far as to advance the idea that the only country representing a threat to the region was none other than Japan.[70]

Facing an intensification of demonstrations and witnessing China's firm stand, Japanese officials confirmed they would not recognize the lighthouse, but they emphasized that this gesture was not to be interpreted as a renunciation of Japan's right to the Senkaku Islands. Several days after this announcement, Chinese and Taiwanese demonstrators again attempted to land on the islands. In response, Japanese dispatched E-2 AWAC (Airborne Warning and Control system) planes toward Okinawa and more coast guard ships toward the islands.

In the spring of 1997 the Senkaku crisis entered its second phase and provided the scene for a variation in Japanese behaviour, as a journalist and a politician from Ishigaki went to the islands. The Japanese government claimed to regret the incident and spoke as though the visit was unauthorized and not advised by the Maritime Security Force.[71] The fact that a Japanese politician had landed on the Senkakus provoked a renewal of activity by foreign fishermen near the islands. Mobs demonstrated in front of Hong Kong's Japanese consulate, and there were even attacks on Japan's economic mission in Taipei. In China, there were fewer demonstrations, because the government refused to authorize them. The Japanese government confirmed that it would not consider using SDF ships and that it would refuse to deploy military troops to the islands. It repeated that the dispute would not be heard by the International Court of Justice, since Beijing would not request it.[72] Soon, even Japanese citizens were forbidden from going to these islands, in order to avoid an escalation. Shortly thereafter, China's ambassador to Japan, Xu Dunxin, confirmed that the resolution of all territorial disputes in the China Sea would be postponed. Since then, only sporadic attempts by the Taiwanese to land on the islands have been observed, the last of them in April of 2000, when the Seinensha erected a Shinto temple.

To manage this dispute – since it did not endeavour to settle it at the time – Japan did not seek recourse to any security institutions other than the alliance. In calling upon the ARF, for instance, Japan would have opened the door to outside arbitration, which would have resulted in the invalidation of its current policy to the effect that there is actually no dispute. The ARF, which was already preoccupied with many disputes involving China, could not really interfere.[73] Japan had nothing to gain and much to lose by diverting itself from its policy. The Senkaku dispute could not be resolved by an international body because, basically, none of the countries involved ever implied that they recognized its existence.

Japan's behaviour was interesting because, even though the Japanese were in possession and control of the islands, they retreated at times to a somewhat ambiguous discursive level. In a few press conferences, it was declared that the Senkaku islands were "administered" by Japan. Administration of a territory by a state by no means implies its sovereignty over that territory.

Japan and China never hid the fact that they did not want this issue to damage their relations. In 1997 Japan resumed granting ODA funds to China, and for the first time, it refrained from signing a UN report denouncing Chinese violations of human rights. In 2001, Japan and

China agreed to implement a mechanism for informing both parties of the activities of search ships in the unofficially disputed waters of the Senkaku Islands. However, China has not always respected this agreement, and on five occasions in August 2001 one of its exploration ships penetrated waters the Japanese considered to be theirs.[74] These apparently trite events are worthy of attention, because the Prime Minister's Office made a special point of ordering the JDA not to reveal anything about the incidents and not to intervene, in order not to harm relations with China.[75]

The fact that Japan officially avoided recognizing the lighthouse constructed by the Seinensha, and refused its citizens access to the Senkaku Islands reveals its cautious approach. For any democracy, restricting access to parts of its territory is unusual. Japan also took great care not to allow the SDF to intervene, in order to avoid criticism – domestic and foreign – and a confusion of the use of force, or the threat to use force, with a revival of militarism. Japan's moderation and restraint thus showed its will to behave in accordance with its postwar pacifist identity and its determination not to send signals that Asian countries could distort to make Japan look like an aggressive power.

It is important to note that the crises of 1996–97 were not interstate crises. Private actions provoked public reactions. The Senkakus were the theatre of crises that in fact addressed the question of the two Chinas, their relations with Japan, and their rapport with history,[76] and that highlighted China's strategies for ensuring its domestic authority through nationalism.[77] In fact, the recurring historical problems have little to do with intentions on either side, or even with changes in the structural relationships: they have deeper roots in human psychology.[78] Just before Hong Kong's retrocession to China and before that of Macao, private groups had used the Senkaku issue to show their loyalty to China or to embarrass Taiwan. The fact that Taiwanese flags flew next to those of China in trawler flotillas in the area also demonstrates how Japan can still be both a scapegoat and a catalyst that instils feelings of unity in the Chinese people.[79] The Senkaku Islands issue thus remains one where security and economics may well matter less for the parties that provoked the crises of 1996–97 than the stakes of sovereignty, national prestige, and history.[80]

CONCLUSION: AT THE CROSSROADS?

Since the beginning of the postwar era, Japan has conceived military security through the prism of a pacifist identity that is anchored in its

Constitution and reinforced by its alliance with the United States. While participating in and promoting multilateral diplomacy and multilateral frameworks in the 1990s, Japan maneuvered so as to satisfy the most pressing American demands without stirring up the fears of an easily irritated China. These two countries, which were at the centre of Japanese preoccupations, grant bilateralism a strategic importance that generally overshadows multilateralism. In some matters, the United States and China also act in ways that border more and more on unilateralism. In order to avoid the insoluble dilemma that would result from a return to an unequivocal balance of power system in East Asia, Japan has kept its security policy in alignment with that of the United States – and sometimes with that of South Korea – while searching for an alternative multilateral way of easing tensions between the rival regional powers. Was Japan's behaviour in line with the realist, the neorealist, or the neoliberal institutionalist approach? Japan certainly demonstrated a firm will to maintain the current political climate, but its desire to preserve the regional equilibrium is not to be explained solely by reference to its national interest: Japan may be trying to avoid placing itself in a position where it could be forced to redefine its role and identity. Can safeguarding one's identity be a superior kind of national interest?

Japan lacks foreign and security policy objectives that can achieve consensus, but it has invested in international security institutions since the 1990s to counter the increasing frictions between the major powers. It avoided those frictions during most of the postwar and Cold War eras and does not wish to have to take sides or be caught between the United States and China. Because it is risk averse, Japan truly is caught between a rock and a hard place. Multilateralism seems to be a safe strategy, but is it a rewarding one?

Holding a permanent seat on the Security Council, along with veto power, is of tremendous importance for Japan, since it could then more legitimately intervene between the great powers and make its voice heard more assertively. The 1991 Gulf War and its aftermath have transformed Japan's idealistic vision of the UN. In a way, the Japanese felt that the ideals of their Peace Constitution were not very different from those of the UN. But after 1991 Japan's pacifism was no longer in tune with the UN. Faced with the impossible choice between renouncing its postwar pacifist identity and the pretence of practising a UN-centred foreign policy, Japan opted for a halfway solution that did not satisfy anyone in the end. The fluctuations in Japanese positions result from the lack of consensus in the political arena. The Ministry of Foreign Affairs profits from this lack of consensus, but its bureaucrats, whose capacity for independent action – already immense – has been reinforced since 1993 by the relative weakness of coalition governments, are being challenged more and more by elected politicians in government.[81]

The decision to create KEDO was certainly not Japan's. Its lack of success in establishing a dialogue with North Korea and its powerlessness to influence Pyongyang in any way encouraged Japan to support a U.S. initiative that Tokyo did not believe in at first. Maintaining harmony in the alliance was without doubt among its most important motives for participating in KEDO. Japan was rewarded by the creation of new multilateral structures and dialogue frameworks, but this reward has not to this day translated into measurable political gains.

Japan did not get security institutions involved in the Senkaku Islands issue, but the dispute did reveal significant elements of Japanese behaviour with regard to the use of force, since the SDF were never called in to protect Japan's claim to sovereignty over the islands. Although the ships of the Maritime Security Force were lightly armed, the symbol represented by the promise not to use military means underlined Japan's determination to stay true to its pacifist identity. Japan chose not to respond to the provocation of those who, in threatening its sovereignty, wanted to reveal its alleged militarist face. History coloured all the dynamics surrounding the dispute, in which the only legitimate nationalism became Chinese, while that of Japan did not even have the right to exist, since it threatened to mutate into imperialism in the minds of those who perceived it through the lenses of the past.

During the 1990s, international security institutions gained in importance for Japan, but always as a complement to the alliance with the United States. However, Japan is changing. It has been demonstrating a lack of confidence in and some impatience towards its American ally since the Okinawa crisis and the Taepodong test launch. The tactless reaction of the United States following the accident in which the USS Greeneville sank the Ehime Maru and the events surrounding the EP-3 incident of 2001 irritated Japan. Deployment of Japanese surveillance satellites in 2002 and the creation of a small intelligence section in 1999 both testify to a desire for emancipation from the alliance, which has resulted from Japanese displeasure with the American management of North Korea – whose sales of missiles apparently never did cease. Despite a growing anxiety over the direction China will take, Japan persists in not becoming a traditional military power.[82] Consensus to this effect remains constant and strong in Japanese society, even though the generation that experienced the founding traumas of Japan's actual security identity is quickly vanishing, a sign that the pacifist norms remain firmly rooted in the national political and social cultures, even if the strength of those norms might gradually dwindle. In the future, security institutions may no longer complement Japan's alliance. They may either act as a counterbalance to the alliance, or the imperatives of alliance politics may cause Japan to turn on them. It is too soon to tell how Japanese behaviour will evolve, especially since 9/11 and the subsequent war on terrorism have transformed the basis upon which the great powers view their security.

CHAPTER SIX

The Institutional Security Policy Reorientation of China

LOÏC TASSÉ

The institutional security policy of China is intriguing not only because there is a marked difference between its theoretical policy and its actions but also because the decision-making process remains obscure – due to the secretive nature of China's regime – even though a certain analytical progress has been made since the Mao period.[1]

In China itself, the question of the country's security policy is divided between two main schools of thought.[2] The reformist school believes that the United States is slowly declining and predicts that China may surpass the United States in a few decades. The orthodox school, on the other hand, contends that the world is witnessing a rapid American decline, one that would lead to a loss of the American alliances, as well as an increase in world multipolarity. This school announces that China is on its way to surpassing the United States. These two schools have different impacts on the analysis of China's institutional security policy. The first one leads to a defensive vision of security, arguing that China must protect itself from an American hegemony that could dominate the world without any rival for a long time to come, even with the existence of secondary poles such as Europe and Japan. The second school derives a contrary analysis, arguing that, because the United States would in reality be less powerful than it appeared, it would be inclined to neutralise a rising power such as China to prolong its domination. China would thus have an interest in conducting a discrete policy of power reinforcement, without letting itself be intimidated by the United States. This debate between experts takes on particular importance because it probably reflects the current discord between the security policy decision makers themselves. Indeed, due to the particular nature of China's communist regime, each school is intimately tied to a faction of China's Communist Party (CCP): the reformist school to Deng Xiaoping's faction and the orthodoxist school to Jiang Zemin's faction. The first faction dominated the country in the early 1990s, and the second took power around 1995.

In the West the debate on China's security policy has taken a political and theoretical turn. A fascination for China, the American Republican Party's concerns, and Western observers' habit of splitting the world in two, has led to a series of commentaries that all generally take a defiant attitude towards China. This attitude has led, in turn, either to containment policies[3] or, on the contrary, to a benevolent view that promotes exchanges with the country.[4] This argument concerning the Chinese threat informs the discussions between the various schools that concentrate on the examination of China's actions in the international security institutions. The constructivists and the neoliberal institutionalists are often inclined to promote trade with China, while the realists and structural realists – who are more pessimistic – embrace containment policies.

The Chinese and Western points of view concerning the institutional security policy of China are less difficult to reconcile than they would at first appear. China's actions in three cases involving international security institutions, or ISIS (the UN Security Council reform, the Nuclear Test Ban Treaty (NTBT), and the Spratly Islands conflict), can be explained by a realist theory and by a structural-realist theory: the balance-of-threat theory, as defined by Stephen Walt, explains China's institutional security policy between approximately 1990 and 1995, and the power maximization theory, as defined by authors such as John Mearsheimer, explains subsequent years. Each theory can be linked to the two dominant factions of the CPC. Before 1995 China seems to have pursued balance-of-threat diplomacy: it was constantly concerned with preventing a rupture of the balance that would occur to China's disadvantage. This style of diplomacy corresponds to the vision of the reformist faction. After 1995 China progressively abandoned its defensive diplomacy and reoriented itself towards an offensive diplomacy, while seeking to maximize its military advantages, territorial and technological, which brought it closer to the view of the orthodox faction. These actions imply that, contrary to the assumptions made by structural-realist analysis to explain China's actions in the ISI, the change from balance-of-threat diplomacy to power-maximization diplomacy rested initially not only on external variables but also on internal variables such as the succession of dominant factions at the head of the CPC.

WESTERN THEORETICAL APPROACHES
TO CHINA'S INSTITUTIONAL SECURITY POLICY

China's institutional security policy is approached differently by neoliberal, constructivist, and realist institutional perspectives. For almost twenty years, many characteristics of China's diplomacy have contributed to the emergence of analysis from the neoliberal institutional school. In keeping with this perspective, since the end of the 1970s China has pursued policies of trade liberalisation. Furthermore, it committed itself as early as 1986 to multilateralism and under Deng Xiaoping's regime power has been decentralised.[5] China finally officially joined the World Trade Organisation in January 2002.

Constructivist analyses, however, were encouraged by China's increasingly active participation in multilateral organisations: under Deng Xiaoping, China adhered to more than a hundred multilateral treaties and to more than fifty international governmental organisations, and it cooperated in almost a thousand NGOs.[6] And realist explanations have constantly been fed by Beijing's stiff attitude towards its own population and towards Taiwan – and towards the United States, as well, during for example, the Tiananmen Square incidents in 1989, the missile testing in Taiwanese waters in the mid-1990s, the escalation of anti-American discourse after the Chinese embassy bombing of 1999, and the collision between Chinese and American planes in April 2001. Consequently, it is not very surprising that perceptions of China's conduct in the ISIs vary according to the different viewpoints of the three schools of thought.

Many analyses of Asian security[7] follow the neoliberal institutional school of thought.[8] As such, they insist on the growth of economic interdependence between China and other countries, which, if well supported, would contribute to a rapprochement between them, rather than exacerbating old rivalries.[9] In accordance with the postulate of irrationality of the actors, the supporters of this school often highlight the opposition between China's official policies and the irresistible pressures towards globalisation. Furthermore, failures of the international bipolar system, Deng Xiaoping's modernisation policy, and economic growth have all contributed to China's emergence at the international level. Under these circumstances, Chinese foreign policy is compelled to be more and more interactive, participatory, and cooperative.[10] This does not necessarily imply a rapprochement between all the powers. On the contrary, according to some observers, since 1997 China might have been looking for a way to discredit the American alliances in Asia and might possibly be striving to replace them with a collective security agreement.[11]

According to the neoliberal school, it should be expected that China's security objectives will become more and more subordinate to various economic interest games, since regulation by the markets would provide a substitute for the regulations set in place by the Chinese state. However, China remains dependent on various sectors, since it acts according to a dual logic. On the one hand, it would like to diminish its security dependence, for instance, in order to enjoy the advantages of interdependence, and it would like to consolidate its comparative advantage in a way that would reinforce its negotiation power. On the other hand, Beijing would increasingly like to commit itself to a multilateral policy, in order to continue to enjoy external advantages.[12] The net result of interdependence is not clear. It could lead to greater regional stability, or it could lead to greater instability, given that China would favour the immediate advantages of interdependence to those of a strengthening of its negotiation policy.[13]

Consequently, the NTBT can be seen as a way for China to consolidate its relative nuclear power advantage or as a way for the country to obtain mutual advantages, namely in the scientific and technological fields. In a reform of the United Nations Security Council, China could seek to preserve its permanent membership advantages in order to achieve ulterior advantages or in order to benefit from cooperating on the council, especially in the economic field. Following a similar logic, the Spratly Islands conflict could evolve in two different directions. It could be exacerbated in the short run, with a consolidation of China's military strength being aimed to reinforce Beijing's negotiation power in the newly emerging order of regional interdependence. Or it could calm down under the various pressures of dependence, particularly those relating to the economy, and it could then give way to very formal and structured institutions in which sanctions against deviant states would be very costly.[14]

The constructivist approach is rarely used to analyse China's behaviour in the ISIS, even though it is frequently used to explain states' behaviour in international institutions.[15] This rarity stems from the fundamental principles of this school: constructivists base their observations on Kant's vision of alliances between democracies and on concepts of pluralist societies.[16] However, China is not a democracy, and its communist regime causes problems, because it is ideologically incompatible with other countries in the region, with the possible exceptions of North Korea and Viet Nam. This difficulty is surmountable, however. Although China is not democratic, as long as a democratic faction exists, its influence could well be reflected in the country's security policy.[17] Furthermore, the Chinese leaders' habit of sharing international consultation guidelines in international institutions, including the ISIS, should push the country towards more cooperation in that area.[18] Many authors do not hesitate to integrate China into their constructivist analysis of, for instance, the UN and peacekeeping missions.[19] Others have derived an Asian approach from this constructivist school,[20] but most of them limit themselves to ASEAN policies and the South-East Asian region.[21]

Following the principles of the constructivist school, it would be expected that China would support the Security Council reforms and the NTBT, as well as the setting up of a cooperative security system in Asia that would encompass the Spratly Islands problem, given that international guidelines would be respected.[22] In addition, it should be observed that since China is opening itself to the world, Chinese leaders should encounter increasing difficulty in ignoring pressures in favour of peace from their own citizens.

The third approach used to explain Chinese behaviour in the ISIS is the realist one. Classical realism, in its most offensive version, believes that states are seeking to increase their power, to preserve their highest prerogatives and, occasionally, to maximise their security. The increase in power that is implied here does not really apply as much to the increasing capacity and absolute competence of states as it does to the way they are able to perform in comparison to their enemies. This approach emphasizes the importance of international status and prestige, which supporters of a realist tendency call positional goods.[23] According to this last tendency, states strive to increase their powers in terms of status and prestige, in order to ensure their national security, and they are not content with a respectable margin of power, as postulated by structural-realists.

The presupposed pessimism of the realist approach leads certain authors to assume that a conflict between China and the United States is highly likely since rising powers tend to assert themselves and defy dominant powers.[24] A conflict is regarded as likely especially because China perceives itself as a historical victim of Western powers. Considering its economic and military potential, it should thus attempt to become a hegemonic regional power, and from its regional base, it could even attempt to defy the international order dominated by the United States.[25] Of course, this hegemonic regional goal would follow a successful resistance of the strategic containment strategy that the United States seems to pursue against China. According to this perspective, international institutions are secondary for China,[26] considering that they serve to facilitate interstate relations.[27] For example, the United States' use of the United Nations during the Korean conflict and the isolation of China when the country was represented by the nationalist regime of Taiwan were notoriously negative experiences for

Chinese diplomats. Thus, it is not surprising that at that time Peking adopted a profoundly sceptical attitude toward security institutions, since they did not favour the development of its positional goods.

In the three cases under study in this chapter (Security Council reform, the Nuclear Test Ban Treaty, and the Spratly Islands dispute), the classical realist approach draws on a China that constantly seeks to increase its relative power. In the Spratlys[28], Beijing is regarded as wanting to obtain strategic military advantages (island occupation),[29] resources (presumed or real), and diplomatic advantages (preventing the creation of an anti-Chinese regional alliance.)[30] On this approach China would be acting in the region as a hegemonic power, striving to consolidate its partnerships, to rival other major powers,[31] although some observers believe that the u.s. presence in the region is for now a stabilizing factor for China, because it diminishes the perceived threat to other Asian countries and thus slows down the military build-up.[32]

In the case of the NTBT, the rivalry between China and other powers should be weak, since China is only a weak nuclear power. In other words, it would act in this case as a secondary power. However, because the NTBT touches on what is held to be most fundamental for China, it should do everything to preserve its established nuclear power status. Only pressures from the United States, Russia, or France could force it to back away from its position, and an eventual Chinese retreat would be accompanied by compensations or would result from threats. Finally, in the case of Security Council reforms, China is seeking to preserve its existing alliances within the United Nations, to increase its institutional power by opposing interventions in internal affairs of a state, and to pressure the dominant power while seeking the predominance of its own international code of conduct.[33]

The structural-realist approach claims to complete and refine the realist approach. Considering that the resources and capacities of each state are different and that states are in competition with each other, it would be to their advantage to mitigate the dominance of more powerful states. This result could be obtained either through a military race, the creation of alliances, or the sharing of resources with other countries.[34] A state that feels threatened by the increasing power of other states would try to reestablish equilibrium in the international system through alliances. A very different view of balance of power is provided by the balance-of-threat perspective, which assumes that states react, not against the increase of power of other states, but against a real threat. The nature of the threat remains fairly vague, however, since it can come from a group of powers, from geographical proximity to a power, from an offensive power, or from aggressive intentions.[35] The threat can also be directed against the internal stability of a regime or against a country's boundaries. Following the balance-of-threat theory, China could increase its military capacity by enjoying either a decrease in military costs or membership in a military coalition with other threatened countries or by seeking short-term gains.[36]

Globally speaking, it follows from the balance-of-threat theory that China would force itself to counter the potential threat that comes mainly from the United States, because of its marked tendency to consider the rise in Chinese power as having a negative effect on its political strength in the world. This threat is particularly dangerous, given that the u.s. capacity for intervention is strong. The situation in the Asian region is more complex. Regionally speaking, the current dynamics in international relations would be shaped by the domination of a single country: the United States. China should thus ally itself to other countries in order to diminish, if not to counteract, the threat that the United States poses, and it should, at the same time, avoid the creation of anti-Chinese alliances in the Asian region. China has the advantage of being able to prevent the creation of ISIS, or at least it could preserve them from American domination.[37] In this context, China should be expected to resist negotiating any military security agreement that would include the Spratlys, while simultaneously increasing its military capacity to maximise its control over the islands.

While the NTBT is an international institution, it represented a regional challenge for China, since Peking sought first and foremost to reduce the risk of nuclear proliferation in Asia. Keeping a balance-of-threat perspective, Peking's participation in the NTBT depended on the predominant influence that China can exercise over the regional security institutions and on the efficiency of the counterweight that it can impose on other powers, mainly on the United States. China's exclusion from similar institutions could push forward an arms race, as in the case of the American intention of building and deploying an antimissile system (AMD) covering u.s. air space.[38] China should thus insist on actively participating in the negotiations concerning the revision of the current antimissile system, since it could benefit from eventual gains such as technological transfers and a relative reduction in external threats.

In terms of the ISIS, always in the framework of the balance-of-threat theory, China should join with other states in order to limit American influence in the debates about Security Council reforms, as well as to prevent other powers from benefiting from these reforms at its expense. The status quo would be acceptable for Beijing, assuming that it would remove the threat of a Council disequilibrium that was favourable to Washington. The multilateral Nuclear Test Ban agreement should preserve or increase the economic and military capacities of China.

CHINESE APPROACHES TO SECURITY
AND FEUDS BETWEEN FACTIONS

The thought control exercised by the CPC over Chinese society forces Chinese researchers to construct their analyses based on the direction given by Chinese propaganda, since the degree of freedom enjoyed by researchers varies with the strength of the dominant party faction's control of the discourse. The Cultural Revolution, which officially lasted from 1966 to 1976, has heavily handicapped social science research in China, since social science faculties reopened their doors only at the end of the 1970s, at which point teaching remained very closely wedded to Maoist principles. It was only during the 1980s that international relations research reached an interesting level in Chinese universities, even if debates between experts still reflected the divisions between the main factions of the Communist Party.[39] Consequently, a look at internal policy is doubly interesting: it not only allows us to understand Chinese experts' arguments but also helps us to understand the motivation behind the Chinese leaders' defence policy.

From the start, it is important to put aside the argument that any Chinese government would have acted in the same sensible way with regard to foreign policy.[40] This interpretation is not substantiated by the evidence. For instance, the autarky policy of Mao, which was put in place and sustained by a propaganda campaign and which warned against an imminent military invasion of China, opposed the policy of Liu Shaoqi's faction. The latter sought to diversify China's trading partners, focusing on Japan. At the end of the 1970s, the commercial autarky policies of Hua Guofeng's faction, by provoking a reduction of China's access to foreign currency, would have slowed down the modernisation of the Chinese army if the policy had been completed.[41] Deng Xiaoping's faction, opposing Hua Guofeng's, had as one of its main objectives the opening of China to the world, which effectively accelerated army modernisation. This opening was a prerequisite for the increased multilateralism of Chinese foreign policy beginning in 1986. In fact, the debate concerning the importance of the army over the economy – or the opposite debate – has reappeared periodically over the last fifty years.[42]

Chinese behaviour in the ISIs in the 1990s also varied in accordance with which faction was in power.[43] Two main types of security policies must be distinguished, since they correspond to the dominant factions of two periods: Deng Xiaoping's reformists (1992–95) and the orthodox coalition established around Jiang Zemin (1996–2002). Deng Xiaoping's faction differed from that of Jiang Zemin in many ways: it was, among other things, not very authoritative ideologically, but it was respected by the military. Jiang Zemin's faction, on the contrary, placed great importance on ideology but commanded little respect from the army when it came to power (unlike Mao and Deng, Jiang was not a veteran military hero). The impact of ideology under Jiang Zemin manifested itself, among other things, in a resurgence of nationalist sentiment. Also, the Chinese president's need for support from the army caused it to increasingly intrude in the economy and in China's foreign policy.[44] While under Deng Xiaoping the importance of economic development over the army had been clearly established, this hierarchical structure started to reverse itself as early as the fall of 1995.[45]

Post-Tiananmen China, although dominated for a short period by a conservative faction (1989–1991), followed with some initial hesitation the security policy of the 1980s, but with some rearrangement. During these years, China's leaders worried that their country would take the place of the USSR as the main enemy of the United States, a role that would have considerably isolated it from other countries.[46] Chinese diplomats therefore actively worked to dissipate the worries caused by the strengthening of China's military capacity, and they showed an increasing desire to cooperate with the international community, more particularly in Asia.[47] A substitution of China for the USSR not only could have slowed down the economic growth of the country but also would have considerably complicated the modernisation process of the army. However, the official military doctrine did not change during this period and Peking still gave the army the role of economic reconstruction and of defence of the country against a massive invasion.

Jiang Zemin's orthodox faction came to power around 1995 and made changes in Chinese security policy, which became much more aggressive: there was missile testing close to Taiwanese waters, and a strategic cooperation treaty with Russia was announced in 1996. The army's military doctrine also changed. Instead of preparing itself for economic reconstruction in times of peace or for defending the country against a massive invasion, tasks that were the main fundamental orientations of the army under Deng, it prepared itself to face local wars in an advanced technological military environment.[48] Finally, the Chinese position towards the United States hardened and American policies were more vigorously denounced.[49]

There were both internal and external reasons for these changes. Jiang Zemin, who is not a career military man, did not have as strong a grip on the army as Mao Zedong or Deng Xiaoping had. Jiang was much criticized by the army on many occasions in 1995 for having lacked firmness towards Taiwan in different areas,[50] but generally speaking, his faction's alliance with the military remains essential if it is to stay in power.[51] However, the military often had firmer positions concerning China's security policy than did the Ministry of Foreign Affairs.[52] The American-Japanese rapprochement in 1996 and the election of a proindependence party in Taiwan reinforced the Chinese leaders' hard line.

Following the recent classification by Michael Pillsbury, in *China Debates the Future Security Environment*, reformists think that the United States will remain for the next three decades the only world superpower, which will allow them to maintain their main alliances, namely, with Germany and Japan, as well as to decide on their key orientation in any region of the world, consequently reducing the possibility of great local wars. Furthermore, China possibly does not possess the necessary qualifications to become a rival international centre of power in the near future, nor do any of the third world nations. The orthodox believe, on the contrary, that the United States' decline is rapid and that this decline is already affecting the intervention capabilities of Washington, which not only implies increasing friction between the United States and its allies but also increases the risk of local wars. For the reformists, China must be allied with various countries to counterbalance the United States' power, while awaiting its decline; for the orthodox, Washington will attempt by any means at its disposal to preserve its international leadership, and China, whose relative power is increasing, could attract attention and fall victim to desperate actions from the United States. In this context, China must hide its power to delay as long as possible any potential confrontation with the United States.

Pillsbury observes, as well, that Marxism remains the fundamental theory that pervades all research in China. Following this Marxist logic, China competes for diverse resources, namely, energy resources and new technologies. One of the objectives of Chinese political security thus consists of, classically, ensuring access to these resources. On the other hand, following Marxist-Leninist logic, multilateralism is a tactical weapon destined either (following reformist precepts) to give China access to resources vital to its economy or (following orthodox precepts) to weaken the United States alliance network.

The way researchers envision China's participation in the ISIS should consequently vary from school to school, and the viewpoints of each should appear in the official position of China's government, depending on whether the reformists or the orthodox dominate the party. As indicated above, the reformist school of thought is close to balance-of-threat theories, and the orthodox school is close to power-maximisation theories.

FOR A REALIST AND STRUCTURAL-REALIST APPROACH TO INSTITUTIONAL SECURITY POLICY IN CHINA

The validity of realist and structural-realist theories was strongly criticised following the end of the Cold War.[53] More recently, on the opposite side of the debate, many critics, seeing the absence of solidarity between Asian countries during the Asian crisis, have considerably weakened the credibility of the constructivist and institutionalist approaches.[54] An examination of China's policies regarding the Security Council reform, the NTBT, and the Spratly Islands dispute, supports this observation. As we shall see, not only does the institutional security policy of China not correspond to the expectations derived from these approaches, but the observations on which these theories rest contradict the evolution of China's policy during the 1990s. While it would have been expected within the context of constructivist theories that China's public opinion would be more and more influential, it appears, on the contrary, that since the events in Tiananmen Square in 1989, the Chinese government has refined its propaganda system, which has occupied an increasingly important place.[55] In addition, the Chinese government warns that its reinforcement of the role of ideology will be directly proportional to the deepening of reform, to the opening and development of markets.[56]

Contrary to what the institutional neoliberal theorists believe, the decentralisation process in China seems to have stopped and reversed itself around 1993, which diminished the possibility of finding any complex interdependence in China's foreign policy.[57] Far from favouring the country's decentralisation, as predicted by the institutional neoliberals, the multiplication of economic, cultural, and political exchanges has been accompanied by a hardening of the Chinese regime and by greater centralisation.[58] Fundamentally, neoliberal institutional theories assume implicitly that the Chinese market is similar to the market in capitalist countries. Even if China has not largely planned its economy, the fact remains that it is still shaped by the presence of the Chinese Communist Party, which plays a part in most of the decision making processes of the country. Furthermore, the traditional and very particular nature of the relations between individuals falsifies the usual logic of supply and demand and favours instead the development and maintenance of a network of alliances between individuals. In this sense, it would be tempting to assume that the security field has always escaped the logic of neoliberal institutionalism and to go further and assume that economic exchanges with foreign entities also fall outside neoliberal institutionalist theories. The economic changes of the 1990s in China were not sufficient to lead to a profound modification of the Chinese economic system. It is not proven yet that China's adherence to the WTO is significantly weakening CCP control over the economy.

In the final analysis, it appears that constructivist and neoliberal approaches do not take into account the immense pressures caused by the changes imposed on the CCP and Chinese society. These changes force a rethinking of the status of the domination of the CCP over Chinese society, since they threaten its very existence. It must thus be expected that the party will fight against these changes, rather than embrace their philosophy. We cannot exclude the possibility that some day these changes will eliminate the party altogether, but Communist leaders will do everything in their power to avoid such an event.

Constructivist and neoliberal institutionalist theories do not currently seem to apply to China's security policy; it corresponds better with realist and structural-realist approaches. The institutional political security of China led by Deng's faction during the first part of the 1990s corresponds fairly well to the predictions of the balance-of-threat theory. As mentioned earlier, during those years Chinese diplomacy was constantly concerned with preventing a rupture of this balance that might work to China's disadvantage. During the subsequent period, led by Jiang Zemin's orthodox factions, China followed an institutional security policy closer to the power-maximisation theory, with a few variations; in particular, it practised power dissimulation.

Important differences distinguish the two approaches, even if it is possible to find similarities between them. The United States constitutes a threat as much for proponents of the balance-of-threat theory as for those of the power-maximisation theory. For the first school, the threat that the United States represents is real, because its power corresponds to the super power status they are seeking. The threat is thus minimal in the sense that there is only a small chance that the United States would use its power openly and specifically against China, but there is a threat nevertheless. It is the threat of what Chinese leaders call "the pacific evolution," meaning a slow overturning of the Communist regime and its alignment with the United States. China can thus allow itself some leeway for a certain level of confrontation with the United States in the ISIs without having to fear its potentially harsh reaction.

For the second school, on the other hand, this threat is illusory, because the United States' power is declining. Washington would thus attempt desperate actions to maintain this illusion. The threat would thus be weak in the sense that increasingly limited means of intervention would be at Washington's disposal, implying a probable pending conflict. Part of China's strategy consists of pushing back this confrontation for as long as possible, which could lead Beijing to some sort of compromise with the United States in the ISIs.

During the Deng and the Jiang periods, China sought to increase its military power but also to hide it, in order to diminish the dissuasive capacity of the country. Hiding this power is less important for balance-of-threat diplomacy than for power-maximisation diplomacy, in which China can hope to increase its regional power through dissuasion, without stirring much insecurity in the United States. It can thus openly request more benefits for its participation in ISIS. On the opposite side, the orthodox faction does not want to seem able to take advantage of too many benefits from its participation in ISIS and must increase its power by other means.

The alliance game differs from one theory to the other. While from a balance-of-threat perspective China cannot hope that the allies of the United States will turn against it, in a power-maximisation situation it can, on the contrary, attempt to speed up the disintegration process of the U.S. network and create new alliances. In the first case, ISI multi-lateralism provides a way for China to fight against the U.S. threat by forming an opposing force along with other countries, including countries that are its allies. By assuming that the common threat of a relative increase in the power of the United States would displease other countries, China can appear to play by the rules of the international game and help to counterbalance Washington's power. In the second case, multilateralism must, more than ever, be used to promote China's good behaviour and to entertain the illusion that Peking's interests are close to those of the United States. In reality, this multilateralism is aimed at exacerbating conflict between the United States and its allies, which could provoke realignment in favour of China.

Whether it follows balance-of-threat or power-maximisation diplomacy, Peking uses three main tactics to sustain its policies within the ISIS. They can be summarised as follows:

1 Pursuing a reassurance tactic. China, fully aware of its increasing-power within the international system, would demonstrate to other states that this increase is marginal and should not be interpreted as a threat. Following this approach, Beijing made efforts to inform other countries of its peaceful intentions. This tactic gives China many advantages. Its perceived weakness reassures its neighbours, reaffirms its relation with the United States, and allows

Peking to pursue military development without attracting too much attention.

2 Creating an image of good behaviour. In other words, China seeks to demonstrate that it is interested in its socialisation within the institutional security networks, either to extinguish fears that other states could entertain against it or to become an "unavoidable player," that is, a player everyone has to deal with. This image of good behaviour that China wishes to project stems essentially from the country's insistence on respecting international laws, as long as these laws conform to the five principles of peaceful coexistence – mutual respect for sovereignty and territorial integrity, mutual nonaggression, noninterference in each other's internal affairs, equality and mutual benefit, and peaceful coexistence. This tactic is linked to the perception that other international actors have of China. The image of a China that respects and defends a certain number of international norms reassures the different Chinese interlocutors and helps to convince them that Peking will respect its commitments and will follow the path of institutional conflict resolution. This respect for norms allows China to increase its authority within the ISIs since it tends to depict the Chinese government as a moral authority beyond suspicion.

3 Stopping the emergence of institutions in which China cannot exercise some control. The goal here is to ensure that China will not be forced to make concessions that it is not willing to make, while minimising contradictions between its discourse and its actions and avoiding rules that risk diluting its power by forcing it to share it. This tactic would help China to preserve a dominating position, even if in some cases this domination is shared with a few other countries.

The change in China's strategy and the use it makes of the three tactics can be observed in its behaviour within the ISIs discussed so far.

Security Council Reform

China made an initial, timid commitment to Security Council reform in 1992 and offered to base reform on four principles: state sovereignty, peaceful international conflict resolution, the economic development of all countries, and the establishment of a new world order that would go beyond the exclusive interests of rich and powerful countries.[59] The first two principles presuppose that China has committed itself to restrict the use of force in the case of international conflict, since it would agree to act in accordance with principles established by international law. The third and fourth principles seem to say that China will accept neither an American nor a Western hegemony, which would be to its disadvantage. This position indicates a certain concern for the preservation of developing countries. Beijing demonstrated a real intention to cooperate in the reform project, but it also defined its limits. China's strategy reflected an alliance flexibility against domination by one or many countries, which corresponds to Walt's balance-of-threat approach, even though Beijing did not limit hegemonic power to the United States exclusively. At the time, China's apprehensions were not simply of a military nature: references to domination by rich countries were based from the beginning of the commitment to reform on Beijing's fear of not fully benefiting from the economic advantages related to UN institutions.

China's position changed only in 1997, when the Chinese authorities warned that conditions were not yet quite ripe for reform.[60] At that point Beijing began to defend the status quo, which meant that China chose not to modify the equilibrium of power on the Security Council. China was able to adopt positions that were aligned with those of the United States, while exacerbating tensions between Washington and its allies. This behaviour, which is in line with the power maximisation theory, seems to have been initially designed to alleviate the United States' fears about China. China's position evolved from that point in two directions that, although seemingly on opposite sides of the spectrum, are really complements. On the one hand, Chinese diplomats insisted more heavily on the disequilibrium of the representation of third world countries on the Security Council. The United Nations could not play an effective role without the fair representation of these countries.[61] On the other hand, the Chinese representatives underlined the specific historical responsibilities of the five permanent members. Tight cooperation and coordination of actions between the five permanent members are essential factors, among others, for the sustainability of the Council's authority and for strengthening the role of the United Nations.[62]

Either way, according to Chinese diplomats, there is no need to rush. The reforms should be discussed at length by all members of the United Nations, and they must correspond to the fundamental interest of all countries, not only to those of a minority.[63] Furthermore, the reforms should not deepen the differences between countries or aggravate conflicts.[64] The Chinese government seems to want to get the best of both worlds. It reaffirmed its alliances with countries under development and also reassured the other five permanent members of its real intentions by reaffirming its solidarity towards them and the particular and prestigious role they play on the Council.

The change in the Chinese strategy was gradually revealed in speeches concerning some of the main elements of reform. The first element is the veto power. Initially, the Chinese diplomats did not formally object to the "two plus three" formula (Germany and Japan plus three developing countries, with a veto right for each of them), but they remained very vague concerning the exact methods that would determine which third world countries would be used. China does not have a clear position on an eventual country rotation or even on the number of members to be added.[65] This vagueness has allowed for great flexibility when playing the alliance game by giving the impression that an alliance will eventually arise between China and other rising powers against the United States. In addition, it has fostered the image of good behaviour that China wanted to project. China justifies all of its important interventions on the Security Council by invoking the conformity of its actions to the UN Charter.

In 1997, however, Beijing put forth a new principle to justify its positions: the regional-equilibrium principle.[66] According to this principle, China claims that developed countries are disproportionately represented on the Security Council. But what is more interesting for China, is that this equilibrium principle implies that it will continue to be the sole representative of the Asian region. This claim implies that Japan and Germany would no longer qualify to enter the Security Council either from an economic or from a regional point of view.[67] Beijing's and Tokyo's positions are so irreconcilable that, by common agreement, on Zhu Rongji's visit to Japan in October 2000 he and the Japanese prime minister chose not to tackle the question of Security Council reform.[68] As for problems with India, nuclear testing by that country led Chinese leaders to say that it is not appropriate at this time to discuss the admission of India to the Security Council as a new permanent member.[69] Since then, in spite of an initial attempt to engage in a dialogue on the issue, both countries have remained firm in their respective positions.[70]

China is thus preventing the entry of new permanent members to the Security Council. As the power-maximisation theory predicts, China is attempting to modify existing alliances, particularly with developing countries for which China demonstrates particular concern. It must be noted that the promotion of the status quo, even if it is done in the name of conditions that are not yet quite properly defined really reasserts China's power as a permanent member. More subtly, the inability of Germany and Japan to become permanent members of the Security Council can create tensions between the United States and its two allies, which implies for orthodox China an acceleration of the decline of the United States. Similarly, alliances against the interests of the United States that China creates with developing countries can be perceived as less threatening than those that China could attempt to make with more powerful countries.

The second reform issue that China recognises is that of peacekeeping activities. On this issue China's policy also demonstrated a reorientation that was in line with the power-maximisation theory. In the early 1990s China wanted a smaller number of peacekeeping missions so that greater sums of money could be invested in development efforts: this approach corresponded to expectations of the balance-of-threat theory. China justified its position by arguing that, when they involved the use of force, peacekeeping missions were contradictory, useless, and harmful.[71]

In 1997, Beijing's position changed completely. China then used its reassurance tactic to announce that it would now participate actively in peacekeeping missions in the hopes of creating a more stable international environment and a fair and reasonable political order.[72] With this tactic which could only reassure, China seemed to be better able to meet its responsibility regarding peace and world security. Furthermore, the interests of China have become "identical or similar" to the United States' in many different areas, and consequently, Beijing said it would be willing to increase its cooperation with Washington at the UN, especially on the issue of Security Council reform.[73] Even after the Chinese embassy bombing by the Americans in Belgrade, Beijing's position remained almost the same. According to Jiang Zemin, peacekeeping missions contributed to peace around the world. These missions did not, however, offer a panacea and must not be used, under the pretence of humanitarian intervention, as a mean of intervening in the internal affairs of other countries.[74]

Once again, China seems to prefer a reassurance tactic towards the United States. Agreement between China and the United States has certainly not been concluded, because of tensions between the two countries generated by the American bombing of the Chinese embassy in Belgrade and by the election in Taiwan of a proindependence government, among other factors. But the issues have been left open to discussion. While the events of September 11 2001 may have encouraged the exchange of information between Beijing and Washington, they do not seem to have provoked a reopening of the Security Council negotiations. From the perspective of power-maximisation theory, these two events have provided great pretexts for slowing down cooperation, for which China seems to have no real interest anyway, since cooperation could slow the decline of the United States.

The third issue is the question of United Nations financing, which irritates China because it perceives a desire on the part of Western countries, and in particular the United States, to divert the organisation from its development mission to benefit organisations better controlled by these countries.[75] As mentioned above, China's position, which is consistent with its tactic of slowing down the emergence of institutions where it cannot ensure a certain domination, has not changed on this issue since 1992. China's position on this aspect of reform conforms to balance-of-threat theory and to power-maximisation theory, but for different reasons. China, according to the first theory, must fear a strengthening of American and Western power within these organisations and consequently must seek to shape a common opposition front along with other poorer countries such as the Group of 77. Following the second theory, it has nothing to gain from organisations led by the United States and so can afford to denounce their functioning, as long as they do not make the great powers too uncomfortable.

The Nuclear Test Ban Treaty

The case of the NTBT is somewhat simpler than that of the Security Council reforms. In the name of the preservation of the interest of non-nuclear countries, China has refused for more than two decades to sign the agreement on nonproliferation of nuclear weapons, because of insufficient reductions in the arsenal of the USSR and the United States.[76] It was only in August 1991, on a Japanese tour, that Prime Minister Li Peng announced that his country would sign the nuclear nonproliferation treaty, which it did in March 1992. The signing of the treaty not only marks a reversal in the Chinese nuclear strategy but also implies a new step in the use of the balance-of-threat theory for security policy. Indeed, Beijing agreed to negotiate its nuclear-power capacity by entering in multilateral alliance games with other nuclear powers.

China came to the NTBT negotiating table in the winter of 1994 by declaring that a treaty should certainly be associated with complete nuclear disarmament.[77] This behaviour was in conformity with its reassurance tactic. China committed itself from the start to the NTBT by pretending to continue to defend the interests of small and middle powers, as long as certain conditions were respected, and by underlining the weakness of its own nuclear arsenal. The Chinese negotiators quickly focused on two main points. The first stated that the nuclear testing ban would be acceptable to China only if nuclear powers gave up their fighting power. China made sure to remind everyone that the signing of the treaty should not prevent the sale of conventional weapons, which would infringe on the sovereignty and integrity of individual states.[78] In this way, Beijing was reassuring the other states by demonstrating its will to refrain from using its military strength as a first recourse, but it was also emphasizing the limits of such a treaty. However, China proposed a certain number of restrictions on the treaty and in particular a clause which would allow for nuclear explosions for civilian reasons.[79] This proposal could have justified China's refusal, along with a few other countries, to adhere to the treaty, but it turned out to be an excellent negotiating tool for Peking. It allowed China to enter into the NTBT discussions by pretending to represent the interests of the small powers against the large ones, which constituted a variation in the Chinese balance-of-threat theory, since Beijing was demonstrating its intentions of allying itself to countries that would oppose the threat emanating from the four other declared nuclear powers, and not only from the United States.

China's position softened during the course of the negotiations. In May 1996, in the name of world peace, security, and the progress that had been made in the destruction of nuclear arsenals, China abandoned its request for nuclear explosions to be permitted for civilian reasons.[80] Then, in the months that followed the signing of the NTBT, China actively defended the measures imposed by the treaty. China seemed once again to be using its good-behaviour tactic, to be projecting an image of good behaviour. In reality, Beijing had abandoned its alliance game with small and middle powers, which opposed the treaty, in order to create an alliance with the declared nuclear powers.

Why did China's policy change from reserved to cooperative? Like the United States, which imposed a moratorium on nuclear testing because it had developed a system of computer simulation (along with France, which also developed such a technique, in January 1996) China does finally possess its own simulation software. It is even possible that the United States supplied it to China.[81] The change in China's policy started to appear in the NTBT in the spring of 1996, when China started renouncing the prerequisites it had imposed for signing the treaty. It was then that it became clear that it would have access to the simulation software for nuclear testing. The software would reaffirm its nuclear strength vis-à-vis the vast majority of countries that would not have access to this technology. China also made a few other concessions, but they pale in comparison to the gains it received: it agreed to authorise cross-border surveillance flights, but the Surveillance Commission established by the treaty[82] and the signature of the treaty was linked to a total disarmament schedule.[83] For China, the heart of the negotiations surrounding the NTBT would now be attached to the possibility of developing third-generation weapons and to its preoccupation with diminishing the risk of nuclear proliferation, especially by neighbouring states.[84]

The American Senate's refusal in 1999 to ratify the treaty, the events of September 11, 2001, and the ease with which the Bush administration is able to control American public opinion – particularly in regard to the ABM treaty and the reinforcement of the American nuclear arsenal – provide a sombre prognosis for the future of the treaty. The Senate's refusal to ratify has led China to denounce the "hegemonistic and selfish" policies of the United States.[85] According to Peking, the real United States policy is to contain China and Russia: Washington's condemnations of "rogue states" serves only to hide the real intentions of the White House. China, however, has maintained its support for the NTBT. The construction of a new international security environment based on cooperation concerning control could prevent another nuclear arms race.[86] Nevertheless, China has yet to ratify the treaty. Since February 2001 it has entered into negotiations with India for a normalisation of security relations outside the context of the NTBT.[87] India's nuclear arsenal would make it the sixth nuclear power in the world, and the Indian arsenal could reach any Chinese city.[88]

China has consequently switched from a balance-of-threat policy to a power-maximisation policy. The NTBT ensures that China can possess a nuclear arsenal that will be able to follow the technological progress of other nuclear powers, especially Russia and the United States. Better yet, China will now belong to the very select club of declared nuclear powers that will exercise surveillance over other countries and will lower the relative power of states sharing a common border – with the exception of Russia – by making it more difficult for them to gain access tosecond- and third-generation nuclear weapons. However, the failure of the United States to ratify the treaty puts this advantage in peril. If the treaty does not take effect, China will need to turn again to mechanisms of bilateral negotiation or even to take part in a costly nuclear arms race. Thus, in practice China would lose its advantage of having the initiative, and the faction in power, whichever one it might be, would need to return to a policy of power maximisation.

In terms of nuclear security, China seems to place only limited importance on multilateralism, which is consistent with the suspicions of the orthodox faction regarding the actual success rate of the NTBT. Accordinging to this analysis, the United States will not be able to contain nuclear arms development for much longer, and other nuclear powers remain too weak to assume such a role. India's refusal to adhere to the treaty under Washington's conditions proves this. Despite all appearances, nuclear cooperation between China and Pakistan constitutes for Peking a way to counterbalance India and can serve as a means of security negotiation between Beijing and New Delhi.

However, the situation could change. The rapprochement between Russia and the United States since the Shanghai Summit of the fall of

2001, apparently to ensure Russia's entrance into NATO, poses a new problem for Chinese leaders. Indeed, the new alliance between Washington and Moscow can only reinforce China's strategy of power maximisation. In the end, China's insistence on upholding the principles of the NTBT can be explained by its high level of control in the organisation of the treaty, by the costs of relaunching the nuclear arms race, and by the short-term reduction of the relative power of China in the event that the United States and other Asian countries fail to ratify the treaty.

The Spratly Islands

The case of the Spratly Islands provides an example of China's refusal to engage in a process of security institutionalisation, even in the presence of international pressures. Again, the Chinese policy goes from a balance-of-threat approach to a power-maximisation approach.

China legitimises its position within international law, which constitutes for China one of the main ways to project a good-behaviour image. From a juristic point of view, the occupation of the Spratly Islands by various countries is justified by the absence of treaties on their ownership.[89] China has adhered to approximately thirty treaties elaborated by the International Naval Organisation and has ratified the United Nations Law of the Sea Convention.[90] Peking has always maintained that the Spratly archipelago was in its territorial waters, which does not prevent it from offering the other countries having a claim on the area the opportunity to jointly exploit the resources.

In the early 1990s, China's position on the Spratlys conformed to ASEAN's position. In 1990 the members of the organisation called for a military de-escalation in the region to strengthen the trust relationship between countries there, and they voiced their hopes that China, the United States, and Japan would become a part of the discussions.[91] The following year, ASEAN countries called for a peaceful resolution of the conflicts, an institutional meeting process, and an informal exploration of the possibilities of cooperation in the fishing, navigation, nonrenewable resources, harvesting, and environmental domains.[92] In 1992 three cooperation mechanisms were suggested: the first one, based on the Law of the Sea Convention, dealt with questions relating to environmental protection, scientific research, nonrenewal resources, and ties with international organisations or states interested in further cooperation.[93] The second encouraged solidarity between ASEAN countries. The goal of the third mechanism was, through discussion forums, to find new solutions to help in the institutionalisation process.[94]

In 1995, China proposed six conditions to guide ASEAN discussions:

1 China would have incontestable sovereignty over the Spratly Islands and surrounding islands; 2 the Chinese government was prepared to resolve the conflict in a peaceful way in accordance with international law; 3 territorial disputes must be set aside to allow cooperation; 4 discussions must be bilateral, not multilateral; 5 free circulation in the seaways must be preserved; and 6 the United States must be kept away from the conflict.[95] In appearance, the discussion forums went so well that at the end of 1997, Jiang Zemin himself was participating and calling for a better use of mechanisms of cooperation and dialogue between China and other ASEAN countries. Three years later, the situation seemed to be stalled in a dead end.[96]

China takes part in three ASEAN cooperation mechanisms, but its military actions intimate that this cooperation might stop, particularly cooperation in the informal working group on the South China Sea issue, even though China's adherence to the Law of the Sea Convention and its regard for international law provide some reassurance.[97] Actually, China has agreed to discuss all questions related to cooperation within these groups, with the exception of those relating specifically to security in the South China Sea.[98] It is likely that Peking will let it be known that it might leave the cooperation mechanisms on the South China Sea issue if security issues are brought up, effectively removing the temptation of some countries to broach the topic.

China, which clearly uses the Spratly Islands case as a slow-down strategy, as well as to project a good behaviour image, has more and more trouble convincing its neighbours of its will to use nonmilitary means to resolve the conflict. China's reassurance tactics have some limits. Certainly China has offered to develop the Spratlys in cooperation with other countries.[99] In March 1999, Chinese diplomats refused a proposal from Viet-Nam and the Philippines that sought to establish a code of conduct for the countries in the region, a code that would cover the Spratlys, as well as other naval territories, including Japan, the United States, and both Koreas. These proposals included the removal of some Chinese infrastructures from some reefs and the joint use of the other infrastructures, as well as a Chinese guarantee that it would not build new infrastructures on the territories claimed by the Philippines. In response to this proposal, China required the Philippines to stop arresting Chinese fisherman, to cease the intrusion of Philippine ships into the contested waters, and to put an end to unfriendly remarks on the issue.[100]

However, China's actions in the region have caused concern more than they have reassured, and Chinese government discourse on the problem is ambiguous.[101] Beijing rejected the proposal of Viet Nam and the Philippines in the winter of 2000, and earlier, a Chinese national defence proposal in 1998 made no mention of the naval border problem.[102] Since the end of 1994, China has pursued an increasingly aggressive occupation policy in the Spratlys. In April of 2000, Peking even announced that it had reinforced its military strength on the islands, presupposing that the Chinese army would want to defend its territory.[103] However, the Chinese government claims that it will not let the Spratlys Islands conflict affect its bilateral relations with the other countries involved.[104]

In the Spratlys China applies a balance-of-threat strategy that is changing more and more into a power-maximisation strategy. This can be explained by the country's limited means of military intervention and by the perception the Chinese population has of the Spratlys. The Chinese means to intervene are very limited compared to those of bordering countries, in particular Singapore and Malaysia, and it seems that in general Peking simply does not possess military means that are appropriate to its territorial sea claims.[105] In China, defence of the Spratlys Islands provides one of the arguments of elements in the army for the purchase of an aircraft carrier. In the case of the Spratlys, the balance-of-threat strategy seems to be a back-up plan, while the country waits to acquire the means to fully apply a strategy of power maximisation.

On the other hand, there is very probably very little difference between the reformist and the orthodox faction on the question of the islands, both factions considering that they are part of the national territory. In the framework of a policy of balance of threat, it is plausible that the reformists had less to fear than the orthodox faction from a reaction of the United States following military actions in the Spratlys (which explains Chinese aggression under Deng Xiaoping). On the contrary, the orthodox faction has every reason to demonstrate its good intentions, to dissimulate as much as possible the Chinese military build-up in the southern seas and to explain Jiang Zemin's desire to cooperate.[106] However, in the case of the Spratlys, as in the two other cases discussed here, China was pushed to reaffirm its power-maximisation policy. Indeed, the tightening of the security relationship between Japan and the United States and the uncertainty that both countries portray regarding the inclusion or noninclusion of the South Sea territories force China to further develop its naval power. Only such a military build-up can allow China to hope to increase its influence over these territories.

CONCLUSION

With the end of the Cold War, the departure of the conservatives at the end of 1991, and the return to a policy of reforms and openness, China has renewed its balance-of-threat policy. Following this logic, it is advantageous to maintain the existing Security Council equilibrium, as well as the curent equilibrium between the declared nuclear powers. Indeed, Beijing could not, in one case or the other, modify this advantage, but in the case of the NTBT it could have lost its status if it had been unable to properly refine its simulation software or if it had taken the place of the USSR as the United States' main enemy. The relative multilateral opening that Beijing pretends to have regarding the Spratlys can be seen as an attempt to maintain the balance of threat in the region, since China does not yet possess a strong enough military capacity to really impose its presence on the territory. This power-of-threat diplomacy faded after 1995, but it did not disappear completely. For instance, it is in the name of the balance of threat against India that China will justify its feeble condemnation of Pakistan's nuclear testing.

The other tendency, the power reinforcement of the country, marks the Jiang Zemin era, with an accent on the reinforcement of its dissuasive capacity as of 1996. In accordance with the theory of the imminent desegregation of American alliances, China multiplied its military coalitions[107] and took the opportunity given by Russia's need for currency to purchase weapons at low cost.[108] Similarly, China reaffirmed it policy in the Spratlys to the point where it now gives the impression that in the coming years it will occupy them militarily, yet it continued to reassure its neighbours of its intentions.[109] Beijing's position regarding the Security Council reforms gave the impression that China accepted more easily that five countries dominate it. All of this happened as if China progressively accepted its rival-power status with the United States in Asia, while it hesitated to manifest its power in the rest of the world.

While there is no existing ISI in Southeast Asia, it is stunning to consider the extent to which China has adopted a defiant attitude towards the powers in the region and towards the United States in regard to the Spratlys. China's attitude is much more nuanced on Security Council reform and the NTBT, even though in Security Council votes, China abstains more and more and increasingly uses its veto power, even if its condemnation of India was very harsh following India's nuclear tests in 1999.

In sum, before 1995, as issues became increasingly international, the institutional security policy of China increasingly corresponded to the balance-of-threat approach. After 1995, as the issues at stake become increasingly regional, this security policy increasingly shifted toward a power-maximisation approach.

Looking for New Voice Opportunities: Canada and International Security Institutions after the Cold War

LOUIS BÉLANGER AND NELSON MICHAUD

While the preceding chapters have analyzed the institutional strategies of major powers in the area of international security, this chapter examines a middle power: Canada. Why should we be interested in middle powers? Is it because they exercise a real influence on institutionalized forms of collective security? According to some authors, this influence not only exists but sometimes proves to be important.[1] But beyond the question of influence, middle powers deserve attention in the context of this book for one very simple reason: they allow us to say something about the impact of power, or the lack thereof, on the institutional choices of states, which is difficult to do when major powers are compared exclusively to each other.

Generally speaking, those who have examined this question have viewed the "lack of power" of middle powers as the reason behind the institutional activism practised by many of these states. In fact, a number of studies tend to confirm the hypothesis that middle powers, such as Canada, have a particular predilection for institutional forms of international cooperation.[2] Thus, for example, Alan Henrikson has observed that the "affinity of middle powers for institutional roles and responsibilities is now fairly well established."[3] This affinity could be explained in terms of the search by weaker states for protection through a well-established collective security system. According to Carsten Holbraad, this is the argument that Canadians would have made to describe their own foreign policy following the Second World War. Holbraad quotes the explanation given at the time by a senior civil servant:

Their [the middle powers'] relatively large size, coveted resources and strategic importance, he explained, endangered their security without giving them the means to defend themselves single-handed. The best arrangement for their protection was a successful international organisation. Since they had more to gain from such an organisation than the great powers, who in the last resort could do without it, and the small powers, whose independence always was more precarious, they could be relied on, he concluded, to play a particularly large part in its work.[4]

However, without rejecting the purely security-related factor, most scholars explain the attitude of middle powers in terms of the benefits that they stand to gain from an international environment that is highly institutionalized in terms of power relationships. As Henrikson put it, "middle powers often rely for influence on their roles in international institutions. Membership, participation, and leadership within international organisations can provide the bargaining power which they themselves lack." From Robert Keohane's 1969 definition (i.e., "a middle-power is a state whose leaders consider that it cannot act alone effectively, but may be able to have a systemic impact in a small group or through an international institution") to Cooper, Higgott, and Nossal's use of the notion of nonstructural forms of power and influence to describe the type of diplomatic leadership exercised by middle powers, the idea that middle powers are able to use the resources offered by a highly institutionalized international environment to their advantage has been widely accepted.[5]

But although everyone appears to see eye to eye on this matter and to understand intuitively why, generally speaking, middle powers opt for institutional solutions to international problems, we do not have a theory to explain why certain states with equivalent power conform to the model while others do not; nor do we understand why, in similar situations, middle powers deploy different institutional strategies. This is not really surprising, insofar as the problem of selecting an institutional design, that is, of choosing suboptions within the institutional option, has received little attention from international relations specialists, who in recent years have simply sought to understand why international institutions were created and why they survived. Yet not only must states, whether intermediate or not, make a choice between the use of an ad hoc or institutionalized process when faced with an international security problem; they must also decide whether their action requires adapting existing institutions or creating new ones and whether these institutions should be strong or weak and wide or narrow in scope.[6] Thus, as suggested by Wallander and Keohane, the level of institutionalization reached by security coalitions varies "from minimal to substantial," as measured by the degree of specificity of rules, of commonality among participants, and of differentiation of functions assigned to members.[7] In other words, for any one problem of cooperation, various institutional strategies and designs are available.

Yet, as Cooper demonstrates in his review of the post–Cold War foreign policy of middle powers, although these states remain faithful to their specific form of statecraft favouring collective, institutionalized action, there are clear differences in their preferred institutional strategies, both between states and even within the same state from one situation to the next.[8] Thus, Cooper shows that certain states, such as Canada, pursue strategies aimed at demanding strong, integrated institutions, whereas others, such as Australia, prefer a weaker, more detached form of institutionalization of international relations.[9] Of course, a middle power like Canada exerts only a very marginal degree of control over the general supply of institutional arrangements on the international scene, and this is probably especially true in the field of security. However, an intermediate power may be led to prefer one forum over another when a specific problem occurs, and it may, from that point on, express a preference, for example, for regional rather than multilateral management of a crisis. In particular, a middle power is often in a position to choose, within a given organizational structure, between different options that will influence the institutional trajectory of this organization.[10] Thus, an understanding of the factors that shape the institutional preferences of a middle power such as Canada may prove to be useful, not only in terms of understanding the strategic choices available to it but also, as will be seen below, because the actions of intermediate powers like Canada often have a determining influence on the institutional trajectory of an international regime or organization.

EXPLAINING THE INSTITUTIONAL STRATEGIES OF MIDDLE POWERS

Studies of middle powers often lack theoretical rigour. Indeed, Black describes the theoretical propositions regarding the role of middle powers in international affairs as "notoriously slippery and imprecise."[11] As Neack has pointed out, this fuzziness can be attributed, in part, to the fact that analysts often adopt a behaviouralist definition of middle powers, the result being that they limit their observations to middle powers that behave like good "middle powers," that is, those displaying a form of institutional leadership.[12] This leads to circular, tautological reasoning. Yet it seems to us that there is a "lowest common denominator" in all these studies, based on which a number of relatively simple, but illuminating, theoretical propositions can be formed. In fact, the current state of knowledge tends to explain the apparent attraction of middle powers to highly institutionalized solutions in terms of a certain number of factors that, a contrario, also provide an explanation of the situations in which middle powers may prefer arrangements that are ad hoc or characterized by a low level of institutionalization.

At the risk of oversimplifying, it can be said, in light of the analyses referred to above, that the preference of middle powers for highly institutionalized structures may be related to their attachment to valuing their participation in the interest-articulation mechanisms found in certain regimes, participation that is not directly linked to the immediate "tangible" or "material" benefits of institutional arrangements. The key idea here is that the issue for middle powers goes beyond the search for security and involves the capacity for action afforded them by a highly institutionalized international environment. This can be expressed in the vocabulary of international relations theory as follows: in addition to the net gains generated by their participation in institutionalized cooperative arrangements (substantive benefits), middle powers attach a greater value than other states to the voice articulation opportunities offered by these arrangements (voice benefits).

This distinction between two types of gains is clearly established by J.M. Grieco in his explanation of why France and Italy chose to advocate a complex institutional trajectory when the European Monetary Union was created, even though this choice clearly consolidated Germany's dominant and potentially hegemonic position. According to Grieco, France and Italy considered not only the material gains ("substantive results") of cooperation but also a second type of benefit that he describes as "the level of policy influence partners have or might attain in the collaborative arrangement."[13] In the case of the European Union, this effective voice benefit took the form of a decision-making method based on majority voting on the common monetary policy. These dynamics led Grieco to formulate the following hypothesis: if "states share a common interest and undertake negotiations on rules constituting a collaborative arrangement, then the weaker but still influential partners[14] will seek to ensure that the rules so constructed will provide sufficient opportunities for them to voice their concerns and interests and thereby prevent or at least ameliorate their domination by stronger partners."[15]

This distinction is important because it leads to the hypothesis that middle powers are not more interested than other states in institutionalization per se but in a specific form of institutionalization, one that provides for voice articulation mechanisms. But why, exactly, and in what circumstances will middle powers attach importance to this type of benefit? In this chapter, we offer five analytical propositions that address this issue.

First, let us consider Grieco's thesis. Drawing on Hirschman he suggests that the voice gains sought by second-rank powers in institutional arrangements compensate for a distribution of the substantive gains of cooperation judged to be advantageous for a more powerful partner.[16] Or, put another way, voice gains represent an alternative to defection (exit) when a state is faced with an agreement from which it expects to draw substantive absolute gains but from which it also expects to suffer a loss of substantive relative gains vis-à-vis a more powerful partner that is likely to take advantage of this situation to bolster its dominant position. According to structural-realist theory, middle powers, because they feel permanently insecure about their status, are more likely than others to be concerned about such a distribution of the substantive gains of cooperation.[17] It can therefore be said that they will more often be interested by voice gains. But they will not necessarily be always or absolutely interested. Their interest in this type of gain will vary according to the advantages to be derived from the institutional arrangement by a dominant power[18] or by same-rank powers with which the middle power is competing for the maintenance or improvement of its status.[19] In the former case there is vertical competition, while in the latter there is horizontal competition.[20]

Second, it should be noted that Hirschman's approach suggests that middle powers are likely to attach more importance to voice benefits than do major powers, not only to compensate for a disadvantageous distribution of the immediate substantive gains of negotiations, as anticipated by Grieco but also and more generally because it is more difficult for them to rely on the threat of withdrawal (exit) as an effective means of obtaining future adjustments to the institutional arrangements, should these arrangements prove to be disadvantageous. Voice can be seen as an alternative to exit, but it can also be seen as a residual to exit: "In this view, the role of voice would increase as the opportunities for exit decline."[21] Given that the supply of security on the international scene is, if not monopolistic, at least highly oligopolistic, a middle power like Canada is continuously confronted with the fact that it can rarely use withdrawal. Even when withdrawal is an option, the threat to defect does not in itself provide the bargaining power needed by a middle power to obtain change in the institutions to which it belongs. Because a middle power knows that, unlike a major power, it cannot rely on an exit strategy to press its point of view, it will normally seek to ensure that the interest-articulation mechanism is designed in a way that allows the institutions to be influenced from within. This is a refinement of the more general and widely held proposition that although middle powers rarely initiate institution building, they tend to influence the institutional trajectory of arrangements towards a stronger and broader institutionalization, simply because this is a more appropriate terrain for middle-power activity. Once again, this varies, since not all middle powers are equally or constantly confronted by the same lack of opportunity to exit. For example, we can imagine that some middle powers are more able than others to choose their allies.

Third, we need to consider the specific capacity of middle powers to assume the transaction costs linked to the establishment of institutionalization. The institutionalization of interest-articulation procedures within a regime (or other type or organizational arrangement) makes it cumbersome and unavoidably implies transaction and participation costs.[22] As Hirschman states, "voice is costly and conditioned on the influence and bargaining power customers and members can bring to bear within the firm from which they buy or the organizations to which they belong."[23] This may constrain the negotiation of highly institutionalized arrangements, but at the same time the question of costs may explain why middle powers, which have the means to take advantage of voice opportunities, differ from smaller powers. The latter would also benefit from promoting voice-opportunity mechanisms to protect themselves from the risk of the dominant state unduly profiting from its position in the coalition, but they do not have the resources to effectively use such mechanisms. Cooper, Higgott, and Nossal have put considerable emphasis on the fact that middle powers have tailored their diplomatic capacities so as to derive benefits from their participation in the institutionalized processes of consultation and bargaining, particularly in the case of cooperation on sectorial issues, which require a certain capacity to master a particular field of knowledge.[24] Even though it involves "non-structural forms of power and influence," this type of capacity is nevertheless limited.[25] It is therefore to the advantage of middle powers to promote functionalism and "niche diplomacy." "Functionalism," Cooper argues, "legitimized the application of issue-specific strengths and skills possessed by individual countries," and it allows certain middle powers to concentrate on fields of cooperation in which they have significant nonstructural leverage.[26] Thus, a middle power's interest in developing highly institutionalized solutions in a particular field of cooperation will depend on its abilities to exercise diplomatic and scientific leadership in that field. It may even be hypothesized that the costs associated with participation in voice articulation mechanisms may serve to create a barrier between middle powers and weaker states that do not have the capacity to support effective voice politics.

This brings us to our fourth proposition. Rather than being absolute, the value of voice benefits is necessarily relative. In other words, intermediate powers are interested in voice-articulation mechanisms because they hope to mobilize more than their share of voice in the process. The raison d'être of these mechanisms is, after all, to provide voices in a way that does not simply reflect the distribution of power. Moreover, it should be noted immediately that, in a variety of ways, the voice-articulation mechanisms within international institutions effectively weight voices. The best example of this, which will be considered in more detail below, is that of the UN Security Council, whose operating rules hierarchize the voices of the states. From this it must be concluded that the logic structuring the institutional strategies of intermediate powers will be one of relative gain or of a zero-sum game and that what we have here is a problem of distributive bargaining. The reasoning in terms of relative gains, set out above in our discussion of substantive gains, therefore applies to voice-articulation gains. Once again, middle powers are in the special position described by Grieco: occupying an intermediate and ill-defined position between the great powers and small states, they are more concerned than other states about preserving or increasing their status through their participation in the life of institutions. Their commitment to substantial institutionalization and voice-articulation mechanisms, even if presumably and potentially greater than for small and major powers, is therefore not absolute. Instead, it will vary according to the expected distribution of voice benefits. Not only will an intermediate power generally seek a distribution of voice benefits that reduces the capacity of more powerful states to act unilaterally (vertical competition), it will also seek to maintain or improve its position among recognized or potential middle powers (horizontal competition).

In the following pages, in line with the agreed strategy of this book, we will explore the validity of these analytical propositions in the immediate post–Cold War context. The interest of intermediate states in strategies that promote the institutionalization of international relations, rather than ad hoc interventions, appears to have survived bipolarity.[27] However, the conditions in which intermediate powers seek to deploy these strategies have changed dramatically. According to some observers, such as Ravenhill[28] and Cooper,[29] the new international context leaves more room for the initiatives of intermediate powers, which should be able to take advantage of the lack of leadership on the part of the major powers. Others, such as David and Roussel, argue that the post–Cold War order is likely to considerably reduce the opportunities of countries like Canada to deploy their preferred strategy, and they predict nothing less than the disappearance of the functions traditionally attributed to middle powers, functions such as mediation.[30] Similar conclusions are reached by Laura Neack, who maintains that the unipolar system constructed after the Cold War, with the United States as the "hub" and some strategically selected regional powers as "spokes," leaves the traditionally allied middle powers like Canada and Australia hanging in the air.[31] This is clearly both an empirical and an analytical puzzle. The propositions that we introduced above prompt us to take a closer look at the consequences of international transformations for the position of intermediate powers and for the insecurity they feel in relation to their status within the international system; for the distribution of the voice benefits offered by existing or proposed institutional arrangements; and for the evolution of the costs of participating in institutions and the capacity of intermediate powers to assume these costs.

CASE STUDIES

Thus, the three cases we have selected for this study reflect priorities Canada set for its foreign policy agenda in the latter part of the twentieth century. It should first be noted that from the end of the Cold War until the Kosovo crisis, Canada's initiatives in foreign policy and its institutional behaviour have been made principally on the fringe of traditional questions of military security. Canada's increasing disengagement as a military power is therefore an important contextual element that must be taken into account. The disengagement that we witnessed until the Kosovo crisis was particularly evident in relation to NATO and the European military theatre after Canada gave up its defence of the northern front in 1987 and withdrew from Germany in the early 1990s. Whether for economic reasons linked to budget restraints or for purely logistical supply reasons – which had nevertheless first militated in favour of an increase in resources[32] – the promises of an involvement made in the late 1980s did not even survive until the early 1990s. Instead, the deep cuts that have taken place did and still do limit Canada's capacity to intervene in the more traditional defence institutions: not only is Canada's ability to intervene in a meaningful way restricted by lack of resources, but the majority of decisions related to this type of involvement are made in a framework of pure realpolitik, even though policymakers and politicians now like to sell the idea of wars fought on behalf of values, not to promote or defend interests. In a context such as this, in which striking-power essentially determines decision-making influence, Canada is relegated to the rank of a player with little influence: the Kosovo crisis and, perhaps more importantly, the "war against terrorism" provide eloquent examples.[33]

Canada therefore has had to redefine its intervention priorities, in

order to avoid a complete exclusion from the multilateral fora in which
it used to play a role, a role that was often described as more influential than would have been expected based on Canada's power alone.
Already, the factors we have identified can be seen at work: Canada
needs to find ways other than relying on military power alone to maintain its status in the forum of nations. Its diplomatic tradition and
network, its reputation as a noncolonial, selfless international partner,
are the values on which it can build its strategy in order to keep its
position. Moreover, based on the theoretical framework presented in
the first part of this chapter, we would expect Canada to give priority
to institutional trajectories that will favour a specific form of institutionalization, one that offers voice-articulation mechanisms through
which the state will be able to maintain, if not enhance, its stature and
influence.

The following three cases have been chosen since they reflect important Canadian foreign policy commitments of the period: the intervention in solving the Haitian crisis, the Personnel Landmines Ban Treaty,
and UN Security Council Reform. For each of these cases, which are
well documented elsewhere,[34] we will first present a brief overview of
the issues at stake and show what options were available, identifying
the one that, according to our theoretical framework, Canada would
be most likely to choose. We will then review the path chosen by
Canada, and, finally, offer an explanation for such a choice. The
general reading thus obtained will provide a picture that will allow us
to evaluate the potential of our analytical framework for contributing
to an understanding of Canada's and other middle powers' institutional behaviour in a world in upheaval.

The UN Security Council Reform: A Voice against Sidelining

As we mentioned in the first part of this chapter, the UN Security
Council is perhaps the forum par excellence in which the voices of
states are hierarchized. In fact, the power status of a country is often
perceived as being equivalent to its rank at the UN and, more specifically, within the UN Security Council. Because the General Assembly
"considers," "invites," and "takes notes," while the Security Council
"decides," "calls upon," or "directs," membership in the latter means
that a country has the opportunity to play a more influential role in the
debates on key security questions by voicing its options. Moreover, the
privileged few countries that enjoy the status of permanent member –
France, Great Britain, China, Russia, and the United States, or the Permanent 5 (P5) – are considered to be the only ones that have access to
the inner sanctum. With this status comes a veto power that basically

allows these countries to "run the show." The UN structure was built to respond to post–World War II needs, but over half a century later, the international situation has evolved dramatically, especially during the last decade. This raises many questions, such as, Why are Germany and Japan, the "defeated countries," still ostracized? What about the developing countries, such as Nigeria, an influential regional player on the African continent? What about the newcomers in the nuclear club, such as India and Pakistan? Or, from the Canadian point of view, what about the countries that regularly take on responsibilities and exercise an influence above and beyond what would be expected based on their intrinsic military power?

All these questions are at the centre of a lagging reform process. Other chapters in this book have referred to different aspects of the UN Security Council reform. The options being considered have been the subject of a number of studies.[35] Our purpose here is to look at the reform from the Canadian point of view. It is first necessary to consider the different options that are presently being discussed. However, instead of listing all of them,[36] we suggest that an analytical review of the possibilities would be more meaningful. For it is not the number of new members or their selection process that really matters here but the status of these new members, since it is this status that determines whether or not one's voice will be heard.

As of now, all of the options except Canada's aim at increasing the number of members around the Council's table without changing its structure. This would allow more countries to have input into the Council's deliberations, some from a permanent-status stance, others not. Ultimately, as a result of diluting the weight of a vote in this way, there would be more countries involved, but each with a lesser influence, except in the case of the countries that would have a veto power. A variant of these options recommends not only increasing membership but also inserting a new tier in the Council's organization, one that would comprise permanent members without veto powers, presently two undissociable concepts. Such a proposal would accommodate, for instance, the admission of Germany and Japan to the Council on a permanent basis without granting them veto power. The continuity in membership would help these countries to acquire an intermediate status, but at the same time, countries that need to be elected in order to become a member of the Council would no doubt be pushed towards the sidelines.

For Canada, three options are possible: supporting a general increase of the membership with more members having a veto power, supporting the three-tier apparatus, or supporting neither of these two options while promoting a third way. According to our theoretical framework, Canada would prefer an institutional strategy that helps it make gains in voice opportunities. A review of the first two options reveals that neither of them would help Canada gain institutional benefits or even maintain its current level of voice opportunities. In fact, in the first case Canada would have no chance of being selected as one of the new members, and certainly not as a permanent member. Most options would grant seats to Japan and Germany and three seats to countries from the South. In the best scenario, Canada would become a member of the Council only when it succeeded in getting elected. Although it might be presumed that more seats would mean increased opportunities of becoming a member of the Council, this is not the case.

First, in most proposals, the majority of the new seats would be permanent. Canada belongs to a group that is already overrepresented on the Council: four of the nine or ten permanent seats would be occupied by countries from the North America–Western Europe group.[37] Therefore, its chances of obtaining a permanent seat are nil, since proposals refer to three South seats (with the exception of France's proposal for two) plus two more seats, which would, understandably, go to Germany and Japan. (The exception to the latter is China's proposal for one more seat only.) Canada's chances would remain, at best, approximately equivalent to its current chances of obtaining a nonpermanent seat. Thus, there are no new voice opportunities in this institutional arrangement. It could even be considered as a relative loss, since a number of countries currently competing with Canada for second-rank positions would acquire permanent recognition.

The second set of options is even worse. Since Canada would remain in what could now be seen as a third layer of influence and since the agenda of the Security Council is in large part controlled by the permanent members, such an arrangement would mean the worst possible institutional return for Canada. Its voice would be heard only from the back of the room, and its influence would be marginal. Our theoretical framework therefore suggests that Canada would oppose the two types of options on the table and instead favour a third option.

The importance of these reforms for Canada can be more fully understood by referring to a context that has been well described by Legault: "The end of the Cold War brought a new dimension in the [UN Security Council] reform process. The impressive growth of peacekeeping activities tipped the scale in favour of transformations in this domain. In fact, such reforms were initiated by Secretary General Boutros-Ghali with his Agenda for Peace."[38] The main goal of the reform is to make the Council more representative, hence improving its legitimacy. As Lloyd Axworthy underscored, speaking in 1997 as minister of foreign affairs, "Canada wants to see a Security Council that is more effective, transparent and broadly representative, and above all less elitist and more democratic."[39] Canada has a lot at stake in this exercise. Neither at the founding of the UN nor in the subsequent years has Canada ever been able to have its or, for that matter, other countries' middle-power status recognized. Nevertheless, Canada is still an important contributor to the organization and an influential, if not always a decision-making, actor.

In fact, the case of UN reform validates our theory. Canada has made it clear that none of the options put forward by other actors would be satisfactory. Minister Axworthy insisted that several parameters must be respected in any proposed reform, that is, the Council should be representative, efficient and credible, and the reform should be equitable. He clearly referred to the need "to move away from vestiges of the past – such as permanent status on the Security Council or the veto – which prevent the Council from coming to grips with a problem before it deteriorates into crisis," adding that "Canadians believe that emphasis on conflict prevention and peacebuilding, enhancing human security, fostering democracy and good governance, strengthening humanitarian law and action, reflect the real needs of UN member states and the proper exercise of responsibility by the Security Council."[40]

In promoting these values, Canada is advocating a reform of the processes more than a reform of the structures. According to the Canadian rhetoric, more seats and more veto-holding members will not ensure better representation, nor will they increase the credibility of the organization. Speaking as Canada's foreign minister, Lloyd Axworthy stated that "The Council needs to broaden its horizons in addressing emerging threats which impact on our security. Thematic debates on these issues, where all member states can participate, is a good step. The addition of peacebuilding in the Council's range of responses to threats to peace and security is also welcome."[41] Such a reorientation addresses not only the topics to be discussed but also the manner in which the Council should debate them. In fact, Canada promotes the idea that decision making at the Council should be more open and more transparent and strongly opposes the permanent members' control over the agenda. Axworthy's objective is clearly that "the distinction between permanent and elected members needs to be narrowed rather than widened. In sum, the Council we need for the next century must be more responsible, more accountable and less impenetrable."[42]

In this specific instance, Canada is aiming particularly at increasing the weight of its voice. Canada is a prime contributor to various UN efforts, but it has no guarantee of being able to exercise its influence – in other words, to have its voice heard – as much as it wishes. This is why Axworthy proposed that "member states involved in and affected by matters before the Council must be allowed to exercise their

Charter rights. Far from constraining the Council's efficiency, this will improve the decisions it takes and render its actions more effective."[43] By trying to inject a dose of functionalism into the Council's decision-making process, Canada is suggesting that states like itself, which are able to participate in costly and diplomatically sensitive UN operations like peacekeeping, could "earn" voice at the Council table.

Transaction costs are thus a key factor to be considered here, since they usually prevent nonmajor powers from innovating. In the case of the UN Security Council reform, it would appear at first glance that Canada can afford the transaction costs involved in voicing its interests. In this sense, Canada's rich diplomatic resources and network are not insignificant. In fact, the value of this diplomatic network is already strenghtened by reaching the highest ranks of the UN hierarchy. Moreover, should this third way prevail, Canada could also count on the support of "like-minded" countries that are ready to share the costs in order to increase their leverage in an institution that has left many on the outside looking in.[44]

The very nature of UN Security Council reform calls for an institutional rearrangement. Thus, should Canada wish to again pursue an innovative avenue, it could do it within the framework of intervention required by the situation. Nevertheless, Canada stands out by advocating a process reform instead of an institutional reform per se, the latter being the object of all other reform proposals. In so doing, Canada is clearly trying to protect, if not enhance, the value of its voice at the UN. Until now, Canada has served a two-year term on the Council once every decade. When not actually serving, it has nonetheless been active, working towards the implementation of Council resolutions, advising on peacekeeping, and so on. What Canada wants is a formal recognition of this contribution. The other proposed solutions, as we have seen, would push Canada to an outer circle of influence, which would be contrary to the country's interests and goals. Could one then say that Canada wishes to mobilize more than its share of influence? Based on Canada's past record, we can say that this is already the case. What Canada is seeking here is to entrench this reality, thereby obtaining a statutory credit for it. In this sense, Canada's behaviour with regard to this issue is a perfect illustration of the country's dissatisfaction with a momentary gain in influence and its preference for working towards a continuous reward of this nature. To borrow Dewitt's image, Canada prefers to be a marginal actor at the centre rather than a central actor at the margin.[45]

A last point needs to be flagged here. Canada's position on the UN Security Council reform is but one element in a larger scheme to enhance Canada's position and influence in world affairs by widening the security agenda and thus reducing the centrality of military power in world politics. Canada is asking that the Council not limit itself to issues solely related to the usual strategic questions. In this sense the "sustainable human security" agenda becomes a prime asset for Canada. Canada's foreign affairs minister argued in 1997 that, by considering this concept and acting in accordance with its principles, conflict could be avoided. Hence, he concluded that "the issues we once dealt with separately are in fact interlinked" and that any efficient action has to take both dimensions into consideration.[46] Should the Council agree to take this route – which is essentially another process reform – Canada, as its primary proponent and a country with very reliable expertise in the domain (from peacekeeping to campaigning against light weapons proliferation), would find itself in an advantageous position. It could then make much greater gains than could be expected given its share of power. Furthermore, this would be in agreement with the theoretical proposition that a middle power will promote institutionalization when it has the capacity to assume diplomatic and scientific leadership, which is clearly true in Canada's case.

This is an evolving situation, and it is therefore difficult to draw sharply defined conclusions. However, if we read the cards being played by Canada in this round, we can see a general tendency that is likely to confirm what was predicted by our theory. Our theoretically defined criteria are clearly recognizable, although in some instances it remains to be seen whether their accuracy will be confirmed as the situation evolves.

The Anti-Personnel (AP) Landmines Ban Treaty: Voicing New Alternatives

The Ottawa Protocol on the anti-personnel landmines ban is probably one of the most visible successes in recent Canadian foreign policy history. Many see it as the expression of the purest Pearsonian peace-seeking tradition. In many respects, not only is this case representative of recent Canadian institutional foreign policy, but it offers interesting elements for our analysis. As for the preceding case, we will first briefly describe the context and then evaluate the available options. We will also identify the option predicted theoretically and, finally, review Canada's stance and explain this specific choice.

The first contextual element to consider is that the question of banning anti-personnel (AP) landmines was to be discussed in a multilateral forum of which Canada is a member. In 1977 the United Nations Diplomatic Conference negotiated the Convention on Certain Conventional Weapons (CCW), and in May 1996, it held a review conference in Geneva. Although AP landmines were a topic on the agenda, the conference failed to reach an agreement. As Manon Tessier has noted, the failure can be attributed to "the combined opposition of countries objecting to discussion on this matter or considering that nuclear disarmament should have precedence over all other disarmament talks."[47] Once more, a UN initiative fell victim to the consensual approach favoured in such circumstances.[48]

This is a classic example of Canada not being in a position to influence the outcome of the meeting, although the country had aligned itself strongly and clearly in favour of a ban. What, then, were Canada's options? First, Canada could continue to work in this same institutional framework, trying to convince other countries to address the issue. Second, it could identify other international, regional, or multilateral fora in order to have the question discussed. Third, a more original route could be followed by proposing an extra- or neo-institutional solution.

According to our theory, middle powers are interested in institutionalization that allows some level of voice articulation. Therefore, the theory invalidates the first two options, since in both cases, Canada's voice would be weaker. Experience has proven that Canada would not be able to voice its concerns in the multilateral forum in which these questions were to be discussed. Moreover, bringing this topic to another already existing forum would have presented one more level of obstacles: countries that were opposed in the first instance to debating the question could have achieved the same result by asking the simple question, "Why here?" Given Canada's status in these fora as a credible, but not a key, actor, the costs involved in convincing these recalcitrant countries would have been much too high without offering any guarantee of success.[49] In other words, if Canada wanted to succeed in this endeavour, it had to do so without the major powers, or even some competing middle powers, both of whom were the very ones who had frustrated Canada's efforts to obtain effective voice opportunities. Therefore, the recourse to a new setting in which these obstacles would be absent seems to be a more appropriate context in which it could voice its interests much more easily. Such a context would meet our theoretical condition. Moreover, the theory also states that a middle power's interest in developing a heavy institutional solution would depend on its capacity to exercise diplomatic and scientific leadership in the chosen domain. Canada also met this condition. Thus, based on our theory, we would expect Canada to opt for the new avenue as its preferred institutional strategy.

In this second case also, our theoretical framework provides an interesting interpretation, since the recourse to a process paralleling the established institutions – the Ottawa process – quickly appeared to be the most suitable strategy for obtaining as many institutional benefits as possible. In fact, Canada was not taken by surprise in May 1996 when the Geneva meeting was not able to reach an agreement on AP landmines. Canada knew it would not have much influence on the process. Indeed, this is an interesting case in that it allows us to simultaneously measure the impact of the exit option played by major powers, which in this case was their refusal to discuss the issue of AP landmines, something that a middle power would never be in a position to do. Canada knew this and acted accordingly.

As early as January 1996, Canada had unilaterally declared a total ban on AP landmines.[50] In the days following this announcement, it held a first meeting where 8 countries (to be known later as "the core countries") joined with thirteen NGOs to prepare the action to be taken. Thus, on the Geneva conference doorsteps Canada announced it would host "an international meeting to develop a strategy for achieving a comprehensive ban on AP landmines."[51] The following months were used to muster supporters of the Canadian initiative, including more "like-minded" governments and NGOs, among them the International Campaign to Ban Land-Mines (ICBL) chaired by Jodi Williams, in an exercise defined by Richard Price as "public diplomacy."[52] At the end of this October meeting that launched the Ottawa process, the Canadian foreign affairs minister made a statement that took most participants by surprise:[53]

I am convinced that we cannot wait for a universal treaty. I am convinced that we can start now, even though we may have to proceed with a treaty that does not, in the first instance, include all of the states of the world ... Making it universal will be the ongoing challenge for each of us. And so, Mr Chairman, I have one final point to add to your action plan. That point comes in the form of both an invitation and a challenge. The challenge is to see a treaty signed no later than the end of 1997.[54]

Fourteen months after the first Ottawa meeting, fast-track diplomacy bore fruit when 122 countries returned to Ottawa to sign the convention. Minister Axworthy continuously applied pressure in order to have more countries sign and ratify the treaty.[55] As a result, as of February 2002, 133 countries had signed the convention, 122 had ratified it, and it was in force in 112 of them. There are still 71 countries that have not ratified or acceded to the convention; however, 20 of them have signed the treaty and are in the process of ratifying it, and 34 have voted in favour of United Nations General Assembly resolutions supporting the implementation of the Ottawa convention.

Viewed from the perspective of "voicing" Canada's concerns, this issue reveals many of the elements predicted by our theory. First, we stated that voice gains were intended to compensate for the substantive gains made by more powerful states. In this case, it seems clear that Canada was not able to influence the disarmament talks because of the prominence given to nuclear disarmament on the agenda. Moreover, having no nuclear armament itself, Canada had nothing to bargain in order to put forward its own priorities. Substantive gains were definitely out of question, and Canada was faced with the possibility of being completely marginalized, a situation that would jeopardize its status as a middle power.

Moreover, at the end of the Cold War, Canada was searching for a new cause to champion and seeking to voice new concerns in order to maintain a role and stance on the world stage. The AP landmines ban was an issue in which Canada could defend its "sustainable human security" agenda. This orientation has long been part of the policy agenda,[56] and it got new prominence at the end of the Cold War in the last days of the Mulroney government.[57] It was put in the shadow under André Ouellet's ministership when UN rapid-intervention capacity enhancement got most of the attention. The concept, however, returned in force as the cornerstone of Lloyd Axworthy's foreign policy. In fact, this new policy is an example of how Canada "voiced" its concerns when the institutional route threatened to obscure Canada's identity and role on the international scene.

Another element of our theory relates to the transaction costs associated with establishing a new course rather than taking advantage of existing institutions. The route chosen by Canada, that is, the establishment of a new institutional entity, is by far the most costly of all. Canada met the challenge by getting involved in "fast-track diplomacy" and "public diplomacy." While major powers rely on their military influence to make things happen, middle powers, which are deprived of such a tool, need to use other means. Thus, Canada relied on its reputation as a noncolonial, non-empire-building nation associated with a far-reaching network of well-respected diplomats. In other words, Canada had sufficient resources to be able to pursue its course of action and buy itself effective voice opportunities. Moreover, these resources were used as leverage to garner resources from other "like-minded" countries and NGOs to build what Kathryn Sikkink describes as a necessary complement of action.[58]

As a result, Canada was able to set the stage for the important meeting in October 1996 in Ottawa at which fifty countries, including some UN Security Council permanent members (UNSCPMs) such as France, Great Britain, and the United States, launched the Ottawa protocol. The success of this first meeting was due in large part to the networking and circulation of a draft of the final conference communiqué during the summer. Moreover, the fourteen months between the two conferences held in Ottawa were used efficiently to gather the support needed to take up Minister Axworthy's challenge.

Again, Canada was able to muster the necessary resources to put both public and classic diplomacy to work. Canada itself participated in as many international meetings as it could in order to convince other governments to rally to the movement.[59] It also ensured that NGOs were active on the ground and that the honours, the visibility, and, of course, the bill associated with the exercise would be shared with most of the other "core group" countries. Such an approach was dictated by a strategic use of the available resources. Because opposition was expected from some countries, including some UNSCPMs, it was deemed appropriate to start by gaining the support of lesser powers, in the hope that strength in numbers would help reach the final goal and bring the last reluctant governments on side. In so doing, Canada avoided having to throw away its ammunition. Hence, it "shared the cost" by enlisting the aid of influential regional players – such as Mexico in Latin America, the Philippines in Asia, and South Africa on the African continent – which were in a position to invest time, resources, and energy. These countries used their regional leverage to bring aboard some of their neighbours, thus reducing costs to Canada, since it did not have to acquire this influence. To complement this action, Canada organized a series of meetings that would pave the way for the drafting, adoption, and ratification of a "legally binding" document that would forbid the production, diffusion, and use of AP landmines. In order to maximize the use of available resources, each one of the core countries had to carry out part of the exercise while reaping part of the political benefits associated with it. Austria offered the secretarial support, for example, and important technical meetings were held in Vienna, Geneva, and Bonn. The two key meetings at which the treaty was drafted and adopted, which led directly to the treaty being signed in Ottawa, were held in Brussels and Oslo.

Canada therefore not only had the moral and physical resources necessary to make this endeavour a success, but it also built on its own resources as a multiplying factor to reach more efficiently the goals that it set for itself and for the international community. This type of behaviour is characteristic of a middle power. A major power would have imposed its agenda based on its military capability and smaller powers would not have been in a position and would not have had the resources and the international credibility to reach these goals. It can also be said that the transaction costs were assumed not only by Canada but also by other similar powers that were dedicated to the implementation of the new order.

A last element that we wish to consider relates to the fact that in this type of "voice" process, middle powers hope to mobilize a share of influence that is greater than what their power level would normally allow. Here again, Canada's behaviour confirms what the theory predicted. By assuming the leadership of a widely successful operation, Canada took on the appearance of a major player in the concert of nations, its role being much greater than what would have been expected based on its conventional military power. Canada was even able to counter efforts by the United States, whose endorsement of the treaty was vague, very qualified, and applied to a relatively distant future, but which, for all intents and purposes, was opposed to the immediate banning of AP landmines.[60] Canada's concession was to share the forefront with other countries in order to lower the transaction costs and, at the same time, ensure that core group countries would be dedicated to the issue. This gave Canada vertical gains over the countries that lagged behind in the process. Since Canada maintained its leadership through "gentle strategic guidance" in international meetings, coordination of public diplomacy, and more traditional diplomatic lobbying, it was also able to make some horizontal gains, rising above the "crowd" of other middle powers without crushing them.

This case study therefore also tends to confirm what the theory predicted. Canada was not in a position to make any substantive gains by fighting its point at the UN conference. It therefore opted for a solution in which it could voice a new alternative to the more orthodox institutional negotiations. Canada had the resources to bear the transaction costs associated with this initiative, which in turn gave Canada greater benefits than what its military power alone could have generated.

Working towards a Solution to the Haitian Crisis: A New Forum, a Renewed Voice

Although Haiti is the oldest independent country in the Caribbean, its history has been characterized by political instability, which has often resulted in external political intervention. Recent history has been no different. On 16 December 1990, president Jean-Bertrand Aristide was democratically elected. However, as early as 5 January 1991, there was a first attempt at a coup, led by Duvalier regime sympathiser Roger Lafontant. This first attempt failed, but in April, rumours about a new conspiracy were spreading, and in May mutiny within the army and police ranks added to the burden faced by the new president. In July the arrest of Lafontant and of several of his followers, as well as the establishment of a commission of enquiry on crimes perpetrated since Duvalier's exile in 1986, did nothing to ease the political climate. On

30 September 1991, Aristide was forced into exile after a coup brought the military back to power. The international community did not recognize General Raoul Cedras' government; several attempts to restore President Aristide were studied and some of them were implemented with varying levels of success.

There are several interesting aspects of the role played by Canada in resolving the Haitian crisis. For instance, this case spans several years, during which Canada experienced a change in government and, within the same government, a change in foreign affairs ministers, each of whom advocated different foreign policy priorities.[61] This being said, it is well known that the United States, including President Carter's mission, must be credited much more than Canada with bringing about the turning point in the resolution of the latest Haitian crisis. Moreover, at first glance it is difficult to see what Canada's interests were in getting involved in this crisis. After all, Canadian security was not at risk; nor did Canadian economic interests in the Caribbean justify major involvement. Why, then, of the many crises around the world, would Canada intervene in this particular one?

It was often mentioned that Canada was home to the Haitian diaspora that settled mainly in Montreal (about sixty to seventy thousand people). Norton's propositions regarding the influence of internal factors on foreign-policy making, might lead one to think that the sheer political weight of the concentration of Haitian people in Canadian foreign affairs Minister André Ouellet's home riding for thirty years might have played a role.[62] Such a conclusion tends to ignore the fact that the Haitian community represented only about 12 per cent of the riding's electorate, making it an important, but not a key, group.[63] Nor does it take into account the fact that Canada was involved in working towards a solution both before Ouellet and the Liberal team came to power and after he retired from politics. Moreover, the fact that four exiled members of the Aristide government had chosen to seek refuge in Montreal did not seem to be of immediate consequence to Canada's involvement, since, as we will see, Canada had started to play a role before the coup.[64]

What then was Canada's interest? And more importantly, what motivated its choice of actions? It is true that throughout history missionaries, as well as governmental and NGO development aid, helped to forge links between the two countries. However, based on our theoretical framework, we would argue that at most this historical background served as a justification, whereas Canada's involvement in Haiti was motivated by its preference for a given institutional arrangement. In other words, Canada's long-established relationship with Haiti made it almost impossible for the Canadian government to simply turn away, but since some action was in order, the type of involvement was chosen according to the institutional development expected to be more favourable in terms of voice opportunities for Canada.

In fact, there were several options to consider. First, recourse to a regional forum such as the Organisation of American States (OAS) was possible. A second option could have been to bring the whole thing before a multilateral forum such as the UN. Finally, as was seen in the two cases above, a third possibility was to establish a parallel response to existing institutions.

Beyond the general statement already made regarding Canada's motivations, elements of our theoretical framework do not lead to a clear and definite conclusion in the present case. In fact, the theory suggests that Canada would have had good reasons to work within the framework of either the OAS or the UN. For instance, on the regional stage Canada had finally joined the OAS in January 1990, after offering resistance over a long period to pressures from both the United States and the Latin American countries.[65] Among the rationales preventing Canada from joining was, on the one hand, its unwillingness to simply add weight to the other countries' opposition to Washington's desiderata. On the other hand, Canada did not want its presence to be used as a rubber stamp for U.S. policies and interventions in the hemisphere. Rather, Canada wanted to craft its own niche and preserve its status. This goal was achieved at the first OAS meeting Canada attended as a voting member, when it presented an amendment to the organization's charter.[66] This amendment opened options that deviated from the original mandate of the OAS, allowing member countries to intervene in another member country when it was considered that democracy in the latter country was threatened.[67] In promoting and defending this new mandate, Canada wanted to confirm its status as an independent but influential player in this new forum. Haiti provided Canada with a situation in which its voice would be valued if the Canadian approach was successful in bringing about a resolution to the conflict. However, should the approach fail, Canada would probably lose more than it could have gained.

Canada was much more familiar with the multilateral solution, and since its network was already in place and functioning, its transaction costs would be minimal. If the UN peacekeeping forces became involved, Canada's long-lasting relationship with Haiti would have added value to its technical expertise, making it an unavoidable actor whose voice would be prized. However, the question of whether or not the Haitian crisis qualified under chapter 7 of the UN Charter remained. Some countries did not seem to think so. Would Canada then gain more by raising its voice against the countries who did not consider such a condition to be met, or would important losses be incurred in terms of voice opportunities and influence by opposing them?

Finally, the two cases we have already studied in this chapter have proven that Canada was in a position to gain much more than its share when acting in a parallel forum with fewer actors. There is no reason to believe that this situation was different this time around, especially since Canada would have been able to afford the transaction costs – which were higher in this type of institutional arrangement – due to its open links with Haiti and its resources and expertise. The downside of such a solution was that, as we have seen, if Canada decided to go against the stance of major powers such as the United States, it risked being isolated and paying a very high price for its independence, since the United States was much more sensitive to an issue that could strategically affect its national security interests in the region.

Contrary to the two previous cases, our theory does not overwhelmingly favour any one of the three options. While this may seem disconcerting, in fact, since no option is clearly favoured or ruled out by the theory, a combination of the three levels of response may be the most appropriate solution. This will only be revealed by examining the events involved.

The OAS was the first institutional actor to intervene and Canada had a high interest in the success of this intervention. As early as 5 June, almost three months before the coup, Canada supported the Santiago Declaration, which provided a framework for the OAS intervention by making it possible to counter threats to democracy in a member state.[68] The Canadian foreign minister was sent to Haiti as a member of an international observers' group, and Canada bore the cost of air transportation for the whole delegation. Canada also worked towards the implementation of OAS-voted sanctions. In the House of Commons, Minister MacDougall presented a seven-point plan of action that Canada would follow in order to back the OAS's measures.[69] In a word, Canada continued to play an active role in support of OAS actions. However, after a few months the hemispheric forum was deemed insufficient to settle the problem. For instance, it was easy for an OAS member to use a non-OAS country as an intermediary to contravene sanctions or, in the case of the United States, which controlled much of the Haitian economy,[70] to do it even more directly with Washington's blessing.[71] Moreover, as Domingo Acevedo concludes, the OAS did not have the legal authority to implement the measures needed to achieve the objectives, including removing the military from power.[72] One might also point to institutional weaknesses, such as the use of a quasi-impossible consensus. In this last instance, the transaction costs, that is, the time, resources, and energy invested to convince OAS members who had so many opportunities to skirt the organization's resolutions, might have prevented Canada from going further with the OAS approach. As Hugo Loiseau points out, "after having exhausted all diplomatic means, the OAS had to call in the UN"[73] and Canada was part of that call; it joined its voice with other OAS members in requesting a UN intervention. The need for a larger multilateral forum had materialized.

The question was then submitted to the UN. To illustrate that this action would be carried out in cooperation with the OAS, Dante Caputo, Argentina's former foreign affairs minister, was chosen as a joint emissary. Canada contributed knowledge and financial and human resources, in order to help find a solution to the situation, playing a very active role in the phases leading to President Carter's mission. Afterwards, through the different peace missions, Canada also played an important role in stabilizing, if not enhancing, the democratic process in Haiti, which corresponds to the diplomatic and scientific leadership referred to in our theory.[74] In this specific case, Canada's experience in Namibia provided it with the basis for benefiting fully from an institutional strategy that it obviously favoured, since this allowed Canada to make gains.

As well, as we have seen in the other cases, Canada was in a position to absorb the transaction costs related to voicing this course of action. Canada had many more resources (human, material, and, most importantly, knowledge resources) than smaller powers. Thus, Canada was able to be involved in the UN missions because it had the capacity to back its voice with concrete actions.

Although in terms of voice and influence, the involvement with UN institutional action offers the most visible example of Canada being able to benefit from voice articulation, it is not the most important one. In fact, Canada's role was even more effective in making gains within a small group of actors that had come together through the initiative of President Carlos Andres Perez of Venezuela, in response to a request made to the UN by President Aristide two weeks before the coup. This group was composed of representatives of France, Venezuela, the United States, and Canada. As David Malone notes, "these four countries were to form a loose alliance in support of democracy in Haiti and later constituted the 'Group of Friends' of the UN Secretary General."[75] The group was very active during the whole crisis and is still monitoring the situation on the western tip of Hispanola Island, holding regular meetings at the OAS headquarters in Washington. Thus, this is another instance of Canada preferring to take a route that runs parallel to established international security institutions without denying their legitimacy.

In so doing, Canada opted for an institutional strategy that was beneficial in many respects. First, by evolving in a smaller group, Canada's
voice was given much more weight, proportionally, even though this
voice was not properly "institutionalized." Moreover, due to Canada's
good relationship with France and the United States, this weight was
multiplied when Canadian proposals were adopted and then echoed by
these major powers. Canada then had an advantage over both these
two countries, since Prime Minister Mulroney was on good terms with
both President Bush and President Mitterrand, whereas these two
leaders did not necessarily get along with each other on their own.
Third, the fact that the United States and Canada were working
together in this small group alleviated the heavy transaction costs that
would have resulted had the United States not been involved. As for the
other costs associated with the work of the "group of friends," Canada
lived up to its word by participating in and supporting UN missions.

Could the gains acquired through a voice strategy compensate for
substantive gains that were, in theory, virtually inaccessible to Canada?
In this regard, this case calls for a much more nuanced conclusion than
that of the landmines case or the case of Security Council reform. Some
of the most important substantive gains would be related to the exercise of some control over the political stability of the region. The American hegemon at first showed no interest in sharing its power over this
issue. However, for reasons related to recent American military intervention in the region, it soon appeared that the United States was not
in a position to take command of the UN missions aimed at restoring
democracy in Haiti. One can therefore see why Washington asked
Ottawa to get involved in the process to the extent that it did. Thus,
there were indeed some substantive gains for Canada. However, the
country's most important gains were made through the credo on which
Canada's inaugural contribution to the OAS was based and its implementation by the UN through the work and monitoring of the "group
of friends." We can conclude, therefore, that gains made through voice
complemented some substantive gains, instead of merely compensating
for the lack of them.

Finally, it may be tempting to conclude that the prominent role
Canada played throughout the process, whether at the OAS or the UN,
with the "group of friends," or in the field, clearly demonstrates that
the country played a greater role and made much greater diplomatic
gains than would have been expected based on its power alone.
However, this conclusion needs to be qualified. What makes Canada a
middle power is that in certain respects the country has characteristics
of both greater powers (in terms of its economy and peacekeeping
expertise, for instance) and of smaller powers (for example, in terms of

its population and military striking power). In the Haitian crisis we have seen that Canada was particularly well placed to intervene. Indeed, it can be said that Canada was closer to a greater-power than a middle-power status. This interpretation was further supported when, in July 2000, Canada threatened to withdraw all support except humanitarian aid from Haiti unless democratic principles were respected in the ongoing elections.[76] It will be recalled that, according to our theory, exit is a strategy that has been identified mainly with major powers. However, it should also be pointed out that this very much depends on the circumstances. Thus, it may be concluded that in the Haitian crisis Canada mobilized its fair share of power by voicing an innovative avenue at the OAS and through the group of friends. However, put into the context of Canada's action more generally on the international scene, its influence with regard to Haiti, as is often the case, was greater than its power alone would have allowed.

To sum up, although Canada's role in the effort to resolve the Haitian crisis presents many nuances, it nevertheless corresponds to the criteria identified theoretically. It is also interesting to note that Canada's actions were consistent during the entire period from May 1991, when the OAS first considered intervening, until November 1997, when the transitional United Nations Mission in Haiti (UNMIH) ended. This is all the more striking given that during this period there were four different ministers at the helm of the foreign affairs department, each with his or her own specific agenda. Despite these differences, however, they all sustained Canada's role as a middle power.

CONCLUSION

Very likely as a reaction to a loss of influence in the realm of security issues, Canada has carved out a niche for itself by focusing on questions that are peripheral to the military domain, such as the ban on certain types of weapons (AP land mines, but also, more recently, small-calibre weapons; these bans seem to be starting a tendency for Canada to focus on these issues), the defence of democracy when it is endangered by the threat linked to security, or the operational reform of the security forum par excellence, the United Nations Security Council. Other, more recent initiatives also tend to confirm that Canada is definitely moving in this direction: for example, its opposition to the concept of child soldiers and its active support for the creation of an international court of justice to judge those responsible for war crimes and crimes against humanity.

Studying Canada's institutional behaviour therefore presents interesting challenges. First, our study is in agreement with Paul Gecelosky, who argues that "states with skills and resources in uncertain issue-areas take on greater responsibility in those areas in the international system."[77] These areas are what Miller identified as "functional areas."[78] The theoretical framework we have used in this chapter specifies that a middle power's choice of behaviour would be determined by what it anticipates in terms of institutional results, or, in other words, by what it values in terms of institutional developments.

The three cases we have studied illustrate the options that were available to Canada. In the first case, the reform of the United Nations Security Council, all of the solutions put forward were detrimental to Canada, for they would have rearranged voice distribution in a way that would have lessened Canada's own voice. Faced with these "unrewarding" reforms to the institutional structure, which would have undermined its influence, Canada chose instead to advocate a third way, an institutional-process reform that would have helped to enhance Canada's role and influence.

The second case, in which Canada promoted the AP landmines ban treaty, also offers an example where Canada did not expect much in the way of institutional benefits, either from the status quo or from any process closely related to the status quo. Canada therefore opted for a completely different trajectory. In so doing, it was able to define the new rules of a new game and to benefit from its participation in that game.

In the third case, the Haitian crisis, the options were much more complex. The nuances relate to the fact that, unlike in the previous two cases, Canada needed a good return on its actions in a regional forum and could expect positive returns from the old multilateral order. However, in order to minimize any uncertainty, Canada was inclined to gamble on a new framework with the "group of friends." Again, the prevailing dynamics of international relations in the immediate post–Cold War period suggest that Canada has a need to enhance the institution's value in accordance with its own interest.

Nevertheless, it has not entered into this new field by means of an orthodox or traditional institutional strategy. Rather, as we have seen, Canada opted for the creation of new instruments on the periphery of existing institutions. Yet the theory of regimes specifies that the creation of new institutions generates significant costs and that states therefore prefer to fashion a new arrangement within an already-established organization, should one exist. The analyst is therefore faced with the following problem: why is it that a middle power like Canada, which, theoretically, should be sensitive to the problem of the transaction costs generated by creating a new institution, would take this route? In fact, as we have seen, Canada was able to favour an institutional arrangement that kept transaction costs to a minimum by sharing the burden with other "like-minded" countries. On the other hand, we provided an explanation for this apparent support for transaction costs associated with new institutions. They are costs middle powers are ready to assume in order to differentiate themselves from weaker states. Consequently, the avenue chosen does not offer an interest-articulation mechanism similar to those offered by ordinary multilateral solutions. However, it seems clear that in all the cases we studied, the cost-benefit forecast indicated that Canada has chosen an extra-institutional voice-opportunities channel.

At first glance, this focus on new alternatives may appear puzzling. Why would Canada abandon its traditional multilateral stance and opt increasingly for unconventional and creative para-institutional arrangements? Here again, our theoretical framework may offer some insights.

If Canada continued to pursue its traditional options in favour of international security institutions, it might very well find itself facing an important voice deficit. In this sense, the first two cases we examined are enlightening. In the case both of the UN Security Council and the UN conference on disarmament, Canada was pushed towards the sidelines or gagged, and its influence was, at best, marginal. In these cases, opting for a new avenue was the immediate and only viable option. The third case, the Haiti crisis, is also telling, in that Canada played its cards at three different tables simultaneously. We also saw that it was in this case that Canada's influence was most visible, active, and best assured. Based on this evidence, we can hypothesize, at the least, that since the Canadian voice was not challenged as much by the traditional institutional arrangement, Canada could rely more on its classic foreign-policy management practice through multilateral and regional institutions.

In other words, Canada displayed its growing concern and dissatisfaction towards the institutions it had hitherto supported. This concern and dissatisfaction was a result of Canada no longer being able to derive the same level of expected institutional benefits from its use of these institutions. This does not mean that Canada is exiting multilateral fora, involvement in which is the recognized hallmark of its foreign policy.[79] In fact, it is interesting to note that all of the new avenues promoted by Canada still have a multilateral component, although often with fewer actors (as, incidentally, was the case during the "golden age" of Pearsonian diplomacy). It is also interesting to note that Canada is crafting these parallel institutions in a way that it can benefit from them.

Although it is true that a new context appears to have changed the role played by intermediate powers,[80] the idea that they are disappearing[81] or that they do not exist[82] appears to be debatable, at least from the evidence gathered from the cases we studied. Indeed, our analysis leads us to believe that, given their specific characteristics, intermediate powers will seek to carve out institutions for themselves. In this sense, the behaviour of Canada, which, as we have clearly demonstrated, is attempting to operate on the periphery of existing organizations, may be explained by a search for greener pastures: that is, chased, as it were, from their traditional fields by the greater powers, middle powers are establishing new fora, defined in particular by innovative issue areas that will allow them to act more autonomously and thus preserve their status. Therefore, the question to ask in order to understand the role of middle powers in the post-Cold War period is not so much, Do we still need "bridge-builders"? but instead, Is institutional development evolving in a direction that is depriving middle powers of the gains they were accustomed to expect? A positive response to this question throws open the door to exploring the post–Cold War behaviour that Canada clearly adopted in the cases that we examined in this chapter and that should be examined further in other studies, in order to determine whether the phenomenon extends to other cases, including other middle powers.

Canada still clearly faces a new challenge of the kind described in our study. Potentially, it could be a much more dramatic one. Pressed by a u.s. administration that was strengthened by the 9–11 attack in its willingess to go ahead with its homeland security initiative, again Canada sees one Cold War institution in which it managed to acquire some voice opportunities, NORAD, threatened. And up to now, Ottawa has not been assured that the new broader Canada-u.s. defence system proposed by Washington would give Canadians a role in the structure of command similar to the one it enjoys in NORAD. This move toward a growing continentalization of security arrangements places Canada in a situation where its dependency on the United States is growing, thus limiting its capacity to use multilateral fora in order to counterbalance the American influence. Indeed, there are no serious exit options from the u.s.-led North American defence system for Canada; and there are fewer and fewer voice opportunities for Canada outside this system.

Minimalism and Self-Interest: Comparing Principal-Power Performance in Security Institutions

ONNIG BEYLERIAN

All did not bode well for the emerging world political order after the dissolution of the Soviet Union. There was a high demand for security around the world, but the response of the principal powers was far from adequate. As the main providers of security institutions, they were generally responsive to security crashes. However, considering the magnitude of human tragedies and considering that a sizeable majority of countries remained exposed to insecurities, their response was by and large minimalist and mindful first and foremost of their own security. Major Western powers worried about instabilities in their immediate periphery and sought to expand their global influence and consolidate their democratic and liberal identity. Throughout much of the 1990s Japan remained unsure of its institutional security tasks. Russia found itself relegated to the Eurasian hinterland, waiting for better days to come and still convinced of the leading role it could play in security institutions. China spent some time licking its wounds from Tiananmen Square while trying to discover the benefits of multilateral security institutions. Canada ventured into new grounds to find relevant and useful roles in international security institutions.

In this concluding chapter, I compare the institutional security behaviour of principal powers, based on the findings of the preceding chapters. My comparison uses two scales to measure the extent to which extent principal powers engaged in security institutions. I then build a typology of security behaviour as a step towards eventually developing a typological theory about the logic of behaviour of principal powers with respect to international security institutions.

MEASUREMENT FOR COMPARISON

The first scale indicates the extent to which security institutions mat-
tered to principal powers. At the upper end of the scale, principal
powers appear most interested in security institutions, and at the lower
end, least interested. This scale is based on three indicators. The first
reflects the extent to which a principal power gives high or low priority to institutions as a means for solving conflicts and regulating security relationship: in the case of the Security Council, it reflects the
extent to which reform is viewed as a high or a low priority. The
second indicator represents the strong or weak expression of preferences over what a security institution can accomplish and the functions
and roles it can play in the regional and world security structure. In the
case of the Security Council, it is the level of interest and articulation
shown in the debates surrounding its reform. The third indicator refers
the extent to which a security institution is a substitute for or complement to achieving international and national goals. When it is a substitute, an institution will matter more than it would if it was a complement. An institution is a substitute when it is a starting point and
vehicle of a principal power's security policies. It is a complement when
it is another means by which a major or middle power intends to reach
international security goals. In the case of the Security Council, reform
is a substitute if it helps the principal powers to change their security
strategies or identity;[1] it is a complement if it offers the principal
powers additional means to reach their international security goals.

The second scale measures the quality and level of institutional
engagement of principal powers. At the left end of the dimension, principal powers appear most passive and reactive towards security institutions; at the right end, most active and constructive. Like the first
scale, it is based on a set of three indicators. The first assesses the
extent to which principal powers were active or passive in searching
for institutional solutions to security problems by being responsive and
innovative in designing institutional mechanisms. A second indicator
reflects the range of activities principal powers engage in to solve conflicts, create security arrangements, and reform existing institutions.
The third indicator reflects the degree to which the principal powers
change their security strategy as a result of their participation in the
institutional process. A change in strategy indicates that principal
powers highly value their investment in security institutions, while
awaiting future benefits. They may also change their strategy because
of their interest in adapting to a changing security environment and in
learning from past positive and negative experience.[2] If the former type
of change is a modification to suit new emerging security policy con-

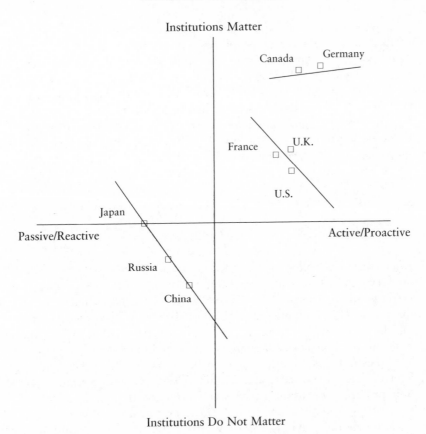

ditions within the institution, the latter represents a change in their fundamental security preferences. If the security strategy remains unchanged during the search for a solution to a conflict or negotiations on regulation of security relationships, their engagement level will likely not exceed the average performance.

The two scales are interrelated. If institutions matter greatly, we would expect principal powers to invest more in security institutions. However, the level of engagement is not always symmetrical with the level of interest in security institutions. There are instances where institutions matter more than would be expected from the low level of resources invested in security institutions. This instance may correspond to the free-rider problem, since principal powers may seek to pass on to their peers the costs of producing security goods. Inversely, principal powers could invest substantial resources in institutions but seldom act through them. This preference indicates the willingness of principal powers to incur governance costs, which are perceived as part of their international responsibilities.[3] If institutions matter little to principal powers, then we should not expect any major investment in them. Nevertheless, there might be instances where institutions do not matter to principal powers but where they would be willing to invest in them as a means to increase their influence in global security affairs. Finally, principal powers might be interested in institutions but unable to invest resources in institutional security processes because they might be marginalized or ostracized by other powers of the international community.

SEARCHING FOR SOLUTIONS TO CONFLICTS

Forced to Lead

After years of hesitation (1992–95), the United States finally agreed to intervene to put an end to the bloodshed and massacres in Bosnia-Herzegovina by sponsoring an accord to end the violence and establish the peace. The Dayton Accord committed the United States to ensuring the consolidation of peace and the stabilization of economic and political life in a society shattered by war and intercommunal hatred. The question that soon arose in Congress was exactly when did the United States plan to leave Bosnia. Congress was already quite unhappy that the administration had arranged the peace terms and sent troops without asking for its official approval.[4]

Although the Dayton Accord was essentially an American peace enforced with allied and U.S. forces, it would have been inconceivable for the United States to intervene in Bosnia without NATO. Washington would have preferred to see Europeans leading peace efforts in Bosnia and thus to save itself the effort to pacify the Balkans. But none of the belligerents in Bosnia-Herzegovina trusted the major European powers, since they appeared to be pursuing distinct agendas. Furthermore, the project of stabilizing the peace in Bosnia was supposed to give NATO a new role in European security. As Racicot and David show in chapter 1, creeping instability in the Balkans, coupled with horrendous massacres, would have smashed the NATO expansion project into smithereens. Moreover, there was the Russian factor to consider. Indeed, it would have been difficult for Europeans to bring security to war-torn communities in Bosnia with Moscow either relentlessly criticizing them from afar or, if it was allowed to participate in the actual peace efforts, playing a disruptive role on the ground, in the absence of U.S. forces. The United States ultimately agreed to lead peace-enforcing operations, but it insisted that its European allies play a bigger part in the expenses of peacebuilding and in dealing with the risks to Bosnia's political future.

Neglecting Institutional Initiatives

In the Senkaku Islands dispute, Japan did not try to build new security mechanisms, nor did it use existing institutional structures. It could have seized the opportunity to establish a security mechanism with either Beijing or Taipei. It could have, for instance, called upon Taiwan to establish a dialogue to manage this dispute. However, no such initiatives were taken, since this strategy might have produced unintended effects that could have further divided the ruling Liberal Democratic Party. But Tokyo did try to use the bilateral U.S.-Japan security arrangement, only to find out to its dismay that Washington intended to remain neutral in this dispute. Its preoccupations were somewhat dissipated when the U.S. Defense Department, contradicting earlier statements of the State Department, confirmed that the U.S.-Japan Security Arrangement did after all cover the Senkakus.[5] Japan could have asked the UN to mediate, but again it did not. Nor did China, which arguably had its own reasons to play down the gravity of this dispute. Both countries preferred not to broaden this issue beyond the dimension it had already reached, since each side was confronting its own nationalist groups, who were staging various demonstrations near the islands. Taking into account other aspects of Sino-Japanese relations, Japanese leaders considered that stakes of this dispute did not warrant an all-out confrontation with Beijing; hence, their reluctance to make the Senkakus one of the central issues dividing the two major Asian powers. In the end, the dispute remained bilateral, with no sign of ever being brought up in other forums such as the ASEAN Regional Forum or in the ASEAN+3 summits.

Limited Involvement

China did not show sustained interest in resolving the Spratlys dispute in a multilateral framework. Beijing's first preference in the early 1990s was to deal with it on a unilateral and, if need be, bilateral basis with other states claiming the Spratlys. But in 1992 it chose to adhere to the Manila Declaration issued by the ASEAN states on the necessity of resolving differences peacefully. Despite notable progress in establishing a dialogue on this matter, China's collaboration with ASEAN states to find a durable solution remained limited, accompanied as it was by its creeping military expansion in the archipelago. Still, Beijing was keen to explore various avenues by maintaining open multilateral channels. Again, the same ASEAN states helped China to overcome certain institutional misgivings by broaching the subject informally in the ASEAN Regional Forum (ARF). Notwithstanding the rise of tensions with the Philippines as a result of the construction of several Chinese structures in the Mischief Reefs in 1995, China agreed to slow down its expansion in the area. Episodically, China seemed to pursue a multi-institutional strategy; resorting to bilateral channels when it wanted to get tangible results and to multilateral venues when it sought to reassure ASEAN states of its peaceful intentions. Eventually China agreed to negotiate a code of conduct suggested by the ASEAN states and the Philippines. China made some conciliatory gestures by proposing the joint development of economic resources of the South China Sea without specifying what that meant. In sum, China underwent an evolution: from a concerned onlooker at the beginning of the 1990s – but with a view to gaining ground in this strategic area – to an active seeker of a solution and an institutional player. Beijing did not, however, go as far as proposing to build a multilateral mechanism to oversee the management of this dispute, nor did it reveal its views as to what the conditions were for its final settlement.[6]

Forging a Security Identity

A principal power seeking to forge a new security identity through security institutions needs a strategy to express its new beliefs about global security. However, it can achieve this goal only by relating the new international identity to the identity of other powers. In Somalia, Germany sought to prove that it possessed the fundamental requirements of a major power that was willing and able to undertake peacekeeping missions in far-flung areas of the world. Other states were generally forthcoming towards Germany, giving it a chance to prove its capacity to assume modest international security responsibilities. In fact, some states were expecting to see Germany provide some evidence that it could earn a permanent seat at the UN Security Council. Once in Somalia, Germany did not distinguish itself by solving civil war problems. But while the UN failed to reach its peacekeeping goals, Germany was able to reach an important goal of its own. Shortly after its peacekeeping mission in Somalia, the German Constitutional Court ruled in favour of allowing Germany to deploy its forces outside NATO areas, provided that it conformed to resolutions of the Security Council.

Unlike the response of Germany in Somalia, various states remained sceptical about and not very impressed by Gorbachev's defence of international law and his promotion of new international norms of conduct. In the diplomacy surrounding the first Gulf War, the Soviet

Union sought to consolidate the cooperative security identity that Gorbachev had outlined with the first arms-control and disarmament initiatives of 1986. Seizing on the strength that the UN had acquired towards the end of the 1980s, he sought to empower the Security Council. However, Soviet musings on Council empowerment fell on deaf ears, since no major Western power thought that the Military Staff Committee should be given the mandate to co-ordinate the coalition's military efforts to drive Iraq from Kuwait.

Gorbachev did not achieve tangible objectives in the Gulf crisis, because several factors conspired against his institutional strategy. First, there was domestic upheaval in the Soviet Union. Gorbachev was about to launch his last attempt to reform the Soviet economy. The Baltic states were agitating even more strongly for their independence; elsewhere in the Soviet Union most of the republics were firmly entrenched in their demand to fundamentally reconfigure the terms of the Union. The domestic crisis reached a climax when Shevardnadze resigned as foreign minister in December 1990, in the midst of the Gulf crisis, right at the moment when Gorbachev was expecting to reason with Saddam Hussein.

Second, Gorbachev could not get Saddam to budge from his position, despite the numerous diplomatic peace initiatives Moscow mounted during the autumn of 1990 till the very eve of the outbreak of hostilities in January 1991. Evidently, the mediator role that Moscow sought to play did not quite catch the imagination of Saddam, who must have felt abandoned by his patron. Moscow did not even contemplate forming a common position with China, since Beijing was still reeling from Western ostracism and actively seeking to strike a deal with the United States to end it. By the time of the Paris Summit of the Conference on Security and Cooperation in Europe (CSCE) in November 1990, Gorbachev found himself thoroughly dependent on Western support in order to remain politically alive at home. Gorbachev's aim to reinvigorate the Security Council could have helped him to defend his shaky domestic position. Indeed, for the Soviet Union the plan acted as a substitute and not as a complement. The fervour with which Moscow was defending international law and other norms and principles stood in contrast with the minor role it eventually played in planning the military campaign against Iraq.

Expressing Strong Preferences

Kosovo turned out to be an opportunity for France to express its preferences about what security institutions must achieve. During the Kosovo conflict it expressed its preference for defining and reinforcing the European Union's security mandate, even while advocating the defence of the Security Council's authority and striving to limit NATO's role to that of peace-enforcer. The handling of the conflict was marred by the fact that the Security Council was bypassed as a result of Russian and Chinese objections to using force against a sovereign state. Although France was uncomfortable with this result, it did, however, stand by the Alliance, and it called for forceful action against Milosevic's forces in Kosovo. But it also sought to sharply differentiate itself from other allies by pointing out its preferences during the conflict. Thus, it sought to preserve the Security Council's authority with respect to the final settlement of the conflict and insisted that civilians should not be targets, and it sought to prevent the conflict from extending to neighbouring Montenegro. France also seized the opportunity provided by the conflict to reinforce the security and defence identity of the European Union, and it strove to assign to the European Union the task of administering the rehabilitation of Kosovo once a settlement had been reached.

At times France seemed to play the role of "conscientious objector" among Western powers. Through statements of its leaders during the conflict, it succeeded in projecting the image of a major power ready to limit possible excesses of American "hyperpower." France's insistence on playing a balancing antihegemonic role was perhaps an important source of its security identity, linked as it was to the institutional development of the European Union's security identity. In sum, of all the principal powers that entertained preferences for one institution over another, France clearly stood out for the vigour and sophistication of its expression, as attested by its nuanced views on the roles that the Security Council, NATO, and the EU had to play.

Multi-institutional Strategy

In the Haitian civil war, Canada resorted to a three-pronged institutional strategy. It used it in sequence and, at a later stage, simultaneously. First, Canada sought to mark its presence in and influence over the solution of the conflict through the OAS, where it had insisted, as a condition of its adherence to the regional organization, on the principle of intervening in another member's domestic affairs should its democratic institutions fail. When the OAS proved insufficient to deal with the Haitian crisis, the matter was then sent to the UN. Even here Canada voiced its capability and willingness to contribute to the solution of the conflict. The UN venue was finally complemented by a third institutional alternative, the Group of Friends, composed of four countries that monitored Haiti's domestic stabilization. In the end, as

Bélanger and Michaud point out (chapter 7), Canada exercised more influence than its power could ever have allowed in other circumstances. Although not possessing the material capabilities of a major power, Canada brought to bear its institutional competence, which was greater than that of some of the major powers studied in the present volume. Canada showed a similarity with France's strong institutional preferences insofar as Ottawa advanced nuanced views about the potential of each institutional trajectory and demonstrated that it had the capabilities and competence to leverage one institution after another in order to achieve clear-cut goals. But there was a noteworthy difference: Canada's institutional preferences might not have been as well-articulated and forceful as France's preferences, but they were open to adaptation and learning, in order to ensure optimal results.

REGULATING SECURITY RELATIONSHIPS

Insisting on Leading

Expanding NATO was not originally a European project, even though Germany stood to gain from it. The United States led practically all aspects of NATO's expansion. When the project was conceived in Washington, the major European powers had already demonstrated their incapacity to manage the Yugoslav conflict. It was the White House that sustained the project early on against the views and advice of the Pentagon and the State Department. It was also the United States that negotiated the NATO-Russia Founding Act, even though the actual negotiation was assigned to Solana, in order to accommodate European and Russian sensitivities.[7] Compared to the case of the Dayton initiative, the United States in this case devoted more resources and energies to succeeding in this endeavour. However, expanding NATO was not a foregone conclusion at the time of its conception. Several obstacles had to be lifted, hence Washington's more careful approach to investing more resources than in its search for a solution to the Bosnian conflict. In Bosnia, America's leading role was a given for the major European powers, which were willing to incur most of the cost of bringing peace to Bosnia under the aegis of NATO. In the expansion of NATO, the nature of the challenge was different: the Clinton administration sought to ensure that obstacles to security integration in Europe would be lifted, hence its greater willingness to spend the required political capital. Insofar as NATO's expansion was not an indispensable political project for the Clinton administration, it was a complement, since it was one way of renewing America's primacy and presence in Europe. But NATO's enlargement can also be seen as a substitute when the administration raised the stakes and continued to insist upon the completion of the project, despite vehement opposition within the American administration. The Clinton administration did not greatly modify its strategy: its two-track enlargement strategy remained unchanged despite Russia's opposition to the project and its willingness to pursue a pro-Western orientation.

Fear of Marginalization

Despite Yeltsin's determination to place Russia on a pro-Western course, he found himself in a dire situation during his re-election campaign in late spring of 1996. By that time NATO's enlargement was well under way, and the United States was ever more interested in bringing this project to a successful denouement. Yeltsin's predicament derived from the strong opposition the expansion had raised among both the public and the political elites in Russia. Indeed, there was unanimous agreement in the Russian strategic community that NATO's enlargement would have a negative impact on Russia's security. Furthermore, Russia confronted tremendous odds in building the Commonwealth of Independent States (CIS), in which few of the former Soviet republics were interested. Moscow would have preferred to receive token support from the Western powers for its institution-building efforts in the Eurasian space, but none was forthcoming, since a majority of the newly independent states declined to commit themselves in a security institution dominated by Russia.

Despite the opposition to NATO's enlargement, Russia did not elaborate institutional alternatives, since it had lost considerable power in Europe and was losing influence and prestige in its own region. Moreover, Russia was not as active as it could have been in the Organisation for Security and Cooperation in Europe (OSCE). As Lavoie and Lévesque argue in chapter 2 of this volume, Russia could have pursued a more activist policy towards the OSCE, especially during its formative period in 1992–93, in order to make it a leading security institution in Europe.[8] Russia might have found in Germany a supporter of the OSCE's reinforcement and primacy in the European security complex.[9] In the end, Russia had to agree to a NATO-Russia Founding Act and a seat at the annual G7 summits. These were modest gains, but Russia's security concerns were still not addressed. In this case, NATO's expansion can be seen as a substitute, for it entailed important externalities to Russia's security and its project to develop the CIS. Finally, for all the truculence exhibited by Russian strategists about the expansion project, Moscow did not elaborate a strategy to either slow down the project or present alternatives (e.g., insisting on joining NATO).[10]

Caught in an Institutional Bind

Let us now consider the case of a major power that did not have an independent institutional security strategy. Japan found itself relegated to a secondary role in sustaining the creation of the first North East Asian security institution. However, it was also a major power that considered institutions important for its global strategy. In the early 1990s Japan tried informally to establish a dialogue with the North Korean leadership before the nuclear crisis broke out in 1994. In this venture, the Japanese leadership was seeking to develop its credentials as a power determined to develop an independent stance at a time when there was a total absence of contact between Washington and Pyongyang. But the latter soon lost interest in pursuing its half-hearted dialogue with Tokyo. It preferred to have the United States as the main interlocutor, along with Seoul and Beijing. To Tokyo, this must have been disappointing, since it confirmed the limits of its security diplomacy. Not only did it not participate in the elaboration in the 1994 Agreed Framework with the United States and North Korea, but it had to agree to defray part of the cost of building light-water nuclear reactors in North Korea and to help run a new security institution, the Korean Peninsula Energy Development Organisation (KEDO).

It should be emphasized that Japan was called upon to contribute to the building of the reactors without any assurance from North Korea that it would cease being a threat to Japanese national security. In August 1998, when Pyongyang tested its Taepodong missile by trespassing into Japanese airspace, Tokyo suspended its participation in KEDO, only to resume it a month and a half later. One would be tempted to characterize Japan's performance in KEDO, or the process that led to the formation of this institution, as a substitution case, since Japan had to participate in KEDO. Japan had little to gain in KEDO, since its subordinate position did not help it to acquire a decisive voice in the determination of the Korean peninsula's political future.

Bypassing Established Institutional Structures

Instead of resorting to an existing UN framework, like the Conference on Disarmament in Geneva, Canada lent its resources and international prestige to a coalition of nongovernmental actors and middle and lesser powers in order to negotiate and conclude one of the most difficult disarmament conventions, the Anti-Personnel Landmines Ban Treaty. Its participation in this process and its stewardship in bringing about a successful outcome brought international support and legitimacy to this convention. Canada could not have reached this goal if it had not been for its institutional competence and experience about when, where, and how to undertake initiatives that can yield tangible diplomatic and political benefits. Creating a brand new security institution is not an easy task, but then this was not the first time Canada was lending a hand to create a new security institution. The process that led to the formation of banning AP land mines was also path-breaking in that Canada, along with other actors in the coalition, demonstrated that NGOs and other civil society groups could also play a central role in promoting human security. As Bélanger and Michaud have shown (chapter 7), Canada did not engage in this venture for altruistic reasons. The investment of its resources was well-placed and well-timed. Canada was able to gain political benefits from the process that led to the adoption of this security regime.

Conditional Engagement

Initially China posed a number of conditions on joining the Comprehensive Test Ban Treaty (CTBT). Two important issues stood out particularly. China wanted to include a clause on peaceful nuclear explosions (PNE), and it opposed national means of technical verification and advocated instead the formation of an international monitoring mechanism that would be empowered to undertake wide-ranging verification, including on-site inspections.[11] More particularly, China asked that countries with advanced verification technologies transfer them to those that did not have such capabilities. For almost two years China maintained its PNE demand against all odds, considering that PNEs had long since lost their legitimacy and usefulness. Eventually, Beijing made a last-minute concession on the PNE issue.

Why China changed its position is still a question that needs to be researched. Holding too much to its position on the PNE exposed China to the risk of ridicule before the G7/G8 countries that were visibly losing patience with their senior ally. There may have been – as Alastair Johnston points out – some learning on the part of the Chinese foreign relations and security bureaucracy as it grew more sensitive to negative images that China's refusal to adhere to the CTBT would have generated in the international community.[12] And to be sure, China's refusal could also have jeopardized Beijing's successful anti-ostracization strategy.

On the whole, China demonstrated a slightly less than average interest in the CTBT as it presented outlandish conditions for the creation of this regime. Joining the CTBT was thus instrumental in bringing an end to its isolation and in beginning its institutional socialization. The level of engagement in this case was relatively high, since China also modified its institutional security preferences as a result of its involvement in the institutional security process and agreed to join the CTBT, which is arguably the most constraining international security treaty to which China has adhered so far.

Expressing Strong Preferences

At first, France was not very keen to transfer parts of its jurisdiction to international institutions to fight terrorism more efficiently (chapter 3). France attempted to deal with this threat through bilateral operations with its European partners. Only after a spate of terrorist bombings did France agree to implement the 1991 convention to create the Europol. In early 1996, France widened its fight against terrorism by joining other states and major powers (the United States, Russia) to discuss the ways in which states could co-operate to combat terrorism. In March 1996 the Sharm el-Sheikh Conference adopted most of the measures suggested by France. Three months later, it returned to the same theme at the G7 Lyon Summit with even more extensive counter-terrorist principles and norms. But the subsequent ministerial meetings on terrorism brought out strong differences between France and the United States. If the Americans were calling for the creation of a counter-terrorist international organization targeting terrorist groups and "rogue" states, the French advocated a critical dialogue with "suspect" states. Furthermore, France argued that socioeconomic and political conditions, which give rise to the scourge of terrorism, needed also to be addressed. Despite numerous divergent viewpoints, these meetings did not create a security institution devoted to counterterrorism. States did agree, however, to coordinate their antiterrorist policies and operations. As Macleod and Viau show (chapter 3), France realized the extent to which terrorism had developed sophisticated methods and had become more transnational, hence the need to coordinate counter-terrorist operations. But this coordination did not include investing tangible resource in creating a new institution. Despite its wide-ranging activities, France kept itself at a distance from the creation of an institution that could conceivably weaken its strategic autonomy.

Despite Germany's relative weakness at the very beginning of the unification process, Chancellor Kohl presented a far-reaching strategy, and Germany stuck to its principles while adapting to the rapidly changing security environment in Europe. To Germany it was important to preserve its relationship with the existing institutional system that had provided domestic stability and political development. No one knew what Germany's choice would be for its political future when East Germans in their vast majority expressed massively and in no uncertain terms their wish to join the Bundesrepublik. As Cloutier,

Lemay, and Létourneau show in their review of the German unification through the lenses of the three main theoretical approaches (chapter 4), Kohl's strategy was composed of many strands.

First, he set out to reassure Germany's Western allies that a unified Germany had no intention of defecting from the alliance, since it was one of the pillars that supported the German state. Second, he also sought to reassure Moscow that a unified Germany did not intend to exclude the Soviet Union from the new European political order. In his negotiations with Gorbachev, Kohl gave assurances that Germany would seriously seek to enhance the CSCE as the first security institution in Europe. Third, remaining firmly a member of existing institutional frameworks while negotiating at the same time with the Soviet Union gave Kohl an excellent argument against those in Germany who were opposed to a hasty and costly unification. Finally, Kohl quickly steered Germany to a position where it became the only interlocutor with the Soviet Union in what was to become the last Soviet-German negotiations of the century. This was no small feat, since it provided Germany with influence and, indeed, more power in developing the European community. Henceforth Bonn, and later Berlin, would be more self-assured in its designs for enlarging the European Union. Germany was thus at long last master of its destiny and intimately tied to Europe and its institutions. Institutions were substitutes for Germany, since much of its legitimacy derived from them; Kohl did not see how unification could proceed without them. Enhancing the CSCE and remaining in NATO, where indeed Germany stood the chance of increasing its power,[13] were not antithetical, a prospect that was lost on Gorbachev, who thought he had heard Kohl say that Germany would leave NATO as soon as possible.

PATTERNS OF REFORM BEHAVIOUR

Before characterizing the conduct of the principal powers in the reform of the Security Council, it is important to review the central issues as discussed in the Open-Ended Working Group (OEWG). In 1993 this group was tasked by the General Assembly with finding a formula to improve the representativity of the Security Council and its working methods. The group considered two clusters of questions. Cluster 1 examined the expansion of permanent and nonpermanent Security Council memberships. At issue in the selection of new permanent members was how to make the Council more representative geographically, while at the same time respecting new world-power realities. At the core of this issue were the attributes of new permanent members: the level of their financial contribution to the organization, their commitment to arms control and nonproliferation, their possession of experienced and well-trained forces capable of undertaking peacekeeping and peace-enforcing operations, their willingness to accept human losses, and their readiness to defend human rights. Cluster 1 included changes in veto rights held by the permanent members. In this case the question was whether present permanent members should continue to use the veto indiscriminately without providing reasons and whether veto rights should be limited to chapter 7 of the United Nations Charter and extended to the new permanent members.[14]

Cluster 2 was about working methods of the Security Council. The OEWG was searching for transparent working procedures that would be more sensitive to the concerns of the large majority of UN member states that do not stand a chance of becoming members of the Security Council. Central to present working methods were informal consultations, since most of the negotiations take place outside the chambers of the Security Council. Traditionally, the Security Council presidency holds informal consultations without the knowledge of parties not directly concerned with the issues at hand, in order to speed up the process of reaching compromises and building consensus among the permanent members of the Council. But since the increase of security disasters and the rise of the democratic ethos at the United Nations, states are less willing to accept this state of affairs. Hence the necessity of devising ways and means by which nonmembers can participate in the Council's proceedings, have access to its decision-making process, and monitor its operations during times of crisis.

The search for greater democracy and openness intersects with the interests of troop-contributing countries that are essentially middle powers; they do not frequently sit on the Security Council, and they seek to increase their access to it. Improving methods of work would therefore give them more voice in the Council, especially if their peacekeeping expertise and capabilities are required. But transforming the Council into a more transparent executive body also has its downside, as the defenders of efficiency have argued in the OEWG. Too much transparency can make its decision-making process more time-consuming. The defenders of efficiency advocated that although transparency was a worthy objective from the viewpoint of fostering openness and democracy, the Council was still expected to take timely decisions. What would be the point of having a Security Council if its operations were contingent on the scrutiny of the members of the General Assembly?

As will be discussed below, four important patterns of institutional behaviour can be observed in this case. For the established permanent members, the issue was to remain in the Security Council: indeed three of the five permanent members (Russia, France, and the UK) were initially candidates for removal of their permanent status. For the major powers with no permanent tenure in the Council, such as Germany, Japan, and India, the goal was to gain permanent status or, alternatively, find a way to remain permanently in it even without veto rights. All of the three had every reason to seek permanent tenure at the Security Council, since it could enhance their power in all international security networks. For middle powers, such as Canada, that did not conceivably stand a chance of gaining permanent status, the goal was to increase their access to the Security Council's decision-making process and in due time build a lasting influence on it.

Protecting Status

All permanent members defended the status quo. They invoked efficiency of working methods, promoted a limited expansion composed mainly of new permanent members and defended the preservation of their veto rights. They warned against "hasty steps" to reorganize the Council.[15] They called for taking into account the opinions of UN members, but ultimately the design of a new Security Council rested on the consensus among the permanent members. And they also lacked a sense of enthusiasm and urgency for finding a compromise solution for restructuring the Council. Their statements at the OEWG were routinely nonevents marked by a reminder that permanent members had veto privileges they were not ready to part with.[16]

Decidedly, among permanent members of the Council, China was the only power expressing reservations about the wisdom of enlarging the permanent membership, since this enlargement implied a seat for Japan and possibly even for India, two Asian powers with which China maintains less than perfect cordial relationships. Speaking as the only representative of the developing countries in the P5 group, China favoured increasing nonpermanent seats in order to ensure a wider representation for countries of Asia, Africa, and Latin America and the Caribbean. But China avoided staking out its position on the ratio of permanent and nonpermanent seats. Just like its peers, China was also against restricting veto rights, because restrictions could have a negative impact on its status in the decision-making process in the Council.[17]

Contrary to the two previous American cases, the United States abstained from leading in the Council's reform. As Racicot and David show (chapter 1), the Clinton administration changed its stance throughout its tenure. From being an early enthusiast of UN reform, it quickly became sceptical and agnostic towards any restructuring formula. It reiterated its long-time view that Germany and Japan should be given permanent-member status. Washington was also willing to consider three more permanent seats for underrepresented regions. The maximum number of seats it could tolerate was twenty-one.

For much of its tenure, the Clinton administration defended a limited expansion of the Security Council. But with Richard C. Holbrooke at the head of the U.S. delegation in 1999, the United States was now prepared to consider a slightly larger number of seats than twenty-one.[18] Whether the slight increase meant a larger number of permanent seats only was not clearly stated, since Washington seemed to be searching for a fallback position on the ideal size and composition of the enlarged Council.[19] To be sure, reform of the Council was not a top priority for the administration or for Congress. Congress prevented the administration from paying the arrears that the United States owed to the UN, and invoked bad administrative practices in the UN for its lack of support for Council reform. Behind this refusal stood its preoccupation with the fact that an improved Security Council could rival its legislative prerogatives, since the president of the United States would be keener to deploying U.S. troops abroad if Security Council resolutions called for such deployment.[20] Congress was also concerned that the Security Council could well become a forum where major powers and other lesser powers would criticize and single out the United States as a unilateralist power bent on world hegemony.

To Russia, Security Council reform was partly a complement and partly a substitute, since on the one hand it wanted to secure a permanent seat in an enlarged Council as a way of preserving its great-power status at a time when its power was rapidly dwindling. On the other hand, as Lavoie and Lévesque argue (chapter 2), it also needed its permanent status in order to assert its legitimacy to build the Commonwealth of Independent States as a security institution in the Eurasian space.[21] Moscow therefore defended a conservative expansion of the Council and stuck to its position all along. It could not bear the idea of seeing an excessive enlargement that could hamper the Council's efficiency. France shared the same preoccupation. It too sought to secure its *rang* at a time when many countries in the OEWG thought that France and Britain should retire from the Council to pave the way for a single European Union seat.[22] However, France defended its seat by supporting a more liberal expansion of the Council, bringing the total number of seats to twenty-four, with five new seats reserved for permanent members.

Contrary to the Russian position, France accepted the principle that veto rights should be restricted to chapter 7 but considered that in no

circumstances should it be abolished. Acting consistently with its entre-
preneurial norms, as Macleod and Viau point out (chapter 3), France
wanted to specify the circumstances during which permanent powers
could invoke their veto rights. Again, expressing its strong preference
as to how an institution should function, France suggested that these
circumstances should not include instances where there were massive
abuses of human rights in a state that was incapable of stopping them
effectively.[23] France expected its peers to accept this fundamental
requirement in a reform package, a tall order, indeed, considering
Russia's and China's propensity to use their veto rights precisely in circumstances where state sovereignty would be put to test by an overpowering Security Council.

No consensus was achieved between the P5 and the UN membership
on veto rights, as all five warned that "any attempt to restrict or curtail
their veto rights would not be conducive to the reform process."[24]
Russia thought it was wrong to suggest that concurring votes would
lead to a paralysis of the Council. The right to veto was even seen as
an irreplaceable tool for well-coordinated activities of the Security
Council and balanced decisions. Finally, if the United States and France
were willing to extend veto rights to new permanent members, Russia
wanted to decide on the issue only after the concrete composition of
the enlarged Council had been agreed upon.[25]

Claiming a New Status

Germany and Japan both asked for and received support for becoming
permanent members of the Security Council. The main support came
from the four permanent members. Both major powers heavily lobbied
inside and outside the United Nations to earn the support of a sizeable
majority of the General Assembly. On balance, Germany spent more
political capital and resources than Japan to prove that it met most of
the attributes of a permanent member. By refusing to rewrite article 9
of its constitution, which prohibits Japan from deploying its soldiers
far away from its territories, Japan failed to emulate the German
example. Like Japan, Germany advocated three additional permanent
seats for Asian, African, and Latin American and Caribbean states and
at least five nonpermanent seats for underrepresented regions.
Germany even supported India's claim to permanent status, while the
European Union preferred to see India join the CTBT before articulating any views on granting India permanent status at the Council.[26]

Moreover, both Japan and Germany did not wish to become second-
class permanent members with limited veto rights or none at all.
However, both were sensitive to the fact that granting veto power to

five new permanent members might create the perception that the Council could become even more exclusionary and elitist. Hence, Germany suggested that permanent members should state clearly why a veto is necessary when they chose to use their veto powers.[27]

Differing slightly from Germany, Japan proposed to increase the permanent-member category more than the nonpermanent category. In this case, Germany's proposal coincided with the French and the American proposals. Japan lobbied with the Asian nations to acquire a permanent seat, since China seemed opposed to its quest to become a permanent member. But Japan had reservations about supporting India, a major power vying for a permanent seat. It agreed, however, to consider granting permanent seats to developing countries.[28] Tokyo could not understand why other middle powers, such as Canada, Italy, Mexico, and Brazil, were against increasing the number of permanent seats, since adding only nonpermanent seats "would not enhance the legitimacy and effectiveness of the Council."[29] To Germany and Japan, the Council's reform was largely a substitute for the enhancement of their international security roles and identities. Without access to permanency, they could not hope to widen their influence in other crucial areas of the world political agenda. If Germany was more active in articulating its views to various audiences, Japan was more conspicuous and preferred to resort to development assistance as a method of gaining support among UN members. If anything, Japan continued to be a major power that was reluctant to embed new international security responsibilities in its Constitution; it relied instead on its chequebook to earn a permanent seat.[30]

While Germany and Japan strove to become full-fledged permanent members, Canada opposed both their claim and enlargement of the permanent-member group in general. It would only agree to an expansion of at least ten new nonpermanent members through election. Furthermore, it insisted that veto rights be limited strictly to chapter 7 decisions. To Canada, this proposal would enhance the Council's representativity, credibility, and accountability and increase its legitimacy in the eyes of the majority of states.

Harbouring no ambitions to gain a permanent seat, Canada did not claim a new status, nor did it present, like Italy, intricate proposals concerning the selection of new nonpermanent members. It did, however, advocate very strongly opening up the Council to UN membership. True representativity and accountability meant that member states could access the Council without resorting to Byzantine tactics.[31] This demand for better accessibility to the Council was not altogether selfless as Bélanger and Michaud argue (chapter 7). As a major troop-contributor, Canada already enjoyed an entry to the Council; what it

needed was to remain in it almost permanently by becoming its emi-
nence grise. Ottawa could not find a better way than advocating
democratization and the establishment of processes that would ensure
its own informal permanence in the Council.

Promoting Transparent Working Methods

Transparent working methods were advocated by Germany and Japan,
which campaigned for permanent seats, and most of all by Canada,
which, as a troop-contributing state, was seeking to enhance its access
to the Security Council. It is relatively easy to understand why
Germany and Japan were advocating transparency, since they were
soliciting the support of member states that must, in the end, vote at
the General Assembly on the reform package. Making the Council
more democratic and accountable in its decision-making and making
its international security operations more efficient were major
demands of the general UN membership, which Canada understood
quite well.

As a measure for promoting transparency that was linked to becoming permanent members, Japan and Germany also supported periodic
review meetings of permanent members' performance every ten or
fifteen years. In their view, this policy would ensure that permanent
members would become more accountable to the General Assembly.
They also supported regular and constant briefings of the Council to
nonmembers and new participatory procedures. For Germany, transparency was as important as efficiency; Japan was much less eloquent
on both issues, since it was more obsessed with gaining approval for its
bid for permanency.

Elected to sit on the Council for a period of two years (1999–2000),
Canada promised to promote human security, strive for a more transparent Council, and work towards a more effective and credible institution. For Canada, transparency was more important than making
the Council more efficient; the reform had first to address the requirements of the United Nations and its member states and the needs of its
membership. Since this was a fundamental principle from which everything flowed, the Council had first to be more transparent so as to be
more representative, open, and accountable to its members. Furthermore, Canada considered that a measure of openness could be
achieved by reducing veto rights to only Chapter 7 decisions. Because
the OEWG was still deliberating on a reform package, Canada also promoted introducing new transparent practices to the Council. Some of
the measures consisted of getting the presidency of the Security Council
to hold briefing sessions immediately after informal consultations. It

also included broadening the Council's established views through thematic debates, such as debates on human security, and offering nonmembers the opportunity to present their views to the Council before major decisions were taken.[32]

Advocating Efficient Working Methods

Most of the established permanent members defended the principle of efficiency over transparency, but with different emphasis. Although it initially expressed reservations about a more open Security Council, France eventually embraced transparency, but with the qualification that it must serve effectiveness, and not the other way around. France wanted to preserve informal consultations for substantive negotiations and for resolving acute tensions between members of the Council: public debates would be reserved only for broad issues, statements from the secretary-general, and general policy matters. More importantly, France favoured a dialogue between the Council and troop-contributing states in private settings where practical issues can be resolved expeditiously.[33]

Both the United States and Russia were united in their quest to keep working methods as they were.[34] The United States saw a greater priority for providing the Security Council with a new set of mechanisms to respond more efficiently to international security contingencies. The U.S. delegations under the first and second Clinton administrations were heedless of transparency issues until Richard Holbrooke arrived on the scene and began supporting such measures in the context of wide-ranging reform of peace-keeping operations. However, even Holbrooke did not forget that working methods should primarily serve to make the Council more effective in dealing with international security challenges.[35]

Russia defended the principles of efficiency while occasionally giving in to demands for greater transparency. It actually linked efficient working methods with the preservation of veto rights.[36] Effectiveness was synonymous with respecting the Security Council as the organ entrusted with the primary responsibility for the maintenance of international peace and security."[37]

Differing slightly with Russian views, China advocated the necessity of holding extensive and lengthy informal consultations before the Security Council took any decision. In many ways, this was business as usual and a convenient way of preventing other permanent members, notably the United States and the United Kingdom, from hastily deciding on a course of action that could jeopardize the principle of sovereignty. China's ambassador told the working group that one way to

improve the working methods of the Council was to develop its relations with the members of the General Assembly. The views of all
Council members, as well as of the broad UN membership, should be
taken into consideration so that decisions and actions taken by the
Council would enable it to reflect the will of the overwhelming majority of member states.[38]

CONCLUSION

Three theoretical statements can be formulated on the basis of the
above typology of institutional security behaviour. First, principal
powers act through security institutions if it suits their interests. This
statement gives credibility to the realist approach, which sees security
institutions as instruments in the hands of principal powers. But once
in the institutional loop, principal powers behave quite differently. This
is where the institutionalist approach is useful, because it informs us
that principal powers remain within institutions as long as they can
draw benefits. But this engagement depends very much on their institutional know-how. Canada created a new security institution and
used a multi-institutional strategy to achieve its goals. China inched
towards multilateral security institutions in a cautious, limited, and
conditional way because of the benefits it could gain from the process.
When a dominant state insists on leading security institutions to a
course of action, it will spend whatever resources are necessary to
make that happen, regardless of whether it reaps large benefits or sus-
tains important losses.

Second, principal powers can be reluctant players in international
security institutions. Apart from restraining the security behaviour of
principal powers, security institutions can place constraints on other
behaviour, and not for the reasons suggested by institutionalist theory.
They may provide constraints when principal powers must invest more
than they should, when they are at a loss about what to do with institutions, or when they are bound by an institutional arrangement that
overrides other security initiatives. The United States under the Clinton
administration was reluctant to lead stabilization efforts in Bosnia,
because it thought Europeans should incur the costs of the operation.
Russia found itself marginalized in the NATO expansion project, mainly
because the Yeltsin government had no institutional security strategy
on its agenda. Japan could not play a crucial role in Northeast Asian
security, because of its strategic dependency, and it was thus caught in
an institutional bind.

Third, security institutions are construction sites where new security
identities are built. They act as forums where principal powers strongly

voice their preferences and test their new security identities against those of their peers. Institutional contexts allow security preferences to change, but in the end most of the changes are sought and made by the principal power. Security institutions may represent a fundamental condition for the principal power's identity, but much depends on how that power develops and renews its security and national identity. Germany used security institutions successfully; but Moscow could not match German performance. Principal powers, like France, for whom security institutions do not constitute a fundamental condition of international behaviour, voice their preferences at different decibel levels, as a method of preserving their rank and prestige in the world order.

Notes

INTRODUCTION

1 Alastair I. Johnston and Paul Evans, "China's Engagement with Multilateral Security Institutions," in *Engaging China: The Management of an Emerging Power*, edited by Alastair I. Johnston and Robert S. Ross (Routledge: London 1999), 235–72; Yong Dong, "The Asianization of East Asian Security and the United States' Role," *East Asia* 16, nos. 3–4 (1998): 87–110.

2 United Nations General Assembly, *Report of the Open-Ended Working Group on the Question of Equitable Representation on and Increase in the Membership of the Security Council and Other Matters Related to the Security Council*, Fifty-fourth Session (25 July 2000), Supp. No. 47, (A/54/47), http://www.globalpolicy.org/security/reform/oewg/wg00a11+.htm.

3 While member states were debating this possibility, the secretary general, Kofi Annan, was able to introduce administrative and organizational changes. For an overview, see United States, General Accounting Office, *United Nations: Reform Initiatives Have Strengthened Operations, but Overall Objectives Have Not Yet Been Achieved* (Washington, DC: Government Publishing Office 2000), 19.

4 See for instance Jarat Chopra, "The UN's Kingdom of East Timor," *Survival* 42, no. 3 (2000): 27–39.

5 Richard Price, "Reversing the Gun Sights: Transnational Civil Society Targets Land Mines," *International Organization* 52, no. 4 (1998): 613–44.

6 For a brief review of the Sixth NPT Review Conference, see Rebecca

Johnson, "The 2000 NPT Review Conference: A Delicate, Hard-Won Compromise," *Disarmament Diplomacy*, no. 46 (2000), http://www.acronym.org.uk/46npt.htm.

7 This is particularly true because all three approaches are basically American. See Ole Wæver, "The Sociology of a Not So International Discipline: American and European Developments in International Relations," *International Organization* 52, no. 4 (1998): 687–727.

8 In this case the expected benefits are low compared to costs that major powers must share. In such cases, it is more like paying dues to keep one's own status as a major power.

9 Celeste Wallander, Helga Haftendorn, and Robert O. Keohane, Introduction to *Imperfect Unions: Security Institutions over Time and Space*, edited by Celeste Wallander, Helga Haftendorn, and Robert O. Keohane (London: Oxford University Press 1999), 1–18; Lisa L. Martin, "Interests, Power, and Multilateralism," *International Organization* 46, no. 4 (1992): 765–92.

10 Jacques Chirac, "La France dans un monde multipolaire," *Politique étrangère* 64, no. 4 (1999): 797–801.

11 Robert D. Putnam, "Diplomacy and Domestic Politics: The Logic of Two-Level Games," *International Organization* 42, no. 3 (1988): 427–59.

12 See John G. Ikenberry, "Institutions, Strategic Restraint, and the Persistence of American Postwar Order," *International Security* 23, no. 3 (1998): 43–78.

13 See also Michael N. Barnett, "Identity and Alliances in the Middle East," in *The Culture of National Security: Norms and Identity in World Politics*, edited by Peter J. Katzenstein (New York: Columbia University Press 1996), 408–9.

14 Martha Finnemore, *National Interests in International Society* (Ithaca, NY: Cornell University Press 1996), 20–1.

15 Keith Krause and Andrew Latham, "Constructing Non-Proliferation and Arms Control: The Norms of Western Practice," in *Culture and Security: Multilateralism, Arms Control and Security Building*, edited by Keith R. Krause (London: Frank Cass 1999), 23–54.

16 Constructivists have not yet been able to work out a feasible method by which this two-way, or dialectical, relation works, especially since most of its proponents think that this happens simultaneously. See Jeffrey T. Checkel, "The Constructivist Turn in International Relations Theory," *World Politics* 50 (1998): 324–48.

17 Thomas Risse, "Let's Argue! Communicative Action in World Politics," *International Organization* 54, no. 1 (2000): 1–39.

18 Paul W. Schroeder, "Did the Vienna Settlement Rest on a Balance of Power?" *American Historical Review* 97 (1992): 683–706.

19 See, for instance, Kenneth Waltz's latest reiteration on this issue, "Structural Realism after the Cold War," *International Security* 25, no. 1 (2000): 5–41.

20 William C. Wohlworth, "The Stability of a Unipolar World," *International Security* 24, no. 1 (1999): 5–41.

21 G. John Ikenberry, "Constitutional Politics in International Relations," *European Journal of International Relations* 4 (1998): 147–78.

22 For an account on the role played by security institutions during the Cold War, see David A. Lake, "Beyond Anarchy: The Importance of Security Institutions," *International Security* 26, no. 1 (summer 2001): 129–60.

23 Randall Schweller, "Realism and the Present Great Power System: Growth and Positional Conflict over Scarce Resources," in *Unipolar Politics: Realism and State Strategies after the Cold War*, edited by Ethan B. Kapstein and Michael Mastanduno (New York: Columbia University Press 1999), 28–68.

24 Gideon Rose, "Neoclassical Realism and Theories of Foreign Policy," *World Politics* 51 (1998): 144–72.

25 See a recent statement on analytical eclecticism by Peter J. Katzenstein and Nobuo Okawara, "Japan, Asia-Pacific, and the Case for Analytical Eclecticism," *International Security* 26, no. 3 (winter 2001/02): 153–85.

26 See for instance Andreas Hasenclever, Peter Mayer, and Volker Rittberger, *Theories of International Regimes* (Cambridge: Cambridge University Press 1997), especially the concluding chapter, where the authors are pleading for a "synthetic approach." See Lisa L. Martin's views on the problematic nature of this methodology in "Theories of International Regimes," *American Political Science Review* 94, no. 1 (2000): 241–2.

27 We believe just as much that the core assumptions of each approach, as well as their respective inferential logics, must continue to be refined.

28 For nesting and sequencing see Ronald L. Jepperson, Alexander Wendt and Peter J. Katzenstein, "Norms, Identity, and Culture in National Security," in *The Culture of National Security: Norms and Identity in World Politics*, edited by Peter J. Katzenstein (New York: Columbia University Press 1996), 68–71. Our nesting is equivalent to their second form of nesting; whereas *sequencing* would be equivalent to their "stage-complementarity."

29 For a recent classification of international security institutions, see Celeste Wallander, Helga Haftendorn, and Robert O. Keohane, "Risk, Threat, and Security Institutions," in *Imperfect Unions: Security Institutions over Time and Space*, edited by Celeste Wallander, Helga Haftendorn, and Robert O. Keohane (London: Oxford University Press 1999), 21–47; Robert Jervis, "Realism, Neoliberalism, and Cooperation: Understanding the Debate," *International Security* 24, no. 1 (1999): 55–62.

30 For a description of strategic partnerships, see Avery Goldstein, "Structural Realism and China's Foreign Policy: A Good Part of the Story," paper presented at the Annual Meeting of the American Political Science Association, 3–6 September 1998, 45–6.

31 Glenn Snyder, *Alliance Politics* (Ithaca, NY: Cornell University Press 1997); John Duffield, "The North Atlantic Treaty Organization: Alliance Theory," in *Explaining International Relations since 1945*, edited by Ngaire Woods (Oxford: Oxford University Press 1996), 337–54.

32 Alexander L. George, Philip J. Farley, and Alexander Dallin, eds., *U.S.-Soviet Security Cooperation: Achievements, Failures, Lessons* (New York: Oxford University Press 1988).

33 Charles A. Kupchan and Clifford A. Kupchan, "The Promise of Collective Security," *International Security* 20, no. 1 (1995): 52–61; George Downs, ed., *Collective Security beyond the Cold War* (Ann Arbor, MI: University of Michigan Press 1994).

CHAPTER ONE

1 We identify international security institutions (ISIS) as all institutions concerned basically with international security matters. We have decided to adopt a narrow view of the security concept. Hence, economic instituions such as the World Bank and the World Trade Organization, although strategic in nature, are not considered ISIS. ISIS can be formal (NATO and the United Nations) or loose (a collection of states such as the Contact Group).

2 For brief presentations of realism see Sean M. Lynn-Jones and Steven E. Miller, preface to Michael E. Brown et al., *The Perils of Anarchy* (Boston: MIT Press 1995), ix–xxi; Sean M. Lynn-Jones, "Realism and Security Studies," in Craig A. Snyder, ed., *Contemporary Security and Strategy* (New York: Routledge 1999), 53–76; Benjamin Frankel, "Restating the Realist Case: An Introduction," in Benjamin Frankel, ed., *Realism: Restatements and Renewal* (London: Frank Cass 1996), x–xv; Joseph M. Grieco, "Realist International Theory and the Study of World Politics," in Michael W. Doyle and John G. Ikenberry, eds., *New Thinking in International Relations Theory* (Boulder, CO: Westview Press 1997), 163–201; Frank W. Wayman and Paul F. Diehl, "Realism Reconsidered: The Realpolitik Framework and Its Basic Propositions," in Frank W. Wayman and Paul F. Diehl, eds., *Reconstructing Realpolitik* (Ann Arbor, MI: University of Michigan Press 1994), 3–29; and Timothy Dunne, "Realism," in John Baylis and Steve Smith, eds., *The Globalization of World Politics: An Introduction to International Relations* (Oxford: Oxford University Press 1997), 109–24.

3 See William C. Wohlforth, "Realism and the End of the Cold War,"

International Security 19, no. 3 (winter 1994/95): 91–129; and Paul Schroeder, "Historical Reality vs. Neo-Realist Theory," *International Security* 19, no. 1 (summer 1994): 108–48.

4 See Steve Smith, "New Approaches to International Theory," in John Baylis and Steve Smith, eds., *The Globalization of World Politics: An Introduction to International Relations* (Oxford: Oxford University Press 1997), 165–90.

5 Robert Jervis, "Realism, NeoLiberalism and Cooperation: Understanding the Debate," *International Security* 24, no. 1 (summer 1999): 42–63.

6 John Mearsheimer, "The False Promise of International Institutions," *International Security* 19, no. 3 (winter 1994–95): 5–49.

7 Randall L. Schweller and David Priess, "A Tale of Two Realisms: Expanding the Institutions Debate," *Mershon International Studies Review* 41 (1997): 1–32.

8 Barry Buzan, Charles Jones, and Richard Little, *The Logic of Anarchy: Neorealism to Structural Realism* (New York: Columbia University Press 1993), 20.

9 For excellent overviews of this debate, see Charles W. Kegley Jr, *Controversies in International Relations Theory: Realism and the Neoliberal Challenge* (New York: St Martin's Press 1995), and David A. Baldwin, ed., *Neorealism and Neoliberalism: The Contemporary Debate* (New York: Columbia University Press 1993).

10 Kenneth Waltz, *Theory of International Politics* (New York: Addison-Wesley 1979).

11 Michael Mastanduno and Ethan B. Kapstein, "Realism and State Strategies after the Cold War," in Ethan B. Kapstein and Michael Mastanduno, eds., *Unipolar Politics: Realism and State Strategies after the Cold War* (New York: Columbia University Press 1999), 7–8.

12 Gideon Rose, "Neoclassical Realism and Theories of Foreign Policy," *World Politics*, no. 51 (October 1998): 144–72.

13 For a quick survey of constructivism see Alexander Wendt, "Constructing International Politics," *International Security* 20, no. 1 (1995): 71–81; "Collective Identity Formation and the International State," *American Political Science Review* 88, no. 2 (1994): 384–96; "Anarchy Is What States Make of It: The Social Construction of Power Politics," *International Organization* 46, no. 2 (1992): 391–425; and Peter J. Katzenstein, ed., *The Culture of National Security: Norms and Identity in World Politics* (New York: Columbia University Press 1996).

14 Other neoclassical realists include Fareed Zakaria, *From Wealth to Power: The Unusual Origins of America's World Role* (Princeton, NJ: Princeton University Press 1998); Randall L. Schweller, *Deadly Imbalances: Tripolarity and Hitler's Strategy of World Conquest* (New York: Columbia University Press 1998); William C. Wohlforth, *The Elusive*

Balance: Power and Perceptions during the Cold War (Ithaca, NY: Cornell University Press 1993); Thomas J. Christensen, *Useful Adversaries: Grand Strategy, Domestic Mobilization, and Sino-American Conflict, 1947–1958* (Princeton, NJ: Princeton University Press 1998).

15 For various interpretations of where the offensive/defensive debate lies theoretically, see Lynn-Jones and Miller, preface, xi; and Lynn-Jones, *Realism and Security Studies*, 62; Rose, *Neoclassical Realism*, 148–9; Joseph M. Grieco, "Realist International Theory and the Study of World Politics," in Michael W. Doyle and John G. Ikenberry, eds., *New Thinking in International Relations Theory* (Boulder, CO: Westview Press 1997), 163–201; Jeffrey W. Taliaferro, "Security-Seeking under Anarchy: Defensive Realism Reconsidered," paper prepared for panel DF-02, Intra-Realist Debates: Theoretical Progress or Degeneration? annual ISA meeting, Washington, DC (15–20 February 1999): 2.

16 Lynn-Jones, *Realism and Security Studies*, 62.

17 See Jack Snyder, *Myths of Empire: Domestic Politics and International Ambition* (Ithaca, NY: Cornell University Press 1991).

18 See Stephen Van Evera, *Causes of War* (Ithaca, NY: Cornell University Press 1999); "Offense, Defense, and the Causes of War," *International Security* 22, no. 4 (spring 1998): 5–43; Charles L. Glaser and Chaim Kaufmann, "What Is the Offense-Defense Balance and Can We Measure It?" *International Security* 22, no. 4 (spring 1998): 44–82; and James W. Davis Jr et al., "Taking Offense at Offense-Defense Theory," correspondence, *International Security* 23, no. 3 (winter 1998/99): 79–206.

19 Fareed Zakaria, "Realism and Domestic Politics," *International Security* 17, no. 1 (summer 1992): 177–98.

20 Fareed Zakaria, *From Wealth to Power: The Unusual Origins of America's World Role* (Princeton, NJ: Princeton University Press 1998), 41–2.

21 Ibid., 21.

22 Zakaria believes his "state-centred realism" explains the behaviour of states during periods of peace and stability better than defensive realism does. See Zakaria, "Realism and Domestic Politics," 181–7.

23 Sean M. Lynn-Jones, "Realism and America's Rise," *International Security* 23, no. 2 (fall 1998): 170.

24 Van Evera, "Offense, Defense and the causes of War," 7–16.

25 See Stephen A. Walt, *The Origins of Alliances* (Ithaca, NY: Cornell University Press 1987); Glen A. Snyder, *Alliance Politics* (Ithaca, NY: Cornell University Press 1997); Randall L. Schweller, "Bandwagoning for Profit," *International Security* 19, no. 1 (summer 1994): 72–107.

26 Stephen Van Evera, "Offense, Defense, and the Causes of War," 44–69.

27 See Charles A. Kupchan, "After Pax Americana," *International Security* 23, no. 2 (fall 1998): 40–79, and Michael Mastanduno, "Preserving the

Unipolar Moment," *International Security* 21, no. 4 (spring 1997): 49–88.

28 See the conclusion of Samuel Huntington, "The Lonely Superpower," *Foreign Affairs* 78, no. 2 (March/April 1999): 49.

29 Mastanduno and Kapstein, "Realism and State Strategies," 16.

30 For a survey of the different theories see Timothy Dunne, "Liberalism," in John Baylis and Steve Smith, eds., *The Globalization of World Politics: An Introduction to International Relations* (Oxford: Oxford University Press 1997), 147–63.

31 John J. Mearsheimer, "The False Promise of International Institutions," *International Security* 19, no. 3 (winter 1994–95): 5–49.

32 Robert Keohane and Lisa Martin, "The Promise of Institutional Theory," *International Security* 20, no. 1 (summer 1995): 39–51.

33 Daniel Deudney and John G. Ikenberry, "Realism, Structural Liberalism, and the Western Order," in Ethan B. Kapstein and Michael Mastanduno, eds., *Unipolar Politics: Realism and State Strategies after the Cold War* (New York: Columbia University Press 1999), 103–37.

34 Ibid., 105–23.

35 John G. Ikenberry, "Institutions, Strategic Restraint, and the Persistence of the American Postwar Order," *International Security* 23, no. 3 (winter 1998–99): 43–78.

36 Ibid., 54.

37 Thomas Friedman, "Foreign Policy Work," *New York Times*, 14 April 1996, D-19; Chris Hedges, "U.S. and Allies Fail to Strip Top Bosnian Serbs of Power," *New York Times*, 24 May 1996, A-1.

38 Barbara Crossette, "UN Official Urges a Rebuilding Role for Peacekeeping Forces," *New York Times*, 22 May 1996, A-11; and Steven Erlanger, "U.S. Report Says Bosnia Peace is Fragile," *New York Times*, 17 May 1996, A-6.

39 Anthony Lewis, "Bosnia Betrayed Again," *New York Times*, 3 June 1996, A-15.

40 Philipp Shenon, "Defense Secretary Says U.S. Troops May Have to Remain in Bosnia Well into Next Year," *New York Times*, 13 June 1996, A-10; Steven Erlanger, "President Makes It Official: He May Send More Troops to Bosnia Next Year," *New York Times*, 9 November 1996, A-11; Alison Mitchell, "U.S. Ready to Keep a Force in Bosnia 18 Months Longer," *New York Times*, 16 November 1996, A-1.

41 Pat Towell, "Cohen, in Confirmation Hearing, Vows a Timely Bosnia Pullout," *Congressional Quarterly*, 25 January 1997, 247–8.

42 Steven Erlanger, "How Bosnia Policy Set Stage for Albright-Cohen Conflict," *New York Times*, 12 June 1997, A-1.

43 Mike O'Connor, "Bosnians Back Home, with Quiet U.S. Help," *New York Times*, 29 July 1997, A-3.

44 Pat Towell "Pentagon Backers in House Settle for Modest Budget Increase," *Congressional Quarterly*, 28 June 1997, 1533–5; Lizette Alvarez, "Senate is Cool to G.I. Mission in Bosnia but Doesn't Cut Off Funds," *New York Times*, 12 July 1997, A-3; and Pat Towell, "Backers of Tough Stand in Bosnia Urge Clinton to Rally Public," *Congressional Quarterly*, 6 September 1997, 2087–8.

45 Pat Towell, "Hill Unlikely to Block Extension of Bosnia Deployment," *Congressional Quarterly*, 20 December 1997, 3134.

46 Alexander Vershbow, "NATO's Role in Bosnia: Past, Present, and Future," *U.S.I.A. Electronic Journal*, vol.3, no. 2 (April 1998); James Kitfield, "Blueprint for the Balkans," *National Journal*, 14 October 1995, 2561.

47 Craig Whitney, "NATO Looks to Peacekeeping by Europeans on Their Own," *New York Times*, 3 March 1996, A-6.

48 President William J. Clinton, "Address to the Nation on Implementation of the Peace Agreement in Bosnia-Herzegovina," *U.S. Department of State Dispatch* (27 November 1995): 22.

49 Strobe Talbott, "American Leadership and the New Europe: Implementing the Dayton Peace Agreement," *Dispatch* (14 December 1995): 919; "The European Answer to the Balkan Question," *Dispatch* (17 March 1998): 26.

50 Graig Whitney, "With Ethnic Strife, NATO finds that the Enemy is Within," *New York Times*,6 July 1997, A-7; Nicole Gnessotto, "Prospects for Bosnia after SFOR," *Chaillot Papers*, no. 32 (May 1998): 28.

51 "Mr Cohen's Caution in Bosnia," editorial, *New York Times*, 8 December 1997, A-24.

52 Alexander Vershbow, "NATO's Role in Bosnia"; William J. Clinton, "The President's News Conference with President Chirac of France," *Presidential Documents Online* 32, no. 5 (5 February 1996): 119.

53 Steven Erlanger, "U.S. Held Likely to Keep Troops in Bosnia," *New York Times*, 14 November 1996, A-10; Chris Hedges, "NATO Drafts Plan to Extend Its Mission in Bosnia by Two Years," *New York Times*, 11 September 1996, A-7.

54 Gerald B. Solomon, "The NATO Enlargement Debate, 1990–1997: Blessings of Liberty," *Washington Papers* 74 (1998): 2.

55 Ibid., 13

56 James Goldgeier, "NATO Expansion: The Anatomy of a Decision," *Washington Quarterly* 21, no. 1 (winter 1998): 86–7.

57 Although initially proposed by Jeffrey Simon of the National Defense University in 1992, the PfP concept was picked up by the American military in Europe, the Department of Defense, and, later, the State Department. See Solomon, "The NATO Enlargement Debate."

58 NATO, *NATO Handbook*, Brussells, NATO Press and Information Bureau (June 1996): 54–7.

59 Elaine Sciolino, "U.S. to Offer Plan on a Role in NATO for Ex-Soviet Bloc," *New York Times*, 21 October 1993, A-1; Stephen Kinzer, "NATO Favors U.S. Plan for Ties with the East, but Timing is Vague," *New York Times*, 22 October 1993, A-1.

60 Goldgeier, "NATO Expansion," 87–8.

61 Anthony Lake, "From Containment to Enlargement," *Dispatch* (27 September 1993); "A Strategy of Enlargement and the Developing World," *Dispatch* (25 October 1993): 748–51.

62 William J. Clinton, *Public Papers, 1994*, Book 1, 40, in Goldgeier, "NATO Expansion," 102.

63 Goldgeier, "NATO Expansion," 97.

64 "House GOP Offers Descriptions of Bills to Enact 'Contract,'" *Congressional Quarterly* (19 November 1994): 3374.

65 During this period the Senate and the House adopted the NATO Participation Act of 1994, the NATO Expansion Act, and the NATO Participation Act Amendments of 1995.

66 Steven Erlanger, "In a New Attack against NATO, Yeltsin Talks of 'Conflagration of War,'" *New York Times*, 9 September 1995, A-5; Craig Whitney, "NATO Presents Plan to Expand Alliance," *New York Times*, 29 September 1995, A-14.

67 Warren Christopher, "NATO: Reaching Out to New Partners and New Challenges," *Dispatch* (5 December 1995): 903; Jane Perlez, "Bosnia: Proving Ground for NATO Contenders," *New York Times*, 9 December 1995, A-5.

68 Warren Christopher, "Leadership for the Next American Century," *Dispatch* (22 January 1996): 9–12; "A New Atlantic Community for the 21st Century," Dispatch (9 September 1996): 449–52.

69 "House Panel Approves Bill on NATO Membership," *Congressional Quarterly* (13 July 1996): 1984; Pat Towell, "Senate Backs NATO Expansion," *Congressional Quarterly* (27 July 1996): 2132.

70 William J. Clinton, "The Legacy of America's Leadership As We Enter the 21st Century."

71 Solomon, "The NATO Enlargement Debate," 98–9.

72 Alison Mitchell, "Summit Talks End with Agreement but not for NATO," *New York Times*, 22 March 1997, A-1; Steven Erlanger, "Clinton and Yeltsin Manage to Get Along," *New York Times*, 23 March 1997, D-2.

73 Alison Mitchell, "Clinton at West Point, Says Bigger NATO Lessens Chance of War," *New York Times*, 1 June 1997; Steven Erlanger, "Yeltsin Balks at Summit: Some Europeans Are Cool to the U.S.," *New York Times*, 21 June 1997.

74 "Germany Tells the UN It Wants a Permanent Seat on the Council," *New York Times*, 24 September 1992; Geoff Simons, UN *Malaise: Power,*

Problems, and Realpolitik (New York: St Martin's Press 1995), 178–86.

75 George Bush, "The United Nations in a New Era," Speech before the United Nations General Assembly, New York, *Dispatch* (30 September 1991): 718–21.

76 "The UN Assembly: Bush in Address to UN Urges More Vigor in Keeping the Peace," *New York Times*, 22 September 1992; Ivo Daadler, "Knowing When to Say No: The Development of U.S. Policy for Peace-keeping," in W.J. Durch, ed., *UN Peacekeeping, American Politics and the Civil Wars of the 1990s* (New York: St Martin's Press 1996), 35–65.

77 "U.S. to Push Germany and Japan for UN Council," *New York Times*, 13 June 1993.

78 David Callahan, "Fall Back Troops: Clinton's New UN Policy," *Foreign Service Journal* (May 1994), 20–8; Carroll J. Doherty, "United Nations' Newfound Muscle Relieves, Worries Washington," *Congressional Quarterly* (6 March 1993): 525–9.

79 "Clinton May Let U.S. troops Serve under UN Chiefs," *New York Times*, 18 August 1993; "Administration Is Divided on Role for U.S. Peacekeeping," *New York Times*, 22 September 1993.

80 William J. Clinton, "Confronting the Challenges of a Broader World," *Dispatch* (27 September 1993): 649–53.

81 Carroll J. Doherty, "Lawmakers Pummel Christopher over Peacekeeping Setbacks," *Congressional Quarterly* (6 November 1993): 3059–61.

82 This policy would take form later in White House, *A National Security Strategy of Engagement and Enlargement* (Washington, DC: U.S. Government Printing Office 1996).

83 William J. Clinton, "Building a Secure Future on the Foundation of Democracy," *Dispatch* (26 September 1994): 633–6; Madeleine Albright, "Use of Force in a Post–Cold War World," *Dispatch* (27 September 1993): 665–8; Warren Christopher, "Remaking American Diplomacy in the Post–Cold War," *Dispatch* (18 October 1993); William J. Clinton, "American Engagement in a Changing World: A Vital Commitment," *Dispatch* (2 May 1994): 249.

84 Carroll J. Doherty, "Dole's Blueprint Takes Aim at Relationship with UN," *Congressional Quarterly* (7 January 1995): 44–5.

85 Warren Christopher, "The United Nations: The Momentum for Reform Must Accelerate," *Dispatch* (2 October 1995): 711–14.

86 "The UN at 50," *New York Times*, 23 October 1995; William J. Clinton, "Focus on the UN," *Dispatch* (19 February 1996): 57–8.

87 Boutros Boutros-Ghali, *Unvanquished. A U.S.-UN Saga* (New York: Random House 1999); "U.S. Will Oppose Move to Re-Elect Top UN Official," *New York Times*, 20 June 1996; "Choosing the World's Top Diplomat," *New York Times*, 14 November 1996.

88 Madeleine Albright, "The UN, the U.S. and the World," *Dispatch* (26 Sep-

tember 1996): 474–7; Juliana Gruenwald, "GOP Warns Richardson on
UN Overhaul," *Congressional Quarterly* (1 February 1997): 300; Judy
Aita, "U.S. Delegation Pushing Ahead with UN Reform Agenda," *U.S.IA*
(17 November 1997).

89 "The UN at 50: The Challenges," *New York Times*, 22 October 1995;
    Bill Richardson, "Statements in the Open-Ended Working Group of the
    General Assembly on the Question of Equitable Representation on
    Increase in the Membership of the Security Council," Press Briefing, Per-
    manent U.S. delegation to the UN, 12 June and 17 July 1997.

90 William J. Clinton, "Remarks by the President to the 52nd Session of the
    United Nations General Assembly," White House, Office of the Press Sec-
    retary, 22 September 1997.

91 "Kinkel Discusses UN General Assembly, Clinton Speech," *Cologne
    Deutschlandfunk Network* (23 September 1997), in FBIS-WEU-97–266.

92 U.S. Mission to the UN, "Statement by Cameron R. Hume, Minister
    Counselor for Political Affairs, to the Open-Ended Working Group," 23
    May 1996.

93 Edward C. Luck, "The United Nations, Multilateralism, and U.S. Inter-
    ests," in C.W. Maynes and Richard S. Williamson, eds., *U.S. Foreign
    Policy and the United Nations System* (New York: W.W. Norton 1996),
    27–53.

94 Barbara Crossette, "U.S. Ready for Much Larger Security Council," *New
    York Times*, 3 April 2000: A1.

95 Rose, Neoclassical Realism, 146.

96 See Michael W. Reisman, "The U.S. and International Institutions," *Sur-
    vival* 41, no. 4 (winter 1999): 62–80.

CHAPTER TWO

1 In this regard, see Stanislav J. Kirschbaum, *La paix a-t-elle un avenir?
   L'ONU, l'OTAN et la sécurité internatonale* (Paris: L'Harmattan, collection
   Raoul Dandurand 2001).

2 See, in particular, the thesis concerning the dangerous character of power
   transition periods in Robert Gilpin, *War and Change in World Politics*
   (Cambridge: Cambridge University Press 1981); Jack Snyder, "Democra-
   tization, War, and Nationalism in the Post-Communist States," in Celeste
   A. Wallander, ed., *The Sources of Russian Foreign Policy after the Cold
   War* (Boulder, CO: Westview Press 1996), 21–40.

3 Neil MacFarlane, "Realism and Russian Strategy after the Collapse of
   USSR," in Ethan B. Kapstein and Michael Mastanduno, eds., *Unipolar
   Politics: Realism and State Strategies after the Cold War* (New York:
   Colombia University Press 1999).

4 However, certain constructivists assert that Gorbachev's desire to modify

the Soviet Union's security identity can also be explained by institutional factors, that is, by the development of new international ideas based on Western liberal ideas in the upper levels of the bureaucracy responsible for Soviet foreign policy. See, for example, Jeffrey T. Checkel, *Ideas and International Political Change: Soviet/Russian Behavior and the End of the Cold War* (New Haven, CT: Yale University Press 1997). See also Matthew Evangelista's version of the same phenomenon in "The Paradox of State Strength: Transnational Relations, Domestic Structures, and Security Policy in Russia and the Soviet Union," *International Organization* 49, no. 1 (1995): 1–38.

5 On the idea of a Common Home see Jacques Lévesque, *The Enigma of 1989: the USSR and the Liberation of Eastern Europe* (Berkeley, CA: University of California Press 1997), 45–51.

6 Concerning the eastward expansion of NATO, see Charles-Philippe David and Jacques Lévesque, eds., *The Future of NATO: Enlargement, Russia, and European Security* (Montreal: McGill-Queen's University Press 1999).

7 On the statists, see Celeste A. Wallander, "Wary of the West: Russian Security Policy at the Millenium," *Arms Control Today* 30, no. 2 (March 2000): 7–12. Sergunin provides the following account of the *derzhavniki*: "The emergence of *derzhavniki* was the end result of the process of consolidation of three major political forces – the industrial lobby, the federal military and civilian bureaucracies, and the moderate Democrats. This group was quickly labelled the *derzhavniki* or the *gosudarstvenniki* (proponents of state power). The term *derzhavniki* denotes the advocating of a strong and powerful state which can maintain order and serve as a guarantee against anarchy and instability; a relatively traditional Russian view of the state's role." Alexander A. Sergunin, "Russian Post-Communist Foreign Policy Thinking at the Cross-Roads: Changing Paradigms," *Journal of International Relations and Development* 3, no. 3 (September 2000).

8 Yevgeniy Primakov, "Our Foreign Policy Cannot Be the Policy of a Second-Rate State – Interview with ITAR-TASS Special Correspondent Tomas Kolesnichenko," *Rossiyskaya Gazeta* (17 December 1996), in Foreign Broadcast Information Service FBIS-SOV-96-243; "Russia's National Interests – Interview with Yegor Yakovlev," *Obshchaya Gazeta* (14 August 1997), in FBIS-SOV-97-227. "The Role of Follower Is Not for U.S. – Speech at the Moscow State Institute of International Relations," *Trud* (25 June 1996), FBIS-SOV-96-124.

9 "Near abroad" is a translation of the Russian expression *blizhnee zarubezh'e*, the near abroad corresponds to the territories of the former soviet republics.

10 Clinton provided a fine example of Western recognition of Russia's near

abroad during a memorable press conference in which he compared the American Civil War to the war in Chechnya. See *Interfax* (21 April 1996), in FBIS-SOV-96–078; *AFP* (22 April 1996), FBIS-SOV-96–079.

11 Mikhail A. Alexseev, *Center-Periphery Conflict in Post-Soviet Russia: A Federation Imperiled* (New York: St Martin's Press 1999).

12 Anna Kreikemeyer, "Renaissance of Hegemony and Spheres of Influence: The Evolution of the Yeltsin Doctrine." In Hans-Georg Ehrhart and Andrei Zagorski et al., eds., *Crisis Management in the CIS: Whither Russia?* (Baden-Baden: Nomos 1995), 93–114.

13 Anne de Tinguy, "Russie-Asie centrale: La fin d'un étranger proche," *La revue internationale et stratégique* (summer 1999): 117.

14 Rajan Menon, "After Empire: Russia and the Southern 'Near Abroad,'" in Michael Mandelbaum, ed., *The New Russian Foreign Policy* (New York: Council on Foreign Relations 1998), 100–66.

15 Concerning Russia's relations with its bordering region, see also Yevgeniy G. Nikitenko, "Russia's Role, Allies and Threats in the New Eurasian World," *Defense and Foreign Affairs Strategic Policy* 26, no. 6: 9–13.

16 Dmitri Trenin, "International Institutions and Conflict Resolution in the Former Soviet Union," in Marco Carnovale, ed., *European Security and International Institutions after the Cold War* (New York: St Martin's Press 1995), 76.

17 See, among others, the speeches of Fedotov (18 December 1995) and Lavrov (25 November 1997) at the UN General Assembly.

18 See David Law, "The OSCE and European Security Architecture," in Neil S. MacFarlane and Oliver Thränert, eds., *Balancing Hegemony: The OSCE in the CIS* (Kingston, ON: Centre for International Relations, Queen's University 1997), 35–46. See also the comments of Andrei Zagorsky, "The OSCE and the CIS Organization: A Comment," in the same volume, 65–6.

19 Jack Snyder, "Russia: Responses to Relative Decline," in T.V. Paul and John A. Hal, eds., *International Order and the Future of World Politics* (Cambridge: Cambridge University Press 1999), 147.

20 Sergei Rogov, "Russia and the United States: A Partnership or Another Disengagement?" *International Affairs* (Moscow 1995): 3, quoted in Neil S. MacFarlane, "Realism and Russian Strategy after the Collapse of the USSR," in Kapstein and Mastanduno, *Unipolar Politics*.

21 See the summary of the evolution of institutionalist studies and the questions they raise in Robert O. Keohane, "International Institutions: Can interdependence work?" *Foreign Policy*, no. 110 (spring 1998): 82–96.

22 For an empirical study that challenges this analytical vision, see William C. Wohlworth, *The Elusive Balance: Power and Perceptions during the Cold War* (Ithaca, NY: Cornell University Press 1993).

23 For a succinct exposé of the principle elements of the neoclassical realist

approach, see Gideon Rose, "Neoclassical Realism and Theories of Foreign Policy," *World Politics* 51, no. 1: 144–72.

24 See MacFarlane, "Realism and Russian Strategy."

25 Here we borrow the identity realist model proposed by Iain Johnston, "Realism(s) and Chinese Security Policy in the post–Cold War Period," in Kapstein and Mastanduno, *Unipolar Politics*, 261–318.

26 On 1 October 1990 at the General Assembly of the United Nations, Eduard Shevardnadze asserted that he supported the principle of his country participating in the military operations under the control of the UN Security Council. Two months later, however, Prime Minister Ryjkov stated the opposite. *Le Monde*, 2 December 1990.

27 Emad Awwad, "L'évolution des relations États-Unis-URSS au Proche-Orient," *Défense nationale* (August-September 1991): 95–108.

28 Yevgeniy Primakov, "Voïna, Kotoroï moglo ne byt'" (The War that Could Have not Occured), *Pravda* (28 February 1991): 5.

29 On balancing, see MacFarlane, *Realism and Russian Strategy*, 218–60.

30 In this regard, see also Gorbachev's speech before the Supreme Soviet in Moscow on 26 November 1990; *Documents d'actualité internationale*, no. 3 (1 February 1991): 65.

31 Excerpt from Eduard Shevardnadze's speech before the UN Security Council on 25 September 1990.

32 Words of M. Sergeï Ordzhonikidze, representing the USSR at the UN General Assembly; General Assembly, Forty-fifth session, Forty-first meeting, Wednesday (14 November 1990).

33 Jean-Christophe Romer, "L'URSS et la Guerre du Golfe," *Fondation pour les Études de Défense Nationale, Stratégique*, nos. 51–2 (3d and 4th quarters 1991): 147–60

34 *Documents d'actualité internationale*, no. 21 (1 November 1990).

35 Speech delivered on 26 September 1990; *Documents d'actualité internationale*, no. 22 (15 November 1990): 422.

36 Yves Boyer and Isabelle Facon, eds., *La politique de sécurité de la Russie: Entre continuité et rupture* (Paris: Ellipses, Collection Repères Stratégiques 2000).

37 Anna Kreikemeyer, "Renaissance of Hegemony and Spheres of Influence: The Evolution of the Yeltsin Doctrine," in Ehrhart and Zagorski, *Crisis Management in the CIS*, 93–114.

38 United Nations, General Assembly, Fifty-first Session, Forty-fifth Plenary Meeting (30 October 1996).

39 United Nations, General Assembly, Fiftieth Session, Sixtieth Plenary Meeting (15 November 1995).

40 Roger E. Kanet, "La résolution des conflits: Le rôle de la Fédération de Russie," *Revue d'études comparatives Est-Ouest* (1 March 1994): 11; see also *The New York Times*, 1 February 1992, L5.

41 United Nations, General Assembly, Forty-fifth Session, Twenty-First Meeting (23 November 1990).

42 Ibid.

43 Pierre Binette and Jacques Lévesque, "La Russie à la recherche d'un nouveau système international et d'une nouvelle politique extérieure," *Revue Québécoise de science politique*, no. 24 (autumn 1993): 45–73.

44 Speech before the UN General Assembly, 22 September 1992, FBIS-SOV-92-185: 9.

45 See Clive Archer and Lena Johnson, eds., *Peacekeeping and the Role of Russia in Eurasia* (Boulder, CO: Westview Press 1996).

46 "Rossiya v roli'evraziiskogo jandarma'?" (Russia in the Role of Eurasian Policeman?) *Izvestiya*, 7 August 1992. Quoted in Pierre Binette and Jacques Lévesque, "La Russie à la recherche d'un nouveau système international et d'une nouvelle politique extérieure," *Revue québécoise de science politique*, no. 24 (autumn 1993): 65.

47 Some discriminatory policies had been practised with regard to russo-phone populations, notably in Estonia and Latvia. This problem was raised by, among others, Yevgeny Primakov, on 26 September at the UN General Assembly.

48 Quoted in Kanet, "La résolution des conflits," 17.

49 This council was dominated by the centrist wing that wanted the government to reinforce its position in the Eurasian zone. See Binette and Lévesque, "La Russie à la recherche," 45–73.

50 See Margot Light, "Debats sur la politique étrangère russe et l'évolution de la doctrine 1991–99," *La Revue internationale et stratégique*, no. 38 (summer 2000): 121–31.

51 Roy Allison, "Military Forces in the Soviet Successor States," *Adelphi Papers*, no. 280 (1993): 72.

52 Alexei G. Arbatov, "Russia's Foreign Policy Alternatives," *International Security* 18, no. 2 (fall 1993): 5–43. To understand the arguments of those who staunchly opposed Russia's isolation, see Dimitri K. Simes, "The Return of Russian History," *Foreign Affairs* 73, no. 1 (January-February 1994): 67–82; Andreï Kozyrev, "The Lagging Partnership," *Foreign Affairs* 73, no. 3 (May-June 1994): 59–71.

53 Concerning the eastward expansion of NATO, see David and Lévesque, *The Future of NATO*.

54 See Youri Robinski, "La Russie et l'OTAN: une nouvelle étape?" *Politique étrangère*, no. 4 (winter 1997–98): 543–58.

55 Ibid., 545; Andrew Kydd, "Trust Building, Trust Breaking: The Dilemma of NATO Enlargement," *International Organization* 55, no. 4 (autumn 2001): 801–28.

56 D. Vernois, "L'élargissement de l'Alliance atlantique: Une révolution stratégique?" *Défense nationale* (May 1997): 36.

57 On the hopes for the OCSE, see, among others, the speeches at the UN General Assembly by Fedotov (18 December 1995) and Lavrov (25 November 1997).

58 Isabelle Facon, "La Russie, l'OTAN et l'avenir de la sécurité en Europe," *Politique Étrangère*, no. 3 (August 1997): 295.

59 United Nations, General Assembly, fifty-first session, sixth plenary meeting (24 September 1996).

60 To do so, it would have been necessary to obtain the agreement of Russia's partners in the CIS, the majority of whom would most certainly have refused.

61 See: "L'OTAN vue de l'Est," *Le Courrier des pays de l'Est* (Paris: La documentation française, January 2000).

62 Those who had a positive attitude towards the expansion of NATO, like some Westernists, did not play a major political role in the debate. See Tatiana Parkhalina, "Mythes et illusions: L'opinion russe," *Revue de l'OTAN* 45, no. 3 (May-June 1997).

63 "It is clearly no coincidence that the United States and its Western allies chose the eve of the Budapest summit to announce new measures concerning the expansion of NATO. They wanted, of course, to show that they in no way supported Russia's project to transform the OSCE into a universal structure of European security and cooperation similar to the UN." Alexandre Velitchkine, "L'OTAN vue par la presse russe," *Revue de l'OTAN* 43, no. 2 (March 1995): 23. See also Stuart Croft, "Guaranteeing Europe's Security? Enlarging NATO Again," *International Affairs* 78, no. 1 (2002): 97–114.

64 Concerning Russia's desire to become politically and economically integrated within the so-called civilized world, see Binette and Lévesque, "La Russie à la recherche," 48–9.

65 Velichkine, "L'OTAN vue," 20–3.

66 See, among others, Lavrov's speech to the UN Security Council on 8 September 1995, of which the following [statement concerning the bombing of Bosno-Serbian positions by NATO forces] is an excerpt: "I most particularly want to stress that the procedures accepted by the Security Council with respect to the employment of force in Bosnia-Herzegovina have this time been seriously violated. First of all, the necessary consultations among the members of the Security Council required by Resolution 844 (1993) did not take place. Nor were the members of the Security Council informed at an opportune time of the measures taken."

67 This "act" was meant to be a compromise between the treaty demanded by Moscow and the charter wished for by Washington.

68 The council would consist of the sixteen NATO countries and Russia.

69 Anne de Tinguy, "La communauté des états indépendants a-t-elle encore un avenir?" *Défense nationale* (August-September 1999): 35.

70 This informal regional alliance was created in 1996. See de Tinguy, "La Communauté des états indépendants," 29–48; Laurent Rucker, "La Russie et l'opération 'force alliée,'" *Le courrier des pays de l'Est*, no. 1001 (January 2000): 39.

71 De Tinguy, "La communauté des états indépendants," 38.

72 Lucien Poirier, "La guerre du Golfe dans la généalogie de la stratégie," Fondation pour les Études de Défense Nationale, *Stratégique*, nos. 51–2 (3d and 4th quarter 1991): 33.

73 Andrei Zagorski, "Russia and European Institutions," in Vladimir Baranovsky, ed., *Russia and Europe: The Emerging Security Agenda* (Oxford: Oxford University Press 1997), 519–40.

74 Rucker, "La Russie et l'opération," 35.

75 In fact, since the events of 11 September 2001 even NATO no longer seems to be the preferred instrument for actively resolving conflicts. The US intervention in Afghanistan represents a good example. The United States increasingly favours ad hoc coalitions or unilateral actions.

76 Alvin Z. Rubinstein and Oles M. Smolansky, eds., *Regional Power Rivalries in the New Eurasia: Russia, Turkey and Iran* (Amonk, NY: M.E. Sharpe 1995); Jonathan Aves, "The Caucasian States: The Regional Security Complex," in Roy Allison and Christoph Bluth, eds., *Security Dilemmas in Russia and Eurasia* (London: The Royal Institute of International Affairs 1998), 175–87; Menon Rajan, "After Empire: Russia and the Southern 'Near Abroad,'" in Michael Mandelbaum, *The New Russian Foreign Policy* (New York: Council on Foreign Relations 1998), 100–66.

77 Ibid.

78 Onnig Beylerian, "Introduction: Objectifs et méthodes de recherche de la conduite institutionnelle de sécurité," in Onnig Beylerian and Jacques Lévesque, eds., *Les puissances majeures et les institutions internationales de sécurité 1990–1997*, special number of *Études internationales* (June 1999): 220.

79 On this subject, see also Fritz Ermarth, "Seeing Russia Plain," *The National Interest*, no. 55 (spring 1999): 5–14; Dmitri K. Simes, "Russia's crisis, America's Complicity," *The National Interest*, no. 54 (winter 1998/1999): 12–22.

CHAPTER THREE

1 Henry Kissinger typifies this view, describing France as a country that "continues to stand for the policies of *raison d'État*, and for the precise calculation of interests rather than the pursuit of abstract harmony." Henry Kissinger, *Diplomacy* (New York: Simon and Schuster 1994), 823 (italics in the original).

2 Stephen Philip Kramer, *Does France Still Count? The French Role in the New Europe* (Westport, CT, and London: Praeger, Washington Papers/164 1994), 26.

3 As an example of this pessimistic view of the French situation in the post–Cold War, see Robert Coudurier, *Le monde selon Chirac: Les coulisses de la diplomatie française* (Paris: Calmann-Lévy 1998), 21–60.

4 Pascal Boniface, *La France est-elle encore une grande puissance?* (Paris: Presses de sciences po 1998), 50.

5 Marie-Christine Kessler, *La politique étrangère de la France: Acteurs et processus* (Paris: Presses de sciences po 1999), 489

6 Basically, realists (especially of the neorealist variety) claim that states are preoccupied by the relative gains they make in relation to others, rivals or allies; this school emphasizes conflictual behaviour. Neoliberal institutionalists consider that states will often be satisfied with absolute gains and are therefore more inclined to cooperation than the realists would have us believe. For a summary of this debate, see David A. Baldwin, "Neoliberalism, Neorealism, and World Politics," in David A. Baldwin, ed., *Neorealism and Neoliberalism: The Contemporary Debate* (New York: Columbia University Press 1993), 5–6.

7 Martha Finnemore, *National Interests in International Society* (Ithaca, NY, and London: Cornell University Press 1996), 3.

8 Jeffrey T. Checkel, "The Constructivist Turn in International Relations Theory," *World Politics* 50, no. 2 (January 1998): 327–8.

9 Ronald L. Jepperson, Alexander Wendt and Peter J. Katzenstein, "Norms, Identity and Culture in National Security," in Peter J. Katzenstein, ed., *The Culture of National Security: Norms and Identity in World Politics* (New York: Columbia University Press 1996), 54.

10 Alexander Wendt, "Collective Identity Formation and the International State," *American Political Science Review* 88, no. 2 (June 1994), 387.

11 Ibid., 389.

12 Jepperson, Wendt, and Katzenstein, "Norms, Identity and Culture," 62.

13 Peter J. Katzenstein, "Conclusion: National Security in a Changing World," in Katzenstein, *The Culture of National Security*, 518.

14 Ann Florini, "The Evolution of International Norms," *International Studies Quarterly* 40, no. 3 (1996): 375.

15 Thus, in the words of the most recent French government white paper on defence, the UN Security Council is "the only international authority with the right to decide on coercive measures or the use of force against a state, outside actions of legitimate individual or collective defense under article 51 of the Charter," *Livre blanc sur la défense 1994* (Paris: Union Générale d'Éditions 1994), 72.

16 On the question of France's adaptation to the post–Cold War world, see also Marie-Christine Kessler and Frédéric Charillon, "Un 'rang' à réin-

venter," in Frédéric Charillon, ed., *Les politiques étrangères: ruptures et continuités* (Paris: La Documentation française 2001), 101–29

17 Of course, we are not suggesting that France has not long practised the values of liberal democracy domestically but rather that with the emphasis on the norms of sovereignty and national autonomy associated with the Republican tradition, French governments were usually loath to make any comments on the internal politics of another state. By taking the lead in condemning the decision to bring the ultra-right Freedom Party into the Austrian government and Russian actions in Chechnya in 2000, both Gaullist president Jacques Chirac and Socialist prime minister Lionel Jospin have shown that sovereignty is no longer quite the overriding norm of French international behaviour that it used to be.

18 Foreign Minister Alain Juppé summed up this position succintly: "We have made our commitment within the United Nations organisation a fundamental axis of our foreign policy," "Voeux du ministre des affaires étrangères, M. Alain Juppé, aux agents du Département" (6 January 1995). All references to speeches and interviews of French decision makers have been taken from the French Ministry of Foreign Affairs web site at http:/www.france.diplomatie.fr. (author's translation), unless otherwise indicated. The dates refer to the day on which the statements were made.

19 According to the 1994 White Paper on Defence, as a permanent member of the UNSC, France must aim at "strengthening its (France's) influence, at allowing it to meet greater responsibilities, thus contributing to further, in the international community, the principles of law which it seeks to promote," *Livre blanc sur la défense 1994*, 72.

20 As one French political scientist has put it, since at least the 1789 Revolution, French foreign policy has been motivated by a "dual idea: France embodies universal values and has as its mission to spread them across the world," Marcel Merle, *Sociologie des relations internationales* (Paris: Dalloz 1988), 3d edition, 292.

21 Finnemore, "National Interests in International Society," 5.

22 "Conférence de presse du ministre d'État, ministre des affaires étrangères, M. Roland Dumas, devant les journalistes français" (25 September 1992).

23 The list is extrapolated from speeches by various policymakers 1993–1997.

24 "Point de presse du ministre des affaires étrangères, Hubert Védrine, 52e Assemblée générale des Nations Unies" (22 September 1997). The Razali report presented the results of a working group set up by the UN General Assembly in 1993 to examine all aspects of the question of increasing the membership of the Security Council.

25 "Discours du ministre des affaires étrangères, M. Alain Juppé, devant la 49e Assemblée générale des Nations Unies" (28 September 1994).

26 *Livre blanc sur la défense*, 49.

27 For a more detailed account of French involvment in the conflict in Kosovo, see Alex Macleod, "France: Kosovo and the Emergence of a New European Security," in Pierre Martin and Mark R. Brawley, eds., *Allied Force or Forced Allies? Alliance Politics, Kosovo and NATO's War* (New York: St Martin's Press 2001).

28 "Intervention du premier ministre, M. Lionel Jospin, à l'Assemblée nationale" (26 March 1999).

29 "Déclaration du président de la République, M. Jacques Chirac" (24 March 1999).

30 "Remise du prix Charlemagne au Premier ministre de Grande-Bretagne, Tony Blair. Allocution du Premier Ministre, Lionel Jospin" (13 May 1999).

31 "Entretien du Ministre des Affaires étrangères, M. Hubert Védrine, avec le 'Club de la presse' sur 'Europe 1'" (29 March 1999).

32 "Intervention du Premier Ministre, M. Lionel Jospin, à l'Assemblée nationale" (26 March 1999).

33 For example, France was the greatest European contributor to NATO's air raids against Yugoslavia. See John Laurenson, "French pilots fly for NATO," http://news.bbc.co.uk (24 April 1999), and "Entretien du Président de la République, M. Jacques Chirac, avec 'TF1'" (10 June 1999).

34 Ministry of Foreign Affairs, "Point de presse" (26 April 1999).

35 In an editorial, *Le Monde* pointed out that reference to the UN was made in a "vague and fuzzy way" ("La nouvelle OTAN," *Le Monde*, 27 April 1999), whilst its two correspondents at the summit underlined the weakness of European support for France's positions (Patrice de Beer and Luc Rosenzweig, "Le nouveau 'concept stratégique' de l'organisation atlantique," *Le Monde* 27 April 1999). American diplomats appeared to share this narrower view of French "success." See John F. Harris, "Clinton Coaxes Allies to Fragile Consensus," *Washington Post*, 26 April 1999.

36 "Interview du Premier ministre au journal de 20h sur 'France 2'" (8 April 1999).

37 "Sommet de l'OTAN: Conférence de presse du président de la République, M. Jacques Chirac" (24 April 1999).

38 "Entretien du Président de la République, M. Jacques Chirac, avec 'TF1'" (10 June 1999).

39 "Visite en Russie. Conférence de presse du Président de la République, Jacques Chirac" (13 May 1999). One can assume that President Chirac was referring to Britain and the United States, since the Ministry of Foreign Affairs had earlier complained that these two countries were stalling further meetings of G8 foreign ministers on Kosovo. Ministry of

Foreign Affairs, "Déclarations conjointes des porte-parole du ministère des Affaires étrangères et du ministère de la Défense" (5 May 1999).

40 "Entretien avec le ministre des Affaires étrangères, M. Hubert Védrine," *Le Figaro*, 21 April 1999.

41 "Visite en Russie. Conférence de presse conjointe du ministre des Affaires étrangères, M. Hubert Védrine, et du ministre russe des Affaires étrangères, M. Igor Ivanov – propos du ministre" (11 May 1999).

42 President Chirac called Secretary-General Kofi Annan to persuade him to appoint Kouchner over his own personal choice, Finnish President Martii Ahtisaari. See Judith Miller, "French Aide Named to Leading Rebuilding Effort," *New York Times*, 3 July 1999.

43 Ministry of Foreign Affairs, "Point de presse," 16 April 1999.

44 "Entretien du ministre des Affaires étrangères, M. Hubert Védrine, avec le quotidien 'La Croix'" (21 May 1999).

45 "Entretien avec le ministre des affaires étrangères, M. Hubert Védrine," *Le Figaro*, 21 April 1999.

46 Philippe Lemaître, "Europe: 'Pacte de stabilité des Balkans' et intégration des pays de l'Est," *Le Monde*, 30 July 1999.

47 "Conseil européen de Cologne: Conférence de presse conjointe du Président de la République, M. Jacques Chirac, et du Premier ministre, Lionel Jospin" (4 June 1999).

48 "Entretien du ministre des affaires étrangères, M. Hubert Védrine, avec 'L'Hebdo des socialistes'" (18 June 1999).

49 "Entretien du ministre des Affaires étrangères, M. Hubert Védrine, avec 'Le Club de la presse' d'Europe 1" (20 June 1999). President Chirac made a similar observation a few days earlier. See "Entretien du Président de la République, M. Jacques Chirac, avec 'TF1'" (10 June 1999).

50 Alain Richard, "Ce que le Kosovo m'a appris," *Le Nouvel Observateur* (15 July 1999).

51 "Interview télévisée de Monsieur Jacques Chirac, Président de la République à l'occasion de la Fête nationale" (14 July 1999). However, a later account suggests that the NATO commander, General Wesley Clark, deliberately presented the allies with a fait accompli, leaving those opposed to escalation either to avoid questions about their own attitude or to try "to claim they had stopped Gen. Clark escalating further". See the transcript of the BBC 2 program *Newsnight* (20 August 1999): Mark Urban, "Nato's Inner Kosovo conflict," http://news.bbc.co.uk/hi/english/world/europe/news_id425000/425488.stm.

52 These examples are all taken from official statements, speeches, and interviews made during the conflict. For a general presentation of French influence over NATO strategy, see Serge July, "La guerre, version elyséenne," *Libération*, 17 and 18 April 1999.

53 See Antoine Guiral, "Elysée-Matignon, le front uni," *Libération* (8 April 1999).

54 "Kosovo: Entretien du ministre des affaires étrangères, M. Hubert Védrine, avec 'France Inter'" (4 June 1999). See also Pierre Haski, "Kosovo: Dans les coulisses du 'club des cinq,'" *Libération*, 1 July 1999.

55 The French government justified this gesture of national sovereignty by declaring that "suppressing terrorism in our country is first of all our affair ... It's first of all France's responsibility." "Entretien du ministre des Affaires étrangères, Hervé Charrette, au Figaro," 9 October 1995.

56 "Réponse du ministre des Affaires étrangères à une question à l'Assemblée nationale" (10 November 1993).

57 Ivan Rioufol, "Terrorisme intégriste: La France vulnérable," *Le Figaro*, 12 November 1994.

58 Foreign Minister Juppé expressed his satisfaction at his government's success in convincing other members of the EU that "one way of contributing to stability in Algeria, and to its recovery is to help it financially." "Entrevue du Ministre des Affaires étrangères, Alain Juppé, au quotidien *Le Monde*," 6 September 1994.

59 "Entretien de Hervé de Charrette avec Europe 1," 30 July 1996.

60 "Document final – Conférence ministérielle sur le terrorisme, G7–P8" (30 July 1996).

61 "Conférence conjointe du ministre des affaires étrangères, M. Hervé de Charrette, du ministre de l'intérieur, M. Jean-Louis Debré, Conférence ministérielle sur le terrorisme" (30 July 1996).

62 Bruce Hoffman, "Is Europe Soft on Terrorism?" *Foreign Policy* (summer 1999): 69.

63 "Jacques Chirac tire les leçons du 11 septembre," *Le Monde*, 6 January 2001.

64 The fact that many neorealists, falling in step with the ideas of Barry Buzan and the Copenhagen School, now recognize an "extended" conception of international security to include the political, the economic, the societal and the environmental – a view that is still hotly contested by other realists and neorealists anyway – changes nothing in the way they interpret the motives behind state behaviours or the nature of the international system. See Barry Buzan, Ole Wæver, and Jaap de Wide, *Security: A New Framework for Analysis* (Boulder, CO, and London: Lynne Rienner 1998); and, for the more restrictive realist interpretation, Stephen M. Walt, "The Renaissance of Security Studies," *International Studies Quarterly* 35, no. 2 (June 1991): 211–39.

CHAPTER FOUR

1 The authors wish to thank Drs. Phillip T. K. Hughes and Alex Macleod for their helpful comments on the translated version of this manuscript.

2 By "foreign-policy-making elite" we mean Christian Democrat chancellor Helmut Kohl, Liberal foreign ministers Hans-Dietrich Genscher and Klaus Kinkel, and Christian Democrat defence minister Volker Rühe, as well as their advisors.

3 John S. Duffield, *World Power Forsaken: Political Culture, International Institutions, and German Security Policy after Unification* (Stanford: Stanford University Press 1998), 211.

4 For example, in 1991 the number of conscientious objectors doubled, from 74,567 (1990) to 151,212. See Wilfried von Bredow, "Conscription, Conscientious Objection, and Civic Service: The Military Institutions and Political Culture of Germany 1945 to the Present," *Journal of Military and Political Sociology* 20, no. 2 (1992): 297.

5 See Karl Kaiser, "Devenir membre permanent du Conseil de Sécurité: Un but légitime de la nouvelle politique extérieure allemande," *Politique étrangère* (winter 1993 and 1994): 1016–17; and Thomas U. Berger, "The Past in the Present: Historical Memory and German National Security Policy," *German Politics* 6, no. 1 (April 1997): 52. Articles 24 ("International Organizations") and 25 ("International Law and Federal Law") of Germany's constitution, the Basic Law (*Grundgesetz*), speak volumes on that score. For example, article 25 states that: "The general rules of international law shall be an integral part of federal law. They shall take precedence over the laws and directly create rights and duties for the inhabitants of the federal territory."

6 Jeffrey J. Anderson and John B. Goodman, "Mars or Minerva? A United Germany in a post-Cold War Europe," in Robert O. Keohane, Joseph S. Nye, and Stanley Hoffmann, eds., *After the Cold War: International Institutions and State Strategies in Europe, 1989–1991* (Cambridge: Harvard University Press 1993), 24.

7 Germany was criticized by its NATO partners in *Die Zeit*, 1 February 1991, 4: Jürgen Krönig, "Verachtung für die 'Krauts': Kein Angst mehr vor einer deutschen Supermacht" (Contempt for 'Krauts": There's no more Fear for a German Superpower); Ulrich Schiller, "Mißtrauen und Mißverständnisse: Die deutsch-amerikanischen Beziehungen in die Krise" (Mistrust and Misunderstandings: German-American Relations in Crisis); Joachim Fritz-Vannahme, "Schon Frist für den Nachbarn: In Frankreich klingt die Kritik noch verhalten" (Already a Waiting Period for the Neighbour: The Critic Is Still Ringing with Circumspection in France).

8 Paul Létourneau, "La politique étrangère allemande: Style nouveau et fidélité au multilatéralisme," *Revue d'Allemagne et des pays de langue allemande* 31, no. 2 (April-June 1999): 335.

9 Paul Létourneau, "Les États-Unis et la question allemande en évolution 1989–1991," *Relations internationales* 70 (summer 1992): 174.

10 Stephen F. Szabo, *The Diplomacy of German Unification* (New York: St Martin's Press 1992), 11–13.

11 Franz-Josef Meiers, "Germany: The Reluctant Power," *Survival* 37, no. 3 (fall 1995): 83.

12 Ibid.

13 "Boutros-Ghali verlangt von Bonn uneingeschränkte deutsche Beteiligung an allen Aktionen der UN" (Boutros-Ghali Requires from Bonn German Participation Without Restriction in UN Actions), *Frankfurter Allgemeine Zeitung*, 12 January 1993, 1.

14 Anderson and Goodman, "Mars or Minerva?" 24. This article is representative of institutionalist arguments, especially since it focuses exclusively on the Bonn government's institutional conduct at the time of unification.

15 William E. Paterson and Gordon Smith, "German Unity," in Gordon Smith, William E. Paterson, Peter H. Merkl, and Stephen Padgett, eds., *Developments in German Politics* (Durham, NC: Duke University Press 1992), 15–18; Karl Kaiser, "Germany's Unification," *Foreign Affairs* 70 (winter 1991): 184–7, 198–200, 205. This article sums up the main arguments found in Kaiser's book *Deutschlands Vereinigung: Die internationalen Aspekte, Mit den wichtigen Dokumenten* (The Reunification of Germany. The International Aspects, with the essential documents) (Bergisch Gladbach: Bastei Lübbe 1991), 384; Ingo Peters, "The OSCE and German Policy: A Study in *How* Institutions Matter," in Helga Haftendorn, Robert O. Keohane, and Celeste A. Wallander, eds., *Imperfect Unions: Security Institutions over Time and Space* (Oxford: Oxford University Press 1999), 202–3.

16 Anderson and Goodman, "Mars or Minerva?" 33–4, 59.

17 Philip Zelikow and Condoleezza Rice, *Germany Unified and Europe Transformed: A Study in Statecraft* (Cambridge: Harvard University Press 1995), 123ff.

18 Ibid., 111–20.

19 Kaiser, "Germany's Unification," 195–6.

20 Paterson and Smith, "German Unity," 14.

21 Anderson and Goodman, "Mars or Minerva?" 31.

22 Kaiser, "Germany's Unification," 179.

23 Stephen F. Szabo, *The Diplomacy of German Unification* (New York: St Martin's Press 1992), 17.

24 Elizabeth Pond, *Beyond the Wall: Germany's Road to Unification* (Washington, DC: The Brookings Institution 1993), 153–4.

25 Ibid., 154–5, 175, 190, 217–24.

26 Szabo, *The Diplomacy of German Unification*, 53–7.

27 Ibid., 92–3.

28 Timothy Garton Ash, *In Europe's Name: Germany and the Divided Continent* (London: Vintage 1994), 348–9.

29 Ibid., 352. With respect to the financing of the USSR by the Federal Republic, see also 402–3.

30 Ibid., 353.

31 Ibid., 354.

32 Lothar Gutjahr, "Competitive Interdependence: Germany's Foreign Policy in a Changing Environment," *Strategic Review* 23, no. 3 (summer 1995): 30–1.

33 Anderson and Goodman, "Mars or Minerva?" 24.

34 Paterson and Smith, "German Unity," 15–18.

35 Kaiser, "Germany's Unification," 184–7, 198–200 and 205.

36 Garton Ash, *In Europe's Name*, 348–9, 352–3.

37 Kaiser, "Germany's Unification," 195–6; Garton Ash, *In Europe's Name*, 405.

38 Pond, *Beyond the Wall..*, 154–5, 175, 190, 217–24.

39 Richard Kiessler and Frank Elbe, *Der diplomatische Weg zur deutschen Einheit* (The Diplomatic Path to German Unity) (Baden-Baden: Suhrkamp Taschenbuch Verlag 1996), 56–65.

40 Pond, *Beyond the Wall*, 154.

41 Ronald D. Asmus, *German Perception of the United States at Unification* (Santa Monica, CA: RAND 1991), 20.

42 On this matter, see Horst Teltschik, *329 Tage: Innenansichten der Einigung* (329 Days: The Internal Views of the Unification) (Berlin: Siedler 1991), 117, 123, 148–9 and 151–2; Szabo, *The Diplomacy of German Unification*, 56–8, 60–1, 102–4, 116; Zelikow and Rice, *Germany Unified and Europe Transformed*, 173–6, 180, 182–7, 203–4, 427–8.

43 Kaiser, "Germany's Unification," 179; Szabo, *The Diplomacy of German Unification*, 17.

44 Christian Hacke, "Nationale Interesse als Handlungsmaxime für die Aussenpolitik Deutschlands" (The National Interest as a Maxim of Action for German Foreign Policy), in Karl Kaiser and Joachim Krause, eds., *Deutschlands neue Außenpolitik: Interessen und Strategien* (The New German Foreign Policy: Interests and Strategies), Vol. 3 (Munich: R. Oldenbourg Verlag GmbH 1996), 12.

45 Jonathan Stevenson, "Hope Restored in Somalia?" *Foreign Policy* 91 (summer 1993): 138. See also Volker Matthies, "Zwischen Rettungsaktion und Entmündigung: Das Engagement der Vereinten Nationen in Somalia" (Between a Rescue Action and Being Under Supervision: The United Nations Engagement in Somalia) *Vereinte Nationen* 2 (1993): 45–51, which draws a good general picture of UN intervention in the Horn of Africa.

46 UNOSOM-II succeeded UNITAF from April 1993 until March 1995. Chester A. Crocker, "Lessons of Somalia: Not Everything Went Wrong," *Foreign Affairs* (May-June 1995): 4, breaks down UNOSOM-II into two phases, "The nation-building phase (May-October 1993) and a scaled-back, accommodative phase (November 1993 and March 1995)."

47 Matthies, "Zwischen Rettungsaktion und Entmündigung," 46, and "Die

Bundesregierung begrüßt die UN-Intervention in Somalia" (The Federal Government Greets the UN's Intervention in Somalia), *Frankfurter Allgemeine Zeitung*, 10 December 1992, 3.

48 Wolfgang Wagner, "Abenteuer in Somalia: Blauhelme im Einsatz gegen das Chaos" (Adventure in Somalia: The Blue Helmets in an operation against chaos) *Europa-Archiv* 6 (March 1994): 151–3; and Michael Schwelien, "Im Sande verweht" (Scattered in the Sands), *Die Zeit*, 18 February 1994, 8.

49 Ibid., 211; Duffield, *World Power Forsaken*.

50 See no. 5.

51 Wagner, "Abenteuer in Somalia," 153.

52 The statement delivered to the *Bundestag* by Klaus Kinkel, minister of foreign affairs, speaks volumes: "To strengthen peace today means above all to reinforce the United Nations." "Erklärung der Bundesregierung zur deutschen Mithilfe bei Friedensmissionen der Vereinten Nationen" (Declaration of the Federal Government on German Assistance in the UN Peace Missions), 151. Sitzung des Deutschen Bundestages (21 April 1993), *Bulletin Presse- und Informationsamt der Bundesregierung* 32 (23 April 1993): 280.

53 "SPD besteht auf Verfassungsänderung zu Bundeswehr-Einsatz" (The SPD Insists on a Constitutional Revision for an Engagement of the Bundeswehr), *Frankfurter Allgemeine Zeitung*, 21 December 1992, 2. In this article, Defence Minister Rühe asserted that the Somali population was suffering from hunger and could not wait for a decision from Karlsruhe.

54 *1994 White Paper on Defence*, Bonn, Federal Ministry of Defence (1994), 88–96, from Meiers, "Germany: The Reluctant Power," 83. One should not draw any definitive conclusion on that score, as the white paper addresses this issue within a more global discussion of Germany's role in multilateral security institutions. Robert H. Dorff, "Germany and Peace Support Operations: Policy after the Karlsruhe Decision," *Parameters* (spring 1996): 74.

55 *Deutscher Bundestag*, 12. Wahlperiode, 151. Sitzung (21 April 1993): 12 925–30.

56 "Beschluß der Bundesregierung zur Unterstützung von UNOSOM II in Somalia" (The Decision of the Federal Government to Support UNOSOM II in Somalia), *Bulletin Presse- und Informationsamt des Bundesregierung* 32 (23 April 1993): 280.

57 Robert Leicht, "Wenn es knallt, Krieg in Somalia: Was haben Deutsche da verloren?" (When it Bursts, War in Somalia: What have the Germans Lost There?), *Die Zeit*, 11 June 1993.

58 Wolfgang F. Schlör, "The German Security Policy: An Examination of the Trends in German Security Policy in a New European and Global

Context," *Adelphi Papers* 277 (June 1993): 14; Christian Merlin, "L'Allemagne doit-elle participer aux actions militaires des Nations Unies?" *Documents: Revue des questions allemandes* 48, no. 1 (1995): 20–1.

59 Philippe Hébert and Paul Létourneau, "L'institutionnalisme dans la politique extérieure allemande: Ajustements et continuité," *Études internationales* 30, no. 2 (June 1999): 340. Joachim Fritz-Vannahme, "Die Bonner Angst vor dem Rückzug" (Bonn's Fear of a Retreat), *Die Zeit*, 15 October 1993, 5.

60 Fritz-Vannahme, "Die Bonner Angst vor dem Rückzug," 5.

61 Schwelien, "Im Sande verweht," 6.

62 Jonathan Stevenson, 138–54, is quite critical of the type of robust interventions that seem to have become the standard since the Gulf War, and he goes on to suggest that the few results achieved by the military component of the operation – food distribution, partial disarmament; embryonic of political reconciliation – could have been achieved within the framework of a civilian operation. Diametrically opposed to this view is Crocker, "Lessons of Somalia," 2–8, who asserts that one lesson from Restore Hope is that "there is no such thing as a purely humanitarian operation" (8). However, both authors draw a rather negative picture of the United Nations intervention in Somalia.

63 Kaiser, "Devenir membre permanent..," 1011–22; Tobias Debiel and Heiko Thomas, "Natürlicher Anwärter oder drängelnder Kandidat? Deutschland und die Reform des UN-Sicherheitsrats" (A Natural Candidate or a Candidate who Pushes? Germany and the Reform of the UN's Security Council), in UN-*williges Deutschland: Der Weed-Report zur deutschen* UNO-*Politik* (The Goodwill of Germany for the UN: The Weed Report on Germany's UN Policy) (Bonn: Dietz 1997), 28–50; Michael Schaefer, "Die neue Rolle des Sicherheitsrates – Warum soll Deutschland ständiges Mitglied werden?" (The New Role of the Security Council – Why Must Germany Become a Permanent Member?), in Eltje Aderhold, Kurt Lipstein, Cristoph Schücking, and Rolf Stürmer, eds., *Festschrift für Hans Hanisch* (Festschrift for Hans Hanisch) (Cologne: Carl Heymanns Verlag 1994) 191–215; Wolfgang Wagner, "Die ständige Sitz im Sicherheitsrat: Wer brauchen wen, Die Deutschen diesen Sitz? Der Sicherheitsrat die Deutschen?" (The Permanent Seat in the Security Council. Who Needs Whom: The Germans or the Security Council?), *Europa-Archiv* 48, no. 19 (10 October 1993): 533ff.; Winrich Kühne, "Erweiterung und Reform des UN-Sicherheitsrats: Keine weltpolitische Nebensache" (Widening and Reform of the UN Security Council: No Secondary World Policy), *Europa-Archiv* 24 (1994): 685–92; and Gerhard Kümmel, "UN Overstretch: A German Perspective," *International Peacekeeping* 1, no. 2 (summer 1994): 160–78.

64 Kaiser, "Devenir membre permanent," 1015–17; Schaefer, "Die Neue Rolle des Sicherheistrates," 201–2.

65 Kaiser, "Devenir membre permanent," 1015–17; author's translation.

66 Debiel and Thomas, "Natürlicher Anwärter oder," 32–3. That Germany plays a significant role as an economic leader is, indeed, the only argument made by the authors.

67 Kaiser, "Devenir membre permanent," 1019; Kümmel, "UN Overstretch," 174–5.

68 See, in particular, Kühne, "Erweiterung und Reform," 685; Kaiser, "Devenir membre permanent," 1015–17.

69 Schaefer, "Die Neue Rolle des Sicherheistrates," 200, 203–4, 210, 214.

70 Kaiser, "Devenir membre permanent," 1022.

71 Wagner, "Die ständige Sitz im Sicherheistrat," 1002; Kümmel, "UN Overstretch," 166; Kühne, "Erweiterung und Reform," 685.

72 Wagner, "Die ständige Sitz im Sicherheistrat," 1006.

73 Kümmel, "UN Overstretch," 166.

74 Jeffrey S. Lantis, "A United Germany in the United Nations: Promise for the Future?" *German Politics and Society* 26 (summer 1992): 76.

75 They succeded Hans-Dietrich Genscher and Gerhard Stoltenberg respectively.

76 Schlör, "German Security Policy," 9.

77 "Rede des deutschen Außenministers Klaus Kinkel vor der 47. Generalversammlung der Vereinten Nationen am 23. September 1992" (Speech of the German Foreign Minister Klaus Kinkel before the Forty-sixth General Assembly of the United Nations on 23 September 1992), *Europa-Archiv* 20 (1992): D600.

78 Klaus Kinkel, "Keine UN-Mitgliedschaft à la carte" (No à *la carte* UN Membership), *Der Überblick* 4 (1992): 58; Hébert and Létourneau, "L'institutionnalisme dans la politique," 341.

79 Doc. A/51/47, Annex II.

80 Germany's UN Ambassador for the Open-Ended Working Group on the Question of Equitable Representation and an Increase in the Membership of the Security Council, Gerhard W. Henze (5 May 1998).

81 See "Auslandeinsätze der Bundeswehr verfassungsgemäß" (Foreign operations of the Bundeswehr in Conformity with the Constitution) *Frankfurter Allgemeine Zeitung*, 13 July 1994; on Minister Kinkel's interpretation, see "Peacekeeping Missions: Germany Can Now Play Its Part," *NATO Review* 42, no. 5 (October 1994): 3.

82 As cited in Karl-Heinz Börner, "The Future of German Operations Outside NATO," *Parameters* (spring 1996): 69–70. See also, Jens Hacker, "Deutschlands Beitrag zur Stabilisierung der europäischen Ordnung" (The contribution of Germany to the Stabilization of the European Order), in Dieter Blumenwitz and Gilbert Gornig, eds., *Rechtliche und*

politische Perspektiven deutschen Minderheiten und Volksgruppe (Legal and Political Perspectives on the German Minorities and Ethnic Groups) (Cologne: Verlag Wissenschaft und Politik 1995), 119–23.

83 Hébert and Létourneau, "L'institutionnalisme dans la politique," 343. See also, Tobias Debiel and Heiko Thomas, "Was kostet die Welt? Deutschland Drängen in den Sicherheitsrat" (How Much Does the World Cost? The Pressure of Germany on the Security Council), *Blätter für deutsche und internationale Politik* (February 1997): 181.

84 Hébert and Létourneau, "L'institutionnalisme dans la politique," 343–4.

85 The German ambassador at the UN, Dieter Kastrup (8 February 1999).

86 Ibid.

87 As of February 1993, Germany had accepted 250,000 of the 700,000 refugees from the former Yugoslavia. Létourneau, "La politique extérieure allemande et le conflit dans l'ex-Yougoslavie," 83.

88 Kaiser, "Devenir membre permanent," 1015–17 and Schaefer, "Die Neue Rolle des Sicherheistrates," 201–2, also share this view.

89 Kaiser, "Devenir membre permanent," 1022.

90 Duffield, *World Power Forsaken..*, 3.

91 Ibid. See also Berger, "The Past in the Present," 52: "Rather than leaving or weakening NATO and the European Community, Kohl worked to strengthen and deepen the complex web of international institutions that had anchored West Germany for the past forty years and extend it to cover the newly unified German State."

92 Peters, "The OSCE and German Policy," 219.

CHAPTER FIVE

1 Article 9 was interpreted by the LDP as allowing Japan to possess armed forces for defensive purposes. However, the left defended the view that article 9 called for the adoption of a policy of unarmed neutrality. This explains why the existence of the SDF and of the U.S.-Japan alliance were judged by the Left not to respect the provisions of the article. These views, however, were mostly abandoned in the early 1990s.

2 The tasks of the SDF personnel were limited to observation of the cease-fire, and engineers units would rebuild or repair damaged roads and bridges.

3 Jean-Pierre Lehmann, "Japanese Attitudes Towards Foreign Policy," in Richard L. Grant, ed., *The Process of Japanese Foreign Policy: Focus on Asia* (London: The Royal Institute of International Affairs, Asia-Pacific Programme 1997), 123. The expression is that of Funabashi Yoichi.

4 Japan had no obligation to come to the aid of American forces even in the event of an attack on them on Japanese soil.

5 Pressured by the United States, Japan accelerated the modernization of its

forces and the cabinets of Suzuki (in 1980) and Nakasone (1982–87) took it upon themselves to extend Japan's surveillance perimeter and to acquire the means to support the American Seventh Fleet, without, however, increasing military spending, which was frozen at 1 per cent of GNP in 1976. Japanese resistance to playing an enhanced alliance role is one of the reasons it is often seen as a "free rider."

6 This type of assertion has been found in official diplomatic papers since Japan was admitted in the UN in 1956. Ronald Dore, ed., *Japan, Internationalism, and the UN* (New York: Routledge 1997), 95; Ogata Sadako, "Japan's Policy toward the United Nations," in Alger F. Chadwick, Gene M. Lyons, and John E. Trent, eds., *The United Nations System: The Policies of Member States* (Tokyo: United Nations University Press 1995), 234–5; and "United Nations and Japan 1995: In Quest of a New Role" (Tokyo: Overseas Public Relations Division, Minister's Secretariat, Ministry of Foreign Affairs, August 1995), 1.

7 Recent developments make some believe that the taboo has mostly dissipated, though. However, Japan still uses terminology that takes away the offensive character of its military equipment. For example, Japanese destroyers are "escort ships" and the F-2 fighter-bomber is a "support fighter." This terminology is not used by any other military force.

8 Soeya Yoshihide, "Japan: Normative Constraints versus Structural Imperatives," in Muthiah Alagappa, ed., *Asian Security Practices: Material and Ideational Influences* (Stanford: Stanford University Press 1998), 211.

9 The ceiling has been officially abrogated since 1988, when defence spending went over 1 per cent (to 1.008 per cent), but this measure remains a psychological barrier.

10 This practice is extended to sanctions of unwanted behaviour in beneficiary countries. One must consider China's 1995 nuclear test and those of India and Pakistan in 1998. In all cases Japan threatened to cut its economic aid if testing continued, and finally did so. Because of the role Pakistan plays in the war against terrorism, Japan decided to give aid to this country again in October 2001 and did not react as firmly as in 1998 when Pakistan proceeded to new missile tests in June and October 2002.

11 Eric Heginbotham and Richard J. Samuels begin their article with this report. See "Mercantile Realism and Japanese Foreign Policy," *International Security* 22, no. 4 (spring 1998): 171.

12 "Japan-U.S. Declaration on Security: Alliance for the Twenty-first Century – 17 April 1996," in *Japan-U.S. Security Alliance for the Twenty-first Century: Cornerstone of Democracy, Peace, and Prosperity for Our Future Generations*, Ministry of Foreign Affairs, Overseas Public Relations Division (July 1996): 73–6.

13 "The United States Security Strategy for the East-Asia Pacific Region

1998," electronic edition (part 3): 45–6, clearly links these issues with that of security.

14 For a general outlook on the Asian values debate, see David I. Hitchcock, *Asian Values and the United States: How Much Conflict?* (Washington, DC: CSIS 1994); see also Amitav Acharya, "A Security Community in Southeast Asia?" in Desmond Ball, ed., *The Transformation of Security in the Asia/Pacific Region* (London: Frank Cass 1996), 177.

15 Amitav Acharya, "Multilateralism: Is There an Asia-Pacific Way?" *NBR Analysis* 8, no. 2 (1997): 6.

16 Ralph Cossa, "Multilateralism, Regional Security, and the Prospect for Track II in East Asia," *NBR Analysis* 7, no. 5 (1996): 26; Susan L. Shirk, "Asia-Pacific Regional Security: Balance of Power or Concert of Power?" in David A. Lake and Patrick M. Morgan, eds., *Regional Orders: Building Security in a New World* (Pennsylvania Park, PA: Pennsylvania State University Press 1997), 267.

17 Amitav Acharya, "Culture, Security, Multilateralism: The 'ASEAN Way' and Regional Order," in Keith Krause, ed., *Culture and Security; Multilateralism, Arms Control and Security Building* (London: Frank Cass 1999), 59, 80.

18 Peter Drysdale and Andrew Elek, "APEC: Community-Building in East Asia and the Pacific," in Donald C. Hellman and Kenneth B. Pyle, eds., *From APEC to Xanadu: Creating a Viable Community in the post–Cold War Pacific* (New York: NBR, M.E. Sharpe 1997), 30.

19 Ibid., 59.

20 Quoted in Paul M. Evans, "The Prospect for Multilateral Security Co-Operation in the Asia/Pacific Region," in Ball, *The Transformation*, 207.

21 This is the thesis of Itoh Mayumi, *Globalization of Japan: Japanese Sakoku Mentality and U.S. Efforts to Open Japan* (New York: St Martin's Press 1998).

22 Ibid, 13; also see Kenneth B. Pyle, *The Japanese Question: Power and Purpose in a New Era.* 2d Edition (Washington, DC: AEI Press 1996), chap. 9.

23 Kosaku Yoshino, "The Discourse on Blood and Racial Identity in Contemporary Japan," in Frank Dikötter, ed., *The Construction of Racial Identities in China and Japan: Historical and Contemporary Perspectives.* (London: Hurst 1997), 210.

24 The Black Ships of Commodore Perry, which threatened the banks of Tokyo Bay in 1853 and 1854, forced the opening up of Japan and the final collapse of the Tokugawa regime. This image is still largely used today as a symbol of foreign pressure on Japan.

25 Even though the term "race" is politically incorrect in the West, it is still largely used in Japan to highlight cultural differences. The racial element

reinforces the exclusive character of the "inherently Japanese characteristics." See Dikötter, *The Construction of Racial Identities*.

26 *Hinomaru* and *kimigayo* once again became official in 1999.

27 Befu Harumi, *Hegemony of Homogeneity: An Anthropological Analysis of Nihonjinron* (Melbourne: Trans-Pacific Press, 2001), 9 and chap. 5.

28 Michael Weiner, "The Invention of Identity: Race and Nation in Pre-war Japan," in Dikötter, *The Construction of Racial Identities*, 112–13.

29 American decision makers did believe that the Japanese had been indoctrinated and so endorsed the militarists' policies. The Japanese supported the militarists but could not be blamed, because they had no access to the information allowing them to make an enlightened choice. Here we have a naive conception that nevertheless concluded a secret report written by the U.S. Army's psychological warfare unit, dated April 1945. See Orr, *The Victim as Hero: Ideologies of Peace and National Security in Postwar Japan* (Honolulu: Hawaii University Press 2001).

30 Lucian W. Pye, "Memory, Imagination, and National Myths," in Gerrit W. Gong, "Remembering and Forgetting; The Legacy of War and Peace in East Asia," *CSIS Significant Series* 18, no. 2 (Washington, DC: 1996): 29. A lot of ink was spilled in Japan over the 2001 Hollywood production *Pearl Harbor*. The version shown in Japan was censored and did not contain any anti-Japanese commentary. The Japanese reprimands addressed to the United States confirm that it is still a sensitive subject.

31 William Lee Howell, "The Inheritance of War: Japan's Domestic Politics and International Ambitions," in Gerrit W. Gong, ed., *Remembering and Forgetting: The Legacy of War and Peace in East Asia*, (Washington, DC: CSIS Significant Series 1996), 88–9

32 Gavan McCormack, *The Emptiness of Japanese Affluence*, revised ed., Japan in the Modern World Collection (Armonk, NY: M.E. Sharpe 2001), 197.

33 Thomas U. Berger, *Cultures of Antimilitarism; National Security in Germany and Japan* (London: The Johns Hopkins University Press 1998), 32.

34 See Charles Hill, "Fighting Stories: The Political Culture of Memory in Northeast Asian Relations," in Gong, *Remembering and Forgetting*, 2–18. The year 2001 was a time for friction with China and the Koreas concerning the new school history manuals proposed by the Japanese education minister.

35 Soeya Yoshihide, "Japan's Dual Identity and the U.S.-Japan Alliance," Asia/Pacific Research Center Paper, Stanford University, May 1998, 4.

36 See Wakamiya Yoshibumi, *The Postwar Conservative View of Asia: How the Political Right Has Delayed Japan's Coming to Terms with Its History of Aggression in Asia*, LTCB Selection, no. 8 (Tokyo: LTCB International Library Foundation 1999.

37 During the last twenty years, more than a dozen cabinet ministers and a few Defense Agency director generals – like Nishimura Shingo in October 1999 – had to resign after having suggested that Japan could possess nuclear weapons or because of Japan's role in the Pacific war.

38 Prime Minister Murayama Tomichii hesitated before requesting the support of the SDF at the time of the Kobe-Hanshin earthquake. Rescue operations helped dissipate public distrust of the SDF, which was not something he had wished for.

39 Agencies are inferior in rank to ministries. Giving an agency the responsibility for defense ensures its subordination to powerful ministries while publicly downplaying the importance granted to the military. Prime Minister Koizumi Junichiro is considering elevating the Defense Agency to ministerial level.

40 "Japan's Challenge: Setting a New Example as an Advanced Nation," *Ronza* (20 December 1994): 27–32, in FBIS-EAS-95-014.

41 "Survey of the Prime Minister's Office," cited in Sassa Atsuyuki, "Murayama Questioned on Crisis Management Issue," *Chuo Koron*, (7 March 1995): 51–69, in FBIS-EAS-95-044

42 Data in Fujita Hiroshi, "UN Reform and Japan's Permanent Security Council Seat," *Japan Quarterly* 1, no. 4 (October–December 1995): 438.

43 The UN General Assembly voted for a resolution to this effect in 1995, but the clauses have yet to be amended.

44 Cited in Reinhard Drifte, *Japan's Quest for a Permanent Security Council Seat: A Matter of Pride or Justice?* (Oxford and New York: St Anthony's Series, St Martin's Press, 2000), 78

45 Yajima Midori. "Wanting to Throw Off a Nasty Burden, but Suppressing the Urge," in Dore, *Japan, Internationalism, and the UN*, 145.

46 Drifte, *Japan's Quest*, 100.

47 Robert M. Immerman, "Japan in the United Nations," in Craig Garby and Mary Brown Bullock, eds., *Japan: A New Kind of Superpower?* (Washington, DC: Woodrow Wilson Center Press 1994), 182–3.

48 Drifte, *Japan's Quest*, 107.

49 Michael Jonathan Green, *Japan's Reluctant Realism: Foreign Policy Challenges in an Era of Uncertain Power*, A Council on Foreign Relations Book (New-York: Palgrave 2001) 194.

50 Darryl Howlett, "Nuclearization and Denuclearization on the Korean Peninsula," in Colin McInnes and Mark G. Rolls, eds., *Post-Cold War Security Issues in the Asia-Pacific Region* (Ilford: Frank Cass 1994), 178–9.

51 Son Ki-yong, "Japan Expected to Split Reactor Cost," *Korean Times*, 24 September 1994, in FBIS-EAS-94-186.

52 "Press Conference by Press Secretary," Ministry of Foreign Affairs of Japan, electronic edition, 17 February 1995.

53 Fukushima Akiko, "Multilateral Confidence-Building Measures in North-east Asia: Receding or Emerging?" in Benjamin L. Self and Tatsumi Yuki, eds., *Confidence-Building Measures and Security Issues in Northeast Asia*, The Henry L. Stimson Center, Report no. 33 (February 2000): 43.

54 "Hashimoto Answers Questions at News Conference," NHK General Television Network (24 February 1996), in FBIS-EAS-96–038

55 Kim Ho-sam, "Japanese Prime Minister's Remarks on Four–Way Talks Decried," Pyongyang Korean Central Broadcasting Network (4 July 1996), in FBIS-EAS-96–132.

56 Sassa Atsuyuki, "Murayama Questioned on Crisis Management Issue," *Chuo Koron* (7 March 1995): 51–69, in FBIS-EAS-95–044.

57 Murayama Kohei, "Japan and U.S. Agree to Joint TMD Research," *Kyodo* (20 September 1998), in FBIS-EAS-98–263.

58 Christopher W. Hughes, "Sino-Japanese Relations and Ballistic Missile Defence," in Marie Söderberg, ed., *Chinese-Japanese Relations in the Twenty-first Century: Complementarity and Conflict* (New York: Routledge 2002), 79. Also see Matsumura Masahiro, "Deploying Theater Missile Defense Flexibly: A U.S.-Japan Response to China," in Nishihara Masashi, ed., *Old Issues, New Responses: Japan's Foreign and Security Policy Options* (Tokyo: Japan Center for International Exchange 1998), 109

59 Wada Haruki et al., "Diplomacy toward North Korea Discussed," *Sekai* (16 September 1994), in FBIS-EAS-94–180.

60 Inoguchi Takashi, "A Peace-and-Security Taxonomy," in Inoguchi Takashi and Grant B. Stillman, eds., *North-East Asian Regional Security: The Role of International Institutions* (Tokyo: United Nations University Press 1997), 198. A Japanese nuclear force – although improbable – would shatter the current regional strategic equilibrium, stir up tensions, and considerably erode U.S. influence in East Asia.

61 Okazaki Hisahiko, "A National Strategy for the Twenty-first Century," *Japan Echo* 26, no. 5 (October 1999), electronic edition. Okazaki clearly states that TMD would protect Japan against China's ballistic missiles.

62 "Press Conference by the Press Secretary," Ministry of Foreign Affairs of Japan, electronic edition (23 October 1998).

63 Desaix Anderson, "KEDO: Seed for Peace in the Korean Peninsula?" *The ICAS Lectures*, no. 99–226–DEA (26 February 1999), electronic edition.

64 "ROK Pursues Six-Nation Northeast Asia Security Forum," *Yonhap* (17 February 1999), in FBIS-EAS-1999–0217.

65 Sakai Hidekazu, "Continuity and Discontinuity of Japanese Foreign Policy toward North Korea: Freezing the Korean Energy Development Organization (KEDO) in 1998," in Miyashita Akitoshi and Sato Yoichiro, eds., *Japanese Foreign Policy in Asia and the Pacific: Domestic Interests, American Pressure, and Regional Integration* (New York: Palgrave 2001), 72

66 Three years after promoting it, Japan is no longer satisfied with ASEAN+3 and since June 2002 the prime minister has been advocating the formation of an ASEAN+5 structure that would welcome the presence of the United States. Apparently Japan feels it cannot compete with Chinese influence on its own.

67 North Korea normalized its diplomatic relations with Italy in February 2000 and with Australia the following May. Other countries, for example France and Canada, have also initiated a dialogue with the North Koreans.

68 Not to be confused with the Maritime Self-Defense Forces.

69 "Press Conference by the Secretary of the Press," Ministry of Foreign Affairs of Japan, electronic version (19 July 1996).

70 "Spokesman Warns Tokyo on Senkakus, Defense Pact with U.S.," *Kyodo* (24 September 1996), in FBIS-CHI-96-186.

71 "Lawmakers Reportedly to Join Trip to Senkaku in May," *Kyodo* (28 April 1997), in FBIS-EAS-97-118.

72 "Press Conference by the Press Secretary," Ministry of Foreign Affairs of Japan, electronic version (27 April 1997).

73 Alastair Iain Johnston, "The Myth of the ASEAN Way? Explaining the Evolution of the ASEAN Regional Forum," in Helga Haftendorn, Robert O. Keohane, and Celeste A. Wallander, eds., *Imperfect Unions: Security Institutions over Time and Space* (New York: Oxford University Press 1999), 300.

74 "Chinese Oceanic Vessel Violates Advance Warning System for Fifth Time," *Sankei Shimbun* (14 August 2001), in FBIS-EAS-2001-0815.

75 "DA Pressured Not to Announce PRC Ships Activity Near Japan Due to 'Delicate Ties,'" *Sankei Shimbun*, in FBIS-EAS-2001-0715.

76 "Lost at Sea: The Demons of Diaoyu," *FEER* (17 October 1996).

77 Erika Strecker Downes and Phillip C. Saunders, "Legitimacy and the Limits of Nationalism: China and the Diaoyu Islands," *International Security* 23, no. 3 (winter 1998–99), 143.

78 Daquing Yang, "Mirror for the Future or the History Card? Understanding the History Problem," in Söderberg, *Chinese-Japanese Relations in the Twenty-first Century*, 20.

79 Arai Hifumi, "Angry at China? Slam Japan!" *FEER* (3 October 1996), 21.

80 Chung Chien-peng, "The Diaoyu/Tiaoyutai/Senkaku Islands Dispute: Domestic Politics and the Limits of Diplomacy," *American Asian Review* 16, no. 3 (autumn 1998), electronic edition.

81 Two examples demonstrate this capacity for independent action. In 1995, Prime Minister Murayama saw his official visit to the United States partially sabotaged by MOFA bureaucrats. Then, in 2001, the foreign minister at the time, Tanaka Makiko, angered certain elements of her ministry and became the victim of plots aimed at discrediting her, in part because

of her anti-American positions, especially with regard to the TMD. The current anticorruption campaign in this ministry is proof of the decisive battle that is being fought between politicians and bureaucrats to snatch power from them and empower politicians.

82 Japan practises a policy of small steps in matters of military security. In 2000, at the request of India and Vietnam, the Maritime Security Forces – and not the SDF – began patrolling the South China Seas, in order to fill the vacuum left by Indonesia. Japan would defend the sea lines of communication against acts of piracy.

CHAPTER SIX

1 David Bachman, "Structure and Process in the Making of Chinese Foreign Policy," in Samuel S. Kim et al., eds., *Chinese Foreign Policy Faces a New Millennium* (Oxford: Westview Press 1998), 34–5.

2 Michael Pillsbury, *China Debates the Future Security Environment* (Washington, DC: National Defence University Press 2000).

3 See, for example, Chalmer Johnson and E.B. Keehn, "The Pentagon's Ossified Strategy," *Foreign Affairs* 74, no. 4 (July-August 1995): 103–14; Chalmer Johnson, "Containing China: U.S. and Japan Drift toward Disaster," *Japan Quarterly* (October-December 1996): 10–18; Richard Bernstein and Ross H. Munro, *The Coming Conflict With China* (New York: Vintage Books 1997).

4 See for example Joseph S. Nye "The Case for Deep Engagement," *Foreign Affairs* 74, no. 4 (July-August 1995): 90–102.

5 Wang Jiangwei, "Chinese Perspectives on Multilateral Security," *Asian Perspective* 22, no. 3.

6 Number taken from David M. Lampton, "A Growing China in a Shrinking World: Beijing and the Global Order," in Ezra F. Vogel et al., eds., *Living with China* (New York: W.W. Norton 1997), 124.

7 Consult, for instance, Robert Keohane, "Neoliberalism Institutionalism: A Perspective on World Politics," in *International Institutions and State Power: Essays in International Relations Theory* (Boulder, CO: Westview Press 1989), 2–3. See also the summary of Joseph M. Grieco, "Anarchy and the Limits of Cooperation: A Realist Critique of the Newest Liberal Institutionalism," in David A. Baldwin, ed., *Neorealism and Neoliberalism: The Contemporary Debate* (New York: Columbia University Press 1993), 488–90.

8 Some commentators exclude the Chinese security policy from institutional policies because China remains a great power in certain domains, such as arms build-up. See Gerald Segal, "Deconstructing Foreign Relations," in David S.G. Goodman and Gerald Segal, eds., *China Deconstructs* (New York: Routledge 1994), 345.

9 See, for example, Amos A. Jordan and Jane Khanna, "Economic Interdependence and Challenges to the Nation-State: The Emergence of Natural
   Economic Territories in the Asia-Pacific," *Journal of International Affairs*
   (winter 1995): 433–62.

10 Thomas W. Robinson, "Interdependence in China's post–Cold War
   Foreign Relations," in Kim, *Chinese Foreign Policy*, 211.

11 Robert A. Manning and James J. Przystup, "Asia's Transition Diplomacy:
   Hedging Against Future Shock, Survival," London (fall 1999),
   file:///CI/WINDOWS/Profiles/On Foreign Policy/asian diplomacy.htm.

12 For this type of argument, see, for example, Joseph Y.S. Cheng, "China's
   ASEAN Policy in the 1990s: Pushing for Regional Multipolarity," *Contemporary Southeast Asia* 21, no. 2, Singapore (August 1999):
   file:///Al/chi-asean1.htm.

13 For a discussion of these two visions, see Chien-pin Li, "The Political
   Economy in East Asia's Security Prospects: A Critical Review of the Literature," *Issues and Studies* 32, no. 11 (November 1996): 31–49.

14 Michael J. Finnegan, "Constructing Cooperation: Toward Multilateral
   Security Cooperation in Northeast Asia," CANCAPS Paper Number 18
   (July 1998): 3; cf. Segal, "Deconstructing Foreign Relations," 449ff.,
   which develops similar arguments for the Security Council and the
   Spratlys but which expresses doubts that a constraining institutional
   structure could be put in place in Southeast Asia in the short run.

15 See, for example, Thomas Risse-Kappen, "The Culture of National Security: Norms and Identity," in *The Culture of National Security: Norms
   and Identity in World Politics*, edited by Peter J. Katzenstein (1996),
   357–99.

16 Thomas Risse-Kappen, *Cooperation among the Democracies: The European Influence on U.S. Foreign Policy* (Princeton, NJ: Princeton University
   Press 1995), 4.

17 The democratic faction can be assimilated to the one that was regrouped
   around Zhao Ziyang and that Deng Xiaoping referred to as a faction
   which sought the "instauration d'un régime libéral, autrement dit capital-
   iste" ("the establishment of a liberal regime, in other words, a capitalist
   regime") through reforms. See Deng Xiaoping, "Nous avons besoin d'un
   collectif dirigeant d'avenir résolu à mener à bien les réformes," 1 May
   1989, in Deng Xiaoping, *Textes choisis* (Beijing: Xinhua 1992), 301–2.

18 See, for example, Rosemary Foot, "China in the ASEAN Forum," *Asian
   Survey* 38, no. 5 (May 1998).

19 Adam Roberts, "The United Nations: Variations of Collective Security,"
   in Ngaire Woods, ed., *Explaining International Relations since 1945*
   (Oxford: Oxford University Press 1996), 327ff.

20 See, for example, Finnegan, "Constructing Cooperation," for whom this
   approach must nevertheless be completed by a structural-realist approach.

21 Jürgen Haacke, "The Aseanization of Regional Order in East Asia: A Failed Endeavour?" *Asian Perspective* 22, no. 3 (1998): 7–47.

22 Canada and Australia encouraged this particular approach in the early 1990s in the Asian region. See Graig A. Snyder, "Regional Security Structures," in Graig A. Snyder, ed., *Contemporary Security and Strategy* (New York: Routledge 1999), 114.

23 Randall L. Schweller, "Realism and the Present Great Power System: Growth and Positional Conflict over Scarce Resources," in Ethan B. Kapstein and Michael Mastanduno, eds., *Unipolar Politics: State Strategies after the Cold War* (New York: Columbia University Press 1999).

24 Zalmay M. Kkhializad et al., *The United States and a Rising China* (Washington, DC: Rand, 1999), 70.

25 Ibid.

26 John J. Mearsheimer, "A Realist Reply," *International Security* 29, no. 1 (summer 1995), 82.

27 Ibid., 86.

28 For a realist point of view on ASEAN, see, for example, Michael Leifer, *The ASEAN Regional Forum*, Adelphi Paper no. 302 (London: International Institute for Strategic Studies 1996).

29 Some observers doubt that the territorial occupation is really militarily important for China, which should be content simply to be able to project its power.

30 David B.H. Denoon, "China's Security Strategy: The View from Beijing, ASEAN, and Washington," *Asian Survey* 36, no. 4 (April 1996): 240.

31 See Sheldon Simon, "The Limits of Defence Security Cooperation in Southeast Asia," *Journal of Asian and African Studies* 33, no. 1 (February 1998).

32 Evan A. Freigenbaum, "China's Military Posture and the New Economic Geopolitics," *Survival* 4, no. 2 (summer 1999): 80.

33 For an analysis of the UN that follows this logic, see Norman A. Graham, "China and the Future of Security Cooperation and Conflict in Asia," *Journal of Asian and African Studies* 33, no. 1 (February 1998).

34 Ibid., 59–60.

35 We follow here the comments of Alastair Iain Johnston on this school: "Realism and Chinese Security Policy in the post–Cold War Period," in Kapstein and Mastanduno, "*Unipolar Politics.*"

36 For a discussion of structural-realist hypotheses based on Walt, see Johnston, "Realism and Chinese Security Policy."

37 Finnegan, "Constructing Cooperation," 1–2.

38 On this last eventuality see Manning et al., *Asia's Transition Diplomacy.*

39 Other institutions provided training in international relations, namely the Foreign Affairs Ministry. Interview by the author in 1999 with retired manager of the Chinese Foreign Affairs Ministry.

40 Avery Goldstein, "Discounting the Free Ride: Alliance and Security in the Post-War World," *International Organization* 49, no. 1 (winter 1995): 39–72.

41 In 1977 Hua Guofeng called for a China "which rests on its own strengths." Hua Guofeng, "Continue the Revolution under the Dictatorship of the Proletariat to the End: A Study of Volume V of the *Select Works of Mao Tse-tung*," *Peking Review*, no 19 (5 May 1977).

42 James C.F. Wang, *Contemporary Chinese Politics*. 6th edition (Toronto: Prentice Hall 1999), 244–5.

43 For a description of the feud between the factions during that period, see, for example, Willy Wo-Lap Lam, *The Era of Jiang Zemin* (Toronto: Prentice Hall 1999).

44 See Willy Wo-Lap Lam, *The Era of Jiang Zemin*.

45 Wang, *Contemporary Chinese Politics*, 245.

46 Wang Jiangwei, "Chinese Perceptions in the post–Cold War Era," *Asian Survey* 32, no. 10 (fall 1992): 903.

47 Paul H.B. Godwin, "Force and Diplomacy: China Prepares for the Twenty-first Century," in Samuel S. Kim, ed., *China and the World*, 4th ed. (Boulder, CO: Westview Press 1998), 173–4.

48 Willy Wo-Lap Lam, *The Era of Jiang Zemin*, 156.

49 The incident in 1995 in which Lee Teng-Hui was given a visa to get him to the United States symbolized the deterioration of relations between Peking and Washington during those times. See Steven I. Levine, "Sino-American Relations," in Kim, *China and the World*, 93–4.

50 Willy Wo-Lap Lam, *The Era of Jiang Zemin*, 172–3.

51 Ibid., 186.

52 The military had firmer positions, particularly over Taiwan and the Spratlys. Willy Wo-Lap Lam, *The Era of Jiang Zemin*, 171.

53 For a critical summary see, for example, Sean M. Lynn-Jones, "Realism and Security Studies," in Snyder, *Contemporary Security and Strategy*, 65ff.

54 See, for, example Amitav Acharya, "Realism, Institutionalism and the Asian Economic Crisis," *Contemporary Southeast Asia* 21, no. 1 (April 1999): 1–29; (even though for Acharya new theoretical possibilities are being offered to institutionalists). According to Acharya, realists present the Asian crisis as proof of the lack of efficiency of institutionalist approaches because the dependence of smaller countries on larger ones has increased. As a result the great powers have exploited the crisis to their advantage and interdependence has increased the impact of the crisis, while ASEAN and APEC have failed to contain it. Institutionalists would answer by insisting on the importance of modelling Asian institutions on Asian culture.

55 On propaganda see, for example, Guanxqiu Xu, "The Chinese Anti-

American Nationalism in the 1990s," *Asian Perspective* 22, no. 2 (1998): 193–218.

56 See "CPC Propaganda Department Reviews 'three-Stresses' Education," *Xinhua* (1 March 2000), FBIS-CHI-2000–301.

57 See Albert Park et al., "Distributional Consequence of Reforming Local Public Finance in China," *The China Quarterly*, 751.

58 See, for example, Le-Yin Zhang, "Chinese Central-Provincial Fiscal Relationships, Budgetary Decline, and the Impact of the 1994 Fiscal Reform: An Evaluation," *The China Quarterly*, no. 159 (September 1999): 115–41.

59 Hou Zhitong, "Déclaration de M. Qian Qichen," *Beijing Information*, no. 40 (5 October 1992), 13.

60 Qin Huasun, Statement by Ambassador Qin Huasun, Permanent Representative of China to the UN at the Fifty-second Session of UNGA on the Reform of Security Council," ONU, 54 (December 1997), http:www.undp.org/missions/china/12–04975.htm.

61 See, for example, "China: Security Council Does Need Proper, Necessary Reforms," *Xinhua* (31 October 2001), FBIS-CHI-2001–1031.

62 "PRC's Tang Jiaxuan on Jiang's Successs at UN Summit," *Xinhua* (9 September 2000), FBIS-CHI-2000–0909.

63 Li Hongji and Gu Zhenqiu, "PRC's Tang Jiaxuan Speaks on UN Role, Global Stability," *Xinhua* (13 September 2000), FBIS-CHI-2000–0914. This type of position can be interpreted as a defence of the status quo or as a defence of the interests of developing countries.

64 "Chinese FM Tang Jiaxuan Says UN Security Council Reform Needs Consensus," *Beijing Xinhua* (21 January 2001), FBIS-CHI-2001–0121.

65 See comments from Singapore's ambassador, Bilahari Kausikan, "Do the Permanent Members Really Want Reform?" ONU (5 May 1997).

66 Su Xiangxin, "China Diplomatic Achievement in UN in 1997" (interview with Qin Huasun, permanent representative of China at the UN), *Zhongguo Xinwen She* (5 January 1998), FBIS-CHI-98–05.

67 A Japanese press agency interpreted the Chinese position on regional disequilibrium; the information was never denied. See "Japan: Li Peng Toast Relationship as Qian Qichen Slams Japan," *Tokyo Kyodo News Service* (29 September 1997), FBIS-EAS-97–272.

68 Ken Sasahaka, "Japan, PRC Said To Stage-Manage Friendly Relations at Summit," *Sankei Shimbun* (14 October 2000), FBIS-EAS-200–1014.

69 Sha Zukang (General Manager of the Weapons and Disarmement Department at the Ministry of Foreign Affairs), "La position de la Chine sur la non-prolifération, discours prononcé le 11 janvier 1999 à la septième conférence sur la non-prolifération de la fondation Carnegie," *Beijing Information*, no. 6 (8 February 1999): 6.

70 "Jiang Zemin, Indian President Hold Talks; Cites Jiang's Four-Point Pro-

posal on Bilateral Relations," *Hong Kong Xinhua* (29 May 2000), FBIS-CHI-2000–0529.

71 Xia Zhalong *& al.*, "UN Representative Interviewed on Peace Keeping ," *Beijing Xinhua Domestic Service* (2 March 1995), FBIS-CHI-95–42.

72 Han Hua, "China: Shen Guofang Views PRC Diplomacy, Exclusive Interview," Hong-Kong, *Wei Wen Po* (4 February 1998), FBIS-CHI-98–035.

73 " China: Qian Qichen Meets with U.S.' Richardson," *Beijing Xinhua* (15 August 1997), FBIS-CHI-97–227.

74 Jiang Zemin, "Text of PRC President Jiang Zemin Speech at UN Security Council Summit," *Hong Kong Xinhua* (7 September 2000), FBIS-2000–0908.

75 Xu Shiquan, "PRC: Article Criticizes U.S. Policy on UN Reform," *Renmin Ribao* (25 June 1996), FBIS-CHI-96–129. For more details see Yang Yang, "China: Obstacles to UN Reform Discussed," *Beijing Shijie Zhishi* (1 December 1996), FBIS-CHI-96–003. Also see Li and Gu, "PRC's Tang Jiaxuan Speaks On."

76 Banning N. Garrett and Bonnie S. Glaster, " Chinese Perspectives on Nuclear Arms Control," in Michael E. Brown, Sean M. Lynn-Jones, and Steven E. Miller, eds., *East Asian Security* (Cambridge: MIT Press 1996), 233.

77 Also see Gao Jian, "UN Envoy Comments on Nuclear Test Ban Treaty," *Xinhua* (12 November 1995), FBIS-CHI-95–223.

78 "UN Envoy Notes Nation's Stand on Disarmament," Beijing, *Xinhua* (16 May 1995), FBIS-CHI-95–096.

79 Ibid.

80 "Disarmament Envoy Elaborates on Nuclear Test Ban Stand," Beijing, *Xinhua* (8 May 1996), FBIS-CHI-96–082. The Japanese government expresses it more clearly: "Tokyo Welcomes China's shift to 'Flexible Stance' on CTBT," *Tokyo Kyodo* (14 May 1996), FBIS-EAS-96–094.

81 The United States denies giving the software to China in May 1996. An American diplomat declared anonymously that a secret agreement had been signed with France in 1996 and that discussions were under way with Russia but not with China. See Dimitri Antonov, "U.S., Russia Discuss Exchange of Nuclear Security Data," *Moscow ITAR-TASS* (19 June 1996), FBIS-SOV-96–119. This was a minority opinion. For the opposite and main argument, see Nigel Holloway, "Bargaining Counter, U.S. Offers China a Nuclear Carrot," *Far Eastern Economic Review* 28 (March 1996), or Tariq Rauf, *Test-Ban Treaty: Asian Concerns* (Monterey, CA: Center for Non-proliferation Studies, Monterey Institute for International Studies 1997), 3. In 1995 the Chinese failed to develop new nuclear technology, and the army pressured the government to pursue further testing. See "New Nuclear Weapons Said Goal of Current Tests," Hongkong, *Lien Ho Pao* (12 November 1995), FBIS-CHI-95–218.

82 Li Daozhong, "PRC: International Commentary on Test Ban Treaty ,"
   Beijing Liaowang (30 September 1996), FBIS-CHI-96-136.

83 "PRC Official: China Makes 'Great Concessions,' Wants Early CTBT,"
   Hong-Kong, *Ming Pao* (14 July 1996), FBIS-CHI-96-136.

84 Gao Jian, "China: Disarmament Envoy Sha Zhukang on Disarmament
   Talks," *Beijing Liaowang* (16 December 1996), FBIS-CHI-95-218.

85 "RMRB Article Criticizes U.S. 'Egoism,' 'Hegemonic Arrogance,'" *Renmin
   Ribao* (7 July 2000), FBIS-CHI-2000-0707.

86 Duan Jiyong, "Shen Guofang Calls on International Community to Speed
   Up CTBT Entry Process," *Beijing Xinhua Domestic Service* (12 November
   2001), FBIS-CHI-2001-1113.

87 Praynah Sharma, "China to Engage in Security Dialogue in February,"
   The Telegraph (Calcutta), (21 January 2001), FBIS-CHI-2001-0121.

88 "PRC Article Says India Needs to Eliminate 'Anxiety about China,'"
   Huanqiu Shibao (6 September 2001), FBIS-CHI-2001-0906.

89 Frédérique Lasserre, "De la stratégie diplomatique au concept de région:
   représentation historique et conflits en mer de Chine du sud," *Relations
   internationale et stratégiques* (Paris, IRIS, September 1997), 107.

90 " Les progrès des activités navales en Chine ," Information Office of the
   State Council of the People's Republic of China, Beijing, May 1998,
   Beijing Information, no. 24 (15 June 1998), 17. The August 1998 document on the defence policy of China does not mention anywhere the
   problems of naval frontiers. Information Office of the State Council of
   the People's Republic of China, July 1998, Beijing, in *Beijing
   Information*, no. 32 (10 August 1998).

91 Han Hua, "China: Shen Guofang Views PRC Diplomacy," 3.

92 "Bali Workshop 1990," in The South China Sea Informal Working
   Group, *Proposals for Cooperation in the South China Sea* (compilation)
   (Vancouver: University of British Columbia 1993), 34. See also *Project
   Management Plan, Asia Pacific Ocean Cooperation Project (APOC),
   Phase II*, ACDI (April 1996).

93 More specifically for the Spratlys, the labour committee of Bandung proposed in 1991 to form joint research groups to study natural phenomenon, meteorological conditions, and navigation; Bandung Workshop
   1991, in Davies, *Proposals for Cooperation*, 45.

94 Yogyarkarta Workshop, ibid., 45.

95 "China: Article Reaffirms PRC Claim to Spratlys," *Zhongguo Tongxun
   She* (25 January 1999), FBIS-CHI-99-025.

96 See, for example, Herman Joseph S. Kraft, "Unofficial Diplomacy in
   Asia: The Role of ASEAN-ISIS," Toronto, CANAPS Paper Number 22 (February 2000).

97 *The Report of the First Group of Experts Meeting on Hydrographic
   Data Information Exchange in the South China Sea*, South China Sea
   Informal Working Group, Kuching (15–20 June 1997).

 98 Jianxiang Bi, "Making the Impossible Possible: The PLA's Taiwan Oper-
    ation in the Twenty-first Century," Canadian Consortium on
    Asia/Pacific Security, University of Victoria, December 1998, 27.

 99 "Les progrès des activitées navales en Chine," Information Office of the
    State Council of the People's Republic of China, Beijing, May 1998,
    Beijing Information, no. 24 (May 1998): 17.

100 Cathy Rose A. Garcia et al., "Manila Said 'Losing Faith' in Talks with
    Beijing," *Manila Business World* (26 March 1999), FBIS-EAS-1999–0326.

101 China occupied the Eldad reef in 1992 and the archipelago of Mischief
    in 1995.

102 "La défense nationale de Chine ," Information Office of the State
    Council of the People's Republic of China, July 1998, *Beijing Informa-
    tion*, no. 32 (10 August 1998).

103 "China's New Naval Strategy," *Stratford* (26 January 2000),
    http://www.stratfor.com/SERVICES/giu2000/012600.asp.

104 "Envoy: Nansha Issue Not to Affect PRC Ties in Asia," *Xinhua* (15 June
    1999), FBIS-CHI-1999–0615.

105 For a comparison of the Chinese armed forces and those of the other
    countries of the region, see Felix K. Chang, "Beyond the Unipolar
    Moment: Beijing's Reach in the South China Sea," *Orbis* (summer
    1996). The director of the Chinese Military Institute for Naval Research
    also concludes that, given the military reinforcements of neighbouring
    countries, it is necessary to considerably improve the Chinese military
    capabilities in the region. Liu Zhenhuan, "China: Military Scholar on
    UN Law of Sea ," *Beijing Guofang* (15 November 1996), FBIS-CHI-
    97–021.

106 Dana R. Dillon comes to a similar conclusion when she states: "In
    short, China attends international forums and signs pleasant-sounding
    statements but steadfastly refuses multilateral negotiations, insisting
    that each dispute must be resolved bilaterally, and acts unilaterally ...
    Meanwhile, China continues to build up its naval air forces in the
    region," Dana R. Dillon, *How the Bush Administration Should Handle
    China Sea Naval Territorial Disputes*, Heritage Foundation (5 Septem-
    ber 2001), www.heritage.org/library/backgrounder/bg.1470.htm.

107 See the declarations of Chi Haotian on the new era of military coopera-
    tion in "Comments on Military Diplomacy, Sino-U.S. Ties," *Beijing
    China Radio International* (9 October 1999), FBIS-CHI-1999–1027.

108 See, for example, Kenneth W. Allen and Eric A. McVadon, *China's
    Foreign Military Relations*, ed. Ranjeet K. Singh, 1999, 59ff.

109 "China Takes Firm Stance on Spratlys Islands" (April 2000),
    www.stratfor.com/asia/commentary/004200200. On the future military
    capacities of China, see Paul Studeman, "Calculating China's Advance
    in the South China Sea: Identifying the Triggers of Expansionism,"
    Naval War College Review 51, no. 2 (1998).

CHAPTER SEVEN

Louis Bélanger is Associate Professor, Department of Political Science, and Director, Institut québécois des hautes études internationales, Université Laval, Québec, Canada G1K 7P4. Nelson Michaud is Professor and Vice-chair, Groupe d'études de recherche de formation internationales (GERFI), École nationale d'administration publique, Université du Québec, Québec, Canada, G1K 9A5 and Associate Research Fellow, Centre for Foreign Policy Studies, Dalhousie University, Halifax, Canada. The authors would like to thank the Fonds pour la formation des chercheurs et l'aide à la recherche (FCAR) for having provided funding for this research; Evelyne Dufault and Annie Laliberté for research assistance; and Onnig Beylerian, Denis Stairs, and this book's anonymous reviewers for their valuable comments on the earlier version of this chapter.

1 On the role of middle powers as institution-builders within the international system, see Carsten Holbraad, *Middle Powers in International Politics* (London: Macmillan 1984); David Cox, Steve Lee, and James Sutterlin, *The Reduction of Risk of War through Multilateral Means: A Summary of Conference Proceedings* (Ottawa: Canadian Institute for International Peace and Security, 1989); James Cotton and John Ravenhill, eds., *Seeking Australian Engagement in World Affairs, 1991–1995* (Melbourne: Oxford University Press 1997); Bernard Wood, *The Middle Powers and the General Interest* (Ottawa: North-South Institute 1989); Gareth Evans and Bruce Grant, *Australia's Foreign Relations in the World* (Melbourne: Melbourne University Press 1991); and Andrew F. Cooper, Richard A. Higgott, and Kim R. Nossal, *Relocating Middle Powers: Australia and Canada in a Changing World Order* (Vancouver: UBC Press 1993).

2 See, for instance, Robert O. Keohane, "Lilliputians' Dilemmas: Small States in International Politics," *International Organization* 23, no. 2 (spring 1969); Cooper, Higott, and Nossal, *Relocating Middle Powers*; Louis Bélanger, Andrew F. Cooper, Gordon Mace, and Joël Monfils, "Middle Powers, Relative Gains, and Regional Trade Cooperation," paper presented at the Fortieth Annual Meeting of the International Studies Association, Washington, DC, 1999.

3 Alan Henrickson, "Middle Powers as Managers: International Mediation within, across and outside Institutions," in Andrew F. Cooper, ed., *Niche Diplomacy: Middle Powers after the Cold War* (London: Macmillan Press 1997), 48.

4 Holbraad, *Middle Powers in International Politics*, 69

5 Henrickson, "Middle Powers as Managers," 47; Keohane, "Lilliputians' Dilemmas," 296; Andrew F. Cooper, Richard A. Higgott, and Kim R.

Nossal, *Relocating Middle Powers after the Cold War* (Vancouver: UBC Press 1993).

6 See Vinod K. Aggarwal, "Reconciling Multiple Institutions: Bargaining, Linkages, and Nesting," in Vinod K. Aggarwal, ed., *Institutional Designs for a Complex World: Bargaining, Linkages, and Nesting* (Ithaca, NY, and London: Cornell University Press 1998), 1–31.

7 Celeste A. Wallander and Robert O. Keohane, "Risk, Threat, and Security Institutions," in Robert O. Keohane and Celeste A. Wallander, eds., *Imperfect Unions: Security Institutions over Time and Space* (Oxford: Oxford University Press 1999), 23–4.

8 Andrew F. Cooper, "Niche Diplomacy: A Conceptual Overview," in Andrew F. Cooper, ed., *Niche Diplomacy*, 1–24.

9 On this point, see Nelson Michaud and Louis Bélanger, "La stratégie institutionnelle du Canada: Vers une 'australisation'?" *Études internationales* 30, no. 2 (June 1999), 373–96.

10 On the influence of second-rank powers over the institutional trajectory of an organization, see Joseph M. Grieco, "The Maastricht Treaty, Economic and Monetary Union and the Neo-realist Research Programme," *Review of International Studies* 21, no. 1 (January 1995), 21–40; and Joseph M. Grieco, "State Interest and International Rule Trajectories: A Neorealist Interpretation of the Maastricht Treaty and European Economic and Monetary Union," in Benjamin Frankel, ed., *Realism: Restatement and Renewal* (London: Frank Cass 1996), 261–306. The main theoretical elements developed by Grieco are discussed below.

11 David Ross Black, *Australian, Canadian, and Swedish Policies toward South Africa: A Comparative Study of "Middle Power Internationalism"* (Unpublished PHD diss., Dalhousie University 1992), 14.

12 We refer to Laura Neack, *Beyond the Rhetoric of Peacekeeping and Peacemaking: Middle States and International Politics* (Unpublished PHD diss., University of Kentucky 1991); and "Empirical Observations on 'Middle State' Behavior at the Start of the International System," *Pacific Focus* 7 (1992) 5–22.

13 Grieco, "State Interest and International Rule Trajectories," 287.

14 Elsewhere, Grieco uses the expressions "relatively weak but still politically necessary partners" or even "weaker but still salient states" ("State Interest and International Rule Trajectories," 288–9).

15 Grieco, "The Maastricht Treaty," 34.

16 To fully understand the concepts involved here, it may be useful to refer to the concept of "voice" developed by Albert O. Hirschman in *Exit, Voice, and Loyalty: Responses to Decline in Firms, Organizations, and States* (Cambridge, MA: Harvard University Press 1970); and borrowed by Grieco ("The Maastricht Treaty"; "State Interest and International Rule Trajectories"). According to Hirschman's theory, when faced with

deteriorating organizational performance, an actor may opt either to leave (exit) or to express dissatisfaction (voice) through the organization's interest-articulation mechanisms. Because Hirschman is interested in situations in which organizational performance is deteriorating, he conceives of both voice and exit as ways to articulate discontent and reestablish or improve the benefits offered by the organization.

17 "Very powerful states may believe that, at least in the short run, gaps in gains arising from any particular relationship will have little impact on their position of preeminence. Very weak states may believe that they cannot in any event ensure their security through their own efforts and thus can largely ignore shifts in relative capabilities arising from gaps in cooperatively generated gains. In contrast, middle-range states may be extremely sensitive to gaps in gains, for they must simultaneously fear the strong and aspire to their status *and* they must worry that they might slip down into ranks of the weak." See Joseph M Grieco, *Cooperation among Nations: Europe, America, and Non-tariff Barriers to Trade* (Ithaca, NY: Cornell University Press 1990), 46.

18 Joseph M. Grieco, "Understanding the Problem of International Cooperation: The Limits of Neoliberal Institutionalism and the Future of Realist Theory," in David A. Baldwin, ed., *Neorealism and Neoliberalism: The Contemporary Debate* (New York: Columbia University Press 1993), 323–7

19 See Louis Bélanger, Andrew F. Cooper, Gordon Mace, and Joël Monfils, "Middle Powers, Relative Gains, and Regional Trade Cooperation," Paper presented at the Fortieth Annual Meeting of the International Studies Association, Washington, DC, 1999.

20 Ibid.

21 Hirschman, *Exit, Voice, and Loyalty*, 34

22 This may also generate externalities based on which costs will be absorbed, but there are no propositions specific to middle powers on this question.

23 Hirschman, *Exit, Voice, and Loyalty*, 40

24 See Cooper, Higgott, and Nossal, *Relocating Middle Powers*.

25 Ibid. 23

26 Cooper, "Niche Diplomacy: A Conceptual Overview," 5

27 See Andrew F. Cooper, ed., *Niche Diplomacy: Middle Powers after the Cold War* (London: Macmillan Press 1997)

28 John Ravenhill, "Cycles of Middle Power Activism: Constraint and Choice in Australian and Canadian Foreign Policies," *Australian Journal of International Affairs* 52, no. 3 (1998), 309–27.

29 Cooper, "Niche Diplomacy: A Conceptual Overview," 3.

30 Charles-Philippe David and Stéphane Roussel, "'Middle Power Blues':

Canadian Policy and International Security after the Cold War," *American Review of Canadian Studies* 28 (spring/summer 1998): 131–56.

31 Laura Neack, "Middle Powers Once Removed: The Diminished Global Role of Middle Powers and American Grand Strategy," Paper presented at the Forty-first Annual Meeting of the International Studies Association, Los Angeles, CA (March 2000), 14–18.

32 Nelson Michaud, *Genèse d'une politique syncopique: La défense du Canada et le Livre blanc de 1987* (Unpublished PHD diss., Laval University 1998).

33 See Nelson Michaud, "Misères de la politique étrangère canadienne," *Le Devoir*, 15 April 1999, A7; and "La gestion de l'après-attentat: Y a-t-il un rôle pour le Canada?" *Le Soleil*, 3 October 2001, A19.

34 Michaud and Bélanger, "La stratégie institutionnelle du Canada," 373–96.

35 See, for instance, Albert Legault, "Maintien de la paix et réforme des Nations Unies," *Études internationales* 27, no. 2 (1996): 325–52; Maurice Bertrand, "À propos de la réforme du Conseil de sécurité," *Études internationales* 30, no. 2 (1999): 413–22; Olivier Fleurence, *La réforme du Conseil de sécurité: L'état du débat depuis la fin de la guerre froide* (Brussels: Bruylant 2000).

36 Onnig Beylerian, "La variation de l'intérêt des puissances dans les institutions internationales de sécurité," *Études internationales* 30, no. 2 (1999): 411. In his article, Beylerian offers an excellent summary of the proposals presently put forward. For another point of view, see the chapters in Eric Fawcett and Anna Newcombe, eds., *United Nations Reform: Looking Ahead after Fifty Years* (Toronto: Science for Peace 1995). Documents pertaining to the reform can be consulted in Paul Taylor, Sam Dawns, and Ute Adamczick-Gerteis, eds., *Documents on the Reform of the United Nations* (Aldershot, England: Dartmouth 1997)

37 These four seats would be occupied by the delegations from Great Britain, France, Germany, and the United States.

38 Boutros Boutros-Ghali, *An Agenda for Peace* (New York: United Nations 1996), 325

39 DFAIT (Department of Foreign Affairs and International Trade), "Notes for an Address by the Honourable Lloyd Axworthy Minister of Foreign Affairs to the Fifty-second Session of the United Nations General Assembly," 97/36, New York, 25 September 1997.

40 DFAIT, "Notes for an address by the Honourable Lloyd Axworthy Minister of Foreign Affairs on the Occasion of the Thirty-fourth Assembly of Heads of State and Government of the Organization of African Unity," 98/44, Ouagadoudou, 9 June 1998.

41 DFAIT, "Notes for an Address by the Honourable Lloyd Axworthy,

Minister of Foreign Affairs to the Fifty-third Session of the United
Nations General Assembly," 98/59, New York, 25 September 1998.

42 Ibid.

43 Ibid.

44 The expression "like-minded" is used in Canadian foreign policy circles
to designate countries whose concerns are similar to Canada's and which
often, due to their limited military striking power, also find themselves in
a situation where innovative avenues provide the only opportunitie for
making their voice heard.

45 See David B. Dewitt, "Directions in Canada's International Security
Policy: From Marginal Actor at the Centre to Central Actor at the
Margins," *International Journal* 55, no. 2 (2000): 167–287.

46 DFAIT. "Notes from an Address by the Honourable Lloyd Axworthy,
Minister of Foreign Affairs on Sustainable Development in Canadian
Foreign Policy," 97/21, Vancouver (17 April 1997a).

47 Manon Tessier, "La convention sur les mines antipersonnel: Un cri
d'alarme de l'opinion publique," *Le maintien de la paix*, bulletin no. 30
(Québec: Institut québécois des hautes études internationales 1997), 2.
China and Russia are examples of the first position, for they were simply
in favour of continuing using AP landmines, while India and Pakistan
espoused the second position, for instance.

48 See International Red Cross Commitee, "Troisième session de la Conférence d'examen des États parties à la convention des Nations Unies de
1980 sur certaines armes classiques; point de la situation no. 8" (10 May
1996) http://www.irc.org/icrcnouv/34ce.html.

49 In fact, Canada brought the issue before both the United Nations General
Assembly and the OAS, more in order to receive support for the principle
than to have a ban treaty adopted there, according to officials interviewed for this research. In June 1996 the success of these efforts could
be seen at the regional/hemispheric level, where a resolution of the Organization of American States (OAS) asked its members to "work towards
the global elimination of AP landmines and to take steps towards a hemisphere free of these weapons" (DFAIT, "OAS Adopts Resolutions on Continued International Presence in Haiti and on Global Elimination of Anti-
personnel Mines," News Release no. 109, 10 June 1996). Then, on 10
December the United Nations General Assembly included a resolution to
ban landmines, as part of a package of resolutions on disarmament
(United Nations General Assembly 1996).

50 Government of Canada, "Canada Announces Anti-personnel Land Mines
Measures," Press Release, no. 5 (17 January 1996).

51 Robert Lawson, "The Ottawa Process: Fast-Track Diplomacy and the
International Movement to Ban Anti-personnel Landmines," in Fen Osler

Hampson and Maureen Appel Molot, eds., *Canada among Nations 1998: Leadership and Dialogue* (Toronto: Oxford University Press 1998), 84

52 Richard Price, "Reversing the Gun Sights: Transnational Civil Society Targets Land Mines," *International Organizations* 52, no. 3 (1998): 615.

53 The statement the United States, especially, by surprise, since it was opposed to a deadline and thought it had reached an agreement with its Canadian counterpart over the summer. According to Kirkey, Canada acted because other countries might have seized the opportunity and exercised leadership. The chair of the first Ottawa conference is reported to have declared that "we need to do something that keeps the lead on Canada." See Christopher Kirkey, "Washington's Approach to the Ottawa Process and the Elimination of Landmines: A Review of American Political Imperatives and Strategic Interests," paper presented at the Canadian Political Science Association and Société québécoise de science politique special joint Annual Meeting, Québec City (July 2000), 7; quoted with the authorization of the author.

54 DFAIT, "Canada Offers to Host Treaty Conference to Sign Ban on Anti-personnel Landmines," News Release, no. 183 (5 October 1996), Appendix: Final Declaration – Towards A Global Ban on Anti-personnel landmines; Declaration of the Ottawa Conference.

55 DFAIT. "Le ministre Axworthy se félicite de la centième ratification de la convention sur les mines terrestres" (2000) at http://webapps.dfaitmaeci. gc.ca/minpub/Publication.asp?FileSpec=/Min_Pub _Docs/103594.htm.

56 Tom Keating, "The Promise and Pitfalls of Human Security," paper presented at the Canadian Political Science Association and Société québécoise de science politique special joint annual meeting, Québec City (July 2000). Quoted with the authorization of the author.

57 Nelson Michaud and Kim Richard Nossal, "The Conservative Era in Foreign Policy," in Nelson Michaud and Kim Richard Nossal, eds., *Diplomatic Departures: The Conservative Era in Canadian Foreign Policy* (Vancouver: UBC Press 2001), 3–24

58 Kathryn Sikkink, "Transnational Politics, International Relations Theory, and Human Rights," *PS: Political Science and Politics* 31, no. 3 (1998): 517–21.

59 A complete annotated list of these meetings can be consulted at http://www.mines.gc.ca/english/documents.html.

60 An interesting review of the American stance is provided by Kirkey, "Washington's approach."

61 These ministers were Barbara McDougall (Conservative), Perrin Beatty (Conservative) André Ouellet (Liberal-realist), and Lloyd Axworthy (Liberal-idealist inclined).

62 Leslie E. Norton, "L'incidence de la violation flagrante et systématique des droits de la personne sur les relations bilatérales du Canada," *Études internationales* 24, no. 4 (1993): 787–811.

63 See Pierre O'Neill, "Les stratèges fédéraux surveillent la performance de la droite," *Le Devoir*, 20 March 1996, A5.

64 See Darcy Jenish and Ann Mclaughlin, "Watching and Waiting. Worry Grips Haitian-Canadians," *Maclean's*, 3 October 1994, 28.

65 Gordon Mace, "Explaining the Decision to Join the OAS: An Interpretation," in Michaud and Nossal, eds., *Diplomatic Departures*, 142–59 (forthcoming).

66 Canada had enjoyed permanent observer status since 1972.

67 DFAIT, Press Release, no. 191, 1993.

68 Organisation of American States. Document AG/RES. 1090 (XXI-0/91), 5 June 1991, reprinted in *U.S. Department of State Dispatch* (7 October 1991): 750.

69 DFAIT, "Notes for an Allocution for the Honourable Barbara McDougall, Secretary of State for External Affairs," Speech 91/53, 1991.

70 Isabelle Desmartis and Yves Goulet, "Le retour annoncé du Père Aristide: L'emprise américaine," *Le maintien de la paix*, bulletin no. 5 (Québec: Centre québécois de relations internationales 1993): 4.

71 An example is executive order issued on 29 October 1991, less than a month after the coup.

72 Domingo Acevedo, "The Haitian Crisis and the OAS Response: A Test of Effectiveness in Protecting Democracy," in Lori Fisler Domrasch, eds., *Enforcing Restraint: Collective Intervention in International Conflict* (New York: Council on Foreign Relations Press 1993), 119–55.

73 Hugo Loiseau, *Les cas de coopération et le rôle des puissances moyennes en matière de sécurité dans les Amériques* (Québec, Institut québécois des hautes études internationales, Université Laval, 1998), 16.

74 For a good overview of the peace missions (MINUAH, MANUH, MITNUH, MIPONUH), see http://www.un.org/englisj/peace.

75 David Malone, "Haiti and the International Community: A Case Study," *Survival – The IISS Quarterly* 39, no. 2 (summer 1997): 127.

76 Marie-Paule Rouleau, "Les élections en Haïti," *Bulletin de nouvelles*, Société Radio-Canada, 15 July, 8 A.M.

77 Paul Gecelovsky, "Raising Hornets: Middle Powers, Ideas, and Canadian Foreign Policy," paper presented at the Canadian Political Science Association and Société québécoise de science politique special joint annual meeting, Quebec City, July 2000, 2; quoted with the authorization of the author.

78 A.J. Miller, "The Functional Principle in Canada's External Relations," *International Journal* 34, no. 2 (1980): 309–28.

79 Tom Keating, *Canada and World Order: The Multilateral Tradition in Canadian Foreign Policy* (Toronto: McClelland and Stewart 1993).

80 Kim Richard Nossal, "The Outlook for 1993," in Kim Richard Nossal, ed., *Canadian Foreign Policy: Still in Flux*, a special iIssue of *Behind the Headlines* 50, no. 2 (1992–93): 2–9.

81 See Charles-Philippe David and Stéphane Roussel, "'Middle Power Blues': Canadian Policy and International Security after the Cold War," *American Review of Canadian Studies* 28 (spring/summer 1998): 131–56.

82 See Adam Chapnick, "The Canadian Middle Power Myth," *International Journal* 55, no. 2 (2000): 188–206.

CONCLUSION

1 For example, Congress perceives the UN as an alternate source of legitimacy, since the president may be tempted to bypass it and use UN resolutions as a means to justify the use of U.S. armed forces in foreign countries. See, for example, Louis Henkin, "Use of Force: Law and U.S. Policy," in Louis Henkin, Stanley Hoffmann, et al., eds., *Right v. Might: International Law and the Use of Force* (New York: Council on Foreign Relations 1991), 37–69.

2 Jack S. Levy, "Learning and Foreign Policy: Sweeping a Conceptual Minefield," *International Organization* 48, no. 2 (1994): 279–312; Jing-Dong Yuan, "Culture Matters: Chinese Approaches to Arms Control and Disarmament," in Keith R. Krause, ed., *Culture and Security: Multilateralism, Arms Control and Security Building* (London: Frank Cass 1998), 85–128; see also Samuel S. Kim, "China and the United Nations," in Elizabeth Economy and Michel Oksenberg, eds., *China Joins the World, Progress and Prospects* (New York: Council on Foreign Relations 1999), 42–90.

3 For a discussion of governance costs, see David A. Lake, *Entangling Relations: American Foreign Policy in its Century* (Princeton: Princeton University Press 1999), 9–11.

4 For a treatment of executive-legislative relations related to the Bosnian involvement, see William C. Banks and Jeffrey D. Straussman, "A New Imperial Presidency? Insights from U.S. Involvement in Bosnia," *Political Science Quarterly* 114, no. 2 (1999): 195–217.

5 For this episode, see Michael J. Green, "Managing Chinese Power: The View from Japan," in Alastair I. Johnston and Robert S. Ross, eds., *Engaging China: The Management of an Emerging Power* (London: Routledge 1999), 161–2.

6 Tobias I. Nischalke, "Insights from ASEAN's Foreign Policy Co-operation: The 'ASEAN Way,' a Real Spirit or Phantom?" *Contemporary Southeast*

Asia 22, no. 1 (2000): 89–112; Yong Deng, "The Asianization of East Asian Security and the United States' Role," *East Asia* 16, nos.3/4 (1998): 87–110.

7 James Goldgeier, *Not Whether but When: The U.S. Decision to Enlarge NATO* (Washington, DC: Brookings Institution Press 1999), 5.

8 Gregory Flynn and Henry Farrell, "Piecing Together the Democratic Peace: The CSCE, Norms, and the 'Construction' of Security in post–Cold War Europe," *International Organization* 53, no. 3 (1999): 505–35.

9 See, for instance, Ingo Peters, "The OSCE and German Policy: A Study in How Institutions Matter," in Helga Haftendorn, Robert O. Keohane, and Celeste A. Wallander, eds., *Imperfect Unions: Security Institutions over Time and Space* (London: Oxford University Press 1999), 195–220.

10 For the implications of Russian efforts to build a strategic partnership with China, see Bruce Russett and Allan C. Stam, "Courting Disaster: An Expanded NATO vs. Russia and China," *Political Science Quarterly* 113, no. 3 (1998): 361–84.

11 Jing-Dong Yuan, "Culture Matters," 110–11.

12 Alastair Johnston and Paul Evans, "China's Engagement with Multilateral Security Institutions," in Alastair I. Johnston and Robert S. Ross, eds., *Engaging China: The Management of an Emerging Power* (London: Routledge 1999), 251–3.

13 Christian Tuschoff, "Alliance Cohesion and Peaceful Change in NATO," in Haftendorn, Keohane, and Wallander, eds., *Imperfect Unions*, 140–61.

14 Cluster I includes the question of periodic reviews of the enlarged Security Council. Although considered unimportant at a time when no consensus exists on the reform package, periodic reviews may become an important issue if the reform uses a list of permanent members (or even nonpermanent members) selected on a rotational basis; such a list will require a periodic evaluation of states that are on the list and those that are not who seem to better exhibit the attributes of permanent members.

15 "Putin Says Russia Supports Japan's Bid for UN Security Council Membership," *Itar-Tass*, 8 September 2000, Foreign Broadcast Information Service, FBIS-SOV-2000-0908.

16 "Statement by a Representative of the Russian Federation in the Open-Ended Working Group on Security Council Reform on Veto Issue," 24 March 1999, http://www.globalpolicy.org/security/docs/russia99.htm.

17 "Statement on the Veto by Ambassador Shen Guofang, Deputy Permanent Representative of China to the UN at the Working Group on Security Council Reform" (23 April 1998), http://www.undp.org/missions/china/veto.html

18 Richard Holbrooke, Statement before the Open-ended Working Group (3 April 2000), http://www.un.int/usa/00_046.htm.

19 Actually, Washington concurred with the position of most major Western

powers, including Japan, to bring the Council's total membership to twenty-four.

20 See, for instance, Senator Jesse Helms' opening remarks to the visiting members of the Security Council in Washington, DC, 20 March 2000, http://www.un.int/usa/oohelo330.htm.

21 See also, particularly, Igor S. Ivanov, Statement at the Fifty-third Session of the United Nations Assembly (22 September 1998), http://www.undp.org/missions/russia/gen_ass/1998/prb98ef1.htm.

22 Interview with the German foreign minister Joscha Fischer, *Die Zeit*, 12 November 1998.

23 See Hubert Védrine's thinking on this issue in "Entretien du Ministre des affaires étrangères avec le journal *Le Monde*," 24 March 2000, http://www.un.int/France/declarations/PP/pponu/000324F.html.

24 See the statement of the five permanent members on 23 September 1999 to this effect (s/1999/996). See also the report of the OEWG referring to this document, as well as an oral proposal, at the May 2000 session of the OEWG).

25 "Statement of Sergei Lavrov, Permanent Representative of the Russian Federation to the United Nations, to the Fifty-fourth Session of the UN General Assembly," item 38 (The question of equitable representation on and increase in the membership of the Security Council), 20 December 1999, http://www.un.int/russia/statement/ga/54th/plenary/99_12_20.htm.

26 See the German foreign minister's statement during his visit in Delhi, in C. Raja Mohan, "India, Germany to Work for UN Reforms," *The Hindu*, 19 May 2000, http://www.globalpolicy.org/security/reform/indger.htm.

27 See the statement of the German representative at the Open-Ended Working Group, 22 March 1999, http://www.germany-info.org/UN/un_state_03_22_99.htm.

28 "Pakistan, Japan to Continue Talks on UN Security Council Expansion," *Islamabad the News*, 24 August 2000, in FBIS-NES-2000–0824.

29 "Basic Standpoint of the Government of Japan on Security Council Reform," 14 May 1999, http://www.un.int/japan/3–statements/achieves/051499–2–12.html.

30 Michael E. O'Hanlon, "Japan's Not Ready for Permanent UNSC Seat," *Japan Times*, 25 September 2000, http://www.brook.edu/views/op-ed/ohanlon/20000925.htm.

31 "Statement by Michel Duval, Deputy Ambassador and Deputy Permanent Representative of Canada to the United Nations before the OEWG," 11 February 1999, http://www.un.int/Canada/html/S-DUVAL-11FEB99.htm.

32 Statement by Ambassador Robert R. Fowler, Permanent Representative of Canada to the United Nations, Fifty-fourth Session of the United Nations General Assembly, 16 December 1999, http://www.un.int/Canada/html/s-16dec99fowler.htm.

33 Mission permanente de la France auprès des Nations unies, "Intervention de l'Ambassadeur Levitte sur l'examen du rapport annuel du Conseil de sécurité," 17 October 2000), http://www.org.int/France/declarations/AG/Pleniere/REFORME/001017F.html.

34 See, for instance, the "Joint Statement by the Minister of Foreign Affairs of the Russian Federation and the Secretary of State of the United States of America," 7 September 2000, http://www.un.int/usa/us-russia.htm.

35 In his relatively short statement before the OEWG on 3 April 2000, Holbrooke used the term effective and effectiveness five times, http://www.un.int/usa/00_046.htm.

36 "Statement by a Representative of the Russian Federation in the Open-Ended Working Group on Security Council Reform on Veto Issue," 24 March 1999, http://www.globalpolicy.org/security/docs/russia99.htm.

37 "Statement by A. Granovsky, Deputy Permanent Representative of the Russian Federation to the United Nations at the Meeting of the Open-Ended Working Group on Equitable Representation on and Expansion of the Security Council," 22 June 1999, http://www.globalpolicy.org/security/docs/russia.htm.

38 "Statement on the Veto by Ambassador Shen Guofang, Deputy Permanent Representative of China to the UN at the Working Group on Security Council Reform," 23 April 1998, http://www.undp.org/missions/china/veto.html.

Bibliography

CHAPTER ONE

Baldwin, David A., ed. *Neorealism and Neoliberalism: The Contemporary Debate.* New York: Columbia University Press 1993.

Baylis, John, and Steve Smith, eds. *The Globalization of World Politics: An Introduction to International Relations.* Oxford: Oxford University Press 1997.

Brown, Michael E., et al. *The Perils of Anarchy.* Boston: MIT Press 1995.

Buzan, Barry, Charles Jones, and Richard Little. *The Logic of Anarchy: Neorealism to Structural Realism.* New York: Columbia University Press 1993.

Christensen, Thomas J. *Useful Adversaries: Grand Strategy, Domestic Mobilization, and Sino-American Conflict, 1947–1958.* Princeton: Princeton University Press 1998.

Durch, W.J., ed. UN *Peacekeeping, American Politics and the Civil Wars of the 1990s.* New York: St Martin's Press 1996.

Doyle, Michael W., and G. John Ikenberry, eds. *New Thinking in International Relations Theory.* Boulder, CO: Westview Press 1997.

Frankel, Benjamin, ed. *Realism: Restatements and Renewal.* London: Frank Cass 1996.

Kapstein, Ethan B., and Michael Mastanduno, eds. *Unipolar Politics: Realism and State Strategies After the Cold War.* New York: Columbia University Press 1999.

Katzenstein, Peter J., ed. *The Culture of National Security: Norms and Identity in World Politics.* New York: Columbia University Press 1996.

Kegley Jr, Charles W. *Controversies in International Relations Theory: Realism and the Neoliberal Challenge.* New York: St Martin's Press 1995.

Keohane, Robert O., and Joseph S. Nye. *Power and Independence: World Politics in Transition.* 1977.

Maynes, C.W., and Richard S. Williamson, *u.s. Foreign Policy and the United Nations System.* New York: W.W. Norton 1996.

Schweller, Randall L. *Deadly Imbalances: Tripolarity and Hitler's Strategy of World Conquest* (New York: Columbia University Press 1998.

Snyder, Craig A. *Contemporary Security and Strategy.* New York: Routledge 1999.

Snyder, Jack. *Myths of Empire: Domestic Politics and International Ambition.* Ithaca, NY: Cornell University Press 1991.

CHAPTER TWO

Alexseev, Mikhail A. *Center-Periphery Conflict in Post-Soviet Russia: A Federation Imperiled.* New York: St Martin's Press 1999.

Allison, Roy, and Christoph Bluth, eds. *Security Dilemmas in Russia and Eurasia.* London: The Royal Institute of International Affairs 1998.

Archer, Clive, and Lena Johnson, eds. *Peacekeeping and the Role of Russia in Eurasia.* Boulder, CO: Westview Press 1996.

Baranovsky, Vladimir, ed. *Russia and Europe: The Emerging Security Agenda.* Oxford: Oxford University Press 1997.

Boyer, Yves, and Isabelle Facon. *La politique de sécurité de la Russie: Entre continuité et rupture.* Paris: Éd. Ellipses, collection Repères stratégiques 2000.

Carnovale, Marco, ed. *European Security and International Institutions after the Cold War.* New York: St Martin's Press 1995.

David, Charles-Philippe, and Jacques Lévesque, eds. *The Future of NATO: Enlargement, Russia, and European Security.* Montreal: McGill-Queen's University Press 1999.

Ehrhart, Hans-Georg, and Andrei Zagorski, et al., eds. *Crisis Management in the CIS: Whither Russia?* Baden-Baden: Nomos 1995.

MacFarlane, Neil S., and Oliver Thränert, eds. *Balancing Hegemony: The OSCE in the CIS.* Kingston, ON: Centre for International Relations 1997.

Mandelbaum, Michael. *The New Russian Foreign Policy.* New York: Council on Foreign Relations 1998.

Paul, T.V., and John A. Hall, eds. *International Order and the Future of World Politics.* Cambridge: Cambridge University Press 1999.

Rubinstein, Alvin Z., and Oles M. Smolansky, eds. *Regional Power Rivalries in the New Eurasia: Russia, Turkey and Iran.* Amonk, NY: M.E. Sharpe 1995.

Wohlworth, William C. *The Elusive Balance: Power and Perceptions during the Cold War.* Ithaca, NY: Cornell University Press 1993.

CHAPTER THREE

Baldwin, David A., ed. *Neorealism and Neoliberalism: The Contemporary Debate*. New York: Columbia University Press 1993.

Boniface, Pascal. *La France est-elle encore une grande puissance?* Paris: Presses de Sciences Po 1998.

Buzan, Barry, Ole Wæver, and Jaap de Wide. *Security: A New Framework for Analysis*. Boulder, CO: Lynne Rienner 1998.

Charillon, Frédéric, ed. *Les politiques étrangères: Ruptures et continuités*. Paris: La Documentation française 2001.

Checkel, Jeffrey T. "The Constructivist Turn in International Relations Theory," *World Politics* 50, 2. January 1998.

Coudurier, Robert. *Le monde selon Chirac: Les coulisses de la diplomatie française*. Paris: Calmann-Lévy 1998.

Finnemore, Martha. *National Interests in International Society*. Ithaca, NY: Cornell University Press 1996.

Florini, Ann. "The Evolution of International Norms," *International Studies Quarterly* 40, 3. 1996).

Katzenstein, Peter J., ed. *The Culture of National Security: Norms and Identity in World Politics*. New York: Columbia University Press 1996.

Kessler, Marie-Christine. *La politique étrangère de la France: Acteurs et processus*. Paris: Presses de Sciences Po 1999.

Kramer, Stephen Philip. *Does France Still Count? The French Role in the New Europe*. Westport, CT: Praeger, Washington Papers/164 1994.

Martin, Pierre, and Mark R. Brawley, eds. *Allied Force or Forced Allies? Alliance Politics, Kosovo and NATO's War*. New York: St Martin's Press 2001.

Walt, Stephen M. "The Renaissance of Security Studies." *International Studies Quarterly* 35, 2 (June 1991).

Wendt, Alexander. "Collective Identity Formation and the International State." *American Political Science Review*, 88 (1994): 384–96.

CHAPTER FOUR

Aderhold, Eltje, Kurt Lipstein, Cristoph Schücking, and Rolf Stürmer, eds. *Festschrift für Hans Hanisch*. Cologne: Carl Heymanns Verlag 1994.

Asmus, Ronald D. *German Perception of the United States at Unification*. Santa Monica, CA: RAND 1991.

Blumenwitz, Dieter, and Gilbert Gornig, eds. *Rechtliche und politische Perspektiven deutschen Minderheiten und Volksgruppe*. Cologne: Verlag Wissenschaft und Politik 1995.

Duffield, John S. *World Power Forsaken. Political Culture, International Institutions, and German Security Policy after Unification*. Stanford, CA: Stanford University Press 1998.

Garton Ash, Timothy. *In Europe's Name: Germany and the Divided Continent*. London: Vintage 1994.

Haftendorn, Helga, Robert O. Keohane, and Celeste A. Wallander, eds. *Imperfect Unions: Security Institutions over Time and Space*. Oxford: Oxford University Press 1999.

Hébert, Philippe, and Paul Létourneau. "L'institutionnalisme dans la politique extérieure allemande: Ajustements et continuité." *Études internationales* 30, 2 (June 1999).

Kaiser, Karl. *Deutschlands Vereinigung: Die internationalen Aspekte, mit den wichtigen Dokumenten*. Bergisch Gladbach: Bastei Lübbe 1991.

Kaiser, Karl, and Joachim Krause, eds. *Deutschlands neue Außenpolitik*. Vol. 3, *Interessen und Strategien*. Munich: R. Oldenbourg Verlag GmbH 1996.

Keohane, Robert O., Joseph S. Nye, and Stanley Hoffmann, eds. *After the Cold War: International Institutions and State Strategies in Europe 1989–1991*. Cambridge: Harvard University Press 1993.

Kiessler, Richard, and Frank Elbe. *Der diplomatische Weg zur deutschen Einheit*. Baden-Baden: Suhrkamp Taschenbuch Verlag 1996.

Pond, Elizabeth. *Beyond the Wall: Germany's Road to Unification*. Washington, DC: The Brookings Institution 1993.

Smith, Gordon, William E. Paterson, Peter H. Merkl, and Stephen Padgett, eds. *Developments in German Politics* 9. Durham, NC: Duke University Press 1992.

Szabo, Stephen F. *The Diplomacy of German Unification*. New York: St Martin's Press 1992.

Teltschik, Horst. *329 Tage: Innenansichten der Einigung*. Berlin: Siedler 1991.

Zelikow, Philip, and Condoleezza Rice. *Germany Unified and Europe Transformed: A Study in Statecraft*. Cambridge: Harvard University Press 1995.

CHAPTER FIVE

Alagappa, Muthiah, ed. *Asian Security Practices: Material and Ideational Influences*. Stanford: Stanford University Press 1998.

Befu, Harumi. *Hegemony of Homogeneity: An Anthropological Analysis of Nihonjinron*. Japanese Society Series. Melbourne: Trans Pacific Press 2001.

Cha, Victor D. *Alignment, Despite Antagonism: The United States-Korea-Japan Security Triangle*. Stanford: Stanford University Press 1999.

Cossa, Ralph A., ed. *U.S.-Japan Alliance: Toward a More Equal Partnership*. Washington, DC: The CSIS Press, Center for Strategic and International Studies 1997.

Dore, Ronald. *Japan, Internationalism and the UN*. Nissan Institute, Routledge Japanese Studies Series. London: Routledge 1997.

Drifte, Reinhard. *Japan's Foreign Policy for the Twenty-first Century: From Economic Superpower to What Power?* 2d ed. St Anthony's Series. New York: St Martin's Press and St Anthony's College 1998.

Fukushima, Akiko. *Japanese Foreign Policy: The Emerging Logic of Multilateralism*. New York: St Martin's Press 1999.

Grant, Richard L., ed. *The Process of Japanese Foreign Policy: Focus on Asia*. London: Royal Institute of International Affairs, Asia-Pacific Programme 1997.

Green, Michael Jonathan. *Japan's Reluctant Realism: Foreign Policy Challenges in an Era of Uncertain Power*. A Council on Foreign Relations Book. New York: Palgrave 2001.

Inoguchi, Takashi, and Grant B. Stillman, eds. *North-East Asian Regional Security: The Role of International Institutions*. Tokyo: United Nations University Press 1997.

Iriye Akira, and Robert A. Wampler, eds. *Partnership: The United States and Japan 1951–2001*. Tokyo: Kodansha 2001.

Itoh Mayumi. *Globalization of Japan: Japanese Sakoku Mentality and U.S. Efforts to Open Japan*. New York: St Martin's Press 1998.

Klien, Susanne. *Rethinking Japan's Identity and International Role: An Intercultural Perspective*. New York: Routledge 2002.

Luther, Catherine A. *Press Images, National Identity, and Foreign Policy: A Case Study of U.S.-Japan Relations from 1955 to 1995*. New York: Routledge 2001.

Miyashita Akitoshi and Sato Yoichiro, eds. *Japanese Foreign Policy in Asia and the Pacific: Domestic Interests, American Pressure, and Regional Integration*. New York: Palgrave 2001.

Mochizuki, Mike M., ed. *Toward a True Alliance: Restructuring U.S.-Japan Security Relations*. Washington, DC: Brookings Institution Press 1997.

Tae-Hwan Kawk and Edward A. Olsen, eds. *The Major Powers of Northeast Asia: Seeking Peace and Security*. Boulder, CO: Lynne Rienner Publishers 1996.

CHAPTER SIX

Baldwin, David A., ed. *Neorealism and Neoliberalism: The Contemporary Debate*. New York: Columbia University Press 1993.

Bernstein, Richard, and Ross H. Munro. *The Coming Conflict with China*. New York: Vintage Book 1997.

Brown, Michael E., Sean M. Lynn-Jones, and Steven E. Miller, eds. *East Asian Security*. Cambridge: The MIT Press 1996.

Goodman, David S.G., and Gerald Segal, eds. *China Deconstructs*. New York: Routledge 1994.

Kim, Samuel S, ed. *China and the World: Chinese Foreign Policy Faces the New Millenium*. 4th ed. Boulder, CO: Westview Press 1998.

Kkhializad, Zalmay M., et al. *The United States and a Rising China*. Washington, DC: Rand 1999.

Pillsbury, Michael. *China Debates the Future Security Environment*. Washington, DC: National Defence University Press, 2000.

Risse-Kappen, Thomas. *Cooperation among the Democracies: The European Influence on U.S. Foreign Policy*. Princeton, NJ: Princeton University Press 1995.

Snyder, Craig A., ed. *Contemporary Security and Strategy*. New York: Routledge 1999.

The South China Sea Informal Working Group. *Proposals for Cooperation in the South China Sea*. Vancouver: Faculty of Law, University of British Columbia 1993.

Vogel, Ezra F., et al., ed. *Living With China*. New York: W.W. Norton 1997.

Wang, James C.F. *Contemporary Chinese Politics*. 6th ed. Toronto: Prentice Hall 1999.

Woods, Ngaire, ed. *Explaining International Relations Since 1945*. Oxford: Oxford University Press 1996.

CHAPTER SEVEN

Aggarwal, Vinod K., ed. *Institutional Designs for a Complex World: Bargaining, Linkages, and Nesting*. Ithaca, NY: Cornell University Press 1998.

Baldwin, David A., ed. *Neorealism and Neoliberalism: The Contemporary Debate*. New York: Columbia University Press 1993.

Cooper, Andrew F., ed. *Niche Diplomacy: Middle Powers After the Cold War*. London: Macmillan Press 1997.

Cooper, Andrew F., Richard A. Higgott, and Kim R. Nossal. *Relocating Middle Powers: Australia and Canada in a Changing World Order*. Vancouver: University of British Columbia Press 1993.

Evans, Gareth, and Bruce Grant. *Australia's Foreign Relations in the World of the 1990s*. (Melbourne: Melbourne University Press 1991.

Fawcett, Eric, and Anna Newcombe, eds. *United Nations Reform: Looking Ahead after Fifty Years*. Toronto: Science for Peace 1995.

Fleurence, Olivier. *La réforme du Conseil de sécurité: L'état du débat depuis la fin de la guerre froide*. Brussels: Bruylant 2000.

Frankel, Benjamin, ed. *Realism: Restatement and Renewal*. London: Frank Cass 1996.

Grieco, Joseph M. *Cooperation among Nations: Europe, America, and Non-tariff Barriers to Trade*. Ithaca, NY: Cornell University Press 1990.

Hirschman, Albert O. *Exit, Voice, and Loyalty: Responses to Decline in Firms, Organizations, and States*. Cambridge: Harvard University Press 1970.

Holbraad, Carsten. *Middle Powers in International Politics*. London: Macmillan 1984.

Keating, Tom. *Canada and World Order: The Multilateral Tradition in Canadian Foreign Policy*. Toronto: McClelland and Stewart 1993.

Hampson, Fen Osler, and Maureen Appel Molot, eds. *Canada Among Nations 1998: Leadership and Dialogue*. (Toronto: Oxford University Press 1998.

Loiseau, Hugo. *Les cas de coopération et le rôle des puissances moyennes en matière de sécurité dans les Amériques.* Québec: Institut québécois des hautes études internationales, Université Laval 1998.

Michaud, Nelson, and Kim Richard Nossal, eds. *Diplomatic Departures: The Conservative Era in Canadian Foreign Policy.* Vancouver: University of British Columbia Press 2001.

Taylor, Paul, Sam Dawns, and Ute Adamczick-Gerteis, eds. *Documents on the Reform of the United Nations.* Aldershot, England: Dartmouth 1997.

Index

SUBJECTS